DATE DUE

			PRINTED IN U.S.A.

Authors
& Artists
for Young
Adults

ISSN 1040-5682

Authors & Artists for Young Adults

VOLUME 10

Kevin S. Hile,
Editor

Gale Research Inc. • *DETROIT* • *WASHINGTON, D.C.* • *LONDON*

Kevin S. Hile, *Editor*

Anne Janette Johnson, *Contributing Editor*

Sonia Benson, Elizabeth A. Des Chenes, Marie Ellavich, Michelle M. Motowski, Susan M. Reicha, and Kenneth R. Shepherd, *Associate Editors*

Joanna Brod, David M. Galens, Cornelia A. Pernik, Pamela L. Shelton, and Deborah A. Stanley, *Assistant Editors*

Victoria B. Cariappa, *Research Manager*

Mary Rose Bonk, *Research Supervisor*

Reginald A. Carlton, Clare Collins, Andrew Guy Malonis, and Norma Sawaya, *Editorial Associates*

Patricia Bowen, Rachel A. Dixon, Shirley Gates, Sharon McGilvray, and Devra M. Sladics, *Editorial Assistants*

Margaret A. Chamberlain, *Picture Permissions Supervisor*
Pamela A. Hayes, *Permissions Associate*
Karla Kulkis, Nancy Rattenbury, and Keith Reed, *Permissions Assistants*

Mary Beth Trimper, *Production Director*
Mary Kelley, *External Production Assistant*

Cynthia Baldwin, *Art Director*
C. J. Jonik, *Keyliner*
Willie Mathis, *Camera Operator*

Contents

Introduction

Authors and Artists for Young Adults is a reference series designed to serve the needs of middle school, junior high, and high school students interested in creative artists. Originally inspired by the need to bridge the gap between Gale's *Something about the Author*, created for children, and *Contemporary Authors*, intended for older students and adults, *Authors and Artists for Young Adults* has been expanded to cover not only an international scope of authors, but also a wide variety of other artists.

Although the emphasis of the series remains on the writer for young adults, we recognize that these readers have diverse interests covering a wide range of reading levels. The series therefore contains not only those creative artists who are of high interest to young adults, including cartoonists, photographers, music composers, bestselling authors of adult novels, media directors, producers, and performers, but also literary and artistic figures studied in academic curricula, such as influential novelists, playwrights, poets, and painters. The goal of *Authors and Artists for Young Adults* is to present this great diversity of creative artists in a format that is entertaining, informative, and understandable to the young adult reader.

Entry Format

Each volume of *Authors and Artists for Young Adults* will furnish in-depth coverage of about twenty authors and artists. The typical entry consists of:

— A detailed biographical section that includes date of birth, marriage, children, education, and addresses.

— A comprehensive bibliography or filmography including publishers, producers, and years.

— Adaptations into other media forms.

— Works in progress.

— A distinctive essay featuring comments on an artist's life, career, artistic intentions, world views, and controversies.

— References for further reading.

— Extensive illustrations, photographs, movie stills, manuscript samples, book covers, and other relevant visual material.

A cumulative index to featured authors and artists appears in each volume.

Compilation Methods

The editors of *Authors and Artists for Young Adults* make every effort to secure information directly from the authors and artists through personal correspondence and interviews. Sketches on living authors and artists are sent to the biographee for review prior to publication. Any sketches not personally reviewed by the biographee are marked with an asterisk (°).

Highlights of Forthcoming Volumes

Among the authors and artists planned for future volumes are:

Judie Angell	Sue Grafton	Kathleen Wendy Peyton
Isaac Asimov	Deborah Hautzig	Jayne A. Phillips
Margaret Atwood	Robert Heinlein	Meredith Ann Pierce
Peter Benchley	Zora Neale Hurston	Rob Reiner
James Blish	Hadley Irwin	Ann Rinaldi
Francesca Lia Block	Diana Wynne Jones	Sook Nyul Choi
Terry Brooks	Rudyard Kipling	Scott Spencer
J. California Cooper	Louis L'Amour	Joyce Carol Thomas
Susan Cooper	Annie Leibovitz	John Rowe Townsend
Gary Crew	Linda Lewis	Luis Miguel Valdez
John Donovan	Lael Littke	Jules Verne
Loren D. Estleman	Don Martin	Robert Westall
Anne Frank	Lorne Michaels	Simon Wiesenthal
William Gibson	Jill Paton Walsh	Jack Williamson

The editors of *Authors and Artists for Young Adults* welcome any suggestions for additional biographees to be included in this series. Please write and give us your opinions and suggestions for making our series more helpful to you. Direct your comments to: Editors, *Authors and Artists for Young Adults*, Gale Research Inc., 835 Penobscot Building, Detroit, Michigan 48226-4094.

Authors & Artists for Young Adults

Woody Allen

■ Personal

Born Allen Stewart Konigsberg, December 1, 1935, in Brooklyn, NY; legal name, Woody Allen; son of Martin (a waiter and jewelry engraver) and Nettie (Cherry) Konigsberg; married Harlene Rosen, 1954 (divorced, 1960); married Louise Lasser (an actress), February 2, 1966 (divorced, 1969); children: (all with Mia Farrow) Moses (adopted son), Dylan (adopted daughter), Satchel. *Education:* Attended New York University and City College of New York (now City College of the City University of New York), 1953. *Politics:* Democrat. *Religion:* Jewish. *Hobbies and other interests:* Playing jazz clarinet, poker, chess, spectator sports (especially basketball).

■ Addresses

Agent—Rollins/Joffe/Morra/Brezner, Inc., 130 West 157th St., New York, NY 10019.

■ Career

Comedian, actor, director, and writer for television, films, and the stage. Began writing jokes for columnists and celebrities while in high school; staff writer for National Broadcasting Corp., 1952; performer in nightclubs, on television, in films, and on the stage, 1961—. Film acting credits include *What's New, Pussycat,* United Artists (UA), 1965; *Casino Royale,* Columbia Pictures, 1967; *Take the Money and Run,* Palomar Pictures, 1969; *Bananas,* UA, 1971; *Play It Again, Sam,* Paramount, 1972; *Everything You Always Wanted to Know about Sex° (°But Were Afraid to Ask),* UA, 1972; *Sleeper,* UA, 1973; *Love and Death,* UA, 1975; *The Front,* Columbia Pictures, 1976; *Annie Hall,* UA, 1977; *Manhattan,* UA, 1979; *Stardust Memories,* UA, 1980; *A Midsummer Night's Sex Comedy,* Orion Pictures, 1982; *Zelig,* Orion Pictures, 1983; *Broadway Danny Rose,* Orion Pictures, 1984; *Hannah and Her Sisters,* Orion Pictures, 1986; *Radio Days,* Orion Pictures, 1987; *September,* Orion Pictures, 1987; *Another Woman,* Orion Pictures, 1988; *Crimes and Misdemeanors,* Orion Pictures, 1989; *Scenes from a Mall,* Silver Screen Partners IV, 1990; *Shadows and Fog,* Orion Pictures, 1992; *Husbands and Wives,* TriStar Pictures, 1992.

■ Awards, Honors

Sylvania Award, 1957, for *The Sid Caesar Show;* Emmy Award nomination, 1957; Nebula Award for Dramatic Presentation, Science Fiction Writers of America, 1974, for *Sleeper;* Special Silver Bear Award, Berlin Film Festival, 1975; O. Henry Award for best short story of 1976-77, for *The Kugelmass Episode;* Academy Awards for best director and best original screenplay, Academy Award nomination for best actor, British Academy of Film and Television Arts Awards for best film, best director, and best screenplay, National Society of Film Critics' Award, best screenplay, and New York Film Critics' Circle Awards, best director and best screenplay, all 1977, all for *Annie Hall;* Academy Award nominations for best director and best original screenplay, 1978, both for *Interiors;* Academy Award nomination for best original screenplay, British Academy of Film and Television Arts Awards for best film and best screenplay, and New York Film Critics' Award, best director, all 1979, all for *Manhattan;* Academy Award nominations for best director and best original screenplay, and British Academy of Film and Television Arts Award for best original screenplay, all 1984, all for *Broadway Danny Rose;* Academy Award nomination for best original screenplay, British Academy of Film and Television Arts Award for best original screenplay, and New York Critics' Circle Award for best screenplay, all 1985, all for *The Purple Rose of Cairo;* Laurel Award, Writers Guild of America, 1986; Academy Award for best original screenplay, Academy Award nomination for best director, British Academy of Film and Television Arts Award for best director and best original screenplay, British Academy of Film and Television Arts Award nomination for best actor, Directors Guild of America Award nomination for outstanding feature film achievement, Golden Globe nominations for best director and best screenplay, London Film Critics' Award for best screenplay, London Film Critics' Award nomination for best director, Los Angeles Film Critics' Association Award for best screenplay, D. W. Griffith Award from the National Board of Review for best director, New York Film Critics' Award for best director, and Writers Guild of America Award for best screenplay written directly for the screen, all 1986, and Moussinac Prize for best foreign film, French Film Critics' Union, 1987, all for *Hannah and Her Sisters;* Academy Award nomination for best original screenplay, and Writers Guild of America Award nomination for best screenplay written directly for the screen, both 1987, both for *Radio Days;* Academy Award nominations for best director and best original screenplay, both 1990, both for *Crimes and Misdemeanors.*

■ **Writings**

Getting Even, Random House, 1971.
Death: A Comedy in One Act, French, 1975.
God: A Comedy in One Act, French, 1975.
Without Feathers, Random House, 1975.
Four Screenplays: Sleeper, Love and Death, Bananas, Annie Hall, Random House, 1978.

Non-being and Somethingness, illustrated by Stuart Hample, Random House, 1978.
Side Effects, Random House, 1980.
Four Films of Woody Allen, Random House, 1982.

SCREENPLAYS

What's New, Pussycat?, United Artists (UA), 1965.
What's Up, Tiger Lily?, American International Pictures, 1966.
Play It Again, Sam, Paramount, 1972.

SCREENPLAYS; AND DIRECTOR

Take the Money and Run, Palomar Pictures, 1969.
Bananas, UA, 1971.
Everything You Always Wanted To Know about Sex° (°But Were Afraid To Ask), UA, 1972.
Sleeper, UA, 1973.
Love and Death, UA, 1975.
Annie Hall, UA, 1977.
Interiors, UA, 1978.
Manhattan, UA, 1979.
Stardust Memories, UA, 1980.
A Midsummer Night's Sex Comedy, Orion Pictures, 1982.
Zelig, Orion Pictures, 1983.
Broadway Danny Rose, Orion Pictures, 1984.
The Purple Rose of Cairo, Orion Pictures, 1985.
Hannah and Her Sisters, Orion Pictures, 1986.
Radio Days, Orion Pictures, 1987.
September, Orion Pictures, 1988.
Another Woman, Orion Pictures, 1988.
"Oedipus Wrecks," in *New York Stories,* Buena Vista, 1989.
Crimes and Misdemeanors, Orion Pictures, 1989.
Shadows and Fog, Orion Pictures, 1992.
Husbands and Wives, TriStar Pictures, 1992.

PLAYS

(With others) *From A to Z,* produced on Broadway, 1960.
Don't Drink the Water (produced on Broadway, 1966), French, 1967.
Play It Again, Sam (produced on Broadway, 1969), Random House, 1969.
The Floating Lightbulb (produced on Broadway, 1981), Random House, 1982.

OTHER

Woody Allen (recording), Colpx Records, 1964.
Woody Allen, Volume 2 (recording), Colpx Records, 1965.
Woody's First Special, broadcast by Columbia Broadcasting System, September 21, 1969.

Also contributor to various periodicals, including *New Yorker*, *Saturday Review*, *Playboy*, *Esquire*, and numerous other publications.

■ Sidelights

Over a span of almost thirty years, Woody Allen has earned a reputation as a prolific and provocative filmmaker whose movies are considered among the most important, if not always the most commercially successful, in contemporary film comedy. As writer and director of landmark movies such as *Annie Hall* and *Hannah and Her Sisters*, Allen has gained more name recognition than most of the actors who star in his films. As an actor, he has portrayed semi-autobiographical *schlemiel* characters so many times that his fans feel as if they know Allen personally. Despite the adoration of moviegoers and the respect of critics and scholars, Allen has shown surprisingly little interest in the trappings of fame. Scorning the accolades of Hollywood and its obsession with blockbuster fare, Allen continues to produce independent features on small budgets, often just earning back his costs in revenues generated by video cassette rentals. Time and again, that is the way Allen has said he prefers it.

Born Allen Stewart Konigsberg, Allen grew up in the Flatbush section of Brooklyn. As a youth, his interests included magic and card tricks, the clarinet, sports, and movies. He began writing early and had the honor of hearing his papers read aloud to the class from the time he was in first grade. In most ways, young Allen resembled his peers. "I was out in the streets from eight o'clock in the morning," he once told Jack Kroll of *Newsweek*, "playing baseball and basketball. At lunchtime I'd race into the house, eat a tuna-fish sandwich by myself and read a comic book—Superman, Batman or Mickey Mouse. I'd run back out on the street and play ball. Then I'd run back in for dinner, read another comic book, run back out again for two hours, come in and watch the St. Louis Cardinals beat the Dodgers on television."

Like many children, Allen disliked school immensely. "It was a loathsome thing," he recalled for William E. Geist in *Rolling Stone*. Among the scholastic activities which Allen objected to "were the natural things that kids would not like: sitting still, being disciplined, not being able to talk and not being able to have fun." Allen held particular disdain for his former teachers who, in addition to being anti-Semitic, "were stupid and mean. They were unpleasant people and one never wanted to

From 1960 to 1964 Allen wrote for *Tonight Show* host Johnny Carson, made guest appearances, and even became a substitute host.

go to school." The feelings might have been mutual on the part of the teachers, who did not always appreciate Allen's sense of humor. "I used to write things they thought were dirty," he told Geist. Despite his high school teachers' opinions, Allen began sending jokes to columnists such as Earl Wilson and Walter Winchell, who used them by claiming that they were the witty remarks of a celebrity. At this time, he adopted the professional moniker Woody Allen, a nickname his father said he earned by always being the one to bring a stick to neighborhood stickball games.

Finds Unconventional Route to Success

Allen did not find college any more to his liking than high school, but he enrolled in an effort to please his parents. Expelled from New York University in less than a year for poor grades, the aspiring comic did not fare any better at City College of New York. "I was a film major at NYU but I couldn't even pass my major.... I'd ride the train to NYU from Brooklyn and I'd think to myself, 'Don't get off here. Keep going.' And I'd go right up to Forty-second Street, cutting school to go to the movies, hang out at the automat, buy the newspapers and go to the Paramount—and then go in to work in the afternoon," he told Geist. It was in his work, writing comedy, that Allen found the confidence to turn his back on college and the usual routes to success. Allen, however, does not offer his own life as an example to youths eager to follow in his footsteps. "You see, I was lucky," he said in *Rolling Stone*. "I don't think you can count on being lucky. I was lucky in that I had a talent to be amusing. If I didn't have that talent, I would have been in great peril. You can only be independent that way if you luck out."

Fortunately, Allen's own combination of luck and talent allowed him to disregard the well-meaning but misguided advice of those who wanted to make his life and career choices for him. "I always felt people are very quick with advice, fast advice from the man on the street and profound advice from your peers. You read your books and you live your life and you see your friends and make your own evaluation as to what you want to do.... You go your own route," he told Geist.

After catching the attention of columnists with his jokes and one-liners while still in high school, Allen launched a career in television, finding himself the youngest—and quietest—staff writer on shows for Sid Caesar, Art Carney, and Jack Paar, among others. By the early 1960s, Allen was doing stand-up comedy in nightclubs, developing the persona that would make him famous—that of the intellectual bumbler, unlucky in love, adversary of nature and small appliances, a perpetual victim of his own urban angst. With his thick glasses, worried expressions, and slight stature, Allen definitely fit the physical requirements of the part. In one of his stand-up routines from that era, Allen bragged about being discovered by a famous film producer who found him sensual, handsome, exciting—a perfect sex symbol. In his typical, self-deprecating manner, Allen described the producer as "a short man with red hair and glasses." In reality, Allen was discovered by Charles K. Feldman, a film producer who saw the comedian's act at the Blue Angel nightclub in 1964 and shortly thereafter offered him a job rewriting a script for a comedy film. Although the experience was not particularly enjoyable for Allen, who did not have much artistic control, the resulting motion picture, released as *What's New, Pussycat?*, was a great commercial success.

Regardless of Allen's own feelings towards his first screenplay, he admitted that it opened the door to other projects, and allowed him to obtain financing to write, direct, and star in his own film. *Take the Money and Run* became the first in a long line of movies over which Allen had almost complete artistic control. That film, too, enjoyed commercial success while winning kudos from critics who found its good-natured slapstick entertaining, but never offensive. The screenplay follows the misadventures of Virgil Starkwell (played by Allen), a hopelessly inept thief who aspires to become an heroic criminal. Unfortunately, Virgil cannot carry out a bank hold up because he misspells the note he hands the teller. Another time, he finds himself running late for a robbery because he can't decide what color shirt to wear. "Call the other guys," his wife suggests. "See what they're wearing." Of the film, Allen once remarked, "Naturally for my first movie I stayed with my safest stuff, which is stuff I know about: abject humility. I was very timid in that picture. But there was no way I could have been anything else. I had never made a film. I was never the star of a picture before."

Allen relied on the successful slapstick formula of his first film for his next few projects, including *Bananas*. Both films, noted *Film Comment*'s Richard Zoglin, "boast sharp bits of parody (of prison movies, TV commercials, courtroom dramas), with Allen kidnapping the cliches and transporting them into wildly inappropriate settings. The laughs provoked by such scenes are two-pronged: the incongruity of seeing familiar actions in absurdly wrong contexts is topped by the fact that no one onscreen notices it.... The underlying message of Allen's comedy is the tyranny of the cliche, which threatens to dehumanize us, to turn us into reflexive automatons. This is not random gag-writing but social comedy of a subtle subversiveness."

The 1973 film *Sleeper* is the last of Allen's zany, madcap films. In it, he plays Miles Monroe, proprietor of The Happy Carrot health food store, who awakes to find himself in the year 2173 after a disastrous ulcer operation leaves him in cold storage for two hundred years. The film relies heavily on visual humor, such as Miles's encounters with the high technology of the new age—robot servants, mechanical dogs, and even a machinery-made replacement for sex. Despite the film's cartoon-like style, Miles's search for personal and cultural identity gave *Sleeper* a serious undertone as well. As Miles recalls his own past, he becomes an enemy of the current government, which prefers that its citizens subscribe to a fabricated version of history. Although Miles becomes involved with a rebel force, by the end of the film he denounces both science and politics, opting instead for sex and death, "two things which come once in my life—but at least after death you're not nau-

Allen honed his skill with visual gags in *Sleeper*, a 1973 satire of science fiction films that won wide acclaim.

seous." Although *Sleeper* enjoyed success at the box office and was praised by critics as the most cohesive of Allen's work, he was ready for a change of pace. "I believe . . . I came out aggressively a little bit," Allen once remarked about the broad comedy.

Creates Masterpiece with *Annie Hall*

The turning point in Allen's cinematic style came with *Annie Hall*, when he left behind the broad, physical jokes of his early work and concentrated on what Penelope Gilliatt of the *New Yorker* described as "psychoanalytic slapstick" instead. Considered Allen's masterpiece, *Annie Hall* tells the story of the courtship of Alvy Singer (Allen)

and the title character, played by Diane Keaton. Since Allen and Keaton had been linked romantically off-screen, the movie was taken as a thinly-veiled account of their real-life courtship. With its insights into the way romances evolved in the 1970s, *Annie Hall*'s portrayal of one couple's struggles became representative of the age.

The film examines the troubled relationship between Alvy, a Jewish comedy writer, and Annie, his gentile lover. While their similar neuroses draw them together at first, they drift apart when Annie begins to grow, exhibiting a self-confidence and intellectual independence which Alvy is incapable of achieving. As a result, Alvy becomes jealous and the relationship falls to ruins. Despite the film's somber nature, Richard Schickel of *Time* found that "traditionalists need not worry. There are plenty of one-liners about the classic anti-hero's copelessness in sexual and other matters as Allen dips once again into the comic capital that he has been living off for years. It is, however, the best measure of [the movie's] other strengths that even when these gags are very good, they often seem unnecessary and intrusive: mood busters."

Perhaps most praised for its general believability, the film's characters are especially realistic. Allen's "central characters and all who cross their paths are recognizable contemporary types," Schickel observed. "Most of us have even shared a lot of their fantasies. Their world, however cockeyed, is our world. Without abandoning the private demi-demons that have been the basis of his past comic success, Allen has fashioned broad new connections with his audience. Ironically, his most personal film may turn out to have the widest appeal of all."

The film's wide appeal was confirmed when *Annie Hall* swept the 1978 Academy Awards, taking awards for best picture, best director for Allen, best original screenplay for Allen and Marshall

Brickman, and best actress for Keaton. Allen, showing little regard for the highly coveted Oscar, did not appear at the awards ceremony. His key reason for not attending (besides the belief that "the whole concept of awards is silly"), he has said, is that the Oscars are held on a Monday night, and on that evening he has a standing commitment—playing clarinet with the New Orleans Funeral and Ragtime Orchestra at a New York City nightclub. Charles Joffe, the film's producer and an associate of Allen's for years, accepted the award in Allen's name; he told the audience: "It's very hard for Woody to accept laurels for his work. He's interested in how well his work comes out and not in prizes."

Allen's next project, *Interiors,* is another departure from the early Allen formula. Not only was the film serious in tone and subject matter, but Allen himself did not appear in it. *Interiors,* modeled after the work of renowned Swedish filmmaker Igmar Bergman, focuses on a family of repressed and neurotic individuals. "The kinds of films I've always liked, right from the start, were serious movies," Allen told David Remnick of *Saturday Review*. Despite Allen's preferences, "it took a lot

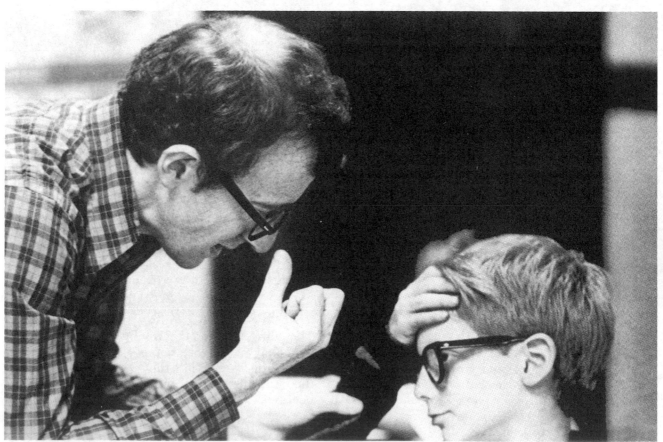

In a classic scene from the introspective 1977 romantic comedy *Annie Hall,* Alvy (Allen) faces his childhood head-on.

of convincing to get the studio to let me make *Interiors*. But it came right after *Annie Hall,* so they were flush with some success. Then I did it and it didn't make any money at all." Allen was not disturbed by remarks that he should have made *Interiors* more like *Annie Hall.* "I don't think I would have been in good shape if, instead of *Annie Hall,* I had made another film like *Sleeper* and then another film like *Bananas* and then another film like *Sleeper.* I don't dislike comedy.... But it can be an artistic dead end for a person," he told Tom Shales in an *Esquire* piece. He further remarked that a filmmaker who continually produces blockbusters is "on a bad treadmill, I feel. You want your films to be successful, but every now and then, when one doesn't work at all, it's a sign of life."

Allen's 1979 film, *Manhattan,* resembles *Annie Hall* more closely than *Interiors.* Allen and Keaton again portray uneasy lovers in contemporary New York City, playing out a romance doomed to failure. Allen plays Isaac, an emotionally stunted, neurotic writer much like Alvy. Isaac, in the process of divorcing a wife who has left him for her lesbian lover, carries on a noncommittal affair with seventeen-year-old Tracy (Mariel Hemingway), who is the most mature character in the movie. Vincent Canby of the *New York Times* found that *Manhattan* "moves on from both *Interiors* and *Annie Hall,* being more effective critically and more compassionate than the first and more witty and clear-eyed than the second." Canby goes on to observe that the film is "mostly about Isaac's efforts to get some purchase on his life after he initiates a breakup with his illegal, teenage mistress ... and his attempt to forge a relationship with the deeply troubled Mary Wilke (Keaton). Unlike all of his friends except the still-learning Tracy, Isaac believes in monogamy. 'I think people should mate for life,' he says, 'like pigeons and Catholics.'"

Allen's next artistic change of pace came with *A Midsummer Night's Sex Comedy,* a pastoral comedy in a turn-of-the-century setting. Allen again drew upon the work of auteur Bergman, as well as William Shakespeare's play *A Midsummer Night's Dream,* but his effort was not critically acclaimed nor commercially successful. Although a *People* magazine reviewer found the film "sumptuously shot, stylishly acted, and fitfully charming.... *Sex Comedy* is still Woody out of water and floundering." Pauline Kael of the *New Yorker* felt that Allen was "trying to please, but his heart isn't in it, and his talent isn't either." While critics agreed that the film was of relatively minor importance in the

canon of Allen's work, it did mark the debut of Mia Farrow in an Allen movie. Farrow, with whom Allen had become involved romantically as well as professionally, went on to appear in a string of Allen movies over a span of ten years.

Cinematic Experiment Wins Praise

In 1983, Allen struck gold with *Zelig,* one of the most acclaimed films of the year. Set in the 1920s, the film explores the assimilation of minorities into mainstream American culture through the tale of Leonard Zelig (Allen), a rather nondescript urban Jew with the amazing ability to adopt the looks and characteristics of any distinct individual or group he encounters. Among fat men, Leonard becomes fat. Among black jazz musicians, his skin darkens. Among gangsters, Leonard adopts the dress, manners and appearance of a gangster. Leonard becomes a national phenomenon when his chameleon-like ability captures the imagination of Roaring Twenties America.

However, like most of Allen's protagonists, Leonard finds that fame does not bring him happiness. He seeks the help of psychiatrist Eudora Fletcher (Farrow), who is convinced she can cure him of his changeable nature. The public, which embraced him for his amazing abilities, does not want to see him cured, and Leonard is driven out of the country into the clutches of Germany's emerging National Socialist party. It's no surprise when Leonard, surrounded by Nazis, becomes one himself. Luckily, when Eudora spots his face among the masses in a newsreel film, she embarks on a daring rescue mission. Zelig's fate after his liberation seems deliberately unclear. As much as *Zelig* is about the assimilation of minorities, it is also a commentary on the nature of fame, a common theme in Allen's work.

Constructed around the plot device of a mock-documentary, *Zelig* includes a series of short interviews with present day social critics such as Susan Sontag and Saul Bellow, who comment on Allen's comic invention as if Zelig were an actual historical figure. But the most impressive aspect of the film is Allen's use of a myriad of modern cinematic techniques to evoke the jumpy, crackling footage of the 1920s and 1930s. Allen spliced his authentically shot black-and-white scenes with actual footage, showing Leonard Zelig with such notables as Babe Ruth, Calvin Coolidge, and even Adolph Hitler. While some critics felt the technical brilliance of *Zelig* overshadowed the movie's message, London *Times* writer David Robinson coun-

1985's *The Purple Rose of Cairo* humorously explores the relationship between fantasy and reality when a 1930s waitress and a fictional film star get mixed up in each other's worlds.

tered that the comedy leaves the viewer "with as many questions about the condition of man as do great tragedies. When you recover from the laughter, this pure, perfect, beautiful comedy leaves a trail of reflections about truth and fiction and the difficulty of preserving one's own personality in a society which offers so many off-the-peg models for being which are so much easier to wear."

Allen's fifteenth film, *The Purple Rose of Cairo*, is another experimental project. This fantasy, about a lonely woman who is amazed to find herself the love object of a character who literally steps off a movie screen and into her life, is the first Allen film since *Interiors* in which he did not appear as an

actor. The story centers around Cecilia (Farrow), a poor New Jersey housewife abused by her insensitive husband, who finds her only solace at the local movie house, where an adventure, *The Purple Rose of Cairo*, is playing. Her need to escape the drudgery of her own life is apparent when she returns to the theater for screening after screening. One day, the film's handsome hero, Tom Baxter, stops the action during the movie to comment on Cecilia's constant presence and, to the surprise of the other characters and Cecilia herself, steps off the screen and into the real world.

Although Tom's appearance is both confusing and exhilarating for Cecilia, it is exasperating for the Hollywood executives who are panicked to discover that Tom Baxters are stepping off movie screens all across America. The studio executives decide that only Gil Shepard, the actor who portrays Tom, can convince the love-lorn adventurer to return to the movie from whence he came. Gil arrives in New Jersey only to fall in love with Cecilia, who is swept away by the gallant movie star's offer to take her back to Hollywood with him. Rebuffed, Tom Baxter returns to *Purple Rose*, allowing the movie to continue. But when Cecilia goes to meet Gil at the movie house, he doesn't show up. It becomes clear that Gil only pretended to love her in order to get Tom to return to the film. Resigned to her fate, Cecilia enters the movie house and waits for another movie to begin.

The dismal ending of *The Purple Rose of Cairo* disappointed many fans and critics who felt the story deserved a happier ending. Pauline Kael of the *New Yorker* found the heroine's fate typical of the morose Allen, who "has a naturally melancholic, depressive quality." The film, she added, reflects Allen's view of life. "The movie casts a spell," Kael wrote, "yet at the end it has a bitter tang. It says sweetness doesn't get you anywhere." In interviews, Allen himself has maintained that the conclusion *was* a happy ending. Other critics found the movie enchanting despite its conclusion. In the *New York Times*, Canby described the film as a "sweet, lyrically funny, multilayered work that again demonstrates that Woody Allen is our pre-

mier film maker." Even Kael conceded that *Purple Rose* was Allen's "most purely charming" film to date.

Celebrates Strong Female Characters

During Allen's next phase of filmmaking, critics noticed a definite trend towards writing female characters who were strong-willed, highly intelligent, and independent. *Hannah and Her Sisters*, a 1986 comedy-drama, demonstrates Allen's affinity for exploring the multi-faceted characters of women in love. Set in present day New York City, the film tells the story of how shifting allegiances and marital strife affect the lives of three grown sisters and their families. "Beginning with a big, festive family celebration . . . the film covers several years in the lives of its six principal characters, moving effortlessly from the mind of one into another. [Allen's] most surprising achievement is the manner by which he has refracted his own, very pronounced screen personality into the colors of so many fully realized characters that stand at such a far remove from the film maker," wrote Canby in the *New York Times*. In *Rolling Stone*, David Edelstein described *Hannah and Her Sisters* as "the summation of—and, in a sense, the justification for—every Woody Allen film since *Annie Hall*."

Despite its serious themes, *Hannah and Her Sisters* is, ultimately, a comedy. Allen may drive each of

The popular 1986 film, *Hannah and Her Sisters*, is what some critics consider a more light-hearted reworking of the themes Allen addressed in his Bergmanesque work, *Interiors*.

his characters "to the edge of tragedy," observed Edelstein, but he pulls them back. "Allen, who has dumped on comedy for almost ten years, comes marching home at last," Edelstein concluded. Intrigued by tragedy, however, Allen ignored the pleas of fans and critics to stick with comedy and forged ahead in 1989 with *Crimes and Misdemeanors.*

Breaking from his tradition of not appearing in his serious movies, in *Crimes and Misdemeanors* Allen plays Cliff Stern, a struggling independent filmmaker whose only claim to fame is an honorable mention at the Cincinnati Documentary Film Festival. Cliff's marriage is in no better shape than his career, and when he accepts a job filming a documentary about his obnoxious brother-in-law, a Hollywood big shot, he hits an all-time low, both personally and professionally. The tragedy of the film, however, lies in its parallel story, about Judah Rosenthal, a celebrated opthamalogist treating Cliff's other brother-in-law. Judah, a prominent citizen devoted to philanthropy, is also the keeper of a nasty secret. For two years, he has been committing adultery with a neurotic woman who is now threatening to reveal the affair. Panicked at the thought of his public image in ruins, Judah agrees to let his shady brother arrange the woman's murder. For the rest of the film, the protagonists come to terms with the moral concessions—both big and small—that they have made. The film's powerfully ironic message is contained in its conclusion, which shows Cliff—the quintessential nice guy—more pathetic than ever and Judah—a morally reprehensible man—more celebrated than ever. "You want a happy ending?" Judah asks Cliff. "See a Hollywood movie."

Despite the film's bleak themes, fans of Allen's humor found satisfaction in its liberal supply of one-liners. For fans of Allen's serious films, *Crimes and Misdemeanors* "provides some enthralling moments, and it is consistently absorbing, even at its lowest points," noted Stuart Klawans in the *Nation.* Klawans praised the film for its lofty aspirations, despite its disturbing and sometimes paradoxical messages. "It's good to watch a film as entertainment," he concluded, "but sometimes it's even better to hold an argument with a movie. A week after seeing *Crimes and Misdemeanors,* I still find myself talking back to it. If that's a measure of the film's problems, then I wish there were more movies with such faults."

The critical success of both *Hannah and Her Sisters* and *Crimes and Misdemeanors* was not repeated with the 1992 film *Shadows and Fog.* "The latest word on Woody Allen," wrote Peter Travers in *Rolling Stone,* "is that he's losing it. Insulated from the rhythms of contemporary life, which gave his work a trendy appeal during the heyday of *Annie Hall* and *Manhattan,* Allen has become less funny and more thoughtful. To his detractors, it's a bum trade-off. They're likely to be particularly pissy about *Shadows and Fog,* a comic lament that is purposefully and defiantly out of step." The film, about a clerk (Allen) who is recruited by a band of vigilantes to help find a serial killer, was described by Travers as "a messy culture clash that's easy to dismiss at first glance." Many fans and critics did just that. "The few isolated laughs recall the burlesque spirit of Allen's early writing.... But here Allen isn't on a roll," wrote Michael Sragow of the *New Yorker.* Despite the negative reviews and poor box office showing, Travers proclaimed the "maddeningly unfocused" film a "noble misfire." Travers praised Allen for having "sketched the outline for a great movie," although he lacked "the inspiration to make it come alive the way he did with *Crimes and Misdemeanors.*"

Turns Cinematic Eye Towards Married Life

While films such as *Shadows and Fog* have allowed Allen to experiment in new directions, he also continues to modify the formula which made *Annie Hall* and *Hannah and Her Sisters* so successful. His 1992 film *Husbands and Wives* adheres closely to the familiar Allen formula with its exploration of the trials and tribulations of two married couples. Filmed as a mock-documentary, the film was described by *Detroit Free Press* movie critic Judy Gerstel as "a primer for people contemplating or experiencing separation or divorce." Ironically, at the time the film was released, Allen and Farrow were involved in a very public break-up which was featured prominently in tabloids and legitimate newspapers alike. As divorcing couple Gabe and Judy, Allen and Farrow speak lines in the film which, to audiences, seemed especially poignant. "Do you ever hide things from me? Feelings, longings, complaints?... Do you think we'd ever break up?" asks Farrow of screen husband Allen. "At these moments," observed Richard Corliss in *Time,* "the masks of fiction drop and seem to reveal two naked, anguished souls: the 'real' Woody and Mia of late notoriety." David Ansen of *Newsweek* admitted that "it's not easy to watch Farrow and Allen in this film.... There are simply too many eerie moments that temporarily throw you out of the movie." Despite the burden of its stars' distracting real life troubles, the movie was applauded

Continuing his keen interest in the nature of art in film, Allen paid homage to the Expressionist movies of the 1920s in the 1992 release, *Shadows and Fog.*

by critics for its accurate insights into marital relations. "It's hard not to identify with these tangled, bungled affairs of the heart," Ansen wrote. "If this movie 'proves' anything, it's that Allen still knows better than most how to turn the demons of domesticity into edgy and hilarious art." Typical of Allen, he did not wait to gauge public reaction to *Husbands and Wives* before setting to work on his next project.

Throughout the critical highs and lows of Allen's career, the filmmaker himself has remained relatively untouched by the judgments—both good and bad—that reviewers have seen fit to bestow upon him. By ignoring the accolades of fickle critics and even more fickle fans, Allen has been able to disregard their disparagements, as well. "Woody Allen is a rare figure in American films— an artist who, early on, won so much good will from his public that it has continued to turn out even for his most radical departures," observed Edelstein. "He has earned the right to make modestly budgeted movies without studio interference, and he has earned the right to fail, which artists need if they're going to grow." Indeed, Allen himself has stated time and again that his main interest is making films, not earning awards. Allen does not value the commercial success of his films any more than critical success. "I've done films that were not commercial successes that I think were much better than ones I've done that

were tremendous commercial successes," he said in a 1987 *Rolling Stone* interview.

Allen himself seems intent on continuing to make "more and better movies than any other American director, comedies with wit and elegance," wrote David Remnick in the *Saturday Review.* Yet the rewards of filmmaking will one day cease to outweigh the hardships, and that's when Allen says he will quit. "It's like the story Groucho told me years ago," Allen told Remnick. "When the Marx brothers were filming *A Night in Casablanca,* he and Harpo had to run, run, run and grab onto the wing of a plane while it was taking off. They were exhausted. Groucho turned to Harpo while they were hanging on and said, 'Well, have you had enough?' Harpo said 'yes' and it was the last film they ever made."

■ Works Cited

Allen, Woody, *Take the Money and Run,* Palomar Pictures, 1969.

Allen, Woody, *Sleeper,* United Artists, 1973.

Allen, Woody, *Manhattan,* United Artists, 1979.

Allen, Woody, *Crimes and Misdemeanors,* Orion Pictures, 1989.

Allen, Woody, *Husbands and Wives,* TriStar Pictures, 1992.

Ansen, David, review in *Newsweek,* September 21, 1992, p. 76.

Canby, Vincent, review in the *New York Times,* April 29, 1979.

Canby, Vincent, column in the *New York Times,* March 1, 1985.

Canby, Vincent, review in the *New York Times,* February 7, 1986.

Canby, Vincent, review in the *New York Times,* February 9, 1986.

Corliss, Richard, review in *Time,* September 21, 1992, p. 64.

Edelstein, David, review in *Rolling Stone,* February 13, 1986, p. 25.

Geist, William E., interview in *Rolling Stone,* April 9, 1987, p. 39.

Gerstel, Judy, review in *Detroit Free Press,* September 18, 1992, p 1C.

Gilliatt, Penelope, review in *New Yorker,* April 25, 1977.

Kael, Pauline, review in *New Yorker,* July 26, 1982, p. 63.

Kael, Pauline, review in *New Yorker,* March 25, 1985.

Klawans, Stuart, review in *Nation,* November 13, 1989, p. 575.

Kroll, Jack, interview in *Newsweek*, April 24, 1978, p. 62.

People, August 28, 1982.

Remnick, David, *Saturday Review*, May-June, 1986, p. 30.

Robinson, David, review in the *Times* (London), October 7, 1983.

Schickel, Richard, review in *Time*, April 25, 1977.

Shales, Tom, interview in *Esquire*, April, 1987.

Sragow, Michael, review in *New Yorker*, April 6, 1992, p. 83.

Travers, Peter, review in *New Yorker*, April 16, 1992.

Zoglin, Richard, *Film Comment*, March/April, 1974.

■ For More Information See

BOOKS

Adler, Bill, and Jeff Feinman, *Woody Allen: Clown Prince of American Humor*, Pinnacle, 1975.

Anobile, Richard, editor, *Woody Allen's 'Play It Again, Sam,'* Grosset, 1977.

Brode, Douglas, *Woody Allen: His Films and Career*, Citadel, 1985.

Burton, D., *I Dream of Woody*, Morrow, 1984.

Contemporary Literary Criticism, Volume 16, Gale, 1981.

Dictionary of Literary Biography, Volume 44: *American Screenwriters, Second Series*, Gale, 1986.

Guthrie, Lee, *Woody Allen: A Biography*, Drake, 1978.

Hample, Stuart, *Non-Being and Somethingness: Selections from the Comic Strip 'Inside Woody Allen,'* Random House, 1978.

Hirsch, F., *Love, Sex, Death, and the Meaning of Life: Woody Allen's Comedy*, McGraw, 1981.

Kael, Pauline, *Reeling*, Little, Brown, 1976.

Lax, Eric, *On Being Funny: Woody Allen and Comedy*, Charterhouse, 1975.

Lax, Eric, *Woody Allen*, Vintage, 1991.

McKnight, Gerald, *Woody Allen: Joking Aside*, W. H. Allen, 1983.

Palmer, M., *Woody Allen*, Proteus Press, 1980.

Quinlan, David, *The Illustrated Guide to Film Directors*, Barnes & Noble Books, 1985.

Welch, Julie, *Leading Men*, Villard, 1985.

Yacowar, Maurice, *Loser Take All: The Comic Art of Woody Allen*, Ungar, 1979.

PERIODICALS

Atlantic, August, 1971; December, 1982; May, 1985.

Chicago Tribune, April 30, 1977; May 11, 1979; October 3, 1980; April 30, 1981; May 31, 1981; June 1, 1981; August 19, 1983; January 27, 1984; January 29, 1984; March 25, 1985; February 7, 1986; February 4, 1987.

Commentary, July, 1979; June, 1982; November, 1983.

Film Quarterly, winter, 1972; March/April, 1987.

Life, April 28, 1967; August 23, 1969; October 6, 1972.

Nation, September 11, 1982; September 17, 1983; March 17, 1984; February 21, 1987.

Newsweek, August 31, 1992, p. 52.

New Yorker, May 15, 1971; June 16, 1975; April 25, 1977; July 26, 1982; July 8, 1983; February 6, 1984; March 25, 1985; February 24, 1986; March 9, 1987; January 25, 1988.

People, August 31, 1992, p. 66.

Spectator, December 9, 1978.

Time, April 30, 1979; August 2, 1982; July 11, 1983; January 23, 1984; March 4, 1985; February 3, 1986; February 2, 1987; December 21, 1987; August 31, 1992, p. 54.°

—*Sketch by Cornelia A. Pernik*

Avi

Personal

Full name is Avi Wortis; given name is pronounced "*Ah*-vee"; born December 23, 1937, in New York, NY; son of Joseph (a psychiatrist) and Helen (a social worker; maiden name, Zunser) Wortis; married Joan Gabriner (a weaver) November 1, 1963 (divorced); married Coppelia Kahn (a professor of English); children: Shaun Wortis, Kevin Wortis; Gabriel Kahn (stepson). *Education:* Attended Antioch University; University of Wisconsin—Madison, B.A., 1959, M.A., 1962; Columbia University, M.S.L.S., 1964.

Addresses

Home—15 Sheldon St., Providence, RI 02906. *Agent*—Dorothy Markinko, McIntosh & Otis, Inc., 475 Fifth Ave., New York, NY 10017.

Career

Writer, 1960—. New York Public Library, New York City, librarian in Performing Arts Research Center, 1962-70; Lambeth Public Library, London, England, exchange program librarian, 1968; Trenton State College, Trenton, NJ, assistant pro-fessor and humanities librarian, 1970-86. Visiting writer in schools across the United States. *Member:* PEN, Authors Guild, Authors League of America.

Awards, Honors

Grants from New Jersey State Council on the Arts, 1974, 1976, and 1978; Mystery Writers of America Special Award, 1975, for *No More Magic*, 1979, for *Emily Upham's Revenge,* and 1983, for *Shadrach's Crossing;* Christopher Book Award, 1980, for *Encounter at Easton;* Children's Choice Award, International Reading Association, 1980, for *Man from the Sky,* and 1988, for *Romeo and Juliet, Together (and Alive) at Last;* Scott O'Dell Award for historical fiction, from *Bulletin of the Center for Children's Books,* 1984, for *The Fighting Ground;* Virginia Young Readers' Award, 1990, for *Wolf Rider: A Tale of Terror;* John Newbery Honor Award from American Library Association, *Horn Book-Boston Globe* Award, both 1991, both for *The True Confessions of Charlotte Doyle;* Newbery Honor Award, 1992, for *Nothing but the Truth.*

Snail Tale: The Adventures of a Rather Small Snail was named one of the best books of the year by the British Book Council, 1973; *School Library Journal,* best books of the year citations for *Night Journeys,* 1980, *Wolf Rider: A Tale of Terror,* 1987, and *The True Confessions of Charlotte Doyle,* 1990. American Library Association, best books for young adults citations, 1984, for *The Fighting Ground,* and 1986, for *Wolf Rider,* and notable book citation for *The True Confessions of Charlotte Doyle,* 1990. Library of Congress, best books of the year citations for *Something Upstairs*, 1989, and *The Man Who Was Poe*, 1990.

■ Writings

Things That Sometimes Happen, illustrated by Jodi Robbin, Doubleday, 1970.

Snail Tale: The Adventures of a Rather Small Snail, illustrated by Tom Kindron, Pantheon, 1972.

No More Magic, Pantheon, 1975.

Captain Grey, illustrated by Charles Mikolaycak, Pantheon, 1977.

Emily Upham's Revenge; or, How Deadwood Dick Saved the Banker's Niece: A Massachusetts Adventure, illustrated by Paul O. Zelinsky, Pantheon, 1978.

Night Journeys, Pantheon, 1979.

Encounter at Easton (sequel to *Night Journeys*), Pantheon, 1980.

Man from the Sky, illustrated by David Weisner, Knopf, 1980.

History of Helpless Harry: To Which Is Added a Variety of Amusing and Entertaining Adventures, illustrated by Zelinsky, Pantheon, 1980.

A Place Called Ugly, Pantheon, 1981.

Who Stole the Wizard of Oz?, illustrated by Derek James, Knopf, 1981.

Sometimes I Think I Hear My Name, Pantheon, 1982.

Shadrach's Crossing, Pantheon, 1983.

The Fighting Ground, Lippincott, 1984.

S.O.R. Losers, Bradbury, 1984.

Devil's Race, Lippincott, 1984.

Bright Shadow, Bradbury, 1985.

Wolf Rider: A Tale of Terror, Bradbury, 1986.

Devil's Race, Avon, 1987.

Romeo & Juliet—Together (& Alive) at Last (sequel to *S. O. R. Losers*) Avon, 1988.

Something Upstairs: A Tale of Ghosts, Orchard Books, 1988.

The Man Who Was Poe, Orchard Books, 1989.

The True Confessions of Charlotte Doyle, Orchard Books, 1990.

Windcatcher, Bradbury, 1991.

Nothing but the Truth, Orchard Books, 1991.

"Who Was That Masked Man, Anyway?", Orchard Books, 1992.

Blue Heron, Bradbury, 1992.

Judy and Punch, Bradbury, in press.

City of Light/City of Dark, Orchard Books, in press.

Also author of numerous plays. Contributor to books, including *Performing Arts Resources, 1974*, edited by Ted Perry, Drama Book Publishers, 1975. Contributor to periodicals, including *New York Public Library Bulletin, Top of the News*, *Children's Literature in Education, Horn Book*, and *Writer*. Book reviewer for *Library Journal, School Library Journal*, and *Previews*, 1965-73.

Translations of Avi's books have been published in Germany, Austria, Denmark, Norway, Spain, Italy, and Japan.

■ Adaptations

A recording of *The Fighting Ground* was produced by Listening Library. *Emily Upham's Revenge, Shadrach's Crossing, Something Upstairs, The Fighting Ground*, and *The True Confessions of Charlotte Doyle*, were produced on the radio programs "Read to Me," Maine Public Radio, and "Books Aloud," WWON-Rhode Island.

■ Sidelights

Avi is known to critics, teachers, parents, and particularly to young readers for his invitably readable novels. His award-winning books include mystery, adventure, historical, supernatural, coming-of-age, and comic novels—and many that are a bit of all of these categories. While captivating even reluctant readers with fast-paced, imaginative plots and plenty of action, Avi's books also offer complex, thought-provoking, and sometimes disturbingly realistic reflections of American culture to adolescents. The author summed up his goals as a young adult novelist in *Twentieth-Century Children's Writers*: "I try to write about complex issues—young people in an adult world—full of irony and contradiction, in a narrative style that relies heavily on suspense with a texture rich in emotion and imagery. I take a great deal of satisfaction in using popular forms—the adventure, the mystery, the thriller—so as to hold my reader with the sheer pleasure of a good story. At the same time I try to resolve my books with an ambiguity that compels engagement. In short, I want my readers to feel, to think, sometimes to laugh. But most of all I want them to enjoy a good read."

Born in Manhattan in 1937 and raised in Brooklyn, Avi grew up in an artistic environment. His great-grandparents and a grandmother were writers, so was an aunt. Two uncles were painters, one a composer. Both parents wrote. Today his twin sister is a writer and many members of his close, if extended, family are active in music, the arts, theatre, film, and television. During his childhood, Avi's family was also quite politically active in ways considered radical, fighting racism and supporting women's rights and labor and other concerns emanating from the Great Depression of the 1930s. The author explained in an interview with *Something about the Author* (SATA) that his extended family comprised "a very strong art community and what this meant for me as a child was that there was always a kind of uproarious sense of debate. It was all a very affectionate sharing of ideas—arguing, but not arguing in anger, arguing about ideas."

Childhood Difficulties in Writing

This early stimulation at home may have prepared Avi for challenges to come in his education. Although he was an avid reader as a child, difficulties in writing eventually caused him to flunk out of one school. He has since learned that he has a dysfunction known as dysgraphia, a marginal impairment in his writing abilities that causes him to reverse letters or misspell words. "One of my aunts said I could spell a four letter word wrong five ways," he told SATA. "In a school environment, I was perceived as being sloppy and erratic, and not paying attention." Despite constant criticism at school, Avi kept writing, and he credits his family's emphasis on books for his perseverance. When papers came back to him covered in his teachers' red ink, he simply saved them, corrections and all. "I think there was so much criticism, I became immune to it," he told SATA. "I wasn't even paying attention to it. I liked what I wrote."

Like many teens, Avi felt like an outsider in many social circles. His family's political views gave him early knowledge of what it meant to be in a minority. "You always assumed that your point of view was quirky or different," Avi told SATA. At school, aside from writing difficulties, he had some typical teenage insecurities. "When I was sixteen or seventeen I looked like I was twelve or thirteen. At that time that means a lot to you. It's hardly anyone's fault but you blame it on everybody, right?" Avi reflected: "I've led a very ordinary life in most respects. I think my adolescence was unhappy in the way that many adolescents' lives are unhappy."

Avi says that the first step on his course to writing professionally was reading. He learned more from reading everything from comic books and science magazines to histories, plays, and novels— than he learned in school. Despite the skepticism of his teachers, he determined while still in high school to make a career of writing. Avi once commented, "After my junior year in high school, my parents were informed that I was in desperate

need of a tutor, for somehow I had never taken the time to learn to write or to spell. That summer I met every day with a wonderful teacher who not only taught me writing basics, but also instilled in me the conviction that I wanted to be a writer myself. Perhaps it was stubbornness. It was generally agreed that was one thing I could not possibly do." Avi told SATA that he still has the diary entry from his senior year of high school in which he logged his decision to be a writer. "I can't wait! I've made up my mind," he wrote.

At Antioch University, Avi avoided English but enrolled in playwriting classes. "That's where I really started to write seriously," he told SATA. "The first playwriting instructor that I had would say, 'this is the way you do it.' You didn't have much choice in it, you had to do it in a very specific way. He even had charts for you to fill out. And I

Avi has written several historical adventures, including this 1977 pirate tale.

think I learned how to organize a story according to this man's precepts. It didn't even matter what [his system] was except that I absorbed it. I think, although I'm not sure of this, that that is still the structure I use when I write." One of the plays Avi wrote in college won a contest and was published in a magazine. The author said that during that time he wrote "a trunkful of plays but I would say ninety-nine percent of them weren't very good."

After working at a variety of jobs, Avi took a job in the theater collection of the New York Public Library. Enrolling in night school to study librarianship, he began a twenty-five year career as a librarian. But his determination to be a writer never flagged. He had written nearly 800 pages of his "great American novel," when, through an odd series of events, he turned to children's literature. It all began with telling stories to his two sons, Avi told *SATA*. "My oldest would tell me what the story should be about—he would invent stuff, a story about a glass of water and so forth. It became a game, and here I had a writing background so I was telling some fairly sophisticated stories."

Along with telling stories, Avi was a doodler, drawing pictures for fun. A friend who was writing a children's book, having seen his drawings, wanted Avi to provide illustrations. When the friend took the book with Avi's illustrations to a publisher, although the book was rejected, Avi was asked to illustrate other children's books. Arguing with the publisher that he was a writer and not an artist, Avi agreed to illustrate if he could also write the book. "Two weeks after this conversation, I was supposed to go to England on a library exchange thing, so I took a week off of work. Some neighbors were gone and I used their apartment. I put down all the stories that I had told my son and drew the pictures, all within one week. So this gets submitted to the publisher and of course she turned everything down. But—seven publishers down the road—Doubleday accepted it."

Avi's first children's book, *Things That Sometimes Happen*, was published—although without his artwork—in 1970. His agent called one day and asked what name he wanted on the book. "That's an odd question to ask," Avi remarked to *SATA*. "It was never an issue, but I thought about it, and I said, 'Oh well, just put Avi down,' and that was the decision. Just like that." *Things That Sometimes Happen*, a collection of "Very Short Stories for Very Young Readers," was designed with Avi's very young sons in mind. For several years he continued to write children's books geared to his sons' advancing reading levels, but he told *SATA*,

"At a certain point they kept growing and I didn't. I hit a fallow period, and then I wrote *No More Magic*. Suddenly I felt 'This is right! I'm writing novels and I love it.' From then on I was committed to writing novels."

Avi's Historical Novels

Avi has written many different forms of the novel. Since several of his early works, including *Captain Grey, Night Journeys,* and *Encounter at Easton,* are set in colonial America, he quickly earned a reputation as a historical novelist. Avi's 1984 novel *The Fighting Ground*, winner of the Scott O'Dell Award for historical fiction for children, presents one event-filled day in the life of Jonathan, a thirteen-year-old boy caught up in the Revolutionary War. The novel begins as Jonathan slips away from his family's New Jersey farm one morning in order to take part in a skirmish with the Hessians (German mercenary soldiers hired by the English). Jonathan sets out full of unquestioned hatred for the Hessians, the British, and for Americans who were loyal to the British—the Tories—and full of hope for a chance to take part in the glory of battle. "O Lord, he said to himself, make it be a battle. With armies, big ones, and cannons and flags and drums and dress parades! Oh, he could, *would* fight. Good as his older brother. Maybe good as his pa. Better, maybe. O Lord, he said to himself, make it something *grand!*"

Avi portrays no grandeur in the war. Jonathan can barely carry his six-foot long musket, and has a worse time trying to understand the talk among the men with whom he marches. The small voluntary group's leader is a crude man who lies to the men and is said to be "overfond of killing." After a bloody and confusing skirmish, Jonathan is captured by three Hessians, and briefly comes to understand them as individual human beings. Later, when he is called upon to be the brave soldier he had yearned to be, Jonathan's harrowing experience reveals the delusion behind his wish. At the close of the novel the reader, along with Jonathan, is brought to an understanding of what war means in human terms. *The Fighting Ground* was widely praised by critics, many of whom expressed sentiments similar to a reviewer for the *Bulletin of the Center for Children's Books* who, describing *The Fighting Ground* as "a small stunner," summarized that the novel "makes the war personal and immediate: not history or event, but experience; near and within oneself, and horrible."

Avi says he is more interested in finding a way to tell a good story and to provide a means of imagining and understanding the past than he is in teaching a specific historical fact. "The historical novel is a curious construction," he told *SATA*. "It represents history but it's not truly accurate. It's a style." He elaborated in an interview with Jim Roginski in *Behind the Covers:* "Somewhere along the line, I can't explain where, I developed an understanding of history not as fact but as story. That you could look at a field and, with only a slight shift of your imagination, suddenly watch the battle that took place there.... You have to have a willingness to look beyond *things....* Take the Battle of Bunker Hill during the Revolution. The leader of the American troops was Dr. Warren, who was killed during the battle. His body had been so dismembered and disemboweled, the only way he could be identified was by the nature of his teeth. And it was Paul Revere who did it. When you tell the story of war that way, a much stronger statement about how ghastly war really is, is made."

In *Something Upstairs: A Tale of Ghosts*, Avi's 1988 combination of historical novel, ghost story, and science fiction, a young man discovers the ghost of a murdered slave in the historic house his family recently moved into in Providence, Rhode Island. He travels back in time to the days of slave trading, where he learns about the murder and, perhaps more importantly, about the manner in which American history is collectively remembered. Although Avi was praised for his historical representation in this work, the author told *SATA* that "the irony is that in those Providence books there is nothing historical at all; it's a kind of fantasy of my neighborhood." Like his narrator in *Something Upstairs*, Avi moved from Los Angeles to Providence; in fact, he moved into the historic house featured in this novel. He told *SATA* that in his neighborhood, just walking down the street can inspire a story. The move to Providence "was truly like going back in history."

Fiction, History, and Edgar Allan Poe

The Man Who Was Poe, Avi's fictionalized portrait of nineteenth-century writer Edgar Allan Poe, intertwines fiction and history on several levels. Historically, Poe went through a period of severe depression and poverty, aggravated by alcoholism during the two years preceding his death in 1849. Avi, whose novel focuses on this period, said he became fascinated with Poe because he was so extraordinary and yet such "a horrible man." In

Along with its sequel, *Encounter at Easton*, this award-winning 1979 novel tells of life in colonial America.

the novel, a young boy, Edmund, has recently immigrated to Providence from England with his aunt and twin sister in order to look for his missing mother. When both aunt and sister disappear, the penniless boy must elicit help from a stranger—who happens to be Edgar Allan Poe. Poe, noticing similarities in Edmund's story to his own life and detecting material for his writing, agrees to help the boy. Between maddening bouts of drunkenness, Poe ingeniously finds a trail of clues. Edmund, who has been taught to defer to adults, alternates between awe of the great man's perceptive powers and despair at his madness.

Vividly reflecting the macabre tone of Poe's fiction, Avi portrays the old port city of Providence as a bleak and chaotic world in which compassion and moral order seem to have given way to violence and greed. The character Poe, with his morbid

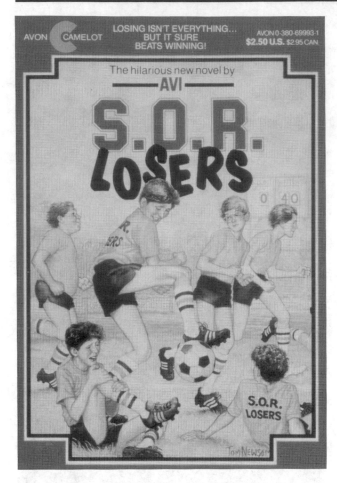

AVON CAMELOT

LOSING ISN'T EVERYTHING...
BUT IT SURE
BEATS WINNING!

AVON 0-380-69993-1
$2.50 U.S. $2.95 CAN.

The hilarious new novel by
——— AVI ———
S.O.R.
LOSERS

S.O.R.
LOSERS

Nerdy kids and an inexperienced coach show how funny losing can be in this 1984 story.

imagination, makes an apt detective in this realm until it becomes clear that he wants the "story" of Edmund's family to end tragically. Edmund's plight is a harsh one, relying on Poe as the only adult who can help him, while at the same time attempting to ensure that Poe's vision does not become a reality. A reviewer for the *Bulletin of the Center for Children's Books,* describing the novel as "a complex, atmospheric thriller," remarked that "Avi recreates the gloom of 1840s [Providence] with a storyteller's ease, blending drama, history, and mystery without a hint of pastiche or calculation. And, as in the best mystery stories, readers will be left in the end with both the comfort of puzzles solved and the unease of mysteries remaining."

In another unique twist on the convention of historical novels, Avi's 1990 *The True Confessions of Charlotte Doyle* presents the unlikely story of a very proper thirteen-year-old girl who, as the sole passenger and only female on a trans-Atlantic ship in 1832, becomes involved in a mutiny at sea. Holding her family's aristocratic views on social

class and demeanor, Charlotte begins her voyage trusting only Captain Jaggery, whose fine manners and authoritative command remind her of her father. She is thus shocked to find that Jaggery is a viciously brutal shipmaster. This discovery, along with her growing fondness for members of the ship's crew, gradually leads Charlotte to question—and discard—the values of her privileged background. As she exchanges her finishing school wardrobe for a common sailor's garb and joins the crew in its work, she reveals the strength of her character, initially masked by her restrictive upbringing.

In the adventures that follow, including a mysterious murder, a storm, and a mutiny, Charlotte's reeducation and emancipation provide a new version of the conventionally male story of rugged individualism at sea. The multi-award-winning novel has received accolades from critics for its suspense, its evocation of life at sea, and particularly for the rich and believable narrative of its protagonist as she undergoes a tremendous change in outlook. The impact of Charlotte's liberation from social bonds and gender restrictions in *The True Confessions of Charlotte Doyle* has a powerful emotional effect on many of its readers. Avi told *SATA* that "many people, mostly girls, and even adults, have told me of bursting into tears" at the book's ending—tears of relief that Charlotte finds the freedom to realize herself as she chooses. In his *Boston Globe-Horn Book* Award acceptance speech, referring to the words of a critic who spoke of the "improbable but deeply satisfying conclusion" of the novel, Avi commented: "I am deeply grateful for the award you have given me today. But I hope you will understand me when I tell you that if the 'improbable' life I wrote lives in someone's heart as a life *possible,* then I have already been given the greatest gift a writer can receive: a reader who takes my story and endows it with life by the grace of their own desire."

Avi, although an enthusiastic reader of history, is by no means tied to the historical novel and delights in finding new ways to structure his stories. He told *SATA:* "People constantly ask 'How come you keep changing styles?' I think that's a misquestion. Put it this way, 'What makes you so fascinated with technique?' You know that there are a lot of ways to tell a story. To me that's just fun." With his extensive background in theater, it is no surprise that many of Avi's novels have roots in drama.

Comedy with a Point

In 1984, Avi published *S.O.R. Losers,* a funny contemporary novel about a group of unathletic boys forced by their school (which is based on Avi's high school in New York City) to form a soccer team. Opposing the time-honored school ethic that triumph in sports is the American way, the boys form their own opinions about winning at something that means little to them. In a team meeting, they take stock of who they are and why it's so important to everyone *else* that they should win their games. The narrator, who is the team's captain, sums it up: "Every one of us is good at something. Right? Maybe more than one thing. The point is *other* things.... But I don't like sports. I'm not good at it. I don't enjoy it. So I say, so what? I mean if Saltz here writes a stinko poem— and he does all the time—do they yell at him? When was the last time Mr. Tillman came around and said, 'Saltz, I *believe* in your being a poet!'"

Avi makes a clear statement with his humor in *S.O.R. Losers.* He told *SATA* that he sees an irony in the American attitude toward education. "On the one hand, our culture likes to give a lot of lip service to support for kids, but on the other hand, I don't think the culture as a whole likes kids. And kids are caught in this contradiction. I ask teachers at conferences 'How many of you have athletic trophies displayed in your schools?' You know how many raise their hands. And I ask, 'How many of you have trophy displays for the best reader or writer?' Nobody raises their hands. And I say 'What is it therefore that stands as the essential achievement in your school?' With test scores falling, we need to make kids better readers, but instead we're interested in a minority of kids, mostly males, whose primary focus is sports."

But with its narrator's deadpan reporting of the fiascos involved in being consistent losers in sports, *S.O.R. Losers* does more than make a point. *Horn Book* contributor Mary M. Burns, who called the novel "one of the funniest and most original sports sagas on record," particularly praised Avi's skill with comedic form. "Short, pithy chapters highlighting key events maintain the pace necessary for successful comedy. As in a Charlie Chaplin movie, emphasis is on individual episode—each distinct, yet organically related to an overall idea." Avi has written several other comic novels, including his sequel to *S.O.R. Losers, Romeo and Juliet, Together (and Alive) At Last,* and two well-received spoofs on nineteenth-century melodrama, *Emily Upham's Revenge* and *The History of Helpless Harry.*

Avi has also written several acclaimed contemporary coming-of-age novels, including *A Place Called Ugly* and *Sometimes I Think I Hear My Name.* His 1992 Newbery honor book, *Nothing but the Truth* is the story of Philip Malloy and his battle with an English teacher, Miss Narwin. With bad grades in English keeping him off the track team, Philip repeatedly breaks school rules by humming the national anthem along with the public address system in Miss Narwin's home room. Eventually, the principal suspends Philip from school. Because the school happens to be in the midst of elections, various self-interested members of the community exploit this story of a boy being suspended for his patriotism. Much to everyone's surprise, the incident in home room snowballs into a national media event that, in its frenzied patriotic rhetoric, thoroughly overshadows the true story about a good teacher's inability to reach a student, a young man's alienation, a community's disinterest in its children's needs, and a school system's hypocrisy.

Avi shows that there is no glory in war in his 1984 tale of the American Revolution.

Nothing but the Truth is a book without a narrator, relating its story through school memos, diary entries, letters, dialogues, newspaper articles, and radio talk show scripts. Presented thus, without narrative bias, the story takes into account the differing points of view surrounding the incident, allowing the reader to root out the real problems leading to the incident. Avi told *SATA* that he got the idea for the structure of this novel from a form of theater that arose in the 1930s called "Living Newspapers"—dramatizations of issues and problems confronting American society presented through a "hodge podge" of document readings and dialogues.

Avi displays his sympathy to the "outsider" position of adolescence with his character, Philip Malloy. In all the national attention Philip receives as a patriotic hero, no one asks him what he feels or thinks, and no one seems to notice that he changes from a fairly happy and enthusiastic youth to a depressed and alienated adolescent. Philip's interest in *The Outsiders*, S. E. Hinton's novel about rival gangs of teenagers (written when Hinton was only seventeen years old herself), reveals that Philip would like to read about a world that looks like his own, with people experiencing problems like his. The Shakespeare plays assigned in school do not reach him. Avi explained to *SATA:* "It's not an accident that in the last decades the book most read by young people is *The Outsiders*. I wish Stephen King's novels were taught in the schools, so that kids could respond to them and talk about them." Avi, too, wishes to write about subjects his readers can respond to meaningfully, and does not hesitate to set complexities and harsh truths before his readers because, as he said to *SATA*, these truths are already well-known to children. "I think writers like myself say to kids like this, 'We affirm your sense of reality.' We help frame it and give it recognition."

Avi's Relationship with His Readers

Although now writing on a full-time basis, Avi maintains regular interaction with children by traveling around the country, talking in schools about his writing. "I think it's very important for me to keep these kids in front of my eyes. They're wonderfully interesting and they hold me to the reality of who they are." Avi told *SATA* that children are passionate and honest readers who will either "swallow a book whole" if they like it, or drop it "like a hot potato" if they don't. In an article in *School Library Journal*, he provides a telling anecdote about his approach to children:

The author combines fiction with fact in his 1989 novel about nineteenth-century writer Edgar Allan Poe.

"Being dysgraphic, with the standard history of frustration and anguish, I always ask to speak to the learning-disabled kids. They come in slowly, waiting for yet another pep talk, more instructions. Eyes cast down, they won't even look at me. Their anger glows. I don't say a thing. I lay out pages of my copy-edited manuscripts, which are covered with red marks. 'Look here,' I say, 'see that spelling mistake. There, another spelling mistake. Looks like I forgot to put a capital letter there. Oops! Letter reversal.' Their eyes lift. They are listening. And I am among friends."

Avi describes himself as a committed skeptic, yet reveals an idealistic center when he discusses children and their role in American culture. He believes that children have a different outlook than most adults. Avi remarked to *SATA:* "When do you become an adult? Sometimes I think the difference is that psychological shift when you start to accept that tomorrow is going to be the same as today.

When you're a kid, there are still options, major options. For a writer like myself, a child is a kind of metaphor for a return to idealism and passionate concern: a metaphor for the ability to change or react, to be honest about all those things that as adults we tend to slide over as we make compromises to obligations and necessities." In an article for *Horn Book* he contrasts children's literature, which generally espouses values such as "sharing, nonviolence, cooperation, and the ability to love," to the adult world where power and self-interest seem to rule. "More than anything else," Avi asserted in *Horn Book*, "children's literature is about the place and role of the child in society.... If we—in the world of children's literature—can help the young stand straight for a moment longer than they have done in the past, help them maintain their ideals and values, those with which you and I identify ourselves, help them demand— and win—justice, we've added something good to the world."

With his success as a professional writer, Avi has proved his childhood critics—his teachers—wrong about his abilities. But he reacts to the surge of critical attention he is now getting in the same skeptical way he responded to the red ink of his teachers many years ago. "I feel awkward about all of this. It's a kind of craziness," he told *SATA*. "I know it's all nonsense. You know, one magazine had a review of a new book of mine and referred to my 'uncanny' insight into character. I mean, the best thing you can say about that line is it's great in a family argument. My wife may say, 'You didn't wash those dishes very well,' and I can say 'Yeah, but I've got an uncanny insight.'" Avi maintains his own perspective on the merits of his work. Although he loves to write and is never at a loss for ideas, he says he never feels secure that his next book will be as successful as the last. This uncertainty, he told *SATA*, keeps him striving to do his best. "The minute you sit back and say 'this is good, this is right,' you've had it."

■ Works Cited

Avi, *The Fighting Ground*, Lippincott, 1984.

Avi, *S.O.R. Losers*, Bradbury, 1984.

Avi, "All That Glitters," *Horn Book*, September-October, 1987, pp. 569-576.

Avi, and Betty Miles, "School Visits: The Author's Viewpoint," *School Library Journal*, January, 1987, p. 21.

Avi, autobiographical statement in *Twentieth-Century Children's Writers*, St. Martin's, 1989, pp. 45-46.

Avi, *Boston Globe-Horn Book* Award acceptance speech, *Horn Book*, January-February, 1992, p. 24-27.

Avi, telephone interview with Sonia Benson for *Something about the Author*, conducted March 16, 1992.

Burns, Mary M., review of *S.O.R. Losers*, *Horn Book*, January-February, 1985, p. 49.

Review of *The Fighting Ground*, *Bulletin of the Center for Children's Books*, June, 1984, p. 180.

Review of *The Man Who Was Poe*, *Bulletin of the Center for Children's Books*, October, 1989, p. 27.

Review of *Nothing but the Truth*, *Publishers Weekly*, September 6, 1991, p. 105.

Roginski, Jim, *Behind the Covers: Interviews with Authors and Illustrators of Books for Children and Young Adults*, Libraries Unlimited, 1985, pp. 33-41.

Something about the Author, Volume 14, Gale, 1978, pp. 269-270.

■ For More Information See

PERIODICALS

Best Sellers, August, 1979, pp. 165-166; June, 1981, pp. 118-119; May, 1982, p. 76.

Bulletin of the Center for Children's Books, July, 1978, p. 170; July-August, 1980, p. 206; June, 1983; December, 1986, p. 61; February, 1986, p. 102; October, 1987, p. 21; September, 1988, p. 2.

English Journal, November, 1981, p. 94.

Five Owls, January, 1991, p. 56.

Horn Book, August, 1979, p. 410; April, 1980, pp. 169-170; October, 1980, pp. 517-518; April, 1981, p. 136; June, 1981, pp. 297-298; August, 1983, p. 439; June, 1984, p. 325; January-February, 1989, p. 65.

Language Arts, October, 1979, p. 822; November-December, 1983, p. 1017; March, 1985, p. 283.

New York Times Book Review, September 11, 1977; March 1, 1981, p. 24.

Publishers Weekly, April 17, 1978, p. 78; December 5, 1980; January 30, 1981, p. 75; November 16, 1984, p. 65; December 26, 1986, p. 61; August 28, 1987, p. 81; September 14, 1990, p. 128; September 6, 1991, p. 105.

School Library Journal, March, 1978, p. 124; May, 1980, p. 64; November, 1980, p. 68; September, 1984, p. 125; October, 1984, p. 164; December, 1986, pp. 111-112; October, 1987, p. 124.

Voice of Youth Advocates, August, 1981, pp. 23-24; August, 1982, p. 27; December, 1984, pp. 261-262; February, 1985, p. 321; February, 1989, p. 293.

—Sketch by Sonia Benson

Clive Barker

■ Personal

Born in 1952 in Liverpool, England; son of Len (a personnel director) and Joan (a school welfare officer) Barker. *Education:* Attended University of Liverpool.

■ Addresses

Home—36 Wimpole St., London, W. 2, England. *Agent*—Creative Artists Agency, 9830 Wilshire Blvd., Beverly Hills, CA 90212.

■ Career

Illustrator, painter, actor, playwright, and author. Executive producer of motion pictures, including *Hellbound: Hellraiser II*, 1989, and *Hellraiser III: Hell on Earth*, 1992.

■ Awards, Honors

Two British Fantasy Awards from British Fantasy Society; World Fantasy Award for best anthology/collection, World Fantasy Convention, 1985, for *Clive Barker's Books of Blood*.

■ Writings

"CLIVE BARKER'S BOOKS OF BLOOD" SERIES

Volume One (contains "The Book of Blood," "In the Hills, the Cities," "The Midnight Meat Train," "Pig Blood Blues," "Sex, Death, and Starshine," and "The Yattering and Jack"), introduction by Ramsey Campbell, Sphere, 1984, Berkley Publishing, 1986.

Volume Two (contains "Dread," "Hell's Event," "Jaqueline Ess: Her Will and Testament," "New Murders in the Rue Morgue," and "The Skins of the Fathers"), Sphere, 1984, Berkley, 1986.

Volume Three (contains "Confessions of a [Pornographer's] Shroud," "Human Remains," "Rawhead Rex," "Scape-goats," and "Son of Celluloid"), Sphere, 1984, Berkley, 1986.

Books of Blood, Volumes 1-3, Weidenfeld & Nicolson, 1985, one-volume edition, Scream/Press, 1985.

Volume Four (contains "The Age of Desire," "The Body Politic," "Down, Satan!," "The Inhuman Condition," and "Revelations"), Sphere, 1985, published in United States as *The Inhuman Condition: Tales of Terror*, Poseidon, 1986.

Volume Five (contains "Babel's Children," "The Forbidden," "In the Flesh," and "The Madonna"), Sphere, 1985, published in United State as *In the Flesh: Tales of Terror*, Poseidon, 1986.

Volume Six (contains "How Spoilers Breed," "The Last Illusion," "The Life of Death," "On Jerusalem Street," and "Twilight at the Towers"), Sphere, 1985, selections published in the United States with the novella *Cabal* (also see below).

Books of Blood, Volumes 4-6, Weidenfeld & Nicolson, 1986.

NOVELS, EXCEPT WHERE NOTED

The Damnation Game, Weidenfeld & Nicolson, 1985, Putnam, 1987.

(Contributor) *Night Visions Three* (includes Barker's novella *The Hellbound Heart*), edited by George R. R. Martin, Dark Harvest, 1986.

Weaveworld, Poseidon, 1987, special edition illustrated by Barker, Collins, 1987.

The Hellbound Heart (novella), Simon & Schuster, 1988.

Cabal (contains novella *Cabal,* and short stories "How Spoilers Breed," "The Last Illusion," "The Life of Death," and "Twilight at the Towers" from *Books of Blood, Volume Six*), Poseidon, 1988.

The Great and Secret Show: The First Book of the Art, HarperCollins, 1989.

Imajica, HarperCollins, 1991.

SCREENPLAYS

Underworld, Limehouse Pictures, 1985.

Rawhead Rex (adapted from Barker's short story), Empire, 1987.

(And director) *Hellraiser* (adapted from Barker's novella *The Hellbound Heart*), New World, 1987.

(And director) *Nightbreed* (adapted from Barker's novella *Cabal*), Twentieth Century-Fox, 1990.

ILLUSTRATOR

(With others) *Fly in My Eye: An Anthology of Unparalleled Confusion*, Arcane, Inc., 1988.

Clive Barker, Illustrator, edited by Steve Niles, text by Fred Burke, Arcane/Eclipse Books, 1990.

Clive Barker's Shadows in Eden, edited by Steve Jones, introduction by Ramsey Campbell, Underwood/Miller, 1991.

OTHER

(Author of introduction) Ramsey Campbell, *Scared Stiff: Tales of Sex and Death*, Scream/Press, 1987.

(Author of introduction), *Night Visions Four* (anthology), Dark Harvest, 1987.

(Author of introduction) *Taboo*, edited by Stephen R. Bissette, Spiderbaby Grafix and Publications, 1988.

(Author of introduction) *H. R. Giger's Necronomicon*, Morpheus International, 1991.

(Author of introduction) Stephen King, *Salem's Lot* (Stephen King Collectors Editions), New American Library/Dutton, 1991.

Author of plays, including *Frankenstein in Love, The History of the Devil, Subtle Bodies,* and *The Secret Life of Cartoons*. Work represented in anthologies, including *Cutting Edge*, published by Futura. Contributor to periodicals, including *Penthouse, American Film,* and *Omni*.

■ Adaptations

"TAPPING THE VEIN" GRAPHIC NOVEL SERIES

Book One, art by Craig P. Russell and Scott Hampton, Eclipse, 1989.

Book Two (adaptation of "In the Hills, the Cities" and "The Skins of the Fathers"), art by Klaus Janson and John Bolton, Eclipse, 1989.

Book Three, Eclipse, 1990.

Book Four, Eclipse, 1990.

BOOKS ON TAPE

The Body Politic (story from volume four of *Books of Blood*), Simon & Schuster, 1987.

The Damnation Game, Warner, 1987.

Cabal, The Great and Secret Show, Imajica, and other stories from *Books of Blood* have all been adapted to audio tape.

OTHER

Alan Grant, John Wagner, and Jim Baikie, *Clive Barker's Night Breed: Genesis* (graphic novel; adaptation of *Nightbreed*), Epic Comics, 1991.

Weaveworld (graphic novel), Eclipse, 1992.

The Candyman (film; adaptation of Barker's short story "The Forbidden"), Tri-Star, 1992.

Characters from *Hellraiser* have also been adapted to graphic novel.

■ Work in Progress

A sequel to *The Great and Secret Show*.

■ Sidelights

"Every body is a book of blood; wherever we're opened, we're red," states Clive Barker's epigraph to his first collection of short stories. With the publication of the first three volumes of *Books of*

"I HAVE SEEN THE FUTURE OF HORROR...
AND IT IS NAMED CLIVE BARKER."
—STEPHEN KING

VOLUME THREE of
CLIVE BARKER'S
BOOKS
of
BLOOD

A BERKLEY BOOK · 0-425-09347-6 · $2.95

Be thankful
if your heart stops.
At least the worst
is over.

One of the volumes of Barker's award-winning anthology series, which got him his start as a published author of horror.

Blood in 1984, the British writer entered the world of horror fiction with a collection of tales based on vivid description, visceral terror, and graphically detailed gore. His work was quickly noticed by some of horror's most notable writers—including Ramsey Campbell and Stephen King—as well as numerous readers. Barker followed this first installment of short stories with the publication of three more volumes of *Books of Blood* and a novel, *The Damnation Game*, in 1985. Over the next two years he published a second novel, *Weaveworld*, adapted and directed his first motion picture, *Hellraiser*, and became one of the most popular fiction authors in the United States and England. He has since written two more novels and a novella, directed another movie, produced two films, and overseen the adaptation of his short stories to graphic novel form. The author's broad

imagination, literary skill, and prolific output led King to proclaim on the covers of *Books of Blood:* "I have seen the future of horror, and its name is Clive Barker."

Born in Liverpool, England, Barker grew up in a country eroding in the wake of the unfulfilled promises of its World War II victory. Facing a community of poverty, unemployment, and despair, the author sought diversion from his surroundings. As a youth he developed an appetite for chimerical literature, reading books by Kenneth Grahame, Herman Melville, and Ray Bradbury. "I never read much material that didn't have some element of the extraordinary or the fantastic in it," Barker told Mikal Gilmore in *Rolling Stone*. "Of course my parents were not really in sympathy with the surreal. I suppose that made it into a vice, which wasn't altogether a bad thing." In addition to his interest in words, Barker was also intrigued by art, and so he studied at the College of Art in Liverpool. However, Liverpool's grim working-class atmosphere precipitated a move to London in the early seventies. In the bustling environment of London, Barker found work as an artist, including a stint illustrating pornography. During this time he began writing for the stage, earning a reputation with plays like *Frankenstein in Love* and *The Secret Life of Cartoons*. Barker had also begun to write fiction, creating short stories for the entertainment of his friends. It was not until he came across a copy of *Dark Forces*, a horror anthology edited by Stephen King's agent, that Barker realized that his short pieces might be marketable. He set to work writing and within the span of a few months had added fourteen stories to his repertoire.

Blood and Beyond

Divided into the first three volumes of *Books of Blood*, those stories became Barker's wake-up call to the readers and writers of horror fiction. As Gilmore described them in *Rolling Stone:* "They were wilder and more wide-ranging stories than the horror world had seen in some time, and their impact on the genre was considerable and rapid." The tales in *Books of Blood* earned their author comparisons to such past masters of horror as Edgar Allan Poe and H. P. Lovecraft, as well as instant access to the elevated ranks of contemporaries like King, Peter Straub, and Dean R. Koontz. The stories contain bracingly open depictions of mutilation, bizarre sex, and graphic violence, but beyond these elements of revulsion, critics and readers were able to discern a talent that transcended the parameters of the genre. "*Books of*

Blood cannot be dismissed as mere splatter fiction," wrote Michael A. Morrison in *Fantasy Review*, "the philosophical and thematic content of these visceral stories elevates them from this category." While the stories vary in settings, plots, and points of view, Barker infuses each of them with detailed examinations of the hideous. "In the Hills, the Cities" tells of a feud between two villages that has evolved to a grotesque extreme; "The Skins of the Fathers," portrays monsters as benevolent, godlike creatures in contrast to coarse, small-minded humans; and in "Son of Celluloid," the malignant spirit of a criminal gives new and twisted life to the celebrity ghosts inhabiting a movie house. "There's always a sense in my work, I hope, of a celebration of the monstrous," Barker told Gilmore, "of beauty found rooted in disturbing imagery—and a sense that finally these confrontations, however dangerous, are enriching and enlightening." Douglas E. Winter saw Barker's stories as a cathartic means to face one's fears, as he described the volumes in the *Washington Post*: "The *Books of Blood* are founded on the proposition that there are no taboos, no mysteries. Barker's eye is unblinking; he drags our terrors from the shadows and forces us to look upon them and despair or laugh with relief."

In 1985 Barker published his second *Books of Blood* trilogy, the first two volumes of which were printed in America under the respective titles *The Inhuman Condition* and *In the Flesh*. Critics noted that this second set of *Books of Blood* reflected a change in Barker's style. As Winter wrote in the *Washington Post*: "These stories reflect a decided maturation of style and find Barker relying more often on craft than sheer explicitness of image to convey his horrors." Stories such as "Twilight at the Towers" and "Babel's Children" examine the horror found beneath the veneer of everyday humanity and often juxtapose fantastic events with reality. In "The Body Politic," human hands decide to secede from the union of anatomy and sever themselves from their owners'arms to lead their own lives. The new volumes expanded Barker's reading audience, and with the publication of his first novel, *The Damnation Game*, his stature among horror aficionados increased.

The Damnation Game spans the decades from the last days of World War II to present day England. As the novel opens, the reader is introduced to two shrouded characters who meet amid the dank death and rubble that was once the city of Warsaw, Poland. One is a cabalistic figure called the Cardplayer, the other an elemental character known as the Thief. They have met to engage in the game for which the former is named: a card game with spiritually perilous stakes. The focus shifts to England several decades later, and the Thief has become a reclusive millionaire named Joseph Whitehead. Whitehead lives on a vast high security estate that provides the setting for the remainder of the book. Despite the measures he has taken to seal his property and himself from the outside world, the millionaire has discovered signs that someone—or something—has penetrated his fortress. Fearing for his safety, Whitehead hires an ex-convict named Marty Strauss as a bodyguard. It does not take Strauss long to learn that his new employer is a man with dark secrets, or that the millionaire's strange afflictions signify something more than mere harassment. The threat to Whitehead stems from his betrayal of the Cardplayer, whose real name is Mamoulian. Whitehead has failed to honor a condition of the card game and has managed to elude Mamoulian's ire up until now. However, the Cardplayer has an arsenal beyond the realm of mortal man; Mamoulian has lived for over two hundred years and possesses, among other powers, the ability to reanimate and command the dead. Events intertwine, drawing in Strauss and Whitehead's disturbed daughter. The novel climaxes with the two men meeting in an apocalyptic culmination of the game they began in Warsaw.

While *The Damnation Game* shares similar settings and themes with other horror novels, some critics felt that Barker instilled elements of style that set the novel apart from books common to the genre. "*The Damnation Game* is an important novel, helping to establish links between graphic horror and high quality literature," wrote Chris Morgan in *Fantasy Review*, adding that the book was "brilliantly executed." *The Damnation Game* made several best seller lists as its author's reputation spread. Laurence Coven lauded the novel in *Washington Post Book World*, and said of Barker: "In pure descriptive power there is no one writing horror fiction now who can match him."

Carpet Magic

Barker followed this wave of critical and popular success with his second novel, *Weaveworld*, which incorporates his horror techniques into a fantasy format. The central figure in the 1987 book is Cal Mooney. Cal is a young man at a crossroads in his life; he knows he must make a decision regarding his future, but he loathes the idea of marrying a dull woman, taking a colorless job, and settling into a torpid loop of domesticity. Then one day, while moving a deceased woman's possessions, he encounters the Weave, and his life changes forever. To most, the Weave is a beautiful, intricately designed rug, but to some eyes it is much more. As Cal studies the designs in the rug and allows his mind to drift, he finds that he has actually drifted into the rug. He is astounded to find that he has been transported to the world depicted in the rug's design, a lush macrocosm of forests and rivers where magic exists at every turn. Cal learns that this world is called the Fugue and its people are known as the Seerkind. The Fugue and its populace have existed in secrecy for years inside the Weave. The Seerkind have their reasons for keeping the Fugue a secluded paradise, for it is the target of the Scourge, a malevolent sect intent upon eradicating magic from the world. The Scourge has succeeded in eliminating vast numbers of Seerkind in its relentless crusade to decimate the Fugue. The survivors were forced into hiding on the earthly plane, often relying on the goodwill of understanding humans. A group of elder Seerkind were able to plait a spell and create the Weave, thus helping to protect their people from further harm. For many generations the Weave has been guarded by a trusted human with the hope that one day, when the world is safe for magic, the Weave will be undone, the Fugue will again be free, and all lost Seerkind will be welcomed home.

Cal experiences but a brief taste of the Fugue's paradise before he is returned to his world. His fleeting exposure to the exciting and fantastic life of the Seerkind is enough to convince him that the Fugue is the place where he wants to spend the rest of his days. In the Weave he has found his future and his purpose; a world beset with danger yet brimming with life—and desperately in need of help. However, before he can attempt a return to the Fugue, the rug is stolen by agents of the Scourge. Cal pursues the thieves but soon learns that he is no match for their ethereal powers. The leader of the Scourge, an alluring and deadly virgin witch named Immacolata, is joined by her two specter-like sisters and a reptilian salesman named Shadwell. In order to rescue the Fugue, Cal joins forces with Suzanna Parrish, the granddaughter of the Weave's last guardian—the woman whose possessions Cal was moving when he discovered the rug. Helping Cal and Suzanna in the fight are a band of wayward Seerkind seeking a return to their stolen home. Their quest takes them to the darkest regions of the real world, into the Weave itself, and

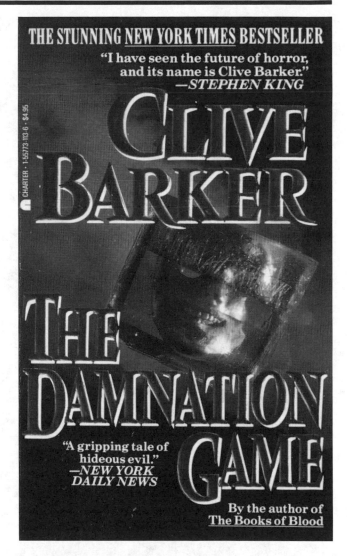

Making the move from short stories and novellas to novels, Barker's first full-length novel was praised for literary quality above that of the typical horror work.

through the liminal cracks that lie between reality and fantasy.

Weaveworld allowed Barker to showcase his writing range. The novel's juxtaposition of genres, varied characters, and epic scale showed the breadth of the author's ability. The novel indicated that Barker was moving beyond the parameters set forth by generations of horror writers before him, and, as some reviewers noted, attempting to brighten the perception of the genre. "*Weaveworld* is clearly Barker's loveliest, most hopeful work," wrote Gilmore in *Rolling Stone*, comparing the novel to the works of noted fantasist J. R. R. Tolkien. Barker explained to Gilmore that *Weaveworld* is a horror book "about the *idea* of fantasy," and further regarded the novel as "a defense of not just my art but of the whole idea of having, to

A number of Barker's short stories have been adapted for this graphic novel series.

quote [philosophical author] Colin Wilson, 'the strength to dream.'" An article in *Kirkus Reviews* proclaimed that *Weaveworld* "manages via its powerful and giddy torrent of invention to grasp the golden ring as the most ambitious and visionary horror novel of the decade."

Mr. Barker Goes to the Movies

In the same year that *Weaveworld* was published, Barker engendered his reputation as a renaissance man of horror by directing his first film. He had previous experience with the cinema, having written both an original screenplay titled *Underworld* and a screen adaptation of his short story *Rawhead Rex*. Barker was unhappy with the results of both films, which he felt strayed from, and lacked the necessary means to realize, his original vision. As he told Jean W. Ross in a *Contemporary Authors* (*CA*) interview, "After those movies I decided to take the law into my own hands." Barker set to work adapting his novella *The Hellbound Heart* into a screenplay that he would direct. The resulting film is *Hellraiser*.

Hellraiser opens with thrill-seeker Frank Cotton purchasing a Chinese puzzle box in a nameless Third World country. When he returns to England, Frank learns that the puzzle box, once solved, opens a gateway to a nightmarish dimension: Rubic's cube goes to hell. The keepers of this netherworld are mutated and mutilated humanoids called Cenobites. The Cenobites take Frank to their realm, where they promise him an eternity of intense pleasure and unbearable pain. Among other indulgences, Frank is treated to such carnal delights as having his flesh pulled apart by thousands of tiny hooks. Meanwhile, Frank's brother, Larry, has purchased Frank's house. In the process of moving in, Larry accidentally cuts his hand in the very room where Frank discovered Cenobite hell. As Larry's blood hits the floorboards it is greedily absorbed into the wood. Later, when Larry's new wife, Julia, returns to clean the blood from the room, she is horrified to find a partially formed human body that she recognizes as Larry's brother—and her former lover—Frank. Frank tells Julia about the anguish and ecstasy of his bondage with the Cenobites and of his subsequent escape from their world. He tells Julia that although the Cenobites destroyed his physical body, he has the ability, with her help, to regenerate. In order to reconstruct a body Frank needs human blood, so Julia must lure men into the room and kill them, their ebbing lifeforce hungrily consumed by the evolving Frank.

Before Frank can fully reconstitute, Larry's teenage daughter Kirsty stumbles into the room. She is mortified to find a skeletal form with raw muscle and nerve growing on it, but she is more terrified when she discovers that this flayed corpse walks and talks and is, in fact, her missing uncle. Despite his deficient physiognomy, Frank still has a voracious sexual appetite and, finding Kirsty attractive, approaches her. The two struggle and Kirsty escapes, taking Frank's puzzle box with her. She later solves the box and the Cenobites appear, ready to take her away. She bargains with the beings, extracting from them a promise to release her if she leads them to Frank. By this time Frank has become completely human, having killed Larry and assumed his brother's features. Kirsty arrives—with the Cenobites close behind—to confront her stepmother and Uncle Frank.

Hellraiser became a cult horror classic. Fans of Barker's fiction were pleased to see the author's penchant for gore translated to the screen. Although some critics complained of problems with the film's pacing and acting, most agreed that Barker's debut as a director was impressive. "The film literally drips with horrific ambience," stated *Motion Picture Guide* (*MPG*), describing *Hellraiser*

Barker adapted his novella, *The Hellbound Heart*, as the 1987 cult classic, *Hellraiser*, which he also directed.

Published in this book along with several stories from his "Books of Blood" series, the title novella to this 1990 work was adapted by the author as the film, *Nightbreed.*

as "head and shoulders above the average horror fare." Calling the film memorable, Gilmore assessed in *Rolling Stone: "Hellraiser* shapes up as a grim parable of modern desire and malevolence that, in its most forceful visual moments, seems to take its inspiration from the art of Bruegel and Bosch: that is, it envisions and makes palpable what hell may actually look and feel like."

For his next project Barker created a novella titled *Cabal,* which was published in a volume of the same title including stories from the sixth *Books of Blood* volume. In 1990 Barker adapted *Cabal* into a script and directed it as the film *Nightbreed.* The film and the book tell the story of a disturbed young man named Boone. Boone is having violent nightmares in which he is the author of a grisly series of murders. He also dreams of a mythical place called Midian, a place where tortured souls are absolved. Frighteningly, the murderous dreams

that Boone envisions are coming true, down to the smallest bloody detail. Boone recounts these dreams to his psychiatrist, Dr. Decker. The doctor gives Boone a vial of sedatives, telling him they will help him sleep while staving off the bad dreams. The next thing Boone knows he is in the mental ward of a hospital, being told that the pills he thought were sedatives were actually a powerful hallucinogen. Boone realizes that Decker has been manipulating his dreams because the psychiatrist is the one committing the murders; Decker is trying to frame Boone for the crimes. Meanwhile, a fellow mental patient hears Boone mention Midian and mistakenly assumes Boone to be a citizen of the fabled city. The man identifies himself as an outcast from Midian and reveals information to Boone regarding the city's location. Boone escapes the hospital in search of Midian. In the meantime Dr. Decker has informed the police that his patient is the one committing the murders, and Decker and the police set off in hot pursuit of Boone.

In the upper regions of Canada, Boone follows the directions to an old cemetery. Before he has time to fully explore the grounds, he is pursued by two monstrous man-beasts. They capture him, and, against the other's warnings, one of the creatures decides to feast upon Boone's flesh, taking a bite out of his shoulder. The second creature tackles his companion and frees Boone, bidding him to escape. As the wounded Boone stumbles out of the cemetery, Decker and the police are waiting and gun him down. However, the creature's bite has had an unusual effect on Boone, and his death is not a permanent one. He awakens in the morgue and returns to the cemetery. There he learns that Midian is real, existing as a labyrinthine underground city. Boone also discovers that the two man-monsters who pursued him are part of the city's population. The denizens of Midian are shapeshifters, creatures that can change their body shape at will, known as Nightbreed. Long ago the Nightbreed inhabited the world alongside humans, but fear and ignorance bred hate and humankind attempted to annihilate the creatures. The race took refuge underground, founding the city of Midian. Boone learns of a prophecy which tells of a human who will become Nightbreed and lead the race back into the world; Boone is the human of that prophecy. In addition to his immunity to bullets, Boone has also acquired shapeshifting abilities. He is given the opportunity to test his new powers and leadership abilities when Decker and the police arrive to destroy Boone, the Nightbreed, and Midian. The *New York Times Book*

Review called *Cabal* "dazzling, captivating stuff," praising Barker's ability to create visual imagery on the page. Reviews for *Nightbreed* again praised Barker's gift for evocation, citing his creative realizations of the Nightbreed monsters. *MPG* noted that Barker's method for horror filmmaking bears "an unmistakable stamp of originality."

Ambitions and the Art

In 1989 Barker began his most ambitious literary undertaking, *The Great and Secret Show: The First Book of the Art,* the initial installment of a trilogy. The sprawling tale begins with Randolph Jaffe, a nondescript man whom Barker describes in the book as "a balding nobody with ambitions never spoken and rage not expressed." Jaffe works in the dead letter office at a post office in Nebraska, sorting through letters that have no return address and no destination. As he sits alone in a room, hour after hour, the letters he opens and reads begin to distill a pattern, a code. Jaffe strains to understand this subliminal current of information travelling through the mail and gradually learns of a quasi-religious sect of people who worship an arcane knowledge. This knowledge is called the Art. Jaffe is consumed with a desire to know the Art, convinced it will bring resonance and power to his bland existence. He begins a quest that leads him to places that exist on no map, to people living between time, and finally to a brilliant evolutionary scientist named Richard Fletcher. Like Jaffe, Fletcher has questions and desires that cannot be quenched by the knowledge of the finite world. With Fletcher's scientific technique and the recondite wisdom Jaffe has accrued through his travels, the two set to work uncovering the inner workings of the Art. Through exhaustive experimentation, Fletcher comes up with a serum called the Nuncio. The Nuncio accelerates the evolutionary process, advancing organisms, in a matter of hours, through adaptations that would naturally take centuries—if ever—to occur. Fletcher has already turned an ape into a crudely evolved, though unmistakably human, young man. When Jaffe learns of this breakthrough he sees the Nuncio as the key to the power and knowledge that he has coveted. Against Fletcher's violent protests and warnings, he consumes the serum. Fearing Jaffe's potential for evil, Fletcher sees no other recourse but to consume the Nuncio as well. Both men are transformed into highly evolved demigods with extraordinary powers. In their reborn state, the men assume new names, Jaffe calling himself The Jaff, and Fletcher calling himself Good Man Fletcher. The two engage in a mammoth battle that spans the country and pushes each man to his super-physical and hyper-mental limits. Eventually they end up in a deadlock, immobile at the bottom of a lake.

Years later a group of teenage girls, all virgins, skinny-dip in the lake. Both the Jaff and Good Man Fletcher see the girls as a means to raise the stakes in the battle. They each immaculately conceive children in the young women. The girls have the babies and the children grow into young adults. Three of the children become key players in the battle for control of the Art. They are Fletcher's son Howie and the Jaff's twins Tommy-Ray and Jo-Beth. Howie has not only inherited Nuncio-enhanced genes but his father's sense of justice as well. While Tommy-Ray sides with his father and assumes the name Death-Boy, Jo-Beth falls in love with Howie and helps him fight the Jaff. As they become immersed in the struggle, Jo-Beth and Howie learn of a dream-sea that exists behind the world. This sea is known as Quiddity, an ocean of tranquility in which the slumbering subconscious swims. As part of his mad scheme to control the Art and the worlds that it influences, the Jaff plans to open a rift between the conscious and subconscious worlds, exposing the delicate balance of Quiddity to the bluntness of the physical realm. Not only will this have disastrous effects on the dream states—and thus the sanity—of every human and animal on the planet, it could also endanger the very fabric that binds the world together. For on the other side of Quiddity exists the monstrous Iad, a nihilistic race that craves negative space and antimatter. The Iad already have agents working in the real world, laying the groundwork for a take-over and consumption of the physical plane. As these issues intersect and tangential storylines weave themselves together, a vast array of players converge on a cataclysmic denouement that involves human and inhuman, the real and the unreal.

Ken Tucker reviewed *The Great and Secret Show* in the *New York Times Book Review* and said of the novel, "it is nothing so much as a cross between [Thomas Pynchon's] 'Gravity's Rainbow' and J. R. R. Tolkien's 'Lord of the Rings,' allusive and mythic, complex and entertaining." Barker's ability to evoke detailed characters and settings within an epic storyline convinced many skeptics of the author's versatility. *The Great and Secret Show* encompassed a variety of genres and made numerous readers aware of Barker's talents. William A. Henry III wrote in *Time* that the novel is "rich and absorbing" and stated that "the images are vivid,

BESTSELLING AUTHOR OF THE GREAT AND SECRET SHOW

CLIVE BARKER

IMAJICA

A secret society seeks to murder magic adepts in Barker's 1991 fantasy novel about parallel worlds.

the asides incisive and the prose elegant in this joyride of a story."

One World is not Enough

Barker again drew from the epic fantasy vein in writing his next novel, *Imajica*. Imajica is the name given to a vast realm which encompasses five dominions, the fifth dominion being the earth. For millennia the first four worlds have been united and travel between them is quick and easy. The earth however, has remained estranged, and travel between the fifth and the other dominions requires the use of special magic. In the book's setting of present day England, the population's majority are more concerned with trivial matters such as making their trains, sleeping with their sexual partners, and complaining about the economy. They do not realize that two hundred years before a great sorcerer, or maestro, attempted a reconciliation of the dominions that ended in catastrophe. In addition to incurring staggering casualties in all five

worlds, the failed reconciliation also spurred an anti-magic movement in the fifth, primarily in the guise of a secret society known as the Tabula Rasa. The Tabula Rasa has collected much of the arcane literature extant in the fifth, and, when they deem it necessary, the order has conducted purges to kill off people with potent mystical abilities. As midsummer approaches, the Tabula Rasa becomes agitated. For two hundred years they have kept magic from flowering in the fifth; they have kept the world safe from another cataclysmic attempt at reconciliation. But on this midsummer it will be two hundred years to the date that the fabled Maestro Sartori attempted his unification. It is a potent date and elements of wonder have already begun to intrude into the fifth, signaling to the Tabula Rasa that another reconciliation is impending.

Barker opens the novel with a tangential storyline that slowly opens into the main narrative. The reader is introduced to John Furie Zacharius, commonly known as Gentle, and Judith, Gentle's sometime lover. Gentle and Judith are both beautiful, ageless people who have trouble remembering their histories beyond ten or fifteen years. As the story begins, Judith's jealous and possessive ex-husband has hired an assassin to kill Judith—if he can't have her, no one can. This assassin is an androgynous, numinous person with the curious name Pie 'o' pah. As fate, or destiny, would have it, on the night that Pie goes to kill Judith in a New York hotel, Gentle has also gone to see her. The three meet in Judith's room and Gentle saves her from death. He pursues the assassin out into the street where they lock gazes across a crowded thoroughfare. Gentle is convinced he knows this otherworldly creature but cannot remember the details. Pie escapes before he can ask, but it is clear the assassin knows Gentle as well. As the days pass, Gentle becomes obsessed with finding Pie. When he finally finds the assassin, he learns that Pie is from another world, a place in the second dominion. Pie is a mystif, a creature neither male nor female who has the capacity to incarnate the deepest sexual desires of its lovers. Pie was also the familiar, or assistant, to the Maestro Sartori during his attempt at reconciliation. Gentle is fascinated by Pie and the creature's descriptions of other worlds. The Mystif agrees to take Gentle on a journey across the dominions. Meanwhile Judith has become involved with her ex-husband's brother, a member of the Tabula Rasa named Oscar. Oscar leads a dual life, acting as both a member of the anti-magic society and as a traveller and trader in the dominions. Through Oscar Judith learns of the other worlds, and she also makes a journey to them.

In the dominions Gentle and Pie see many strange and beautiful things, and they encounter much pain and horror. In addition to several scrapes with bizarre mutants, the pair also learn that the ruler of the dominions, the Autarch, has begun to make murderous sweeps through villages. Gentle and Pie soon discover that the Autarch seeks them, and that he will raze through anything to get to the visitors from the fifth. They decide to journey to the capital city to confront the Autarch and to return to Pie's tribe. As the trek progresses Gentle learns bits and pieces of his past, and also learns that he possesses considerable powers. Events come to a head in the capital city, as both Gentle and Judith learn of their pasts and their purposes. They return to the fifth dominion days before midsummer, with Gentle determined to unite and reconcile the dominions. In order to complete the task however, he will have to contend with evil forces that wish to impede the reunification. Gods and goddesses, a plethora of wizardry, and an evil twin all come into play as the novel reaches its conclusion.

Numbering over eight hundred pages, *Imajica* is Barker's longest single work and emphasizes the author's strong feelings for fantasy. As with his previous books, various other elements are also intertwined. Critics increasingly compared the author to Tolkien, whose *Lord of the Rings* books were cited as spiritual ancestors to *Imajica*. While some critics found the work overambitious and rambling, others were impressed with its unique perspective. *Publishers Weekly* declared Barker's creative talent "prodigious," and called the book a deft blend of "unconventional eroticism and mesmerizing invention." Other critics also commented on Barker's vivid imagination, using terms such as "literary shamanism" to describe the author's ingenuity. Reviewers have also noted that while Barker shares a visionary imagination comparable to the likes of Tolkien, his work is far more modern and realistic in its approach. In comparing *Imajica* to similar, less successful books, Roz Kaveney stated in the *Times Literary Supplement:* "What takes Barker's version out of the rut is his comprehensively jaundiced view of existence and a sense that this journey really is a gamble with damnation."

While books like *Imajica* and *Weaveworld* have attracted comparisons to Tolkien and British author and illustrator Mervyn Peake, passages in those same books have been compared to the hellacious works of Dutch painter Hieronymus Bosch. Barker sees this ghastly content as but one of many facets in a whole creation. "Everyone thinks of me as exploring this terrifically grim material," Barker told Maitland McDonagh in *Film Comment*. "It's the imaginative that's always fascinated me, not just the dark imaginative." While Barker's fiction embraces modern themes and strives for new ground, the author also acknowledges the groundwork laid by horror authors before him and the role it plays in his fiction. "There is no reason why one can't explore and use and celebrate the old forms of strong narrative line which almost conceal their subtext," he told Ross, "so that people can come to a work . . . and read it on several levels."

Good Horror and the Human Condition

"Good horror can do much more than horrify; it can take you places where no fiction has ever been before," Barker told Gilmore in *Rolling Stone*. Barker's work in film and print has attempted to modify the popular definitions of horror. His fiction often eschews the concepts of good and evil, staples in traditional horror, as thematic vehicles. Sometimes Barker will begin a story at an unlikely point and finish it before it reaches a patent conclusion, using the events in between to convey his ideas. He draws on elements that are both familiar and alien, terrifying and humorous. Like many artists, Barker sees his work as more than entertainment. His goal is to fascinate—and even petrify—his audience, but he also wants them to consider *why* they are entertained or scared. Barker summarized his intentions to Jonathan Cooper in *People:* "I do seek to horrify, but I also seek to disturb, amuse, arouse and intellectually challenge." By not averting his—or his readers'—gaze from episodes of intense and graphic horror, Barker hopes to expose facets of humanity that are often repressed. In talking with Gilmore, Barker concluded that he believes that "horror can speak loud and long about the complexity of our experience."

■ Works Cited

Barker, Clive, *Books of Blood, Volume One,* Sphere, 1984, Berkley Publishing, 1986.
Barker, Clive, *The Great and Secret Show: The First Book of the Art,* HarperCollins, 1989.

Barker, Clive, in an interview with Jean W. Ross, *Contemporary Authors,* Volume 129, Gale, 1990, pp. 28-33.

Chambers, Andrea, and Jonathan Cooper, *People,* June 15, 1987, p. 88.

Coven, Laurence, "Unspeakable Acts," *Washington Post Book World,* June 28, 1987, p. 10.

Gilmore, Mikal, "Hell Raiser," *Rolling Stone,* February 11, 1988, pp. 103-108.

Henry, William A. III, *Time,* March 19, 1990, p. 84.

Review of *Imajica, Publishers Weekley,* August 9, 1991. p. 42.

Kaveney, Roz, *Times Literary Supplement,* October 11, 1991, p. 23.

McDonagh, Maitland, "Future Shockers," *Film Comment,* January-February, 1990, p. 61.

Mittelmark, Howard, review of *Cabal, New York Times Book Review,* December 18, 1988.

Morgan, Chris, "Brilliant First Novel," *Fantasy Review,* September, 1985, p. 16.

Morrison, Michael A., "Blood without End," *Fantasy Review,* June, 1985, p. 15.

Motion Picture Guide, 1988 Annual, Cinebooks, 1988, pp. 114-115.

Motion Picture Guide, 1991 Annual, Baseline, 1991, pp. 129-30.

Tucker, Ken, *New York Times Book Review,* February 11, 1990.

Winter, Douglas E., "Clive Barker: Britain's New Master of Horror," *Washington Post Book World,* August 24, 1986, p. 6.

Review of *Weaveworld, Kirkus Reviews,* August 1, 1987, p. 1085.

■ For More Information See

BOOKS

Contemporary Literary Criticism, Volume 52, Gale, 1989, pp. 51-57.°

—Sketch by David Galens

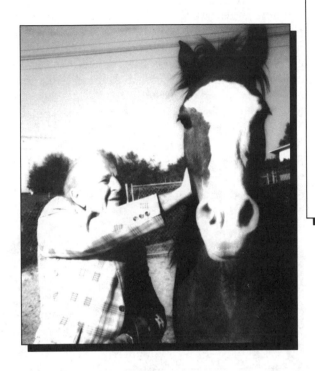

Jay Bennett

■ Personal

Born December 24, 1912, in New York, NY; son of Pincus Shapiro (a businessman) and Estelle Bennett; married Sally Stern, February 2, 1937; children: Steven Cullen, Randy Elliott. *Education:* Attended New York University.

■ Addresses

Home—64 Greensward, Cherry Hill, NJ 08002.

■ Career

Worked as a farmhand, factory worker, lifeguard, mailman, salesman, and other various occupations; writer, c. 1930—. Scriptwriter for radio and television dramas during 1940s and 1950s; novelist, especially for young adults, 1960—. *Wartime service:* U.S. Office of War Information, English features writer and editor, 1942-45. *Member:* Mystery Writers of America, Authors League of America, Writers Guild, Dramatists Guild (life member).

■ Awards, Honors

Edgar Allan Poe Award for best juvenile mystery novel, Mystery Writers of America, 1974, for *The Long Black Coat*, 1975, for *The Dangling Witness;* Variety Award for television script for *Monodrama Theatre;* Shakespeare Society award for television adaptation of *Hamlet.*

■ Writings

Catacombs, Abelard-Schuman, 1959.
Murder Money, Fawcett, 1963.
Death Is a Silent Room, Abelard-Schuman, 1965.
Shadows Offstage, Nelson, 1974.

YOUNG ADULT MYSTERIES

Deathman, Do Not Follow Me, Meredith Press, 1968.
The Deadly Gift, Meredith Press, 1969.
Masks: A Love Story, F. Watts, 1971.
The Killing Tree, F. Watts, 1972.
The Long Black Coat, Delacorte, 1973.
The Dangling Witness, Delacorte, 1974.
Say Hello to the Hit Man, Delacorte, 1976.
The Birthday Murderer, Delacorte, 1977.
The Pigeon, Methuen, 1980, Avon, 1981.
The Executioner, Avon, 1982.
Slowly, Slowly I Raise the Gun, Avon, 1983.
I Never Said I Loved You, Avon, 1984.
To Be a Killer, Scholastic, Inc., 1985.
The Skeleton Man, F. Watts, 1986.
The Haunted One, F. Watts, 1987.
The Dark Corridor, F. Watts, 1988.
Sing Me a Death Song, F. Watts, 1990.

Coverup, F. Watts, 1991.
Skinhead, F. Watts, 1991.
Hooded Man, Fawcett-Juniper, 1993.
Death Grip, Fawcett-Juniper, 1993.

PLAYS

No Hiding Place (three-act), first produced in New York at President Theatre, November 10, 1949.
Lions after Slumber (three-act), first produced in London at Unity Theatre, June 2, 1951.

OTHER

Also author of numerous radio scripts, including *Miracle before Christmas* and *The Wind and Stars Are Witness;* author of television scripts for *Alfred Hitchcock Presents, Harlem Detective, Crime Syndicated, Wide, Wide World, Cameo Theater,* and *Monodrama Theater.* Senior editor of encyclopedias for Grolier Education Corp., c. 1960.

■ Adaptations

One of Bennett's novels for adults was adapted as a film produced by Warner Brothers.

■ Work in Progress

Another young adult suspense mystery.

■ Sidelights

Jay Bennett's suspense stories for young adults have sold over four million copies in some sixteen languages, and they have twice been honored with the prestigious Edgar Allan Poe Award. Bennett, who has been called the "master of short sentences" by a *School Library Journal* reviewer, writes about violent, life-threatening situations from the point of view of the potential victims. Readers suffer and triumph with Bennett's lonely heroes who pit themselves against organized crime, deadly racists, and—especially—sinister adults who seem harmless on the surface. *New York Times Book Review* editor George A. Woods notes that in a Bennett mystery "victims have real blood, not catchup, and the screams aren't caused by the rocking chair coming down on the cat's tail."

One strong theme that runs through most of Bennett's thrillers is the notion that people need to reach out to one another, that solitude and alienation are breeding grounds for fear and anger. "Among other things, I speak to the loner in our society," Bennett writes in the *Something about the Author Autobiography Series* (SAAS). "There are so many loners, especially among the young and I say to them in my novels, You cannot make it alone,

you have to reach out and embrace another human being and human values. There is no other way, or you are lost."

Bennett is also compelled to write out of a fierce passion against life's injustices, a sense that young people are sometimes burdened with guilt or placed in great danger by the actions of their elders. The author's books go beyond the standard murder mystery to explore crises of conscience, psychological trauma, and bitter confrontations between parents and children. In *Voice of Youth Advocates*, Mary K. Chelton calls the average Bennett book "a satisfying read on a complicated topic" and praises the author for his ability to evoke mood and plot "with an absolute minimum of description."

Published in 1974, Bennett won his second Edgar Allan Poe award for this novel about a college student who witnesses a murder.

Life's Little Injustices

Where are the roots of Bennett's long years working as a writer? The author himself is not quite sure. In *SAAS*, he lightheartedly tells of a moment when he discovered how unfair life could be to a child: "I went to my first baseball game at the age of four. My grandfather, Harris Bennett, took me there. He was a neat and kindly man and he wore a straw hat. They called them straw katies in those days. Well, we were sitting behind third base, sitting in the warm afternoon sun, watching this semipro game and a pop foul comes along and hits him right on the straw katie and smashes it. Luckily it was a weak pop foul and it didn't really hurt him. Just the katie. I come home after the game, our team won, and we're both happy and my mother looks at the smashed katie, gasps, and then hugs her father tight to her.... Well, she hugs him and then turns on me and gives me a real hard time for not taking better care of him.

"How did I ever let him sit behind third base? How? I should've taken him behind the catcher where there was a screen. You see, she knew baseball too. Now I loved my mother and she loved her father but this was a great injustice to me. Don't you think so? If I was four and a half I could understand it but I was only four. A mere child. So there you are. Injustice. Maybe that's when it all started."

Bennett was born on December 24, 1912, in Manhattan. His father, Pincus Shapiro, was a Jewish immigrant who left Russia to escape discrimination. In America he found a job in a wholesale dry goods company, gradually working his way up the career ladder until he became vice president of the firm. In time he married the firm's head bookkeeper, Estelle Bennett, a native New Yorker. When the author was still an infant, the Shapiro family left their tenement apartment behind and moved to a large house in Brooklyn. That was the home in which Bennett grew up, and many of his stories are set in similar urban neighborhoods, with brownstone row houses, street lights, and the excitements of New York City within reach by subway.

Bennett remembers in *SAAS* that his father never quite adjusted to city life. "My father came off a very large farm and he rode horses barebacked and all his life he never forgot the birch trees and the spirited horses and the smell of waving, windswept grass. Yet all his life he was trapped in a city and he would drive my mother up the wall with his fierce love of animals. He kept pigeons and chickens in

*Twice winner of the Edgar Award for his suspense mysteries for young people

A teen is framed by terrorists for the murder of his former girlfriend in this typical Bennett thriller, published in 1981.

his backyard and one day he came home with a deer." Bennett's mother put her foot down about the deer, and it was taken away. The smaller animals stayed, though.

From his earliest days as a student, Bennett knew he wanted to be a writer. After one year in public elementary school, he was enrolled in a Hebrew Institute. The curriculum there included lessons in the Hebrew language every morning, with readings in Hebrew from the Old Testament. After lunch the students concentrated on standard school subjects. Bennett prospered under the heavy work load. "I believe that my studies of Hebrew had an influence on my writing style," he says in *SAAS*. He adds that an exposure to the writings of the great Hebrew prophets—Isaiah, Jeremiah, and Amos— became "a life-enduring influence." He calls the heroes of the Old Testament "giant men and tremendous poets."

Another early influence was the work of the English playwright William Shakespeare, whose

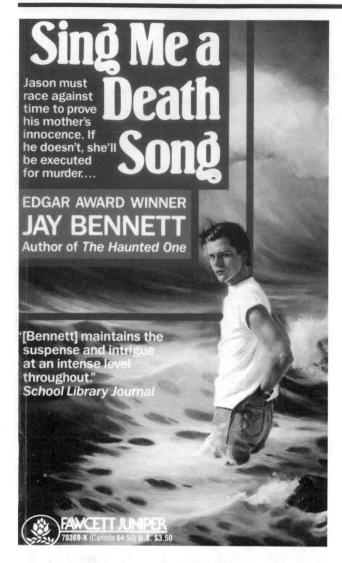

Sing Me a Death Song

Jason must race against time to prove his mother's innocence. If he doesn't, she'll be executed for murder....

EDGAR AWARD WINNER

JAY BENNETT

Author of *The Haunted One*

"[Bennett] maintains the suspense and intrigue at an intense level throughout." *School Library Journal*

FAWCETT JUNIPER
70369-X (Canada $4.50) U.S. $3.50

In this 1990 novel, a woman is slated for execution for a murder she did not commit, but her son gets one last chance to find the killer before it's too late.

tragic plays held all the elements of the best mystery and suspense stories. "Shakespeare taught me an awful lot about writing," Bennett claims in *SAAS*. "He knew how to create mood, atmosphere, character, and action better than any writer I've ever read. His sense of structure is uncanny." Bennett continues, "Every writer should study Old William. Particularly suspense writers. Of which I am one."

Bennett continued his formal schooling at James Madison High School in Brooklyn and then at New York University. Of medium height and strongly built, he loved boxing, played semi-pro football, and was an excellent wrestler who almost qualified for competition in the Olympics. Although he enjoyed the challenge of higher learning—and was already attracted to writing as a career—he lost

interest in his courses at New York University and eventually dropped out after three years. The author says in *SAAS* that a "general malaise" settled over him, a period of rebellion when he questioned all the values he had grown up with. Another factor entered into his decision to quit school as well. As he puts it, "The Depression [was] starting to blow in, first softly and then ... with tremendous force."

Hard Times and Determination

Like so many others, Bennett watched the Great Depression bring hardship to his family. His father became unemployed, along with seventeen million other Americans. Bennett tried to help the family by quitting college to find a job, but nothing was available. After a few months spent searching fruitlessly for work, he hit the road and began to wander across the country. He hopped on empty freight trains and spent nights in flophouses and, occasionally, county jails.

The times were desperate, and Bennett experienced moments of genuine danger. Once he watched in horror as a pair of men fought in an empty box car. The fight ended when one of the men was thrown from the moving train and fell down a cliff. Some time later, Bennett found himself in a crowded flophouse for vagrants in Denver. The man in the next bed spent the night trying to persuade Bennett to help with an armed robbery. Bennett, realizing that if he lived this lifestyle much longer he might become a criminal himself, finally had enough. He slipped away from the shelter during the early hours of the morning and found an empty freight train heading east. He went home to New York, determined to become a writer.

"I remember standing in a snowstorm in a line that stretched around the entire block in downtown New York," the author writes in *SAAS*. "Standing there for eight hours waiting for an application to become a street cleaner. But after eight hours of waiting, we were told that there were no more applications and to go on home. And all the time I was writing."

Bennett drifted through a series of odd jobs, almost always able to find employment somewhere. In 1937 he married Sally Stern, and together they found a small apartment in Manhattan. Bennett's wife encouraged him to keep writing, and he turned out numerous poems, short stories, stage plays, and even six novels. Bennett remembers that he spent fourteen years writing without a single word of encouragement from any established editor or publisher. Yet he never gave up. "With or without a job I would write," he recalls. "A fish swims, a bird flies, and a writer writes. That's the way I put it to myself."

His wife agreed, so when he lost yet another job he began writing full-time while she worked as a beautician. Then the beauty shop closed, and the couple faced bankruptcy and eviction from their tiny apartment. Bennett's wife went home to her parents in Atlantic City, New Jersey, and Bennett continued to struggle to put something into print.

A friend told Bennett that a radio show called *Grand Central Station* was buying scripts. "I knew nothing about writing for radio, so I borrowed a small radio . . . and I sat by the radio for ten hours a day, listening to the dramas and soaps and whatever else was on that I could learn from," the writer remembers. Once he understood the format, Bennett spent a month churning out scripts. He submitted twenty-eight of them before he finally got an acceptance, but that single acceptance opened a door. He could finally earn a living as a writer.

Soon he was working regularly for radio shows on all the major networks. He wrote all sorts of scripts and even did some work with radio soap operas, but his greatest success came with the mystery-suspense format. One of his mystery scripts was so notable that it was produced on four different national shows and then later filmed for the *Alfred Hitchcock Presents* television series. Another was submitted by the Writers War Board to forty countries as a representation of the best of American radio writing.

From radio Bennett moved to television writing, turning out show after show during the early days of the small screen. He was the first writer to adapt Shakespeare's *Hamlet* for television—an effort that won him an award from the Shakespeare Society—and he won a Variety Award for work with *Monodrama Theatre*. For several seasons he was a staff writer for a police drama called *Harlem Detective* that featured two detectives, one white and the other black. The integrated cast was a breakthrough at the time, being produced years before the popular television program *I Spy* drew attention for casting a black actor, Bill Cosby, in a costarring role with Robert Culp.

Television work enabled Bennett to provide a comfortable living for his wife and two sons. Life still held surprises for the family, however. In the late 1950s, the mecca for television productions

A crooked judge tries to conceal a murder and must stop his son's best friend from discovering the truth in Bennett's 1991 tale.

moved from New York City to Los Angeles. Bennett tried to move with it, but he did not like the idea of uprooting his family. He remembered the time when he had wandered across the country during the Great Depression, and he wanted more stability for his own children. Against the advice of his friends in the entertainment business, and after trying to work in California for a short time, he decided to stay in New York City.

From Scripts to Books

Eventually Bennett moved out of television work entirely, taking a job as an editor with an encyclopedia company. In his spare time he began to bend his talents for suspense writing to fit a new format: the novel. He wrote three novels for adults, one of which was adapted for a Warner Brothers movie, and then he turned to writing for young adults.

"All through my years I have been intensely interested in the young and their problems and hopes. Their dreams and despairs," Bennett notes in *SAAS*. "My wife still calls me a child who will never grow up and in one sense she's absolutely right. And that's why it's so easy for me to write my books for that readership. But there's more to it than that. I feel very strongly that it's up to the young to help turn things around. We can't go on much longer the way we are."

Deathman, Do Not Follow Me, first published in 1968, was Bennett's debut novel for teens. Its story, setting, and characters indicate the direction Bennett would follow in other works: teenager Danny Morgan finds himself in mortal danger after a Van Gogh painting disappears from the Brooklyn Museum. A loner by nature, Danny finds he cannot confide his fears of the eerie "Deathman" to even his closest friends and family. A similar experience befalls John-Tom Dawes in the 1969 mystery *The Deadly Gift*. Seemingly by accident, John-Tom acquires a box full of money from a desperate stranger on a rainy night. Soon the teen finds himself under threat from a crime syndicate that claims ownership of the money. "There is something almost epic about John-Tom's struggle with himself ...," writes Sarah Law Kennerly in the *School Library Journal*. "[*The Deadly Gift*] should have much to say to contemporary teen-agers."

The typical hero in a Bennett mystery is a young man in his late teens, thoughtful and nonconformist by nature, who finds himself drawn into danger by events beyond his control. In the book *The Dangling Witness*, Matthew Garth suffers a crisis of conscience when he witnesses a murder but cannot bring himself to tell the police what he knows. Soon he finds himself threatened, and he must confront the violence he detests so much. Phil Brant, central character in *The Long Black Coat*, must outwit his older brother's murderous army buddies who come to Brooklyn looking for stolen money. Both *The Dangling Witness* and *The Long Black Coat* won Edgar Allan Poe awards, making Bennett the first author to earn the honor two years in a row.

Bennett's stories often hinge on implied violence and frightening threats. The heroes fall victim not only to evil stalkers but to their own psychological hang-ups. In *The Birthday Murderer*, for instance, Shan Rourke is convinced that he caused a fatal accident when he was only five. He cannot remember the incident, but he believes the adults who were there. Shan must wrestle with his own imperfect memories as well as a threat to his own life, facing "the seeming unlikelihood of an other-wise respectable adult's madness," to quote the *Washington Post Book World*.

Bennett abhors violence and feels there is too much of it in American culture today, remarking to *AAYA* that "Shakespeare said if you trivialize death you trivialize life." He feels that his work can offer a message to readers and that they can help to make the world a safer and better place to live. "Today with the world, a pretty sick and chaotic one at that, hovering on the edge of extinction," he says in *SAAS*, "the young have to grow up geometrically. Their perceptions must be deeper and quicker. Their grasp of essential knowledge swift and sure. Their search for truth pure and inviolate. In a word, they must grow up fast." He adds, "More important than that, they must get to feel in the very core of their beings that without world peace there is nowhere to go."

Bennett has written well over a million words for radio and television, but he left that field because he felt the need to reach out to a new audience. He notes in *Something about the Author*: "I ... believe that this [young adult] readership is the most vital and alive of all readerships in American literature."

How Bennett is able to craft novel after novel is still a mystery to him. He says he loves each of his "suspense children," the heroes of his thrillers, but the process of creating them comes from deep within—from moments remembered from his past, from passing remarks made by strangers, from feelings he recalls almost at random.

The author concludes in *SAAS*: "They've walked the moon already. They'll walk across Saturn one day. And swing from the rings. Believe me, they will. But they'll never be able to walk across the unknown land that lies deep, so very deep, within the heart and soul of a writer. At least that's how I look at it."

■ Works Cited

Review of *The Birthday Murderer, Washington Post Book World*, October 7, 1979, p. 15.

Chelton, Mary K., review of *I Never Said I Loved You, Voice of Youth Advocates*, August, 1984, p. 143.

Kennerly, Sarah Law, review of *The Deadly Gift, School Library Journal*, May, 1970, p. 92.

Porter, Judie, review of *Coverup, School Library Journal*, August, 1991, p. 195.

Something about the Author, Volume 41, Gale, 1985, pp. 36-37.

Something about the Author Autobiography Series, Volume 4, Gale, 1987, pp. 75-91.

Woods, George A., review of *Deathman, Do Not Follow Me, New York Times Book Review,* July 7, 1968, p. 16.

■ For More Information See

BOOKS

Contemporary Literary Criticism, Volume 35, Gale, 1985, pp. 52-53.

Donelson, Kenneth L., and Aleen Pace Nilsen, *Literature for Today's Young Adults,* Scott, Foresman, 1980, pp. 228-257.

PERIODICALS

Best Sellers, January, 1981, p. 349.

English Journal, February, 1969, pp. 295-296; April, 1970, p. 591.

Kirkus Reviews, April 1, 1973, p. 395.

New York Times Book Review, August 22, 1965; November 10, 1974, pp. 8, 10; May 2, 1976, p. 38.

Publishers Weekly, May 7, 1973, p. 65; June 3, 1974, p. 157; August 12, 1974, p. 58; August 22, 1977, p. 66; July 1, 1983, p. 103; September 27, 1985, p. 97; October 28, 1988, p. 83.

School Library Journal, May, 1974, p. 69; May, 1976, p. 77; May, 1980, p. 86; May, 1982, p. 84; December, 1983, p. 84; August, 1984, p. 80; October, 1986, pp. 185-186; November, 1987, p. 112; April, 1990, p. 139; May, 1991, p. 108.

Times Literary Supplement, August 19, 1988.

Voice of Youth Advocates, August, 1982, p. 28; February, 1984, p. 337.

—Sketch by Anne Janette Johnson

Mary Higgins Clark

◼ Personal

Born December 24, 1929 (some sources say 1927 or 1931), in New York, NY; daughter of Luke Joseph (a restaurant owner) and Nora C. (a buyer; maiden name, Durkin) Higgins; married Warren F. Clark (a businessman), December 26, 1949 (died September 26, 1964); married Raymond Charles Ploetz (an attorney), August 8, 1978 (marriage annulled); children: (first marriage) Marilyn, Warren, David, Carol, Patricia. *Education:* Attended Villa Maria Academy, Ward Secretarial School, and New York University; Fordham University, B.A. (summa cum laude), 1979. *Politics:* Republican. *Religion:* Roman Catholic. *Hobbies and other interests:* Traveling, skiing, tennis, playing piano.

◼ Addresses

Home—2508 Cleveland Ave., Washington Township, NJ 07675; 200 Central Park S., New York, NY 10019. *Agent*—Eugene H. Winick, McIntosh & Otis, Inc., 310 Madison Ave., New York, NY 10017.

◼ Career

Writer. Remington Rand, advertising assistant, 1946; Pan American Airlines, stewardess, 1949-50; radio scriptwriter and producer for Robert G. Jennings, 1965-70; Aerial Communications, New York City, vice president, partner, creative director, and producer of radio programming, 1970-80; D. J. Clark Enterprises, New York City, chairman of the board and creative director, 1980—. Chairman, International Crime Writers Congress, 1988. *Member:* Mystery Writers of America (president, 1987; member of board of directors), Authors League of America, American Society of Journalists and Authors, American Academy of Arts and Sciences, American Irish Historical Society (member of executive council).

◼ Awards, Honors

New Jersey Author Award, 1969, for *Aspire to the Heavens*, 1977, for *Where Are the Children?*, and 1978, for *A Stranger Is Watching;* Grand Prix de Litterature Policiere (France), 1980; honorary doctorate degrees from Villanova University, 1983, and Rider College, 1986.

◼ Writings

Aspire to the Heavens: A Portrait of George Washington, Meredith Press, 1969.
Where Are the Children?, Simon & Schuster, 1975.
A Stranger Is Watching, Simon & Schuster, 1977.
The Cradle Will Fall, Simon & Schuster, 1980.

A Cry in the Night (also see below), Simon & Schuster, 1982.

Three Complete Novels (contains *Weep No More, My Lady,* [also see below], *Stillwatch* [also see below], and *A Cry in the Night*), Wings Books, 1982.

Stillwatch, Simon & Schuster, 1984.

(With Thomas Chastain and others) *Murder in Manhattan,* Morrow, 1986.

Weep No More, My Lady, Simon & Schuster, 1987.

(Editor) *Murder on the Aisle: The 1987 Mystery Writers of America Anthology,* Simon & Schuster, 1987.

(With others) *Caribbean Blues,* J. Curley, 1988.

While My Pretty One Sleeps, Simon & Schuster, 1989.

The Anastasia Syndrome and Other Stories, Simon & Schuster, 1989.

Loves Music, Loves to Dance, Simon & Schuster, 1991.

All Around the Town, Simon & Schuster, 1992.

Also author of syndicated radio dramas. Contributor to *I, Witness,* Times Books, 1978, and *Family Portraits,* edited by Carolyn Anthony, Doubleday, 1989. Work anthologized in *The Best "Saturday Evening Post" Stories,* 1962. Contributor of stories to periodicals, including *Family Circle, McCall's, Redbook, Saturday Evening Post,* and *Woman's Day.*

■ **Adaptations**

A Stranger Is Watching was filmed by Metro-Goldwyn-Mayer in 1982; *The Cradle Will Fall* was shown on CBS as a "Movie of the Week" in 1984; *A Cry in the Night* was filmed by Rosten productions in 1985; *Where Are the Children?* was filmed by Columbia in 1986; *Stillwatch* was broadcast on CBS in 1987; Ellipse, a French production company, is producing *A Cry in the Night,* two stories from *The Anastasia Syndrome* (which will star Clark's daughter Carol), and *Weep No More, My Lady.* Several of Clark's books have been released on cassette tape, including *While My Pretty One Sleeps,* read by Jessica Walter, Simon & Schuster Audio, 1989, and *Loves Music, Loves to Dance,* read by Kate Burton, Simon & Schuster Audio, 1991.

■ **Sidelights**

Suspense writer Mary Higgins Clark's novels reflect the values instilled in her from an early age. Her strong personality, honed by her mother's determination and her own experience with adver-

sity, has proven to be the key to her success. "Mary, she's like the heroines in her books. She's able to prevail over adversity in a positive, wholesome way. She sees the negative in life, but it doesn't get her down," Clark's agent, Gene Winick, told Elizabeth Hill O'Neill in *Publishers Weekly.* Clark's characters share these traits. "I write about strong, nice people—they're ordinary people whose lives have been invaded," she told O'Neill. "The danger comes from outside. They're not looking for trouble, not walking down Eighth Avenue at 3 a.m."

Clark's father died when she was ten, leaving behind a widow with three children and mortgage payments at the onset of World War II. "My mother's occupation and hobby, vocation and avocation, was motherhood," Clark wrote in *Read-*

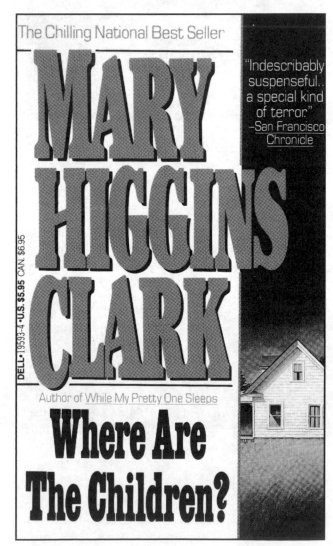

Clark first gained critical acclaim with her 1975 book about a mother accused of killing her children. It was adapted as a Columbia Pictures film in 1986.

er's Digest. "She was determined that her children have everything." She took in boarders to supplement the family's income, but their meager rent payments weren't enough: Clark's mother lost her house and was forced to move the family into an apartment. Adding to her troubles was Clark's brother Joe's illness, diagnosed as osteomyelitis a few months after their father's death. Doctors recommended an operation to remove Joe's hipbone, but Clark's mother refused. "She wouldn't make a cripple of Joe, and she knew God wouldn't take him from her," Clark wrote in *Reader's Digest.* Her faith was well-founded; Joe was well enough to play hockey in school the next year, and announced his intention to join the Navy after graduation. "Instead of trying to dissuade him by pointing out the financial hardship this would cause the family, [Mother] let him enlist with his friends," Clark related. Sadly, Joe died after contracting spinal meningitis six months later. Clark graduated from Villa Maria Academy and her younger brother Johnny completed grammar school the following June.

While material things were at a premium, Mother's love and attention were not. "As the only girl, I was guarded with the vigor of a dragon-slaying St. George," Clark noted. Her husband, Warren, was the only boy her mother approved of. For the first time, Clark returned from a date to find that her mother had not waited up for her.

No Stranger to Adversity

Two hours into her first date with Warren F. Clark, "he was scribbling names on a cocktail napkin," Clark related in *Reader's Digest.* "'I'm making a guest list for the wedding,' he said. 'Now don't get all girlie and cute. You know we'll be great together.'" They married six months later, and had five children before Warren's chest pains began. "Warr had three heart attacks in the next five years, but his sense of humor never stopped," Clark wrote. "'Don't be a blooming widow,' he would tell me. 'Try to look real gaunt.' No one was more graceful in loving life—and leaving it." After fifteen years of marriage, Clark, like her mother, became a widow with children.

Unlike her mother, however, Clark was able to find a good job—times were easier and Clark had some upper-level schooling—and left her children in the care of their devoted grandmother. She worked as a radio scriptwriter and producer, and submitted short stories to women's magazines. "Each [radio script] was four minutes long," she told Herbert

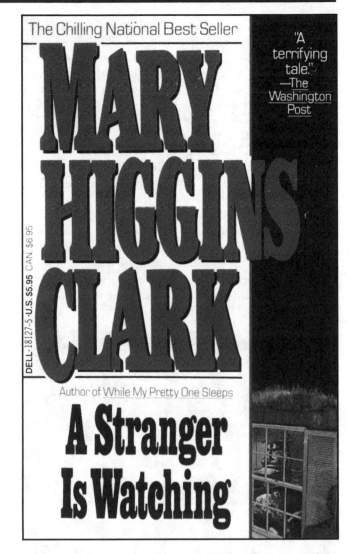

The Chilling National Best Seller

MARY HIGGINS CLARK

"A terrifying tale." —The Washington Post

DELL ●18127-5 ●U.S. $5.95 CAN. $6.95

Author of *While My Pretty One Sleeps*

A Stranger Is Watching

Children are again victims in this 1977 story about a kidnapper who imprisons his quarry in Grand Central Station.

Mitgang in the *New York Times Book Review.* "In that time you had to tell a story and leave room for two messages from the sponsor. It taught me to write tightly." After several years, Clark tried her hand at a very different form of writing. Although her first book, a biography of George Washington entitled *Aspire to the Heavens,* was not a commercial success, it proved that Clark could write in a larger format.

In Clark's first critically and commercially successful work, the suspense novel *Where Are the Children?,* a mother accused of murdering her children is acquitted when a key witness disappears. Suspicions are rekindled, however, when seven years later, after she remarries and has two more children, they too disappear. Clark said *Where Are the Children?* grew out of her childhood memories of the kidnapping of aviator Charles Lindbergh's baby son, a case that kept the country glued to its radios from the abduction and discovery of the child's body in 1932 until the trial and execution of the kidnapper in 1936; many of her stories have since revolved around a kidnapping. Clark told Jo Cooper in *Writer's Digest,* "I still remember the night Bruno Hauptmann was executed. My mother and father had the radio on, and they didn't realize my brothers and I were playing marbles nearby. The radio program was very dramatic. They switched from Death Row to the motel where Mrs. Hauptmann was screaming hysterically. I remembered this and realized that everyone cares about children who disappear." *Where Are the Children?* brought Clark best-seller status in 1975 and a six-figure advance for her next book, *A Stranger Is Watching.* Kidnapping again played a central role in *A Stranger Is Watching,* in which a famous

journalist's children are kidnapped and hidden in New York's Grand Central Station. "It's hard to beat this novel for sheer frights, although it frequently strains credibility," a *Publishers Weekly* reviewer commented.

With the success of her first two novels, Clark's life was at last financially stable. "The [money] changed my life in the nicest way," Clark told Bina Bernard in *People.* "It took all the choking sensation out of paying for the kids' schools." Her next book, *The Cradle Will Fall,* enlarged her rapidly expanding readership. When a woman looking out of her hospital room window sees someone stuffing a body into a car trunk, she chalks it up to a bad dream. The murderer, however, sees her watching and plans her death. "*The Cradle Will Fall* is built of familiar materials, but the hammering and joining are expertly professional," Walter Clemons declared in *Newsweek.* The psychological mysteries *A Cry in the Night* and *Stillwatch* and romantic suspense novel *Weep No More, My Lady* followed.

"The plot [of *A Cry in the Night*] appears to have been put together out of generous borrowings from many familiar sources, *Psycho, Gaslight, Rebecca, Jane Eyre,* among others," Elisabeth Jakab observed in the *New York Times Book Review.* When Jenny MacPartland is rescued from her unhappy, scraping existence by a rich and famous artist, she thinks her life has become a fairy-tale. She soon finds, however, that her new husband is not the loving hero she had believed him to be. Jenny becomes convinced that she is losing her mind when strange things begin to happen at her new home, an isolated farm in Minnesota. Her ex-husband is murdered when he comes looking for her, and a witness swears Jenny, who remembers nothing of it, was at the scene. Psychological intrigue again plays a role in *Stillwatch,* in which a woman moves into the house where her parents died in order to come to terms with her past. *Weep No More, My Lady* incorporates classic whodunit elements to reveal why a famous actress fell to her death from her penthouse balcony. Her sister, convinced that the dead woman's fiance is responsible, works to prove his guilt.

While she sets out to entertain her readers, Clark's writing also contains a message. "I feel a good suspense novel can and should hold a mirror up to society and make a social comment," she once said. A subplot of *A Stranger Is Watching,* described by Patrick Cosgrave in *Spectator* as "an intelligently wrought account of the American argument about capital punishment," is an example of Clark's efforts to explore controversial issues. She told

The painful truth about the death of a young woman's mother is revealed in this 1989 bestseller.

Bernard, "I would like to get across a sense of values. I like nice, strong people confronting the forces of evil and vanquishing them."

When preparing a book, Clark creates biographies of each character and compiles research to make sure each one, particularly the criminals, behaves the way they would in real life. "I go to a lot of trials," Clark commented to Cooper. "I see psychopathic killers on trial. They look perfectly normal." During the trials Clark absorbs the facts of the cases, observing evidence and listening to the stories of the victims. Having two children involved in the legal profession also helps Clark to stay informed: "They let me know when there's a case I shouldn't miss," she told O'Neill.

Clark's daughter, Carol, is poised to follow in her mother's footsteps. Her first novel, *Decked*, was released by Warner in 1992. Her protagonist is, appropriately, a sharp young sleuth and the daughter of a famous mystery writer. An actress as well, Carol Clark will star in the film version of *A Cry in the Night*, and has been contracted to narrate the audio versions of three of her mother's books.

Unprecedented Contract

In 1989, Clark received a contract from Simon & Schuster worth $11.4 million, the largest ever between a publisher and author, to produce four novels and a short-story collection. The first work to result was *While My Pretty One Sleeps*, about a young woman who discovers the bizarre truth behind her mother's murder. *The Anastasia Syndrome and Other Stories* was next, followed by *Loves Music, Loves to Dance* and *All Around the Town*.

Clark drew upon her knowledge of the fashion world in *While My Pretty One Sleeps*, revealing clues "through a trail of fashion dos and don'ts, the giveaways taking the form of a pair of torn hose and a mismatched designer top," a *Publishers Weekly* reviewer noted, and enabling her protagonist, Neeve Kearny, a Madison Avenue boutique owner, to solve the murders of her mother and a client. Clark's mother and aunt were both buyers for clothing stores, "so all my life I heard fashion even when we didn't have a cent," she related to O'Neill, adding that she takes care to outfit each of her characters appropriately, providing clues to their personalities and psychological states through descriptions of their clothing. She opened *A Stranger Is Watching* with a description of the murderer, wearing a green polyester suit, as he checked into a hotel: "Last night at the desk in the lobby, he'd seen the clerk's eyes sliding over his clothes. He'd carried his coat under his arm because he knew it looked shabby. But the suit was new; he'd saved up for it." Not all unsavory characters are fashion failures, however; the impeccable dress of a ruthless designer in *While My Pretty One Sleeps* emphasizes his cold, unfeeling personality: "Meticulously dressed in a tan cashmere jacket over a brown-and-beige Scottish pullover, dark-brown slacks and Gucci loafers, with his blaze of curly brown hair, slender, even-featured face, powerful shoulders and narrow waist, Gordon Steuber could easily have had a successful career as a model. Instead, in his early forties, he was a shrewd businessman with an uncanny knack of hiring unknown young designers and exploiting them until they could afford to leave him."

The propriety and sense of class exhibited by Clark's well-groomed heroes are an integral part of her writing style. Reviewers and readers alike have noticed the lack of gory violence and explicit sexuality in her books. In "Terror Stalks the Class Reunion," which originally appeared in *Woman's Day* magazine and is one of the entries in *The Anastasia Syndrome and Other Stories*, a high school teacher is kidnapped by a psychopathic nerd. "Whereas Stephen King would use this as a stage setting for inspired gross-out gore, Ms. Clark clings to the scrupulous code of magazine morality: the nerd refrains from raping the object of his infatuation. He wants to *marry* her first," Bill Kent commented in the *New York Times Book Review*. Clark's theory on descriptions of violence, she told O'Neill, is that they "should be just enough—vivid but not belabored, just that one stark awfulness." She builds the action to allow for this. "The bomb that blows away an entire room of supporting characters starts a fire that saves her the task of describing the carnage," Kent remarked. The title story of *The Anastasia Syndrome*, based on the true account of a woman who believed she was the daughter of the murdered Russian Czar, Nicholas II, features a character possessed by a restless ghost. A kidnapping in "The Lost Angel," a troubled marriage in "Lucky Day," and a murder in "Double Vision" complete the collection. In a review for *Voice of Youth Advocates*, Catherine M. Dwyer predicted that *The Anastasia Syndrome* will be a hit with young adult fans of romantic suspense. "There are no surprises here, no challenges to the reader," she commented. "But occasionally it is nice to get exactly what you expect."

The *Los Angeles Times Book Review*'s Charles Champlin noted that *Loves Music, Loves to Dance*

MARY HIGGINS CLARK LOVES MUSIC, LOVES TO DANCE

A NOVEL

Responding to personal ads in the newspaper proves deadly in another Clark bestseller, published in 1991.

"was atop the bestseller lists even before its official publication date." Described by Roberta Lisker in the *School Library Journal* as "a terrifying tale of life in the '90s," it begins with two women answering personal ads as research for a documentary. When one is murdered, the other sets out to find the killer by answering the same ads to which her friend had responded. *Loves Music, Loves to Dance* "reaffirms that Mary Higgins Clark deserves her reputation for creating splendid suspenseful fiction," Joyce Cohen remarked in the *New York Times Book Review*.

Clark's maturation as a writer is evident in her latest offering, *All Around the Town,* in which she tackles the complex problem of multiple personality disorder. Laurie Kenyon, kidnapped and sexually abused as a child, develops a number of separate personalities to enable her to deal with the trauma. As a college student, Laurie is accused of murdering a professor, a situation which "poses an interesting problem suggested by modern psychiatry,"

New York Times reviewer Christopher Lehmann-Haupt noted. "If a person suffering from multiple personality disorder were to commit a murder, how would one resolve the questions of responsibility and guilt, and whom would one punish?" While many of the elements familiar to her readers are present, including kidnapping, a female victim, and low-key treatment of sexual situations, "Clark's story sense has grown in sophistication since she began writing of helpless women and children in distress" as in *Where Are the Children?* and *The Cradle Will Fall,* Marilyn Stasio commented in the *New York Times Book Review*.

Besides maintaining a strict writing schedule, Clark accepts invitations to speak at various locations throughout the U.S., including libraries, finds time to give radio and television interviews, and attends functions of the various clubs and groups of which she is a member. She attributes her ability to juggle all of these activities to the enjoyment she gets from them. "I think that there is an expression [for this]," she remarked to Kimberly Olson Fakih in a *Library Journal* interview. "If you want to be happy for a year, win the lottery; if you want to be happy for life, love what you do, and I love what I do."

■ Works Cited

Bernard, Bina, "With Five Kids to Support, Could Widow Clark Find Romance? Life, Like Novels, Does End Happily," *People*, March 6, 1978, pp. 79-80.

Champlin, Charles, review of *Loves Music, Loves to Dance, Los Angeles Times Book Review*, June 9, 1991.

Clark, Mary Higgins, *A Stranger Is Watching,* Simon & Schuster, 1977.

Clark, Mary Higgins, *While My Pretty One Sleeps,* Simon & Schuster, 1989.

Clark, Mary Higgins, "A Husband Beyond Compare," *Reader's Digest,* December, 1989, pp. 92-94.

Clark, Mary Higgins, "My Wild Irish Mother," *Reader's Digest,* July, 1991, pp. 83-86.

Clemons, Walter, review of *The Cradle Will Fall, Newsweek,* June 30, 1980, p. 65.

Cohen, Joyce, review of *Loves Music, Loves to Dance, New York Times Book Review,* June 16, 1991, p. 16.

Cooper, Jo, "Inside Mary Higgins Clark's Bestselling Characters," *Writers Digest,* April, 1988, pp. 46-47.

Cosgrave, Patrick, review of *A Stranger Is Watching, Spectator,* August 19, 1978, p. 22.

Dwyer, Catherine M., review of *The Anastasia Syndrome and Other Stories*, *Voice of Youth Advocates*, April, 1990, p. 26.

Fakih, Kimberly Olson, "The Reassuring Triumph of the Good: An Interview with Mary Higgins Clark," *Library Journal*, March 15, 1990, pp. 35-37.

Jakab, Elisabeth, review of *A Cry in the Night*, *New York Times Book Review*, November 14, 1982, p. 15.

Kent, Bill, "Psychopathic Nerd, Marriage-Minded, Seeks ...," *New York Times Book Review*, December 3, 1989.

Lehmann-Haupt, Christopher, "2 Contrasting Murder Mysteries," *New York Times*, June 4, 1992, p. C18.

Lisker, Roberta, review of *Loves Music, Loves to Dance*, *School Library Journal*, September, 1991, p. 292.

Mitgang, Herbert, *New York Times Book Review*, May 14, 1978.

O'Neill, Elizabeth Hill, "Mary Higgins Clark," *Publishers Weekly*, May 19, 1989, pp. 64-65.

Stasio, Marilyn, review of *All Around the Town*, *New York Times Book Review*, May 10, 1992, p. 23.

Review of *A Stranger Is Watching*, *Publishers Weekly*, December 26, 1977, p. 59.

Review of *While My Pretty One Sleeps*, *Publishers Weekly*, June 2, 1989, p. 58.

■ For More Information See

PERIODICALS

Chicago Tribune, June 12, 1988, Section 14, p. 5.

Library Journal, April 15, 1969, p. 1792; June 1, 1989, p. 170.

Los Angeles Times Book Review, November 4, 1984; May 14, 1989; June 9, 1991.

New Yorker, August 4, 1980, p. 92.

New York Times, July 3, 1987.

New York Times Book Review, December 9, 1984, p. 26; June 28, 1987; June 18, 1989.

People, August 31, 1992, p. 31.

Publishers Weekly, September 7, 1984, p. 70; March 30, 1992, p. 91.

West Coast Review of Books, November, 1982, p. 33.

Wilson Library Bulletin, September, 1987, p. 73.°

—Sketch by Deborah A. Stanley

Ellen Conford

■ Personal

Born March 20, 1942, in New York, NY; daughter of Harry and Lillian (Pfeffer) Schaffer; married David H. Conford (a professor of English and a poet), November 23, 1960; children: Michael. *Education:* Attended Hofstra College (now Hofstra University), 1959-62.

■ Addresses

Home—26 Strathmore Rd., Great Neck, NY 11023. *Agent*—McIntosh and Otis Inc., 310 Madison Ave., New York, NY 10017.

■ Career

Writer of books for children and young adults.

■ Awards, Honors

Best Books of the Year citation, *School Library Journal*, 1971, for *Impossible, Possum;* Children's Books of International Interest citation, 1974, for *Just the Thing for Geraldine;* Library of Congress Children's Books of the Year citation, 1974, for *Me and the Terrible Two;* Child Study Association of America Books of the Year citations, 1975, for *The Luck of Pokey Bloom* and *Dear Lovey Hart, I Am Desperate;* Best Books for Young Adults citation, American Library Association, 1976, for *The Alfred G. Graebner Memorial High School Handbook of Rules and Regulations;* Surrey School award, 1981, Pacific Northwest Young Reader's Choice Award, 1981, and California Young Reader's Medal, 1982, all for *Hail, Hail Camp Timberwood;* Best Books of the Year citation, *School Library Journal,* and Parents' Choice Award, both 1983, both for *Lenny Kandell, Smart Aleck;* Parents' Choice Award, 1985, for *Why Me?*, and 1986, for *A Royal Pain;* South Carolina Young Adult Book Award, 1986-87, and South Dakota Prairie Pasque Award, 1989, both for *If This is Love, I'll Take Spaghetti.*

■ Writings

Impossible, Possum (Junior Literary Guild selection), illustrated by Rosemary Wells, Little, Brown, 1971.

Why Can't I Be William?, illustrated by Philip Wende, Little, Brown, 1972.

Dreams of Victory (Junior Literary Guild selection), illustrated by Gail Rockwell, Little, Brown, 1973.

Felicia the Critic (Junior Literary Guild selection), illustrated by Arvis Stewart, Little, Brown, 1973.

Just the Thing for Geraldine, illustrated by John Larrecq, Little, Brown, 1974.

Me and the Terrible Two, illustrated by Charles Carroll, Little, Brown, 1974.

The Luck of Pokey Bloom, illustrated by Bernice Lowenstein, Little, Brown, 1975.

Dear Lovey Hart, I Am Desperate, Little, Brown, 1975.

The Alfred G. Graebner Memorial High School Handbook of Rules and Regulations, Little, Brown, 1976.

And This Is Laura, Little, Brown, 1977.

Eugene the Brave (Junior Literary Guild selection), illustrated by Larrecq, Little, Brown, 1978.

Hail, Hail Camp Timberwood (Junior Literary Guild selection), illustrated by Gail Owens, Little, Brown, 1978.

Anything for a Friend, Little, Brown, 1979.

We Interrupt This Semester for an Important Bulletin, Little, Brown, 1979.

The Revenge of the Incredible Dr. Rancid and His Youthful Assistant, Jeffrey, Little, Brown, 1980.

Seven Days to a Brand-New Me, Little, Brown, 1981.

To All My Fans, with Love, from Sylvie, Little, Brown, 1982.

Lenny Kandell, Smart Aleck, illustrated by Walter Gaffney-Kessell, Little, Brown, 1983.

If This Is Love, I'll Take Spaghetti (story collection), Four Winds, 1983.

You Never Can Tell (Junior Literary Guild selection), Little, Brown, 1984.

Why Me?, Little, Brown, 1985.

Strictly for Laughs, Putnam, 1985.

A Royal Pain, Scholastic, 1986.

The Things I Did for Love, Bantam, 1987.

A Case for Jenny Archer, illustrated by Diane Palmisciano, Little, Brown, 1988.

A Job for Jenny Archer, illustrated by Palmisciano, Little, Brown, 1988.

Genie with the Light Blue Hair, Bantam, 1989.

Jenny Archer, Author, illustrated by Palmisciano, Little, Brown, 1989.

What's Cooking, Jenny Archer?, illustrated by Palmisciano, Little, Brown, 1989.

Jenny Archer to the Rescue, illustrated by Palmisciano, Little, Brown, 1990.

Loving Someone Else, Bantam, 1991.

Can Do, Jenny Archer, illustrated by Palmisciano, Little, Brown, 1991.

Dear Mom, Get Me out of Here!, Little, Brown, 1992.

Contributor of stories and poems to *Teen, Reader's Digest, Modern Bride*, and other periodicals, and of reviews to *New York Times* and *American Record Guide*. Conford's manuscripts are housed in the Kerlan Collection, University of Minnesota.

■ Work in Progress

I Love You, I Hate You, Get Lost, a collection of short stories for Scholastic.

■ Adaptations

"Getting Even: A Wimp's Revenge" (based on *The Revenge of the Incredible Dr. Rancid and His Youthful Assistant, Jeffrey*) was adapted as an *ABC Afterschool Special*, starring Adolph Caesar and Jon Rothstein, American Broadcasting Companies, Inc. (ABC-TV), 1986; *And This Is Laura* and *The Alfred G. Graebner Memorial High School Handbook of Rules and Regulations* were adapted for television; *Dear Lovey Hart, I Am Desperate* was adapted for television as an *ABC Afterschool Special*, and was distributed as a film by Walt Disney's Educational Media Co. for use in schools; *Dreams of Victory* was adapted into a sound recording disc; *If This Is Love, I'll Take Spaghetti, Lenny Kandell, Smart Aleck, The Luck of Pokey Bloom*, and *The Revenge of the Incredible Dr. Rancid and His Youthful Assistant, Jeffrey*, were adapted into sound recording cassettes.

■ Sidelights

Ellen Conford is one of the most popular authors of realistic fiction for children and young adults. Her books for teenagers usually focus on female protagonists living in modern-day suburbia, dealing with normal adolescent problems. Attempting to reassure young adults that what they are going through is normal, Conford often employs humor as a vehicle for her themes of identity, romance, and success. Her novels are fast-paced and optimistic, and she is able to capture the elusive teenage vernacular in her often witty dialogue. "I don't write to pound home a message, or to teach a lesson, or to convert kids to a particular point of view," explains Conford in a promotional piece by Little, Brown and Company. "I want to write books that are fun to read, books that will help children to realize that there is such a thing as reading for pleasure, and that books do not merely inform and teach, but *amuse*."

Conford was born on March 20, 1942, in New York City. Her childhood years were shy ones, and she remembers herself as being very introverted. "What I liked to do most was read and write," she comments in an interview with *Authors and Artists for Young Adults (AAYA)*. "I was not very social and I hated to go out and play. I had some friends of course, but I wasn't particularly popular and I

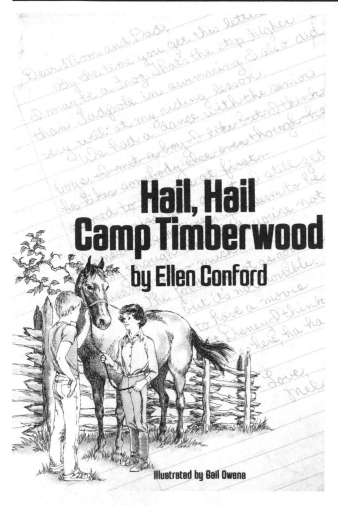

Conford based this 1978 story on her real-life experiences in summer camp.

wasn't particularly good at anything. I was timid and afraid of a lot of things." Because of this overwhelming shyness, Conford spent most of her time reading, especially after she got her library card in the second grade. "I had to pass a public library on my way to school every day," she remembers in her *AAYA* interview. "It was a little tiny storefront library about the size of a small candy store. Every week I would stop there after school on Fridays and pick out eight books because that was all they would let you take out. I would have taken out sixteen if they would have let me. I would pile them on top of my school books and carry them home and I would read all eight books during the week while my mother was yelling, 'Ellen go out and play, you need some fresh air and sunshine,' and I would say, 'Later Mom, later.'"

Aside from all the library books Conford devoured, she also bought her own books. "I was a real Nancy Drew fan, and I read a lot of teenage books, books about popular teenage girls, the kind of teenage

girl I hoped to be, whose biggest problem was whether they would get asked to the prom," remarks Conford in her interview. As she became one of the teenage girls she spent so much time reading about, Conford's social life and activities began to improve. She was still shy, but she became more active in school and had a larger group of friends. "I joined a lot of clubs," she tells *AAYA*, "but I was still mainly interested in reading and writing, so I was on the school newspaper and the yearbook, and I was editor of the humor magazine in high school."

Conford began writing around the same time she began consuming over eight books a week. She started out with poetry, moving on to novels and short stories around the fourth or fifth grade, finally joining the staffs of many of her high school's publications. Looking back at her daughter's writing development, Conford's mother has commented that she knew her daughter was going to be a writer ever since she was in the third grade. "She said she knew because I had started putting rhyming lines together when I was about seven years old. . . . I mean even before I could write them down," relates Conford in her *AAYA* interview. "I started reciting them and she saw that I had the ability to do it. And it was what I was doing all the time. She was an elementary school teacher and recognized that my ability was unusual." Being a writer was not Conford's only dream, though; she also wanted to be an actress. This aspiration was put to rest when she tried out for Manhattan's High School of Performing Arts and wasn't accepted. "So I figured that career was doomed and I'd have to be a writer," she observes in her interview. "I mean there was nothing else that I was good at. This was it. Absolutely no other talent whatsoever. So it was writing or nothing."

Following high school, Conford attended Hofstra College for a little more than two years. And it was on her first day of classes that she met her future husband; they got married during Conford's second year of school, and she got pregnant soon after. Dropping out to have her child, Conford returned to school for a short while before she moved to New Mexico, where her husband was doing graduate work. While in New Mexico she took a few more classes and was able to work on a newspaper during the Cuban missile crisis. Her husband later became an English professor, and the couple moved back to New York with their son Michael.

Possums Swing into First Picture Book

It was Michael who indirectly inspired Conford to write her first children's book. He was four years old, and the Confords were in the habit of reading to him every night before he went to bed, going through seven to eight books a week. During one of these many weeks, Conford was at a local public library and couldn't find anything she wanted to bring home to read to Michael. "Of course we'd been through a lot of books—we'd read to, him since he was a year old," she points out in her *AAYA* interview. "But I couldn't find anything, and I was looking at all these books that people had published and had gotten paid to produce, and I'm thinking, 'Gee, some of these are really awful, and some of them are just not very good, and some of them are boring.' And I thought, 'I can't believe people are getting paid to do this and these things are getting published and I know I can do better.'" Conford returned home in frustration, and with encouragement from her husband she sat down to write her first book, *Impossible, Possum*.

The inspiration for the book came in a somewhat backwards way—Conford came up with the title first, then went from there. After deciding on the subject matter for the book, Conford "did a little research on possums and found out what their habits were," she explains to *AAYA*. "And then I tried to think of a problem, I tried to think of what would have universal appeal; what were the universal themes that kids were interested in? I thought one of the major ones was fitting in and being able to do what the rest of your group or peers or family does. I knew that possums hung by their tails and I thought, 'What if this possum can't?' And that's how I developed the book." Once *Impossible, Possum* was done, Conford sent the manuscript to thirteen publishers before it was finally accepted two and a half years later by Little, Brown. "Everything about *Possum* worked right," maintains John G. Keller (one of Conford's editors) in *Elementary English*. "In a field where it often takes several books before the market begins to know and trust an author, this first book exceeded ... expectations." *Impossible, Possum* tells the story of how Randolph, with the help of his sister Geraldine, overcomes his inability to hang from his tail. A *Publishers Weekly* contributor calls Conford's first picture book a "delightful story" which will "charm" its young readers.

Conford followed her first published work with another picture book—*Why Can't I Be William?* In this short story, young Jonathon spends all of his time envying his friend William only to find out that looks can sometimes be deceiving. *Why Can't I Be William?* is "a painless lesson in how the other half lives, with funny pictures," observes a *Publishers Weekly* contributor. Conford's other books for young children continue the story of the possum family introduced in *Impossible, Possum*. In *Just the Thing for Geraldine*, Randolph's older sister finds that her parents are not the best judges of what her talents are and the kind of future they will lead to. Despite her parents' efforts to direct her toward feminine activities, such as weaving and dancing, Geraldine sticks up for what she enjoys most and does the best—juggling. "This is a gentle story" that "should touch a note of familiarity with most children," points out Barbara Dill in the *Wilson Library Bulletin*. Conford's final addition to her possum stories, *Eugene the Brave*, explores a common fear among young children. Eugene, the

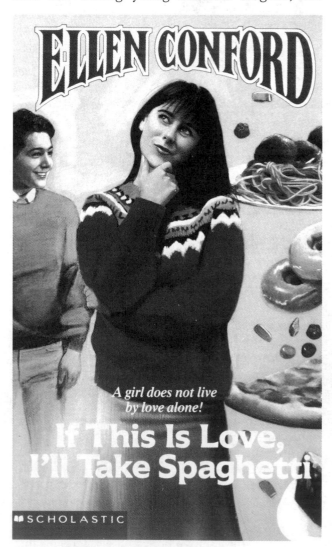

In her 1983 story collection, Conford explores everything from family relationships to first romances.

youngest member of the family, suddenly finds himself afraid of the dark—a fear that will severely limit his ability to function since possums are nocturnal animals. Geraldine saves the day again when she conditions Eugene with small scares and falls into a hole in the process. Eugene must overcome his fear to save his sister, and his discovery of his bravery is "whimsically" portrayed in "this funny tale," concludes Sharon Spredemann Dreyer in *The Bookfinder, a Guide to Children's Literature about the Needs and Problems of Youth Aged 2-15*.

Deft Dialogue Attracts Middle Grade Readers

After publishing her first two picture books, Conford, because of her deft handling of dialogue, was urged by her publisher to try her hand at a novel for middle grade readers. The result was *Dreams of Victory*. Eleven-year-old Victory Benneker thinks she has no talent, so she spends most of her time daydreaming. She only receives six votes when she runs for class president, but in her imagination she is elected President of the United States. In the end Victory finds her hidden talent—her animated imagination, which enables her to be a writer. "Results of a vivid imagination are well-demonstrated in an amusing story about a sixth-grader who describes herself as a loser," relates a *Horn Book* reviewer. And Jane Langton, writing in the *New York Times Book Review*, concludes: "Any young reader who ... does not have the longest blondest hair in the class or who is apt to be given the part of Litter in the pollution play will" appreciate Victory's dreams. "They make a simple and successful book."

Conford got the idea for her next middle grade novel, *Felicia the Critic*, from her cousin Susan Beth Pfeffer, who is also a writer. After hearing about the problems her cousin was having with a particular story line, Susan suggested that Conford make her protagonist someone who has the critical ability to know when something is wrong or isn't going to work. Conford loved the idea, but thought it was a whole book in itself. The resulting novel presents Felicia Kershenbaum, a constructive critic who sees her innate ability as a talent that should be developed. People resent her criticism at first— the butcher insults her when she complains about a cut of meat, the traffic guard is angered by her list of suggestions, and her Aunt Celeste is startled when Felicia critiques the children's book she's written. Felicia's older sister also hates her criticism, and when Felicia's friends form a club they'll only let her in if she doesn't talk. In the end,

however, her friends find Felicia's talents valuable when a winter carnival they've planned fails because they didn't ask for her input. *Felicia the Critic* "is a lively book with some entertaining characters," asserts Dorothy Nimmo in the *School Librarian*. In her *Introducing More Books: A Guide for the Middle Grades*, Diana L. Spirt states that Conford's "sure powers of observation and understanding" enable her to draw "real youngsters in action."

The concept for another of Conford's middle grade novels was inspired by an unusual name. After hearing a distinctive name, Conford often wonders "what somebody with that name would be like, what type of character this would make," she explains in her *AAYA* interview. "The best example I can give is the book I wrote titled *Me and the Terrible Two*, which features twin boys named Haskell and Conrad Conger. I got the idea for this book in 1971 or 1972 when I was watching a football game on television. It was a college football game and one of the players was named Haskell Stanback. I thought, 'What a great name,' because I've always been a name collector.... Now, let's say Haskell Stanback was a character— what would he be like? And I began to think up some traits he might have. He would be mischievous; he could play practical jokes; maybe he could do imitations of John Wayne or Bela Lugosi. And I thought he could be a real pain in the neck to the girl that lived next door.... But wouldn't he have even more fun if there were two of him? And that's when I thought up his brother, I thought of making him a twin."

Me and the Terrible Two, featuring Conford's name-inspired characters, was published in 1974. Dorrie Kimball is the unsuspecting girl terrorized by the terrible twins, Haskell and Conrad, who move in next door when her best friend moves to Australia. In the beginning, Dorrie sees no end to the zany pranks of Haskell and Conrad, but things start looking up for her when she makes new girlfriends at school and is assigned to the Children's Book Week committee. Haskell is also assigned to the project, and he and Dorrie, along with his brother Conrad, end up forming lasting friendships. *Me and the Terrible Two* "seems effortlessly written" and Dorrie's first-person narrative is "wryly" delivered, contends Joyce W. Smothers in *Children's Book Review Service*. And Ethel L. Heins, writing in *Horn Book*, finds the book "appealingly full of school happenings, zippy repartee, and plenty of preadolescent witticisms."

Aside from unusual names and snappy titles, Conford also relies on her own childhood and teenage experiences as resources for book ideas. "What I draw on mostly, more than the experiences themselves, are the emotions that I felt," notes Conford in her interview. "Not so much things that happened to me," she continues, "although a couple of my books are very close to me, and in a couple of books I am very close to the heroine emotionally. There is one book that really is autobiographical." *Hail, Hail Camp Timberwood* "is almost completely true," reveals Conford. "I took experiences of three summers and put them into one summer, and Melanie, the heroine, had triumphs that I never had in camp. But essentially all the people in that book were people that I knew, and I really lived through most of the experiences." The autobiographical nature of *Hail, Hail Camp Timberwood* made the writing much more difficult than Conford expected; she had to keep reminding herself that she was writing a fictional story and could deviate from the reality of her own experiences.

In the fictionalized account of her years at camp, thirteen-year-old Melanie Kessler takes Conford's place. Describing Melanie's first summer away from home, *Hail, Hail Camp Timberwood* also touches upon the topics of first love and self-discovery. Melanie quickly makes friends, but takes longer overcoming her fear of water and learning how to horseback ride. And along the way she falls in love with Steve Tepper and befriends his little brother Dougie. *Hail, Hail Camp Timberwood* "deals with the joys and anxieties of a girl spending her first summer 'on her own' and finding—as I did—that one of the people she gets to know most intimately is herself," describes Conford in the *Junior Literary Guild*. Conford's *Hail, Hail Camp Timberwood* "all rings true" and is "told at [a] lively pace and in an easy, natural style, and . . . has unforced humor," summarizes a *Bulletin of the Center for Children's Books* contributor.

Unlike the majority of her works, Conford's 1983 *Lenny Kandell, Smart Aleck* features a male protagonist. It is also one of the few books she had to research—it's set in 1946. To get a feel for the time period, Conford studied old newspapers and magazines, also drawing on her knowledge of old movies, which gave her an idea of what the slang and the clothes should be like. The main character of the novel is eleven-year-old Lenny Kandell, whose big dream is to be a comedian. His mother and teachers aren't amused by his constant one-liners, but his best friend Artie, who is constantly reading "It Pays to Enrich Your Word Power" in *Reader's Digest*, is duly impressed. Other problems Lenny has to deal with involve his attempts to attract the attention of pretty Georgina, and his efforts to avoid the school bully after he jokingly trips him. By the end of the story, Lenny is able to put his humor aside long enough to acknowledge the fact that his father died accidentally during World War II, not while in active combat. A lively tempo and an amusing portrait of growing up in the 1940s "complement the predicaments, jokes, and comic patter that keep Lenny squarely on center stage," relates *Horn Book* contributor Nancy C. Hammond. And Kathleen Garland comments in *School Library Journal:* "Children looking for a funny story will find it here—and will probably want to try out some of Lenny's jokes on their friends."

Adventurous Jenny Archer Comes to Life

The character of ten-year-old Jenny Archer fills Conford's most recent novels for younger readers. "The Jenny Archer books are wonderful because they're fairly easy to write and I love the character," assesses Conford in her *AAYA* interview. "Her character stimulates me instantly when I start to write about her. She is the kid I wished that I had been, she is so different from me as a child that I get very excited by her adventures." The series of books featuring Jenny also includes her best friend Wilson Wynn, and her large and friendly dog Barkley. In *A Job for Jenny Archer*, published in 1988, Jenny is determined to buy her mother a fur coat for her birthday. Mistakenly assuming that her mother can't afford one because they are poor, Jenny sets out to make money; she babysits, trains dogs, and even attempts to sell her house. Undaunted by the problems she encounters, Jenny acquires the perfect gift just in the nick of time. "Conford's witty, humorous style is in evidence from the first page," maintains *School Library Journal* contributor Martha Rosen, adding: "Younger readers will be entertained by Jenny's bright ideas and the unanticipated problems she creates."

Conford presents more of Jenny's zany adventures and unexpected problems in *A Case for Jenny Archer*, *What's Cooking, Jenny Archer?*, and *Can Do, Jenny Archer*. Faced with a boring summer vacation, Jenny goes to the library and loads up on Missy Martin mysteries in *A Case for Jenny Archer*. Attempting to emulate Missy, Jenny, along with Wilson and Barkley, begins an investigation which eventually alerts the police to a group of thieves trying to rob some vacationing neighbors. "Any library in need of a well-written adventure that will take readers . . . to a place where book fantasies are allowed to come true shouldn't be without this playful mystery,'' points out Joanne Aswell in *School Library Journal. Can Do, Jenny Archer,* published in 1991, has Jenny competing in a school contest; whoever collects the most tin cans for a recycling program wins the right to direct their own movie with the school's new video equipment. Plowing over everyone in her attempt to win, Jenny sees her mistakes in the end when her best friend unselfishly signs over her cans to Jenny so she can win. Maggie McEwen points out in the *School Library Journal,* "Through a feisty main character, Conford touches on typical childhood experiences with humor and sensitivity, and lightly handles the theme of overcompetitiveness."

Early on in her career, after writing for both young children and middle grade readers, Conford moved into the field of young adult literature. "Adolescence is a wonderful time to write about," remarks Conford in her *AAYA* interview. "It's a horrible time to live through, but a wonderful time to write about because their emotions are so strong—the highs are so high and the lows are so low. You're either walking on air or in the depths of total despair, and all this can take place in the space of ten minutes, depending on whether the phone rings or not, or if somebody smiles at you in the cafeteria. So, it's a very ripe time for me since I do work a lot out of emotion in characters, . . . and my memories of these emotions are very vivid, which makes it an easy time to write about."

Conford's first book exploring the emotions of this period of life, *Dear Lovey Hart, I Am Desperate,* was published in 1975. In addition to the normal anxieties of a freshman in high school, Carrie Wasserman must also deal with the new column she's assigned to write for the school paper. The editor of the paper, Chip (whom Carrie has a crush on), convinces her to do an anonymous advice-to-the-lovelorn column, which he believes will help raise circulation. Carrie becomes Lovey Hart, and the column is very successful at first. When Carrie begins to get flip in some of her responses, though, her readers revolt, as does the head guidance counselor, who happens to be her father. In the end, Carrie's younger sister reveals the identity of Lovey Hart, and Carrie offers an apology in her last column. *Dear Lovey Hart, I Am Desperate* is "an imaginative story . . . delivered in swift prose that should win more fans for the popular author," asserts a *Publishers Weekly* reviewer. The credible characters, close family relationships, and "satisfy-

While most of Conford's books view life through the eyes of teenage girls, the author uses a male perspective in this 1985 story.

ing ending make this fun,'' concludes Barbara Elleman in *Booklist.*

The trials and tribulations of Carrie Wasserman's high school years continue in Conford's 1979 *We Interrupt This Semester for an Important Bulletin.* Chip is now Carrie's boyfriend, and she is having trouble writing articles that please him. This becomes a small worry when Southern belle Prudie Tuckerman shows up and steals Chip away. Vowing to forget romance and concentrate on her "career," Carrie puts her all into her reporting, doing an expose on the school lunch program. Her informant turns out to be a disgruntled ex-employee, though, and Carrie and Chip barely hold onto their jobs at the paper. A *Horn Book* contributor comments that "the fast, funny dialogue, the characterization of Prudie as *femme fatale,* and Carrie's self-mocking . . . attitude towards . . . her problems make the book light and amusing."

Conford also uses humor to convey the experiences of a number of young adult characters in her 1983 collection of short stories, *If This Is Love, I'll Take Spaghetti*. The nine short stories included in the book cover such topics as rock stars, jealousy, family relationships, and love and romance. "With a wink and a smile, Conford playfully spins out some familiar scenes and syndromes to their logical—or sometimes delightfully illogical—conclusions," summarizes a *Booklist* contributor. "Each short piece is a gem of characterization, packed full of wry humor and topical illusion, and conveyed by a spare narrative style, plenty of wonderfully believable dialogue, and profound sympathy for the hapless heroine," relates Lois Bragg in *Best Sellers*. And Mary M. Burns concludes in *Horn Book:* "The appealing collection demonstrates the author's versatility with the genre and her ability to isolate those monumental events and problems which dominate a teenager's life."

Why Me?, published in 1985, is similar to *Lenny Kandell, Smart Aleck* in that it is one of only a few books in which Conford portrays teenage adolescence through the eyes of a male. Hobie experiences many of the same worries and anxieties of Conford's female protagonists—he's secretly in love with his beautiful classmate Darlene. At first he's too shy to tell Darlene how he feels, so he pours out his emotions in the poems he writes for her. When he finally works up the courage to actually give her one of these poems, Hobie is delightfully surprised when she asks for more. In the meantime, he's trying to shake the affections of another classmate, G. G. Graffman, who has a crush on him. In the end Hobie discovers that Darlene was telling everyone his poems were from the star athlete she adores. He then realizes that G. G. has many hidden charms, but it's a little too late—she's dating his best friend. "Hobie tells a slightly-slapstick but very funny story about the pitfalls and pinnacles of his young adolescent love life," describes a *Bulletin of the Center for Children's Books* contributor. And a reviewer for *Horn Book* finds that "snappy dialogue and a light hand with character make this glimpse of the teenage world both entertaining and true to life."

Comedy: The Main Attraction

The comic element in *Why Me?*, and a number of Conford's other books, is one of the aspects of her writing that adolescent readers appreciate. "When I get letters from kids who comment on the humor in my writing, they tell me that it appeals to them because they like to laugh at what they recognize,"

Conford tells *AAYA*. "They see reflections of things that have happened to them, and they see the stream of consciousness monologue where the heroine dumps on herself for being so inept and they know they've felt the same way. But when they read hers, and it's done comically, they tell me it makes them laugh at their own problems. It makes them laugh at the experiences they've had, lightening sometimes dark moments for them and the things that seem so serious. And if they laugh over something that seemed horrible at the time they went through it, then they feel better."

This lightness is evident in Conford's novel *A Royal Pain*, which strays from her usual realistic subject matter and incorporates elements of fantasy. The idea for the book was given to Conford by an editor, who wanted her to create a romantic story about an average American teenage girl who suddenly finds out that she was switched at birth with the princess of a small foreign country. Conford was skeptical at first, mainly because she usually writes about realistic situations. "So I thought about it for three weeks," she remembers in her *AAYA* interview, "and finally I was riding home from New York one day on the Long Island Railroad and I thought, 'You know, that's the trouble with what I'm trying to do here. I'm trying to make it believable. That's a mistake. The way to approach this is to make it as unbelievable as possible.' And once I got that idea, I realized that I could do anything I wanted.... Anything was possible, because this was, a) unbelievable, and b) completely my own creation which had no relation in fact to the real world. It was totally imaginary and I loved doing it. It was so liberating; you couldn't do anything wrong."

The novel Conford ended up with features the utterly American character of fifteen-year-old Abby Adams, who was born prematurely while her parents were attending the Gloxinia Festival in the small European country of Saxony Coburn. (The stop was thrown in as a free bonus by their travel agent.) The same royal physician assists in the birth of both Abby and Florinda, the fourteenth princess of Saxony Coburn. Fifteen years later, shortly before Abby's sixteenth birthday, emissaries arrive at her house to tell her that she's the real Princess Florinda. The physician has recently died and left a confessional letter stating that he accidentally switched the babies at birth—Abby is the real princess.

Hesitant at first, Abby soon finds that she can't resist the fantasies associated with being a princess, and is whisked away to Saxony Coburn. Things

A BANTAM STARFIRE BOOK

ELLEN CONFORD
GENIE WITH THE
LIGHT BLUE HAIR

"A deft blending of fantasy and reality."
—Publishers Weekly

Author of THE THINGS I DID FOR LOVE

Another departure for Conford came with this 1989 book, which mixes fantasy and reality with humorous results.

immediately start to go wrong: the tiny country is not very technically advanced, the dethroned Princess Florinda is resentful, and Abby discovers she is to be married to the revolting Prince Casimir on her sixteenth birthday (despite the fact that she has fallen in love with a gorgeous newspaper reporter). As things get worse, Abby hatches a plan to escape, starting a rumor that she is not really the princess. Her parents arrive just in time, and it is finally decided that the rumor she started is really the truth, and Abby returns home to America. What makes *A Royal Pain* "so irresistibly funny are the gut-level adolescent responses, word plays and banter that this decidedly modern princess engages in on her trip to and from the throne," explains Cynthia J. Rieben in the *Voice of Youth Advocates*. Abby's "account of her adventures as a princess are so hilarious that the reader never quarrels with

what is possible and what is not," points out Cynthia Samuels in the *Washington Post Book World*. "In fact, most of the time the reader is too busy laughing to care very much about anything."

Conford delves into the fantasy world once again with her 1989 novel *Genie with the Light Blue Hair*. "The reason I wrote it is because I got this terrific idea and I realized again that this could be pretty much anything I wanted it to be, as long as I maintained a certain consistency," observes Conford in her interview. "Anything could happen and it could be utterly ridiculous, which is what I tried to do." *Genie with the Light Blue Hair* begins on fifteen-year-old Jeannie Warren's birthday. A practical and intelligent young woman, Jeannie appreciates the dictionary she receives from her parents, but doesn't know what to do with the odd-looking lamp with a big blue candle inside it that she receives from her aunt. That night, an electrical storm knocks out all the power, so Jeannie lights the new lamp. To her surprise, a blue genie, who looks remarkably like Groucho Marx, emerges and tells her she can have anything she wishes for, and as many wishes as she wants. Once she believes the genie, Jeannie begins wishing for such things as popularity and the love of a teacher she has a crush on, but her wishes never seem to turn out right. She finally discovers that her genie was meant for her Aunt Jean, and returns the lamp to its rightful owner. But along the way, she gains some well-needed confidence. "The saucy, true-to-life characterizations and dialogue" in *Genie with the Light Blue Hair* "are inevitably comical," points out a *Horn Book* contributor. "This light, humorous novel will amuse readers who enjoy a deft blending of fantasy and reality," concludes a reviewer in *Publishers Weekly*.

What Is Love?

Reality and teenage love, two of Conford's mainstays, can be found in a couple of her more recent works. In *The Things I Did for Love*, Stephanie Kasden tries to analyze the reasons behind love for a psychology project. While working on the assignment, her best friend Amy inexplicably falls for a motorcyclist with an ostentatious mohawk and fixes her up with his friend Bash. In the meantime, the school's Don Juan (Trevor) also develops an interest in Stephanie, as does her long-time friend Jon. Trevor turns out to be a little bit too suave, and Jon is really after Amy, but Stephanie finds herself irresistibly attracted to Bash, who lives in his motorcycle club's house and has dropped out of school. The project that started all the questions about love ends with the conclusion that there is really nothing rational about love at all. "Laced with pithy observations, tense moments of crisis, and lively dialogue, this well-realized agony of love should be an applauded addition to most collections," maintains Katharine Bruner in the *School Library Journal.*

Loving Someone Else, published in 1991, adds a contemporary and timely twist to the basic theme of adolescent love. Seventeen-year-old Holly Campion is getting ready to go off to Sarah Lawrence College in the fall when her rich father suffers a great financial loss after his company falls prey to a hostile takeover. Faced with paying for college on her own, Holly takes a summer job working as a companion for a couple of eccentric elderly women who live on Harmony Island. One attraction of the job is their attractive nephew Avery, who is at least ten years older than Holly. In the course of her job,

author of *Genie With the Light Blue Hair*

ELLEN CONFORD LOVING SOMEONE ELSE

After her father loses his fortune, a college freshman not only learns how to do things for herself, but also how to love someone else in Conford's warm-hearted 1991 novel.

Holly is faced with partaking in a seance, driving an old hearse, learning Esperanto, and cooking and doing the laundry (without all the modern conveniences she's used to). Because she's so caught up in trying to win over Avery, Holly misses out on the affections of Pete, a nice local boy who works at the marina. After she meets Avery's fiancee, Holly is determined to quit, but when a real emergency comes up she realizes just how selfish she has been. *Loving Someone Else* "is an enjoyable light read with snappy dialogue and a sense of humor," sums up Marian Rafal in the *Voice of Youth Advocates.* And a *Publishers Weekly* contributor concludes: "From Holly's witty first-person narrative to the artfully developed conclusion, this book is top-notch."

Conford's 1992 work, *Dear Mom, Get Me out of Here!*, is similar to *A Royal Pain* and *Genie with the Light Blue Hair* in that it combines elements of both reality and absurdity. The story concerns Paul Tanner, who is placed in a boarding school when his parents must go to Europe for several months. The school they choose to place him in is one that his uncle went to thirty years ago and loved. Unfortunately, the school turns out to be one of the worst-run organizations in the entire United States; the food is horrible, the headmaster and the handyman are both deranged, and the other kids there are extremely weird. One of the students has a pet rooster, another is convinced that he could fly if only he had the right equipment, and there is also a kid who is positive that the headmaster is really a killer on the loose. Conford's hero, like many of her previous ones, must deal with the trials and tribulations associated with growing up.

In her *AAYA* interview, Conford describes what she believes is the basic underlying theme for most of her work, regardless of which age group it's written for. "I think pretty much in most of my books what I'm doing is saying that there is a normal growing up process which you, the reader, are going through. And you are not alone. Sometimes you have these bad thoughts about yourself, or you think you're thinking bizarre things, and you think nobody else goes through this stuff and that you must be really, really weird. But you're not, because here's a character who is going through the same thing, who is going to turn out okay in one way or another, who knows what you're going through. And essentially the message is, hey, you're okay. This is not strange, this is not bizarre, this is not unusual; this is normal. Growing up is not easy. It's not necessarily pretty, but you're not crazy, you're not weird; you're special in your own way, but you're not that different from other kids who are experiencing these things. Here's a person in a book who it's happening to, so you know it's more universal than you think. The main thing is that these are the problems of growing up, other people have them. So stand back and watch somebody else go through what you're going through."

■ Works Cited

Aswell, Joanne, review of *A Case for Jenny Archer*, *School Library Journal*, March, 1989, pp. 156, 158.

Bragg, Lois, review of *If This Is Love, I'll Take Spaghetti*, *Best Sellers*, May, 1983, p. 73.

Bruner, Katharine, review of *The Things I Did for Love*, *School Library Journal*, January, 1988, p. 84.

Burns, Mary M., review of *If This Is Love, I'll Take Spaghetti*, *Horn Book*, June, 1983, pp. 309-310.

Conford, Ellen, *Nobody Dies in My Books* (promotional piece), Little, Brown, 1977.

Conford, Ellen, interview with Susan M. Reicha for *Authors and Artists for Young Adults*, August 24, 1992.

Review of *Dear Lovey Hart, I Am Desperate*, *Publishers Weekly*, October 20, 1975, p. 74.

Dill, Barbara, review of *Just the Thing for Geraldine*, *Wilson Library Bulletin*, November, 1974, p. 241.

Review of *Dreams of Victory*, *Horn Book*, August, 1973, p. 378.

Dreyer, Sharon Spredemann, review of *Eugene the Brave* in her *The Bookfinder, a Guide to Children's Literature about the Needs and Problems of Youth Aged 2-15: Annotations of Books Published 1975 through 1978*, Volume 2, American Guidance Service, 1981.

Elleman, Barbara, review of *Dear Lovey Hart, I Am Desperate*, *Booklist*, January 1, 1976, p. 624.

Garland, Kathleen, review of *Lenny Kandell, Smart Aleck*, *School Library Journal*, May, 1983, p. 70.

Review of *Genie with the Light Blue Hair*, *Horn Book*, March, 1989, p. 215.

Review of *Genie with the Light Blue Hair*, *Publishers Weekly*, December 9, 1988, p. 67.

Review of *Hail, Hail Camp Timberwood*, *Bulletin of the Center for Children's Books*, February, 1979, p. 97.

Review of *Hail, Hail Camp Timberwood*, *Junior Literary Guild*, September, 1978.

Hammond, Nancy C., review of *Lenny Kandell, Smart Aleck*, *Horn Book*, August, 1983, p. 442.

Heins, Ethel L., review of *Me and the Terrible Two*, *Horn Book*, August, 1974, p. 375.

Review of *If This Is Love, I'll Take Spaghetti*, *Booklist*, April 1, 1983, p. 1031.

Review of *Impossible, Possum*, *Publishers Weekly*, August 2, 1971, p. 64.

Keller, John G., "Ellen and Me or The Editor as Fisherman's Wife," *Elementary English*, September, 1974, pp. 790-796.

Langton, Jane, review of *Dreams of Victory*, *New York Times Book Review*, June 24, 1973, p. 8.

Review of *Loving Someone Else*, *Publishers Weekly*, June 28, 1991, p. 102.

McEwen, Maggie, review of *Can Do, Jenny Archer*, *School Library Journal*, December, 1991, pp. 80, 84.

Nimmo, Dorothy, review of *Felicia the Critic*, *School Librarian*, September, 1975, p. 228.

Rafal, Marian, review of *Loving Someone Else*, *Voice of Youth Advocates*, August, 1991, pp. 168-169.

Rieben, Cynthia J., review of *A Royal Pain*, *Voice of Youth Advocates*, June, 1986, p. 77.

Rosen, Martha, review of *A Job for Jenny Archer*, *School Library Journal*, April, 1988, p. 79.

Samuels, Cynthia, "I Was a Teen-Age Princess," *Washington Post Book World*, March 9, 1986, p. 10.

Smothers, Joyce W., review of *Me and the Terrible Two*, *Children's Book Review Service*, July, 1974, p. 103.

Spirt, Diana L., "Getting Along in the Family: 'Felicia the Critic'" in her *Introducing More Books: A Guide for the Middle Grades*, Bowker, 1978, pp. 4-7.

Review of *We Interrupt This Semester for an Important Bulletin*, *Horn Book*, February, 1980, p. 59.

Review of *Why Can't I Be William?*, *Publishers Weekly*, August 28, 1972, p. 264.

Review of *Why Me?*, *Bulletin of the Center for Children's Books*, October, 1985.

Review of *Why Me?*, *Horn Book*, January, 1986, pp. 56-57.

■ For More Information See

BOOKS

Children's Literature Review, Volume 10, Gale, 1986.

PERIODICALS

America, December 3, 1977, p. 406.

Booklist, April 1, 1979, pp. 1217-1218; October 15, 1985, p. 334.

Horn Book, December, 1973, p. 591; August, 1974; December, 1974, p. 688; August, 1975, p. 380; April, 1976; June, 1977; August, 1978, p. 389; February, 1980, p. 59; October, 1980, pp. 518-519; May, 1986, p. 329; July, 1988, p. 489.

Junior Literary Guild, September, 1971, p. 17; September, 1973, p. 27; March, 1978; October, 1987-March, 1988, p. 61.

Library Journal, July, 1973, pp. 2191-2192.

New York Times Book Review, June 24, 1973, p. 8; April 17, 1983, p. 28.

Publishers Weekly, August 2, 1971, p. 64; June 18, 1973, p. 70; May 12, 1975, p. 66; February 13, 1978, p. 127; January 16, 1981, p. 77; April 25, 1986, p. 84; April 29, 1988, p. 77.

School Library Journal, February, 1973, p. 57; September, 1975, p. 100; December, 1975, p. 58; September, 1976, p. 130; September, 1977, p. 124; September, 1978, p. 133; September, 1979, pp. 132, 154; September, 1980, pp. 67-68; March, 1981, p. 155; February, 1982, p. 87; April, 1983, pp. 121-122; January, 1985, p. 83; November, 1985, p. 95; December, 1985, p. 98; March, 1986, p. 174; February, 1989, p. 100; August, 1989, p. 118; January, 1990, p. 103; December, 1990, pp. 74-75; June, 1991, p. 122.

Times Literary Supplement, April 4, 1975, p. 371.

Voice of Youth Advocates, April, 1981, p. 32; August, 1982, pp. 28-29; August, 1983, p. 144; February, 1986, p. 383; April, 1986, p. 28; October, 1987, p. 198; April, 1989, p. 26; August, 1990, p. 149.

Washington Post Book World, November 8, 1987, p. 18.

Wilson Library Bulletin, March, 1980, p. 456; March, 1981, p. 530.

—Sketch by Susan M. Reicha

Michael Crichton

Personal

Surname is pronounced "*Cry*-ton"; has also written under pseudonyms John Lange and Jeffrey Hudson, and under the joint pseudonym Michael Douglas; born October 23, 1942, in Chicago, IL; son of John Henderson (a corporate president) and Zula (Miller) Crichton; married Joan Radam, January 1, 1965 (divorced, 1970); married Kathleen St. Johns, 1978 (divorced, 1980); married Suzanne Childs (marriage ended); married Anne-Marie Martin, 1987; children: (fourth marriage) Taylor (a daughter). *Education:* Harvard University, A.B. (summa cum laude), 1964, M.D., 1969.

Career

Salk Institute for Biological Studies, La Jolla, CA, post-doctoral fellow, 1969-70; full-time writer of books and films; director of films and teleplays, including *Pursuit* (based on his novel *Binary*), American Broadcasting Companies, Inc. (ABC-TV), 1972, *Westworld*, Metro-Goldwyn-Mayer, 1973, *Coma*, United Artists (UA), 1978, *The Great Train Robbery*, UA, 1979, *Looker*, Warner Brothers, 1981, and *Runaway*, Tri-Star Pictures, 1984. Mem-

ber: Mystery Writers Guild of America (West), Authors Guild, Authors League of America, Academy of Motion Picture Arts and Sciences, Directors Guild of America, PEN, Aesculaepian Society, Phi Beta Kappa.

Awards, Honors

Edgar Award, Mystery Writers of America, 1968, for *A Case of Need*, and 1979, for *The Great Train Robbery*; writer of the year award, Association of American Medical Writers, 1970, for *Five Patients: The Hospital Explained*.

Writings

NOVELS

The Andromeda Strain (Literary Guild selection), Knopf, 1969.

(With brother Douglas Crichton, under joint pseudonym Michael Douglas) *Dealing: Or, The Berkeley-to-Boston Forty-Brick Lost-Bag Blues*, Knopf, 1971.

The Terminal Man, Knopf, 1972.

Westworld (also see below), Bantam, 1974.

The Great Train Robbery (also see below), Knopf, 1975.

Eaters of the Dead: The Manuscript of Ibn Fadlan, Relating His Experiences with the Northmen in A.D. 922, Knopf, 1976.

Congo, Knopf, 1980.

Sphere, Knopf, 1987.

Jurassic Park, Knopf, 1990.

Rising Sun, Knopf, 1992.

NONFICTION

Five Patients: The Hospital Explained, Knopf, 1970.
Jasper Johns, Abrams, 1977.
Electronic Life: How to Think about Computers, Knopf, 1983.
Travels (autobiography), Knopf, 1988.

SCREENPLAYS

Extreme Close-up, National General, 1973.
Westworld (based on novel of same title), Metro-Goldwyn-Mayer, 1973.
Coma (based on a novel of same title by Robin Cook), United Artists, 1977.
The Great Train Robbery (based on novel of same title), United Artists, 1978.
Looker, Warner Brothers, 1981.
Runaway, Tri-Star Pictures, 1984.

UNDER PSEUDONYM JOHN LANGE

Odds On, New American Library, 1966.
Scratch One, New American Library, 1967.
Easy Go, New American Library, 1968, published as *The Last Tomb,* Bantam, 1974.
Zero Cool, New American Library, 1969.
The Venom Business, New American Library, 1969.
Drug of Choice, New American Library, 1970.
Grave Descend, New American Library, 1970.
Binary, Knopf, 1971.

UNDER PSEUDONYM JEFFREY HUDSON

A Case of Need, New American Library, 1968.

■ Adaptations

The Andromeda Strain was filmed by Universal, 1971; *A Case of Need* was filmed by Metro-Goldwyn-Mayer, 1972; *Binary* was filmed as *Pursuit,* ABC-TV, 1972; *The Terminal Man* was filmed by Warner Brothers, 1974.

■ Work in Progress

Screenplay for Steven Speilberg's film adaptation of *Jurassic Park.*

■ Sidelights

Michael Crichton has had a number of successful careers—physician, teacher, film director, screenwriter—but he is perhaps best known for pioneering the "techno-thriller" with novels such as *The Andromeda Strain, Sphere,* and *Jurassic Park.* Whether writing about a deadly microorganism, brain surgery gone awry, or adventures in the Congo, Crichton's ability to blend the tight plot and suspense of the thriller with the technical

emphasis of science fiction has made him a favorite with readers of all ages. Crichton's fame is not limited to literary endeavors; he has also directed a number of popular films with subjects ranging from body organ piracy (*Coma*) to advertising manipulation and murder (*Looker*). Summing up Crichton's appeal in the *Dictionary of Literary Biography Yearbook,* Robert L. Sims writes: "His importance lies in his capacity to tell stories related to that frontier where science and fiction meet.... Crichton's best novels demonstrate that, for the immediate future at least, technological innovations offer the same possibilities and limitations as their human creators."

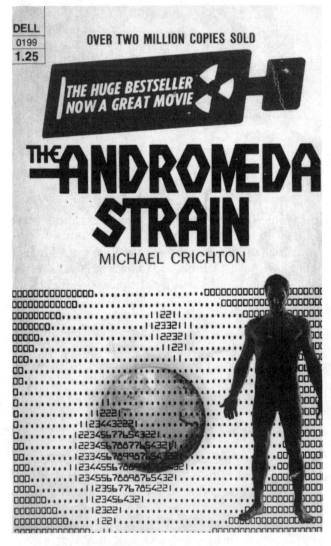

Crichton first gained attention with his 1969 novel about a deadly interstellar disease that threatens mankind's existence.

Lives hang in the balance when a group of greedy surgeons plot to profit from the sale of human organs in the horrifying 1977 film, *Coma*, for which Crichton wrote the screenplay.

Early Ambitions

Crichton spent most of his youth in Roslyn, Long Island. From an early age, he knew that he wanted to write. "This had been my earliest life ambition. It went back almost to the beginning of my ability to read and write at all," Crichton notes in *Travels*. One of his first works had its origins in a third-grade class assignment. The students were told to write a puppet play for presentation. While most of his classmates turned in small skits, Crichton wrote a "nine-page epic." "I had to get my father to retype it for me on multiple carbon copies before it could be performed. My father said he'd never read anything so cliche-ridden in his life," the author recalls in his autobiography.

Crichton's father was a journalist and editor; as a result, all of his children were exposed to the intricacies of English language and usage (often in the form of dinner table discussions). Crichton learned to type by age twelve and began submitting short stories to magazines at age thirteen. He published his first article—a travel piece about a family vacation—in the *New York Times* when he was fourteen. Crichton recalls in *Travels*: "I was ecstatic! I was a published writer! It gave me tremendous encouragement to continue writing. After all, I had been paid sixty dollars, which in those days was a lot of money for a kid."

Over the years, Crichton continued to refine his writing skills. In high school, he covered school sports for his hometown paper, while in college he wrote movie commentaries and acted as book review editor for the *Harvard Crimson*. Crichton maintained a strict writing schedule even after he entered medical school, in large part to help with tuition expenses. "For the next three years ... I wrote paperback thrillers to pay my bills. Of course, there wasn't much time for writing, but I did it on weekends and vacations. And, with practice, I learned to write these spy thrillers quickly.... But I didn't take any particular interest in this work," he remembers in *Travels*.

With time, Crichton's attitude about his writing changed. As his books became more successful, he began to question his commitment to medicine. This conflict came to a head with the publication of *A Case of Need*. Written under a pseudonym, the novel revolves around a Chinese-American obstetrician who is unjustly accused of performing an illegal abortion on the daughter of a prominent Boston surgeon. Critical reaction to the book was very positive. "Read *A Case of Need* now," urges Fred Rotondaro in *Best Sellers*, "it will entertain you; get you angry—it will make you think." Allen J. Hubin, writing in the *New York Times Book Review*, concurs, noting that "this breezy, fast-paced, up-to-date first novel ... demonstrates again the ability of detective fiction to treat

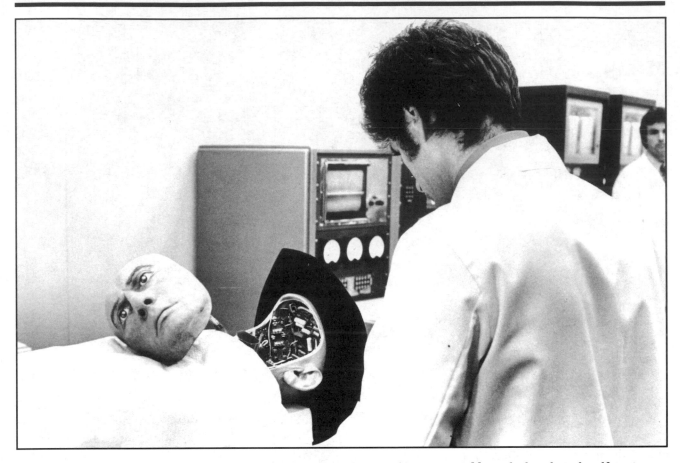

It's a face-off between man and machine in Crichton's successful 1973 film, *Westworld*, in which technical malfunctions cause the android characters of a futuristic amusement part to turn on their human patrons.

contemporary social problems in a meaningful fashion."

Crichton's eventual decision to leave medical school in favor of a writing career was not an easy one (in fact, it took him three tries; each time he decided to leave, an instructor or dean would convince him to give medicine another chance). He recounts in his memoir: "In quitting, I was following my instincts; I was doing what I really wanted to do. But most people saw only that I was giving up a lot of prestige.... To quit medicine to become a writer struck most people like quitting the Supreme Court to become a bail bondsman. They admired my determination, but thought I was pretty unrealistic."

A Deadly Microbe Brings Big Success

Crichton's concerns about leaving medicine were abated somewhat by the success of *The Andromeda Strain*. Published while the author was still in school, *Andromeda* made Crichton a minor celebrity on campus (especially when the book rights were sold to Universal Studios). Crichton had some

difficulty adjusting to his new status—in fact, it made him rather uncomfortable: "The blatant insincerity of the way I was treated troubled me very much. I didn't yet understand that people used celebrities as figures of fantasy; they didn't want to know who you really were," he writes in *Travels*.

A large part of the success of *The Andromeda Strain* lies in the way the story is presented. Part historical journal, the novel uses data such as computer printouts, bibliographic references, and fictional government documents to lend credence to the story of a deadly microorganism that arrives on Earth aboard a NASA space probe. The virus quickly kills most of the residents of Piedmont, Arizona. Two survivors—an old man and a baby—are taken to a secret government compound for study by Project Wildfire. The Wildfire team—Stone, a bacteriologist, Leavitt, a clinical microbiologist, Burton, a pathologist, and Hall, a practicing surgeon—must race against the clock to isolate the organism and find a cure before it can spread into the general population.

Andromeda's mix of science and suspense causes problems for some reviewers. While admitting that he stayed up all night to finish the book, Christopher Lehmann-Haupt of the *New York Times* feels cheated by the conclusion: "I figured it was all building to something special—a lovely irony, a chilling insight, a stunning twisteroo.... The whole business had to be resolved before I could sleep.... It wasn't worth it, because ... Mr. Crichton resolves his story with a series of phony climaxes precipitated by extraneous plot developments." Richard Schickel, writing in *Harper's*, is more concerned with a shortage of character development. "The lack of interest in this matter is ... amazing. Perhaps so much creative energy went into his basic situation that none was left for people," he writes. Not all critics are as harsh in their evaluation of the novel, however. "The pace is fast and absorbing," claims Alexander Cook in *Commonweal*, "the writing is spare and its quality is generally high; and the characters, if not memorable, are at any rate sufficiently sketched in and have been given little personal touches of their own."

Madness, Money, and Monkeys

Crichton also uses the world of science and medicine as a backdrop for *The Terminal Man*. The title refers to computer scientist Harry Benson who, as the result of an automobile accident, suffers severe epileptic seizures. As the seizures grow in intensity, Benson has blackouts during which he commits violent acts. At the urging of his doctors, Benson decides to undergo a radical procedure in which an electrode is inserted into his brain. Hooked up to a packet in the patient's shoulder, the electrode is wired to locate the source of the seizures and deliver a shock to the brain every time an episode is about to occur. Unfortunately, something goes wrong, and Benson's brain is overloaded; as the shocks increase, Benson becomes more irrational, dangerous, and eventually, murderous.

John R. Coyne of the *National Review* finds *The Terminal Man* "one of the season's best." He adds: "Crichton proves himself capable of making the most esoteric material completely comprehensible to the layman.... Even more important, he can create and sustain that sort of suspense that forces us to suspend disbelief." And, in an *Atlantic Monthly* review of the novel, Edward Weeks opines that Crichton has "now written a novel quite terrifying in its suspense and implication."

In *The Great Train Robbery*, Crichton moves out of the realm of science and into the world of Victorian England. Loosely based on an actual event, the book explores master criminal Edward Pierce's attempt to steal a trainload of army payroll on its way to the Crimea. "*The Great Train Robbery* combines the pleasures, guilt, and delight of a novel of gripping entertainment with healthy slices of instruction and information interlarded," declares Doris Grumbach in the *New Republic*. Lehmann-Haupt enthuses that he found himself "not only captivated because it is Mr. Crichton's best thriller to date ... but also charmed most of all by the story's Victorian style and content." And Weeks, writing in the *Atlantic Monthly*, calls the novel "an exciting and very clever piece of fiction."

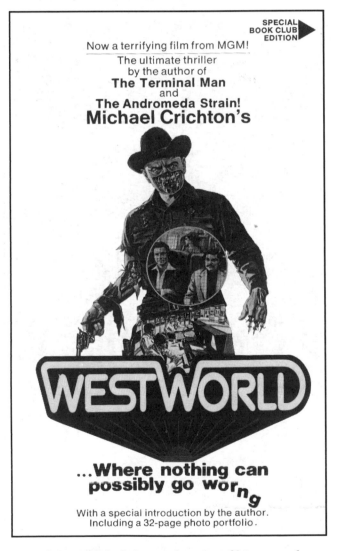

Crichton published the novel version of his screenplay one year after the film's debut.

Congo marks Crichton's return to the field of science and technology. In the novel, three adventurers travel through the dense rain forests of the Congo in search of a cache of diamonds with the power to revolutionize computer technology. The trio is accompanied by an intelligent, linguistically-trained gorilla named Amy, the designated intermediary between the scientists and a band of killer apes who guard the gems. The small band's search is hampered by cannibals, volcanos, and mutant primates; it is also marked by a sense of desperation, as the team fights to beat a Euro-Japanese rival company to the prize. In a review of *Congo* for *Best Sellers*, Justin Blewitt terms the novel "an exciting, fast-paced adventure. It rang very true and at the same time was a terrific page-turner. That's a rare combination.... [*Congo* is] really a lot of fun."

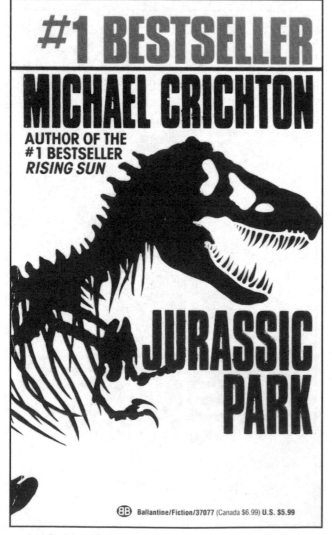

#1 BESTSELLER
MICHAEL CRICHTON
AUTHOR OF THE
#1 BESTSELLER
RISING SUN
JURASSIC PARK

BB Ballantine/Fiction/37077 (Canada $6.99) U.S. $5.99

In typical Crichton fashion, science runs amok in a 1990 novel about bioengineered dinosaurs that turn a tourist attraction into a deadly arena.

Monsters By Land and Sea

A scientific—and monetary—search is also the emphasis in *Sphere*. An American ship laying cable in the Pacific hits a snag; the snag turns out to be a huge spaceship, estimated to be at least three centuries old. An undersea research team is ordered to investigate the strange craft from the relative safety of an underwater habitat. Among the civilian and military crew is psychologist Norman Johnson, whose apprehension about the entire project is validated by a number of increasingly bizarre and deadly events: a bad storm cuts the habitat off from the surface, strange messages begin appearing on computer screens, and an unseen—but apparently huge—squid attacks the crew's quarters.

"Michael Crichton's new novel... kept me happy for two hours sitting in a grounded plane," writes Robin McKinley in the *New York Times Book Review*, adding that "no one can ask for more of a thriller.... Take this one along with you on your next plane ride." While noting that he had some problems with *Sphere*—including stilted dialogue and broad characterizations—James M. Kahn muses that Crichton "keeps us guessing at every turn.... [He is] a storyteller and a damned good one." And Michael Collins of the *Washington Post* notes that "the pages turn quickly." He urges readers to "suspend your disbelief and put yourself 1,000 feet down."

Huge creatures—in this case, dinosaurs—are also integral to the plot of Crichton's next thriller, *Jurassic Park*. *Jurassic Park* chronicles the attempts of self-made billionaire John Hammond to build an amusement park on a remote island off the coast of Costa Rica. Instead of roller coasters and side-shows, the park features actual life-sized dinosaurs bred through the wonders of biotechnology and recombinant DNA. There are some problems before the park opens, however: workmen die mysteriously and local children are attacked by strange lizards. Fearful that the project's opening is in jeopardy, Hammond calls together a team of scientists and technicians to look things over. Led by a paleontologist named Grant, the group is initially amazed by Hammond's creation. Their amazement quickly turns to horror when the park's electronic security system is put out of commission and the dinosaurs are freed to roam at will. What ensues is a deadly battle between the vastly underarmed human contingent and a group of smarter-than-anticipated tyrannosaurs, pterodactyls, stegosaurs, and velociraptors.

Crichton's 1992 tale departs from his usual interest in science to weave a story of international intrigue set in Japan.

John Skow of *Time* considers *Jurassic Park* the author's "best [techno- thriller] by far since *The Andromeda Strain*." He adds that "Crichton's sci-fi is convincingly detailed." In a review of the book for the *Los Angeles Times Book Review*, Andrew Ferguson demurs, remarking that "having read Crichton's fat new novel ... I have a word of advice for anyone owning real estate within 10 miles of the La Brea tar pits: Sell." Ferguson ultimately finds that *Jurassic Park*'s "only real virtue" lies in "its genuinely interesting discussion of dinosaurs, DNA research, paleontology, and chaos theory." Gary Jennings of the *New York Times Book Review* is less harsh, arguing that the book has "some good bits.... All in all, *Jurassic Park* is a great place to visit."

Crichton leaves the world of science in *Rising Sun*. The novel's plot revolves around the murder of a young American woman during a party for a huge Japanese corporation. The case is given to detective Peter J. Smith, who finds himself up against an oriental syndicate with great political and econom-

ic power. As Smith gets closer to the truth, the Japanese corporation uses all it's influence to thwart his investigation, influence that includes corruption and violence. John Schwartz of *Newsweek* recognizes that "Crichton has done his homework," but still feels that *Rising Sun* is too full of "randy propaganda instead of a more balanced view" to be effective.

Real-Life Adventures

Although Crichton is best known for his works of fiction, he has also written a number of nonfiction books that reflect his varied interests. *Five Patients: The Hospital Examined* explores how a modern hospital functions using five case studies as examples. The topics Crichton discusses in *Five Patients* include the rising cost of health care, advancing technology, and the relationships between doctors and their patients. According to Sims, "*Five Patients* is written by a doctor who prefers writing about medicine to practicing it." Some of the issues raised in *Five Patients* are also touched on in Crichton's autobiographical *Travels*. In *Travels*, the author talks with candor about both his personal and professional life, a life that includes journeys to mysterious lands. "I was ultimately swept away, not just by [Crichton's] richly informed mind, but his driving curiosity," remarks Patricia Bosworth in the *New York Times Book Review*.

Crichton's ability to mesh science, technology, and suspense is not limited to novels. Many of the films that the author has directed, such as *Westworld* and *Runaway*, feature a struggle between humans and technology. In *Westworld*, a businessman's expensive vacation at a theme park manned by wish-fulfilling robots turns into a nightmare when a gun-slinging, mechanized employee runs amok. The policeman protagonist of *Runaway* must not only deal with some deadly machines, but their mad creator as well. Despite the often complex and grim nature of both his films and novels, Crichton reveals in an interview with Ned Smith of *American Way* that his primary intention in making movies and writing books is to "entertain people." He notes that one of the rewards he gets from filmmaking and writing lies in "telling stories. It's fun to manipulate people's feelings and to be manipulated. To take a movie, or get a book and get very involved in it—don't look at my watch, forget about other things." As for critical reaction to his work, Crichton tells Smith: "Every critic assumes he's a code-breaker; the writer makes a code and the critic breaks it. And it doesn't work that way at all. As a mode of working, you need to become very uncritical."

■ Works Cited

Blewitt, Justin, review of *Congo, Best Sellers*, February, 1981, p. 388.

Bosworth, Patricia, "Touring the Altered States," *New York Times Book Review*, June 26, 1988, p. 30.

Collins, Michael, "Summer Thrillers from Three Masters," *Washington Post Book World*, June 14, 1987, pp. 1, 14.

Cook, Alexander, review of *The Andromeda Strain, Commonweal*, August 9, 1969, pp. 493-94.

Coyne, John R., "Suspense and Insomnia," *National Review*, June 23, 1972, pp. 700-701.

Crichton, Michael, interview with Ned Smith, *American Way*, September, 1975, pp. 66-69.

Crichton, Michael, *Travels*, Knopf, 1988.

Ferguson, Andrew, review of *Jurassic Park, Los Angeles Times Book Review*, November 11, 1990, p. 4.

Grumbach, Doris, "Fine Print," *New Republic*, June 7, 1975, pp. 30-31.

Hubin, Allen J., review of *A Case of Need, New York Times Book Review*, August 18, 1968, p. 20.

Jennings, Gary, review of *Jurassic Park, New York Times Book Review*, November 1, 1990, pp. 14-15.

Kahn, James M., review of *Sphere, Los Angeles Times Book Review*, July 12, 1987, pp. 1, 13.

Lehmann-Haupt, Christopher, "A Flash Pull for a Fat Pogue," *New York Times*, June 10, 1975.

Lehmann-Haupt, Christopher, "A Hard Five-Days' Night," *New York Times*, May 30, 1969, p. 25.

McKinley, Robin, "Anybody Home?," *New York Times Book Review*, July 12, 1987, p. 18.

Rotondaro, Fred, review of *A Case of Need, Best Sellers*, August 15, 1968, pp. 207-208.

Schickel, Richard, review of *The Andromeda Strain, Harper's*, August, 1969, p. 97.

Schwartz, John, review of *Rising Sun, Newsweek*, February 17, 1992, p. 64.

Sims, Robert L., "Michael Crichton," *Dictionary of Literary Biography Yearbook: 1981*, Gale, 1982, pp. 189-194.

Skow, John, review of *Jurassic Park, Time*, November 12, 1990, p. 97.

Weeks, Edward, review of *The Terminal Man, Atlantic Monthly*, May, 1972, pp. 108-110.

■ For More Information See

BOOKS

Contemporary Literary Criticism, Gale, Volume 2, 1974, Volume 6, 1976, Volume 54, 1989.

PERIODICALS

Horn Book, October, 1975; February, 1981.
Newsweek, November 2, 1981, p. 108.
New Yorker, November 9, 1981, p. 177-180.
Playboy, January, 1988, pp. 142, 181-184.
Publishers Weekly, September, 1990, p. 84.°

—Sketch by Elizabeth A. Des Chenes

Louise Erdrich

■ Personal

Has also written under joint pseudonyms Heidi Louise and Milou North; born Karen Louise Erdrich June 7, 1954, in Little Falls, MN; daughter of Ralph Louis (a teacher with the Bureau of Indian Affairs) and Rita Joanne (affiliated with the Bureau of Indian Affairs; maiden name, Gourneau) Erdrich; married Michael Anthony Dorris (a writer and professor of Native American studies), October 10, 1981; children: Abel, Jeffrey, Sava, Madeline, Persia, Pallas, Aza. *Education:* Dartmouth College, B.A., 1976; Johns Hopkins University, M.A., 1979. *Politics:* Democrat. *Religion:* "Anti-religion." *Hobbies and other interests:* Quilting, running, drawing, "playing chess with daughters and losing, playing piano badly, speaking terrible French."

■ Addresses

Home—Hanover, NH.

■ Career

Writer. North Dakota State Arts Council, visiting poet and teacher, 1977-78; Boston Indian Council, Boston, MA, communications director and editor of *Circle*, 1979-80; Charles-Merrill Co., textbook writer, 1980. Previously employed as a beet weeder in Wahpeton, ND; waitress in Wahpeton, Boston, and Syracuse, NY; psychiatric aide in a Vermont hospital; poetry teacher at prisons; lifeguard; and construction flag signaler. Has judged writing contests. *Member:* International Writers, PEN (member of executive board, 1985-88), Authors Guild, Authors League of America.

■ Awards, Honors

Johns Hopkins University teaching fellow, 1979; MacDowell Colony fellow, 1980; Yaddo Colony fellow, 1981; Dartmouth College visiting fellow, 1981; First Prize, *Chicago* magazine's Nelson Algren fiction competition, 1982, for "The World's Greatest Fisherman"; Pushcart Prize, 1983; National Magazine Fiction awards, 1983 and 1987; *Love Medicine* received the National Book Critics Circle Award for best work of fiction, and the Virginia McCormick Scully Prize for best book of the year, both 1984; *Love Medicine* received the *Los Angeles Times* Award for best novel, the best first fiction award from the American Academy and Institute of Arts and Letters, the Sue Kaufman Prize, and was named one of the best eleven books of 1985 by the *New York Times Book Review;* Guggenheim fellow, 1985-86; *The Beet Queen* was named one of *Publishers Weekly's* best books, 1986; First Prize, O. Henry awards, 1987; National Book Critics Circle Award nomination.

■ Writings

NOVELS

Love Medicine, Holt, 1984.
The Beet Queen, Holt, 1986.
Tracks, Harper, 1988.
(With husband, Michael Dorris) *The Crown of Columbus*, HarperCollins, 1991.

POETRY

Jacklight, Holt, 1984.
Baptism of Desire, Harper, 1989.

OTHER

Imagination (textbook), C. E. Merrill, 1980.
(Author of preface) Michael Dorris, *The Broken Cord: A Family's Ongoing Struggle with Fetal Alcohol Syndrome*, Harper, 1989.
(Author of preface) Desmond Hogan, *A Link with the River*, Farrar, Straus, 1989.

Author of short story, "The World's Greatest Fisherman"; contributor to anthologies, including the *Norton Anthology of Poetry; Best American Short Stories* of 1981-83, 1983, and 1988; and *Prize Stories: The O. Henry Awards*, in 1985 and 1987; contributor of stories, poems, essays, and book reviews to periodicals, including *New Yorker, New England Review, Chicago, American Indian Quarterly, Frontiers, Atlantic, Kenyon Review, North American Review, New York Times Book Review, Ms.* magazine, *Redbook* (with her sister Heidi, under the joint pseudonym Heidi Louise), and *Woman* magazine (with Dorris, under the joint pseudonym Milou North).

■ Adaptations

The Crown of Columbus has been optioned for film production.

■ Work in Progress

The Bingo Palace, a novel; "additions to a republished *Love Medicine.*"

■ Sidelights

Considered the first major author in her generation, Louise Erdrich published her first two books—*Jacklight*, a volume of poetry, and *Love Medicine*, a novel—at the age of thirty. The daughter of a Chippewa Indian mother and a German-American father, the author explores Native American themes in her works, with major characters representing both sides of her heritage. *Love Medicine*, which traces two Native American families from 1934 to 1984 in a unique seven-narrator format, was extremely well-received, earning its author the National Book Critics Circle Award in 1984. Since then, Erdrich has gone on to publish *The Beet Queen* and *Tracks*—two more novels in what she plans to be a four-part series—which explore the roots of *Love Medicine*'s characters, as well as those of their white neighbors. These three novels, which are related through recurring characters and themes, all became national best-sellers, and in 1989 the author penned a second volume of poetry, titled *Baptism of Desire*.

Although Erdrich's name is the only one appearing on the covers of these books, the writing process involves a collaborative effort between Erdrich and her husband, Michael Dorris, an educator who is also part Native American. Both their names appear on the cover of the novel *Crown of Columbus*, which explores the meaning of Columbus's voyage for both Native Americans and white people today. While *Tracks* and *Crown of Columbus* are political in nature, examining the exploitation of Native Americans by those of European descent, the majority of Erdrich's work is concerned with relationships and the human condition. The Native American folklore and myths form a backdrop for stories of individuals struggling against fate and circumstances of birth. While *Love Medicine* is solely concerned with American Indians, *The Beet Queen* expands the focus to include whites and those who—like Erdrich—are of mixed descent.

Storytelling and Erdrich's Early Writing

Erdrich's interest in writing can be traced to her childhood and her heritage. She told *Writer's Digest* contributor Michael Schumacher, "People in [Native American] families make everything into a story.... People just sit and the stories start coming, one after another. I suppose that when you grow up constantly hearing the stories rise, break, and fall, it gets into you somehow." The oldest in a family of seven children, Erdrich was raised in Wahpeton, North Dakota. Her Chippewa grandfather had been the tribal chair of the nearby Turtle Mountain Reservation, and her parents worked at the Bureau of Indian Falls boarding school. Erdrich told *Contemporary Authors* of the way in which her parents encouraged her writing: "My father used to give me a nickel for every story I wrote, and my mother wove strips of construction paper together and stapled them into book covers. So at an early age I felt myself to be a published author earning substantial royalties."

But Erdrich would not feel ready to write about her ethnic heritage until adulthood. In fact, the author stated in an interview with *Publishers Weekly* contributor Miriam Berkley that as she was growing up, she "never thought about what was Native American and what wasn't. I think that's the way a lot of people who are of mixed descent regard their lives—you're just a combination of different backgrounds." It was during her adolescent years that Erdrich first began to think of herself as a writer. In addition to cheerleading, her interests included "dressing funny and listening to [folksinger] Joan Baez and keeping journals and reading poems and trying to be a little different," the author told *Newsday* contributor Dan Cryer. As a creative writing major at Dartmouth University—where she won awards for her poetry and fiction—Erdrich decided to pursue writing as a career.

Erdrich's first year of college—1972—was the year that Dartmouth began admitting women, as well as the year the Native American studies department was established. The author's future husband and collaborator, anthropologist Michael Dorris, was hired to chair the department. In his class, Erdrich began the exploration of her own ancestry that would eventually inspire her novels. Intent on balancing her academic training with a broad range of practical knowledge, Erdrich told Berkley, "I ended up taking some really crazy jobs, and I'm glad I did. They turned out to have been very useful experiences, although I never would have believed it at the time." In addition to working as a lifeguard, waitress, poetry teacher at prisons, and construction flag signaler, Erdrich became an editor for the *Circle*, a Boston Indian Council newspaper. She told Schumacher, "Settling into that job and becoming comfortable with an urban community—which is very different from the reservation community—gave me another reference point. There were lots of people with mixed blood, lots of people who had their own confusions. I realized that this was part of my life—it wasn't something that I was making up—and that it was something I *wanted* to write about." In 1978, the author enrolled in an M.A. program at Johns Hopkins University, where she wrote poems and stories incorporating her heritage, many of which would later become part of her books. She also began sending her work to publishers, most of whom sent back rejection slips.

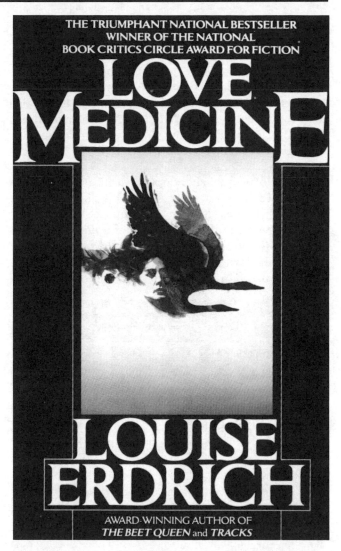

Erdrich's first novel, published in 1984, takes advantage of the author's personal knowledge of the American Indian oral tradition while it weaves a multigenerational tale about two Chippewa families.

Erdrich and Dorris's Collaboration

After receiving her master's degree, Erdrich returned to Dartmouth as a writer-in-residence. Dorris—with whom she had remained in touch—attended a reading of Erdrich's poetry there, and was impressed. A writer himself—Dorris would later publish the best-selling novel *A Yellow Raft in Blue Water* and receive the 1989 National Book Critics Circle Award for his nonfiction work *The Broken Cord*—he decided then that he was interested in working with Erdrich and getting to know her better. When he left for New Zealand to do field research and Erdrich went to Boston to work on a textbook, the two began sending their poetry and fiction back and forth with their letters, laying a groundwork for a literary relationship. Dorris returned to New Hampshire in 1980, and Erdrich moved back there as well. The two began collaborating on short stories, including one titled "The World's Greatest Fisherman." When this story won five thousand dollars in the Nelson Algren fiction competition, Erdrich and Dorris decided to expand it into a novel—*Love Medicine*. At the same time, their literary relationship led to a deeply romantic one. In 1981 they were married.

Dorris had previously adopted three children, and the couple had four more. Erdrich's days became a flurry of babies and manuscripts. She and her husband were building a family of novels alongside their family of children. Erdrich told Berkley, *"The Beet Queen* was written while either rocking, feeding, or changing," and she adds that her two

THE NEW YORK TIMES BESTSELLER
"A PERFECT—AND PERFECTLY WONDERFUL—NOVEL."
—ANNE TYLER

The BEET QUEEN

LOUISE ERDRICH

AWARD-WINNING AUTHOR OF
LOVE MEDICINE and *TRACKS*

The troubled lives of two abandoned children are explored in Erdrich's 1986 offering, which also depicts the interrelationships between American Indians and European Americans.

consecutive pregnancies inspired the many birth scenes in the work. In the couple's interview with Schumacher, Dorris drew a parallel between their children and the characters they have created: "The fictional characters belong to both of us, regardless of who's trotting them out at any given time." Erdrich also spoke of their dual partnership: "Marriage is a process of coming to trust the other person over the years, and it's the same thing with our writing."

The titles Erdrich and Dorris have chosen for their novels—such as *Love Medicine* and *A Yellow Raft in Blue Water*—tend to be rich poetic or visual images. The title is often the initial inspiration from which their novels are drawn. Erdrich told Schumacher, "I think a title is like a magnet: It begins to draw these scraps of experience or conversation or memory to it. Eventually, it collects a book." Erdrich and Dorris's collaboration process begins with a first draft, usually written by whoever had the original idea for the book, the one who will ultimately be considered the official author. But this draft incorporates earlier conversations in which the two participated equally. Before and during the writing process, Dorris and Erdrich have constant discussions about the characters and plot. It is sometimes difficult for them to remember later who contributed a specific idea that influenced the course of the book. Although the author has the original voice and the final say, ultimately, both collaborators are responsible for what the work becomes.

After the draft is written, the other person edits it, and then another draft is written; often five or six drafts will be written in all. Finally, the two read the work aloud until they can agree on each word. As Dorris explained to Schumacher, "We go on a word-by-word basis." The process requires the kind of intimate trust that Erdrich and Dorris share. Both believe that their writing benefits from having been closely scrutinized at every stage. "Nothing goes out of the house," Dorris told Berkley, "without the other person concurring that this is the best way to say it and the best way of presenting it. One of the beauties of the collaboration is that you bring two sets of experience to an issue or an idea, and it results in something that is entirely new."

Erdrich's first major work, *Jacklight*, is a volume of poetry closely associated with the author's mixed heritage. Some of the selections deal with tribal myth and express anger at white people's treatment of Native Americans. The series of poems "The Butcher's Wife" is derived from Erdrich's

German roots and tells the story of an immigrant community. *Jacklight* established the author's gift for language, and reviewers also noted the use of character and setting that foreshadowed her ability as a novelist.

Erdrich's Related Novels

Erdrich's novels *Love Medicine, The Beet Queen,* and *Tracks* encompass the stories of three interrelated families living in and around a reservation in the fictional town of Argus, North Dakota, from 1912 through the 1980s. The novels have been compared to those of William Faulkner—one of Erdrich's favorite authors—on account of Faulkner's fictional county of Yoknapatawpa, as well as the multi-voice narration and nonchronological storytelling which he employed in works such as *As I Lay Dying.* Erdrich's works, linked by recurring characters who are victims of fate and the patterns set by their elders, are structured like intricate puzzles in which bits of information about individuals and their relations to one another are slowly released in a seemingly random order, until three-dimensional characters—with a future and a past—are revealed. As one moves through the novels, one repeatedly discovers surprising connections between the characters in the three books. For example, a character in the third novel, *Tracks,* turns out to be the mother of a woman who, in the first novel, *Love Medicine,* was a grandmother; we also discover in *Tracks* that a pair of lovers in *Love Medicine* are committing incest. Through her characters' antics, Erdrich explores universal family life cycles while also communicating a sense of the changes and loss involved in the twentieth-century Native American experience.

Poet Robert Bly, describing Erdrich's nonlinear storytelling approach in the *New York Times Book Review,* emphasized her tendency to "choose a few minutes or a day in 1932, let one character talk, let another talk, and a third, then leap to 1941 and then to 1950 or 1964." The novels' circular format is a reflection of the way in which the works are constructed. Although Erdrich is dealing with a specific and extensive time period, "The writing doesn't start out and proceed chronologically. It never seems to start in the beginning. Rather, it's as though we're building something around a center, but that center can be anywhere."

Erdrich published her first novel, *Love Medicine,* in 1984. "With this impressive debut," stated *New York Times Book Review* contributor Marco Portales, "Louise Erdrich enters the company of

America's better novelists." *Love Medicine*—named for the belief in love potions which is a part of Chippewa folklore—concerns three generations of two Chippewa families between 1934 and 1984. The novel explores the bonds of family and faith which preserve both the tribal community and the individuals that comprise it. Reflecting the oral tradition in which the author was raised, the work is divided into fourteen stories, told in the words of seven different characters.

The novel begins at a family gathering following the death of June Kashpaw, a prostitute. The characters introduce one another, sharing stories about June which reveal their family history and their cultural beliefs. June's son, King Kashpaw, arrives at the reservation with his white wife, his son, and the new car he purchased with the insurance money from his mother's death. Albertine Johnson, June's niece, introduces her grand-

Erdrich revisits a shameful part of U.S. history in her 1988 story about Native Americans desperately trying to keep the government from stripping them of their ancestral lands and their dignity.

mother, Marie, her grandfather, Nector, and Nector's twin brother, Eli. Eli represents the old way—the Native American who never integrated into the white culture. He plays a major role in *Tracks,* in which he appears as a young man.

The story of Marie and Nector brings together many of the important images in the novel, including the notion of "love medicine." As a teenager in a convent, Marie is nearly singed to death by a nun who, in an attempt to exorcise the devil from within her, pours boiling water on Marie's back. Immediately following this incident, Marie is sexually assaulted by Nector, who is still holding the wild geese he has just shot and killed. Marie and Nector are later married, but in middle age, Nector begins an affair with Lulu Lamartine, a married woman. In an attempt to rekindle Nector and Marie's passion, their grandson Lipsha prepares "love medicine" for Nector. But Lipsha has difficulty obtaining a wild goose heart for the potion. He substitutes a frozen turkey heart, which causes Nector to choke to death.

Reviewers responded positively to Erdrich's debut novel, citing its lyrical qualities as well as the rich characters who inhabit it. *New York Times* contributor D. J. R. Bruckner was impressed with Erdrich's "mastery of words," as well as the "vividly drawn" characters who "will not leave the mind once they are let in." Portales, who called *Love Medicine* "an engrossing book," applauded the unique narration technique which produces what he termed "a wondrous prose song."

After the publication of *Love Medicine,* Erdrich told reviewers that her next novel would focus less exclusively on her mother's side, embracing the author's mixed heritage and the mixed community in which she grew up. Her 1986 novel, *The Beet Queen,* deals with whites and half-breeds, as well as American Indians, and explores the interactions between these worlds. The story begins in 1932, during the Depression. Erdrich has stated that both she and her husband have had close relationships with their grandparents, who lived through this time. These bonds helped the authors to depict this generation in their fiction. *The Beet Queen* begins when Mary and Karl Adare's recently-widowed mother flies off with a carnival pilot, abandoning the two children and their newborn brother. The baby is taken by a young couple who have just lost their child. Karl and eleven-year-old Mary ride a freight train to Argus, seeking refuge with their aunt and uncle. When they arrive in the town, however, Karl, frightened by a dog, runs back onto the train and winds up at an orphanage. Mary

grows up with her aunt and uncle, and the novel follows her life—as well as those of her jealous, self-centered cousin Sita and their part-Chippewa friend Celestine James—for the next forty years, tracing the themes of separation and loss that began with Mary's father's death and her mother's grand departure.

The Beet Queen contains the same sort of recurring and related imagery as *Love Medicine.* As a child, Mary falls on the ice, leaving a pattern the nuns interpret as a miraculous vision of Christ. As an adult, Mary becomes a fortune-teller, reading palms, spitting on bricks, and inevitably predicting the worst. She inherits her aunt and uncle's butcher store, and has relationships which reenact the abandonment she suffered as a child. Sita endures two marriages and the failure of her restaurant, and slowly grows insane. Karl becomes a bisexual salesman/conman and returns to Argus twenty years after he and Mary parted ways. He seduces Celestine, as well as her friend Walter Pfef, who has brought a thriving beet crop to Argus. Celestine gives birth to Karl's child, a girl named Dot, who appears as a large, irritable adult in *Love Medicine.* Celestine rejects Karl, preferring to raise the child alone, and Karl's departure begins a new cycle of abandonment that will plague Dot throughout her life. In the final scene, which brings together all the characters who have been introduced in both books, Dot, a teenager in 1972, is named queen of the sugar beet festival.

The Beet Queen was well-received by critics, some of whom found it even more impressive than *Love Medicine.* Many noted the novel's poetic language and symbolism; Bly noted that Erdrich's "genius is in metaphor," and that the characters "show a convincing ability to feel an image with their whole bodies." Josh Rubins, writing in *New York Review of Books,* called *The Beet Queen* "a rare second novel, one that makes it seem as if the first, impressive as it was, promised too little, not too much."

Other reviewers had problems with *The Beet Queen,* but they tended to dismiss the novel's flaws in light of its positive qualities. *New Republic* contributor Dorothy Wickenden considered the characters unrealistic and the ending contrived, but she lauded *The Beet Queen's* "ringing clarity and lyricism," as well as the "assured, polished quality" which she felt was missing in *Love Medicine.* Although Michiko Kakutani found the ending artificial, the *New York Times* reviewer called Erdrich "an immensely gifted young writer." "Even with its weaknesses," proclaimed Linda

Simon in *Commonweal*, "*The Beet Queen* stands as a product of enormous talent."

Erdrich's Ambitious *Tracks*

After Erdrich completed *The Beet Queen*, she was uncertain as to what her next project should be. The four-hundred-page manuscript that would eventually become *Tracks* had remained untouched for ten years; the author referred to it as her "burden." She and Dorris took a fresh look at it, and decided that they could relate it to *Love Medicine* and *The Beet Queen*. But Erdrich still felt blocked. Then Dorris told her about a tribe of Indians who live in Alaska. He explained that their language has no equivalent for the English word 'I,' and they instead use 'we.' This gave Erdrich the idea to rewrite the narrators' voices as both personal and communal narratives.

While more political than *Love Medicine* or *The Beet Queen*, *Tracks*, Erdrich's 1989 work, also deals with spiritual themes, exploring the tension between the Native Americans' ancient beliefs and the Christian notions of the Europeans. *Tracks* takes place between 1912 and 1924, before Erdrich's other novels, and reveals the roots of *Love Medicine*'s characters and their hardships. One of the narrators, Nanapush, is the leader of a tribe that is suffering on account of the white government's exploitation. The community struggles to survive, to hold on to any land the government has not yet confiscated. As he watches his people succumb to smallpox, tuberculosis, alcoholism, famine, and forced migration, Nanapush feels pressured to give up their land in order to avoid starvation. While Nanapush represents the old way, Pauline, the other narrator, represents change. The future mother of *Love Medicine*'s Marie Lazarre, Pauline is a young half-breed from a mixed-blood tribe "for which the name was lost." She feels torn between her Indian faith and the white people's religion, and is considering leaving the reservation.

Tracks centers on Fleur, a character whom *Los Angeles Times Book Review* contributor Terry Tempest Williams called "one of the most haunting presences in contemporary American literature." Nanapush discovers this young woman—the last survivor of a family killed by consumption—in a cabin in the woods, starving and mad. With "no stories or depth of life to rely upon, all she had," says Nanapush, "was raw power and the names of the dead that filled her." Nanapush adopts Fleur and nurses her back to health. She lives alone in

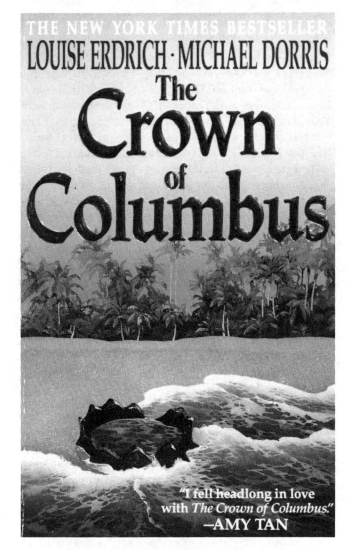

THE NEW YORK TIMES BESTSELLER
LOUISE ERDRICH · MICHAEL DORRIS
The Crown of Columbus

"I fell headlong in love with *The Crown of Columbus*."
—AMY TAN

In her first joint venture with her husband, Erdrich's 1991 novel offers opposite modern perspectives on the significance of Christopher Columbus's voyages to America.

the woods, studying tribal medicine. On several occasions, Fleur has apparently drowned, but miraculously survived; she is rumored to have mated with a creature at the bottom of the lake.

In 1913 Fleur moves to Argus briefly and finds a job as a butcher's meatcutter. Pauline, who sweeps the butcher's floor, also has special powers, but, unlike Fleur, is dull looking and unable to attract men's attention. She attaches herself to Fleur, hoping to learn her secrets. When Fleur marries Eli, a shy boy whom Nanapush coaches in the ways of love, the jealous Pauline casts her own spell, a combination of pagan hex and Christian mysticism. She causes a girl named Sophie to seduce Eli, then substitutes her own soul and sensations for Sophie's. Later, Pauline has a vision of the Virgin Mary and becomes a nun.

Reviewers found *Tracks* distinctly different from Erdrich's earlier novels, and some felt that her third novel lacked the characteristics that made *Love Medicine* and *The Beet Queen* so outstanding. *Washington Post Book World* critic Jonathan Yardley felt that, on account of its more political focus, the work has a "labored quality." Robert Towers stated in *New York Review of Books* that he found the characters too melodramatic and the tone too intense. Katherine Dieckmann, writing in the *Voice Literary Supplement*, affirmed that she "missed [Erdrich's] skilled multiplications of voice," and called the relationship between Pauline and Nanapush "symptomatic of the overall lack of grand orchestration and perspectival interplay that made Erdrich's first two novels polyphonic masterpieces." However, according to *Commonweal* contributor Christopher Vecsey, although "a reviewer might find some of the prose overwrought, and the two narrative voices indistinguishable ... readers will appreciate and applaud the vigor and inventiveness of the author."

Other reviewers enjoyed *Tracks* even more than the earlier novels. Williams stated that Erdrich's writing "has never appeared more polished and grounded," and added, "*Tracks* may be the story of our time." Thomas M. Disch lauded the novel's plot, with its surprising twists and turns, in the *Chicago Tribune*. The critic added, "Louise Erdrich is like one of those rumored drugs that are instantly and forever addictive. Fortunately in her case you can *just say yes*."

Erdrich continued to explore the dual nature of her spiritual heritage in *Baptism of Desire*, her 1989 collection of poems. Many of the selections were composed late at night when Erdrich's pregnancy gave her insomnia, and these works capture both the ordinary and the inspirational in her nightly experience. In the poem "Hydra," Erdrich explores female sexuality, birthing, and mothering, historically and in various cultures. Comparing herself to both Mary and Eve, the poet addresses her unborn child, as well as the mythical serpent, in the lines, "Blessed one, beating your tail across heaven, / uncoiling through the length of my life." The final selection deals with gardening, childrearing, and marriage.

Crown of Columbus Is New Departure

Erdrich and Dorris's jointly-authored novel, *The Crown of Columbus*, which has been optioned for a film production, explores Native American issues from the standpoint of the authors' current experience, rather than the world of their ancestors. Marking the quincentennial anniversary of Spanish explorer Christopher Columbus's voyage in a not-so-celebratory fashion, Erdrich and Dorris raise important questions about the meaning of that voyage for both Europeans and Native Americans today. The story is narrated by the two central characters, both Dartmouth professors involved in projects concerning Columbus. Vivian Twostar is a Native American single mother with eclectic tastes and a teenage son, Nash. Vivian is asked to write an academic article on Columbus from a Native American perspective and is researching Columbus's diaries. Roger Williams, a stuffy New England Protestant poet, is writing an epic work about the explorer's voyage. Vivian and Roger become lovers—parenting a girl named Violet—but have little in common. Vivian judges Roger to be an unfit father and sends him away, but when he learns to appreciate some of her opinions, she forgives him and takes him back. In her research, Vivian then discovers what appear to be two pages from Columbus's lost diary. She believes the remainder of the diary to be in the possession of a businessman living on a Caribbean island. Roger dismisses her findings, but agrees to accompany Vivian, Violet, and Nash to the Bahamas to discover the truth about Columbus.

During their trip, Vivian and Roger struggle to find a common ground in their relationship and have a series of adventures. First Violet is set adrift alone on a raft, and then Roger must battle a shark before becoming trapped in a cave full of bats. Meanwhile, the businessman they have come to see desperately craves the two pages Vivian has found, which may contain directions to the jeweled crown Columbus once buried on the island. The man takes Vivian out in his sailboat, ties her to a bucket of sand, and attempts to throw her overboard. But all is well in the end, as Vivian and Roger rediscover themselves as they rediscover America. Acknowledging the destructive impact of Columbus's voyage on the Native American people, Vivian and Roger vow to redress the political wrongs symbolically by changing the power structure in their relationship. Some reviewers found *The Crown of Columbus* unbelievable and inconsistent, and considered it less praiseworthy than the individual authors' earlier works. However, *New York Times Book Review* contributor Robert Houston appreciated the work's timely political relevance. He also stated, "There are moments of genuine humor and compassion, of real insight and sound satire." Other critics also considered Vivian and Roger's adventures amusing, vibrant, and charming.

Although Erdrich has planned a final sequel to her three related novels, in which the younger characters from *Love Medicine* will interact with those from *The Beet Queen*, her involvement with *The Crown of Columbus* represents a significant departure from that world. Although *The Crown of Columbus* involves interpreting and finding new meaning in history, the Argus characters are themselves living out history and guiding the reader through its changes. It is unlikely that Erdrich will be able to avoid returning to the series for very long. As she once told the *New York Times Book Review*, "I can't stand not knowing what's happening ... [because] there's an ongoing conversation with these fictional people. Events suggest themselves. You have no choice."

■ Works Cited

Berkley, Miriam, "Louise Erdrich," *Publishers Weekly*, August 15, 1986, pp. 58-59.

Bly, Robert, "Another World Breaks Through," *New York Times Book Review*, August 31, 1982, p. 2.

Bruckner, D. J. R., "Books of the Times," *New York Times*, December 20, 1984, p. C21.

Contemporary Authors, Volume 114, Gale, 1985, pp. 146-147.

Dieckmann, Katherine, "Tribes and Tribulations: Louise Erdrich's Family Affair," *Voice Literary Supplement*, October, 1988, p. 37.

Disch, Thomas M., "Enthralling Tale: Louise Erdrich's World of Love and Survival," *Chicago Tribune*, September 4, 1988, pp. 1, 6.

Erdrich, Louise, interview with Dan Cryer, *Newsday*, November 30, 1986.

Erdrich, Louise, *Tracks*, Harper, 1988.

Erdrich, Louise, *Baptism of Desire*, Harper, 1989.

Houston, Robert, review of *The Crown of Columbus*, *New York Times Book Review*, April 28, 1991, p. 10.

Kakutani, Michiko, "Books of the Times," *New York Times*, August 20, 1986, p. C21.

Portales, Marco, review of *Love Medicine*, *New York Times Book Review*, December 23, 1984, p. 6.

Rubins, Josh, "Foundling Fiction," *New York Review of Books*, January 15, 1987, pp. 14-15.

Schumacher, Michael, "Louise Erdrich and Michael Dorris: A Marriage of Minds," *Writer's Digest*, June, 1991, pp. 28-31.

Simon, Linda, "Small Gestures, Large Patterns," *Commonweal*, October 24, 1986, pp. 565, 567.

Stead, Deborah, "Unlocking the Tale," *New York Times Book Review*, October 2, 1988, p. 1.

Towers, Robert, "Roughing It," *New York Review of Books*, November 19, 1988, pp. 40-41.

Vecsey, Christopher, "Revenge of the Chippewa Witch," *Commonweal*, November 4, 1988, p. 596.

Wickenden, Dorothy, "Off the Reservation," *New Republic*, October 6, 1986, pp. 46-48.

Williams, Terry Tempest, "Facing the World without Land to Call Home," *Los Angeles Times Book Review*, September 11, 1988, p. 2.

Yardley, Jonathan, "Louise Erdrich's Lament for a Vanishing World," *Washington Post Book World*, September 18, 1988, p. 3.

■ For More Information See

PERIODICALS

Los Angeles Times Book Review, October 5, 1986, pp. 3, 10.

New York Times, August 24, 1988, p. 41.

New York Times Book Review, October 2, 1988, pp. 1, 41-42.

People, June 10, 1991, p. 26-27.

Washington Post Book World, August 31, 1986, pp. 1, 6.

—Sketch by Joanna Brod

Esther M. Friesner

■ Personal

Born July 16, 1951, in New York, NY; daughter of David R. (a teacher) and Beatrice (a teacher; maiden name, Richter) Friesner; married Walter Stutzman (a software engineer), December 22, 1974; children: Michael Jacob, Anne Elizabeth. *Education:* Vassar College, B.A. in Spanish and Drama (cum laude), 1972; Yale University, M.A. in Spanish, 1975, Ph.D. in Spanish, 1977.

■ Addresses

Home—53 Mendingwall Circle, Madison, CT 06443. *Agent*—Richard Curtis Literary Agency, 171 East 74th Street, New York, New York 10021.

■ Career

Writer. Yale University, New Haven, CT, instructor in Spanish, 1977-79, and 1983. *Member:* Science Fiction Writers of America.

■ Awards, Honors

Named Outstanding New Fantasy Writer by *Romantic Times,* 1986; Best Science Fiction/Fantasy

Titles citation, *Voice of Youth Advocates,* 1988, for *New York by Knight.*

■ Writings

FANTASY NOVELS

Harlot's Ruse, Popular Library, 1986.
New York by Knight, New American Library, 1986.
The Silver Mountain, Popular Library, 1986.
Elf Defense, New American Library, 1988.
Druid's Blood, New American Library, 1988.
Sphynxes Wild, New American Library, 1989.
Gnome Man's Land (first volume in trilogy), Ace, 1991.
Harpy High (second volume in trilogy), Ace, 1991.
Unicorn U (third volume in trilogy), Ace, 1992.
Yesterday We Saw Mermaids, Tor Books, 1992.
Wishing Season (young adult), Atheneum, 1993.
Majik by Accident, Ace, 1993.
(With Laurence Watt-Evans) *Split Heirs,* Tor Books, 1993.

"CHRONICLES OF THE TWELVE KINGDOMS"; FANTASY NOVELS

Mustapha and His Wise Dog, Avon, 1985.
Spells of Mortal Weaving, Avon, 1986.
The Witchwood Cradle, Avon, 1987.
The Water King's Laughter, Avon, 1989.

"DEMONS" SERIES; FANTASY NOVELS

Here Be Demons, Ace, 1988.
Demon Blues, Ace, 1989.
Hooray for Hellywood, Ace, 1990.

■ Sidelights

"Esther M. Friesner," writes Fred Lerner in *Voice of Youth Advocates,* "has established herself as one of the most prolific writers of fantasy fiction, and one of the funniest." She overturns many of the conventions of modern and traditional fantasy in books ranging from *New York by Knight,* in which a dragon and his armored pursuer bring their ages-old battle to the streets of modern-day New York, and *Elf Defense,* in which a mortal woman seeks to escape her marriage to the king of Elfhame by hiring a divorce lawyer, to the "Gnome Man's Land" trilogy—where Tim Desmond, a high-school student from a single-parent home must cope not only with adolescence but with successive invasions of "little people" from folklore, exotic monsters, and gods. Friesner's works, Lerner continues, "open new territory. She has made a specialty of ferreting out obscure creatures from the mythologies and demonologies of the world and turning them loose on unsuspecting places like Brooklyn, New Haven, and Hollywood."

"I was born in New York (Brooklyn, to be specific)," Esther Friesner told an interviewer. "My mother was an English teacher in the Brooklyn public junior high schools. She later became a reading specialist. My father also started out teaching in the Brooklyn junior high schools, then went on to teach in the high schools. His main speciality was Spanish, but he also taught Latin, Italian, algebra, and he coached soccer in the Brooklyn high schools."

An Early Love for Stories

"My mother told me stories when we were going on long car trips—stories from the works of Washington Irving, for instance. She'd tell me 'The Legend of Sleepy Hollow,' and I kept saying, 'I want another story, I want another story.' Finally she said, 'Look, learn to read and you can have all the stories you want.' So I thought 'That sounds like a good idea,' and I learned to read. Instead of bedtime stories, my father would sit down and read me collections of the *Pogo* comic strip by Walt Kelly. That was wonderful. It totally warped my sense of humor in just the right way. I didn't understand a lot but I certainly knew that what Kelly was doing with the language was wonderful.

"I liked to write at an early age. In fact, I started making stories when I was three years old. I couldn't write them down, but I cornered my mother and said, 'Would you please write this down for me?' I'd tell myself a story while drawing

a picture, and that would help me know what to put into the picture next. I'd take a pack of index cards and create a series of cartoons that would tell a story about the characters. The main character started out on the first card and then I went through the character's routines, waking up in the morning, getting ready for school. The character in question was a little stick figure bird for some reason (probably because if I drew wings I didn't have to worry about drawing fingers, which I could not draw; and a bird's legs are stiff so you don't have to worry where the knees go) wearing shorts and a little baseball cap. Of course the mother looked like Mary Tyler Moore on *The Dick Van Dyke Show* drawn as a bird.

"We had books all over the place. My mother said to me, 'Oh, you *have* to read [Frances Hodgson

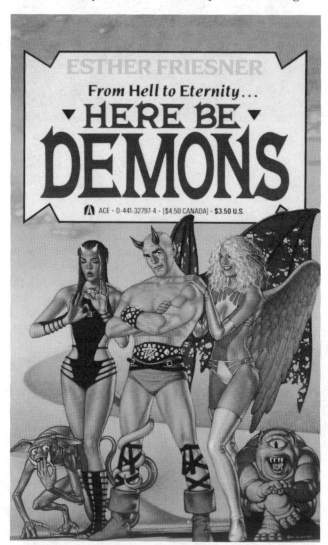

Combining humor and fantasy, Friesner's 1988 work concerns a group of demons who have been banished to earth from Hell for being too good.

Burnett's] *The Secret Garden.*' When a parent says 'Oh, you have to read something,' immediately the child thinks 'Oh yeah?!' But I tried it and it was wonderful. I got to love Kipling. Then as I got a little older my father said 'I adore Jack London,' so I tried some Jack London and wound up reading everything he ever wrote. Another favorite author was E. Nesbitt, who did *Magic by the Lake,* and *The Time Garden.* It was one of the few times that I read something and actually wished it would happen to me.

"Because the bookshelf had my parents' books on it as well, if I got bored I could look at the selection and think, 'Well, this looks kind of interesting; maybe I'll like it, maybe I won't.' One time I wound up reading *Emily Post's Etiquette.* I was fascinated. One of the rules stated that 'young ladies may not accept gifts from a gentleman,' and I thought, 'Why not?' I didn't understand half of what was going on and I never even thought to ask questions about it. I just thought, 'My goodness, things get complicated when you get older.'

"Because I was an only child, I didn't have anyone to tell stories to. Once, however, my parents took me visiting, and the people we were visiting had a girl a little younger than I was. I started to amuse her by telling her stories about the different objects in her room. For instance, she had a very nice statue of a Siamese cat with one eye as a jewel and the other eye as plain white ceramic, so I told her the story of the statue's magical eye: how it would protect people or how the evil people who tried to steal it got fricasseed (the evil people always had to get fricasseed).

"I got a very strange sense of power knowing I could scare somebody else. Of course this came back to haunt me when I was in high school. I once read a story called 'The Screaming Skull' that terrified me so badly that it haunted me. I couldn't get rid of that story until I took a friend aside and said 'I read the worst story, you've got to hear this story,' and told it to her with as much of the horror as I could. That night I slept peacefully for the first time in weeks. The next day she came into school and said, 'Thanks a *lot.*' She hadn't slept."

Drama at Vassar, Marriage at Yale

After graduating from high school, Friesner went on to Vassar College where she studied Spanish and Drama. She chose Spanish, she said, "because I thought that no matter *what* I wanted to be, I ought to have something practical that I could fall back on. I wanted to have a skill that would be

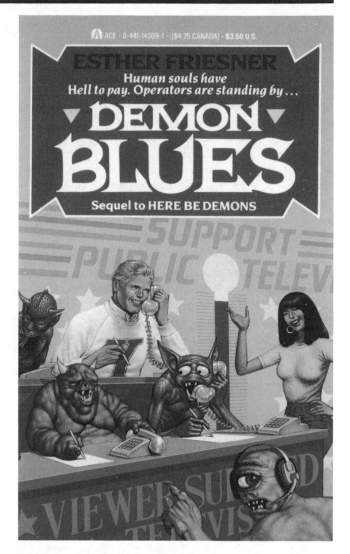

Humorous mishaps ensue in Friesner's middle novel of the "Demons" series when a young college student discovers he has the powers of a sorcerer.

useful, and I knew I could teach Spanish or use it in business. But I enjoy Spanish, both the culture and the literature. I concentrated on Castilian (I wasn't a Latin American Spanish major), and specialized in the Golden Age of the late 16th and early 17th centuries, especially on the playwright Lope de Vega. It was a fascinating time—the romantic movement in Spain was marvelous too—but most people in the United States aren't familiar with it. The story of El Cid is a magnificent epic, but the only thing most people will know about it is if they saw the Charlton Heston-Sophia Loren movie. There is a whole body of literature that people don't know about because they haven't been introduced to it.

"Drama, on the other hand, was the result of a strange occurrence. When I started out at Vassar I took advanced placement examinations in both Spanish and English. Later I found out that if I had taken a third AP exam I could have skipped a whole year of college. I thought that would have been a wonderful saving of money for my parents. So I asked my guidance counselor, 'How can I accelerate?' and we worked out a program. I crammed so many credits into my second year it was appalling. Later, when I told my parents I was accelerating my coursework to save them money, they said 'Dear, college can be some of the best years of your life. We're in no hurry; we've saved our money, we can afford this. *Decelerate!* You're putting yourself under too much pressure.'

"So there I was with a nearly empty program. I found I could do anything I wanted with the next two years of education. I thought, 'Well, I'm enjoying the drama course I'm taking. Maybe I could turn all these empty slots into a second major.' I love drama, and I enjoyed acting, but I was certainly not good enough to make a living at it. Still, I could take the major and enjoy drama just for its own sake instead of looking at it as a possible career.

"And, heaven knows, at the time I was at Vassar there was a shining light of pure talent: Meryl Streep. When you are a drama major you have got to participate in every official drama department production. If you audition and get a part in the particular production, that's your participation; otherwise you have to be on one of the crews: the prop crew, the tech crew, the lighting crew, the publicity crew.... Well, the rule stated that you had to serve on a crew at least once. So I got a part in a departmental production (Rosita, the aging street walker, in Tennessee William's *Camino Real*) once when Meryl Streep had to do her compulsory crew. She was on makeup crew. So there I sat in a crummy aqua satin dress with my hair all bedraggled, while Meryl Streep said things like, 'Now let me put on some black tooth wax so that you'll have a blotted out tooth.' Meanwhile, I sweat bullets because my parents were in the audience. I tried to explain, 'Mom, Dad, just because I'm playing a hooker doesn't mean anything.' They said, 'We know, dear. Just do the best you can.'

"Meryl is a very lovely person, absolutely wonderful. She wound up going to the Yale Drama School at the same time I was in the Yale Grad School. I was always in awe of her, but really she was just another human being. She would have been very friendly, but I was so full of admiration and hero worship that I never even thought to approach her as a potential friend."

Yale also introduced Friesner to her future husband, Walter Stutzman. "When I first came to Yale," she explains, "I couldn't get into student housing. Midway through my first year a woman got married and I got into her room. But I was in a dormitory, I didn't know anybody in the cafeteria and it was very lonely eating by myself. Finally a girl from Vassar who knew me, recognized me and said, 'Come on over to our table' and there was Walter, one of the gang at the table. We became friends, we ate together, went to the movies together and hung out together, and by the second year we weren't just friends anymore. It was sort of a cross between *When Harry Met Sally* and *The Big Chill*, although I never found Walter to be initially obnoxious the way Sally felt about Harry. I thought he was a very charming person. One of the advantages in being nearsighted is that you can really say that looks aren't everything. Walter happens to be incredibly handsome but I had no idea that was so until somebody said 'Oh boy,' and I looked very closely and said, 'Oh my goodness, you're *right!*' I actually liked him for his personality because I couldn't see anything else."

Taking the First Steps toward Writing

"I love reading Dr. Samuel Johnson's quotation about *no man but a blockhead ever wrote, except for money*. I always knew that I wanted to write, but I did want to write for money. I was trying to get published while I was in college, but it wasn't until I was in grad school that I got very serious about it. The first item I ever sold was a nonfiction article with the photos—I sold the photos, too—to *Cats Magazine*. I also sold an article to *Brides Magazine* about how to get through the first year of your marriage without shooting anybody. (It was hard to survive all the advice). The editors of the magazine said 'Put in lots of examples,' so I did, and various people came around and said 'I *know* you meant me.' I'm not up on a murder rap so I think it worked out pretty well.

"But fiction was my main love. I wanted to write fiction and I tried and tried and tried.... I'd written two novels that didn't sell; one was a murder mystery which came close but didn't make it, and the other one was an historical that I really didn't send out much. The first time I got an encouraging rejection slip (saying 'We are not buying this, but this is why,') was from George Scithers of *Isaac Asimov's Science Fiction Magazine*. I continued to send to him and he continued to send me back rejection slips, but always telling me what was wrong. Finally I made my first sale to

IASFM as a result of his encouragement. I appreciated it and I won't forget it. He was very, very good. His criticism was excellent, never the *because I said so* type of criticism.

"That was a short story, but I got into writing full-length fantasy thanks to a group at Yale. In the grad school there was a woman who is now also a published science fiction and fantasy author. She is now famous for the hard science fiction she writes, but she started out writing a fantasy. Her name is Shariann Lewitt, but she publishes under the name S. N. Lewitt because unfortunately at the time there was a lot of prejudice against women writing hard SF. There was a real fear that people would say 'What can a woman know about this? I won't buy the book.' So Shariann was working on her first fantasy novel, and we saw her building a whole world, working out all the details on a big legal pad she had. This was quite different from writing a short story. I thought, 'Oh, building a world. I get to be God! How nice. I'm going to try that.' And that was how I got started on fantasy novels."

Goddess of the Twelve Kingdoms

"The novel I wrote from my first world-building was actually the second book I sold. It was *Spells of Mortal Weaving*, in the 'Chronicles of the Twelve Kingdoms' series. In its original version, however, it was a little too off-the-wall (at least, that was the response I got on it), so I did a rewrite, calming it down a bit, and it came out much better. It did sell eventually, but it was not the first one that sold." Friesner's first published book was *Mustapha and His Wise Dog*, an Arabian Nights-style adventure "enlivened by an exotic and evocative fantasy setting, and a pair of captivating characters," declares Don D'Ammassa in *Twentieth-Century Science-Fiction Writers*. The series, continued in *The Witchwood Cradle* and *The Water King's Laughter*, follows the struggles of various mortals to overthrow Morgeld, an evil demigod. "Although Friesner followed traditional forms for the most part in this series," D'Ammassa concludes, "her wry humor and gift for characterization marked her early as someone to watch."

"What I started out to do with 'The Chronicles of the Twelve Kingdoms,'" Friesner explains, "was a high fantasy series. I wanted it to be a twelve book series. They do not set out to be funny; they simply tell these stories which together form a multigenerational epic. And you don't have to read them in order—it's my little strike against trilogies. When I started reading fantasy seriously I read Tolkien's

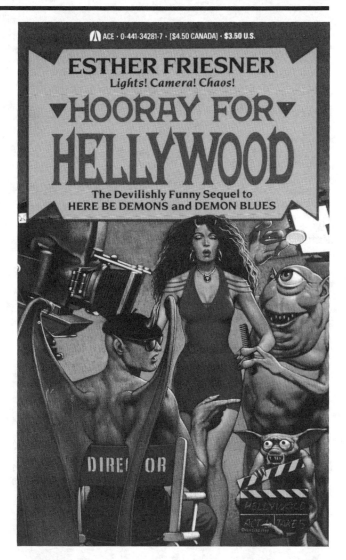

This final novel in the "Demons" series is filled with demonic Hollywood personalities and television evangelists in the process of making a great biblical epic.

The Lord of the Rings beginning in the middle: I finished the second book, then the third, and finally the first. Even though I didn't quite know what was going on at first, after awhile the story was so good, it got me hooked. If you tried to do that with some trilogies, they wouldn't make any sense. I wanted to have a series where if readers started with book three, they wouldn't feel totally lost. Reading book two after book three would be enriching but it wouldn't be a necessity.

"I also wanted to have characters that were not just good and evil. There are several villains in the series, but the main one is a demigod-type known as Morgeld. Morgeld was half god but he was also half of another kind of creature, a night spirit. I tried to explain why he was so horrible, to give a reason for him being so villainish and, in fact, give him a chance to redeem himself from his evil. Most people, unless they are really unbalanced mentally, do not do evil things without a reason. Their reasons seems perfectly good and perfectly justified to them, and they go ahead and do atrocious things in the belief that they are doing the right thing.

"In *The Witchwood Cradle*, the third book in the series, the villain shows up as something other than villainish, while you actually get to see a hero that is not always perfectly sterling silver pure. One of the chief heroes in the book is Ayree the witch king. He has twelve sisters, and *The Witchwood Cradle* is their book. Of course he is fighting evil and, in case you can't tell he's a good guy, he's a big blond with blue eyes and so are all his sisters. Ayree is committed to doing the right thing for the right reason, and it turns into a disaster. There can be a lot of mercilessness behind being a hero, and by the end of that book I had pretty well estab-

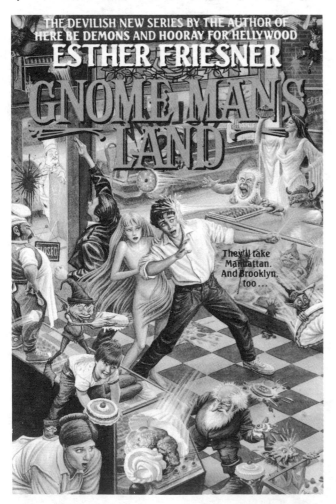

In addition to normal adolescent problems, Tim Desmond must also deal with the recurring appearances of little domestic spirits in this 1991 work.

lished the point that *you can't just accept this guy is the good guy in the white hat.* I think that comes out of the real world too. A lot of people want to believe that so-and-so is our flawless leader, and if our flawless leader all of a sudden decides to do something that isn't right, they will follow it anyway: *our leader is good, therefore everything our leader does must be good, and we must do it; we must not question.*"

Ethnic Elves

"I don't think that I have a particular cause in writing fantasy; I just try to make it interesting and also to say a few things that I feel need to be said. For instance, in *Gnome Man's Land* I was having a good time with the central point of the plot, which was that the little domestic spirits of the hearth (like the brownies) were reappearing, but what I was also saying was, 'Why did they have to go away?'" In fact, Friesner continues, the sprites came from a place called the Leeside "where America has banished them after that horrible embarrassment at Salem Village. 'Yes, we're standing here with egg on our face for having believed in the supernatural. Therefore we will *not* believe in the supernatural anymore, and if you wish to be an American you have to not believe in silly things like that too.' It was because immigrants to the U.S. became assimilation-mad—people became ashamed or embarrassed by their ethnic backgrounds and rejected them. When I was telling my daughter's teacher about *Gnome Man's Land*, I explained, 'Oh, you'll like this book, because the hero is Irish American and he's haunted by a banshee.' The teacher said, 'Well, I'm Irish American and I don't know anything about banshees, because my grandparents did not want anybody to be too Irish. They wanted us to be American.'

"And so in *Gnome Man's Land* I was speaking about the suppression of people's ethnic heritage. In fact, I pointed out how this could get a little dangerous, because every culture has its own domestic spirits. Now, America is a melting pot of ethnicity, so while you can have an American who is predominantly Irish, you often have people who really aren't predominantly anything, and then all the little spirits from their different ethnic backgrounds will fight over them. In America the only little domestic spirits kids ever learn about are in the story 'The Shoemaker and the Elves,' which draws on a British tradition. The kids don't realize that there are the *hinzelmaenner*, little people myths from Germany, and they don't know about the *duende* in the Hispanic culture. When I was in

Hawaii, I totally shocked the tour guide by asking, 'Excuse me, but do Hawaiians have elves?' He looked at me strangely for a while—because usually tourists ask questions like 'Where does Don Ho live?' or 'Is Jack Lord around anywhere?'—and finally he said, 'Well we do actually have the *menehune*, the little people.' The little people of Hawaii are quite active even today—it's still an active belief—but unless you take the time to ask about something other than *why doesn't my drink have a little paper parasol in it,* you can miss out.''

Despite the conflict between the sprites, Friesner states, ethnicity is ''not as much of an issue for the humans. They aren't having to assimilate; they're several generations American already. But they are really unaware of what their background means to them until it's brought home to them by confronting it. What does your name mean? Where do you come from? Tim knows he's got a last name, *Desmond*, but he may never have thought about where it came from. I remember I never thought about what my last name meant until I was given an assignment in seventh grade. I looked up *Friesner* and discovered it was either German or Dutch, and that my family came from Friesland or Frisia, or possibly the Frisian Islands.''

In addition to the warring ethnic spirits, Tim has to deal with his own problems: getting through high school, living in a single-parent family—his father disappeared one evening on his way to buy a paper—and stabilizing a relationship with his girlfriend. ''You've heard of the underlying rule for how to tell a story or how to write a play,'' Friesner declares; ''in Act One, you chase your hero up a tree, and in Act Two, you surround the tree with hungry crocodiles. Tim is up a tree—he's got adolescence on his case, his family situation is not the easiest, and then here come the crocodiles.'' In addition, Tim has to fend off the lusty attentions of his own personal spirit, the Desmond family banshee. ''A lot of the modern American perception of the elfin community in general is very sanitized— you know, Santa's little helpers happily making toys and shoes and whatever—but traditionally most otherworldly sprites were incredibly sexy creatures,'' Friesner explains. ''They did not invite the ladies to come and join them just to have a cup of tea. In addition, there's a whole history of changelings and elfin babies with mortal mothers, and on the other side, the women of Elfhame stealing off men. I think the Irish hero Oisin was taken away to the Land of Youth by a woman, a female elf. There are *selkies*—seal people who come out of the sea, shed their seal coats and dance

as human females. A fisherman captures one by holding on to her skin, and she bears him children until she manages to steal the skin back again.

''The English fairy tale *Coo-my-dove* starts with a girl sitting in her tower. In comes this dove, who is really an enchanted fairy prince. He gets her pregnant and flies away; she has the baby, and the baby is stolen. This goes on for seven babies. Her father keeps saying, 'Why don't you get married?' but she says that she is happy with Coo-my-dove (isn't she just). The ballad of Tam Lyn tells of a mortal man who has been stolen away by the Queen of Elves. He takes a mortal lover who winds up pregnant by him and she saves him from becoming Elfland's tithe to hell, from being sacrificed by the elves to hell. These are not nice elves, so having an amorous banshee is pretty much in

Tim's encounters with the Faerie world continue with this sequel to *Gnome Man's Land* in which his mother is entranced by the Russian witch Baba Yaga.

keeping with the spirit of the otherworldly creatures."

Friesner also presents a variety of small children who are, she states, "little dickenses. They are adorable; they are the most wonderful things in this world. I think so, and I've had two. But even when you love children so much, they're still human beings, not little Victorian Currier and Ives pictures. They are marvelous human beings and we have to help them to become the most marvelous human beings they can be. Some of this does mean telling them when to calm down. But you have to tell them to calm down without doing something horrible to them. You must teach them how to cope with life in a way that will not be painful for anybody, but you must not do this in a way that is painful to them."

Humor (Seriously)

"Humor can make you think, and therefore can be very, very dangerous. There is a long tradition of humorists being regarded as very dangerous people. I researched this for an article about humor in science fiction and why it don't get no respect. It turns out that in Ireland if a chief got the bard mad, the bard would start singing satires about the chief, and if the bard was not bought off and shut up, the chief would have to resign. That was a very, very dangerous use of humor. I think that a country that can stand humorists has got an open mind and is willing to take chances, because humor can be devastating and it can make you stop and question things that you accepted before.

"People don't like to have their sacred cows gored. Once I wrote a humorous article for *Twilight Zone Magazine* entitled 'How To Write Your Own Best-selling Horror Book.' I had been looking at the best selling horror stories and discovered there were certain elements that seemed to show up in most of them, so I gave instructions for what to include: make sure the bullies always get theirs eventually, make sure your hero is a downtrodden underdog, and it really helps if you have an all-American symbol that holds the evil—the family car in *Christine*, the family dog in *Cujo*, Mom in *Carrie*. I didn't think we'd taken care of apple pie yet, but then somebody said, 'Oh, I guess you didn't read *Thinner*, it's about an evil pie.' But I got reactions from horror writers saying 'How *dare* you!' I thought, 'But, but, it was only fun, I was just poking fun and . . .' It wasn't fun to them because it was their sacred cow.

"Now, some people can take fun-poking. I have a short story that hasn't been published yet, in which I took different science fiction and fantasy classics and retold sections of them in the style of established literary figures. I had *Dune* as *The Old Man and the Worm* (Hemingway's work), and *The Hobbit* as *God's Little Shire* and Dark Lord Sauron as something out of Taylor Caldwell—things like that—and one of the selections is Ann McCaffrey's *Pern* done as Jane Austin. And from what I hear she thinks this is hilarious. She can take a joke.

"You should never sacrifice the plot to the humor. If the humor doesn't arise naturally out of the plot, the story's going to resemble one of the really bad sitcoms. We all know there are no such things as those darling little children who get off a wise crack every five minutes, but it's pasted on there because it makes the people laugh. Good humor, and good writing in general, should seem to be pretty natural. There is a lot of humor that does arise out of day to day situations; in fact, humor shows up in places that you wouldn't believe, in some of the most ghastly situations. In times like those laughter could be the saving of us.

"So the plot should lead to the humor. Sometimes it comes with just a little exaggeration, a twist on how things normally happen. For instance, everybody accepts the fact that women go to the bathroom in pairs. In *Harpy High* I decided to use the truism about women going to the bathroom in pairs. Well, why do they go to the bathroom in pairs? It's very simple; they have to go to the bathroom in pairs at the prom so that one of them can take her bra off and turn it into a slingshot to fight a giant out on the prom floor. The giant in this case happens to be Goliath and he takes one look at the slingshot and thinks *oh good lord not again*. So now you know why women have to go to the bathroom in pairs."

Mixing History and Fantasy

"I have always loved history. History is full of incredible trashy gossip that has been legitimized, because it is history: great stories, the things that people did and how they got around to doing them, how they justified them, and some of the things that they actually said. I have learned from some of this. I love reading good historical novels and even bad historical novels if the history is accurate: not just *let's put on costumes*.

"In the middle book of the 'Demons' trilogy, *Demon Blues*, I turned Richard the Lionheart and Saladin loose on the Yale campus. They did the siege of Sterling Memorial Library. It does actually look like a castle (in fact, there is a miniature medieval village on the roof of the library). I called in my friends in the Society for Creative Anachronism to help me on that one and they gave me the most wonderful advice. I now know how to take and hold Sterling Library against all comers using only those handy items I would find in the cleaning closets. Always ask the experts for help.

"In *Sphynxes Wild* I used the Roman Emperors from my old reading of Suetonius. With *Druid's Blood* I got to do something that I liked to do. I like to give parties and invite people from the different facets of my life, from the different facets of the whole family's life. I like to see what will happen when you get the science fiction writers together with the computer people and the neighbors. I have attended Tupperware parties just to see who will mingle, and who will form up into their little groups and not mingle at all. So in *Druid's Blood* I had a perfectly justified way of getting some of my favorite characters from English history together.

"I finally got to use Spanish history for a book which became my first hardback, called *Yesterday We Saw Mermaids.* The title is a direct quote from the diary of the first voyage of Christopher Columbus. He wrote, 'Yesterday we saw mermaids. They are not as beautiful as we have been led to believe.' And you know what he saw—manatees (adorable animals but they have got a face that would make a train take a dirt road). I thought 'Well, what would happen if indeed they saw mermaids but it's not Christopher Columbus who sees it, it's the ship that got there ahead of him.' A ship which has got a bunch of nuns that got on by accident, a genie, a Moorish woman who is married to the genie, a gypsy who used to be the slave of the Moorish woman's father, and a little jewess who has been literally plucked from the flames of an auto-da-fe because she has to be brought to the New World. The reason she has to be brought to the New World is because she is pregnant with the savior of the creatures of the New World, which is not as Columbus found it. Instead, it is a refuge for all fantastic creatures—dragons and griffins. Ruling over them is Prester John, and he says that they have to have a savior, because if they have a savior it will be proof enough that they have souls to be saved.

"Now in history when Columbus got to the New World and discovered the native Americans, a whole chunk of years passed during which the Europeans were debating whether the natives were human or not. 'Do they have souls or not?

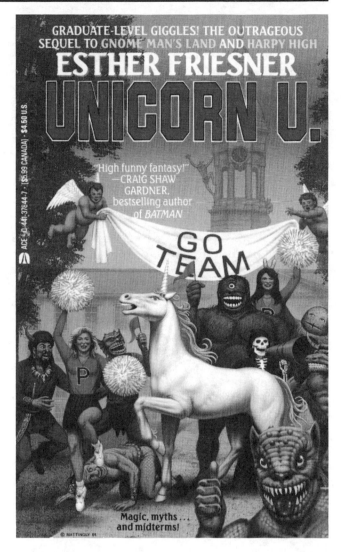

In this 1992 sequel to *Harpy High*, Tim enters Princeton, but he must still deal with the otherworldly when his girlfriend is kidnapped by a rock group from hell.

Because if we decide they are not human and do not have souls, then we can do whatever we want to them without any fear.' Well finally the Europeans published the *Dialogue of the Dignity of Man*, in which they decided 'Oh, well, I guess they do have souls.' They kept on being pretty awful to the natives anyway, in spite of the excellent work of a number of churchmen who kept saying, 'What are you doing? These are human beings, they have souls and we must save their souls.' (If they didn't have their souls saved, they were still semi-fair game.) So that was my little ax to grind with Columbus and the *are they human* people.

"When I write," Friesner concluded, "I try to make the story so interesting that I wouldn't mind rereading it myself. This is actually a very good thing. It's important to interest your readers because if you don't you won't have readers anymore. But if you don't interest yourself in what you're writing.... Well, the process of going from the first draft to the published book takes an awfully long time. You will have to look at that story and those characters a lot—you'll have to do another draft, perhaps even a third, then the editor will go over it, then the copy editor. Every time you're going to be reading the same words. If they aren't good words, you're going to get the feeling of being trapped at a party with people you don't like.

"Now Walter is a published writer too. He is the person who pushed me to go from the typewriter to the computer for writing. Now whenever I have a problem with the computer I don't reach for the manual; I just say, 'Oh *honey!*' And a few years back, while we were sitting around just joking about these ads on TV—the ones for Ronco or Ginsu blades that will cut through anything, or for Elvis Presley's Greatest Hits—we started to write a fantasy parody titled 'But Wait, There's More,' which was later published. He contributed as much as I did. Again, recently I was asked to participate in an anthology called *Whatdunnit: Science Fiction Mysteries*. The editor gave me my choice of scenarios but I said, 'Could I please have Walter help me on this, because he's a mystery fan?' (I'm the one who looks at the last page to find out who done it and then decides if I'm going to read the book or not). I did the actual writing but Walter was the plotter. Now I'm trying to drag him into writing a full length science mystery with me. I'm also going to try and drag our poor innocent thirteen-year-old son in. He's becoming a young computer expert and he likes to do computer gaming and I'd like to make the project a family thing. I may drag my daughter in at some point, too. The cat is still safe."

■ Works Cited

D'Ammassa, Don, "Esther M. Friesner," *Twentieth-Century Science-Fiction Writers*, 3rd edition, St. James, 1991.

Friesner, Esther, interview with Kenneth R. Shepherd for *Something about the Author*, May 11, 1992.

Lerner, Fred, "The Newcomer," *Voice of Youth Advocates*, December, 1991, p. 294.

■ For More Information See

PERIODICALS

Analog, December, 1989, pp. 184-185; September, 1991, pp. 166-167.

Locus, April, 1989, pp. 25-27; January, 1990, p. 25.

Science Fiction Chronicles, June, 1990, p. 37; October, 1991, p. 41.

Voice of Youth Advocates, April, 1991, p. 42.

John Knowles

■ **Personal**

Born September 16, 1926, in Fairmont, WV; son of James Myron and Mary Beatrice (Shea) Knowles. *Education:* Graduate of Phillips Exeter Academy, 1945; Yale University, B.A., 1949.

■ **Addresses**

Home—New York, NY.

■ **Career**

Yale Alumni, New Haven, CT, assistant editor, 1949; *Hartford Courant,* Hartford, CT, reporter and drama critic, 1950-52; free-lance writer, 1952-56; *Holiday,* Philadelphia, PA, associate editor, 1957-60; full-time writer, 1960—. Writer-in-residence at University of North Carolina at Chapel Hill, 1963-64, and Princeton University, 1968-69. *Military service.* U.S. Army Air Force Aviation Cadet Program, 1945, qualified as pilot.

■ **Awards, Honors**

Richard and Hinda Rosenthal Award, American Academy and National Institute of Arts and Let-

ters, and William Faulkner Foundation Award, both 1960, both for *A Separate Peace;* National Association of Independent Schools Award, 1961.

■ **Writings**

NOVELS

A Separate Peace: A Novel, Secker & Warburg, 1959, Macmillan, 1960.
Morning in Antibes, Macmillan, 1962.
Indian Summer, Random House, 1966.
The Paragon: A Novel, Random House, 1971.
Spreading Fires, Random House, 1974.
A Vein of Riches, Little, Brown, 1978.
Peace Breaks Out, Holt, 1981.
A Stolen Past, Holt, 1983.
The Private Life of Axie Reed, Dutton, 1986.

OTHER

Double Vision: American Thoughts Abroad (travel), Macmillan, 1964.
Phineas: Six Stories, Random House, 1968.

Also author of unpublished novel, "Descent into Proselito." Contributor of articles, short stories, and essays to periodicals, including *Cosmopolitan, Esquire, Hartford Courant, Holiday,* and *New York Times.* A collection of Knowles's manuscripts is housed in the Beinecke Library, Yale University.

■ **Adaptations**

A Separate Peace was adapted for film and released by Paramount Pictures in 1972; Knowles's first novel was also adapted for the stage by Nancy Gisenan, Dramatic Publishing Co, 1988.

■ Work in Progress

A memoir of the late Truman Capote, Knowles's friend for over twenty-five years.

■ Sidelights

Although his writing career has spanned more than three decades, his name graces the cover of numerous novels, and his byline appears atop many essays and short stories, John Knowles remains identifiable to most readers as the author of *A Separate Peace*. First published in 1959, this classic novel was the recipient of both the William Faulkner Award for a notable first novel and the

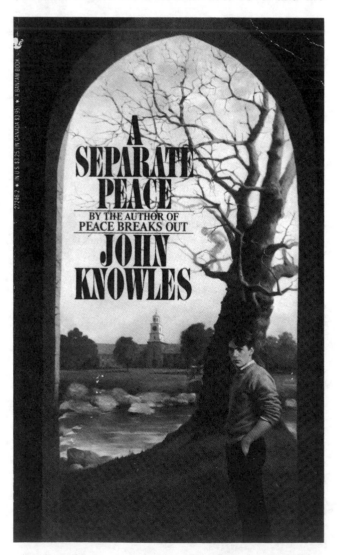

Knowles explores everything from the nature of competition and fair play to questions of morality and guilt in this 1959 story of prep school friendships.

Rosenthal Award, as well as later proclaimed by *Time* to be one of the ten best novels of the 1960s. Even after more than thirty years in print, Knowles's first novel continues to be a perennial favorite among high school and college students. "Think of classic novels of adolescent life written during the last generation," suggested critic Ralph B. Sipper in the *Los Angeles Times*. Placing the book in the company of such classic works as J. D. Salinger's *The Catcher in the Rye* and *Lord of the Flies* by William Golding, Sipper praised *A Separate Peace* as one of those "first novels [that] proves the mysteries of the teen-age heart."

Knowles has continued to pursue his fascination with the World War II-era consciousness explored in his first novel: his work is noted for its sophistication and its rendering of man's inner dualistic nature. Throughout his books, Knowles's protagonists embody what he perceives as a uniquely American paradox. He stated his belief most openly in his travelogue *Double Vision: American Thoughts Abroad,* when he wrote that "the American character is unintegrated, unresolved, a careful Protestant with a savage stirring in his insides, a germ of native American wildness thickening in his throat." Readers of his novels and short stories take part in Knowles's protagonists' struggle to reconcile the "wildness" of man's inner character with the cultural norms imposed upon him by society's institutions. Location plays a significant role in this thesis, according to Robert M. Nelson in *Dictionary of Literary Biography.* Nelson remarked upon the vivid settings Knowles creates within the pages of his novels, stating that "cultures are to a significant degree products of their geographical limitations," that a person's character is formed by the physical landscape around him as much as by his own heredity.

Born on September 16, 1926, Knowles was the third of four children of James and Mary Knowles. He was raised in Fairmont, West Virginia, the center of the state's large coal-mining region. At the age of fifteen, Knowles attended New Hampshire's Phillips Exeter Academy. After graduation, he continued his studies at Yale University where he received his B.A. in 1949. Knowles chose to remain in Connecticut and joined the staff of the *Hartford Courant,* one of the area's two major newspapers, in 1950. There he served as a staff reporter and drama critic until 1952, when he decided to become a free-lance writer. Knowles worked independently for the next five years: "At age twenty-eight, I had published some short fiction and nonfiction, lived for a while in Europe,

Roommates Gene and Finney, played by Parker Stevenson and John Heyl, deal with their feelings about World War II in this 1972 film adaptation of *A Separate Peace*.

read widely, and in general tried to live a varied life preparatory to doing my life's work," the author explained in *Esquire*. During this period, Knowles finished a novel, "Descent into Proselito," but decided against publishing it on the advice of his mentor, author Thornton Wilder. He returned from his travels through Italy and southern France in 1955 and moved into an apartment with a friend, actor Bradford Dillman, in the Hell's Kitchen section of New York City. Still under Wilder's guidance, he began to work on a second novel as well as several short stories. Knowles supported himself by continuing to write drama reviews and other articles for periodicals and his hard work resulted in several achievements. He published several short stories, including "Phineas" and "A Turn with the Sun," and his freelance work led to the offer of a full-time job. Knowles came to the attention of the editors of *Holiday* after they published an article he wrote about his old school, Phillips Exeter Academy, and he was asked to join the travel magazine's staff in 1957. He accepted the job offer and relocated to Philadelphia.

The Writing of *A Separate Peace*

Knowles worked at *Holiday* as an associate editor for several years, in addition to continuing work on his fiction. "What was required was to be home in bed by midnight, get up at a quarter to seven in the morning, throw some cold water at my face, drink a glass of orange juice and a cup of coffee, and then sit down at my desk and take up my pen," Knowles recalled in *Esquire* of those days. "Five or six hundred words later, written in an hour, I would get up and go to work as the editor of a magazine." While working full-time at *Holiday*, Knowles managed to write and publish *A Separate Peace*, a novel that would eventually be ranked among the classics of modern American literature. For Knowles, writing the book would prove to be an event that would change the course of his life.

Knowles found a suitable literary agent who made the rounds of the major publishing houses with his manuscript; he was confounded when no one would agree to publish the book. "It'll never sell a lot of copies," he remembered thinking, "but it is a good book." Not ready to give up on his efforts, Knowles approached the British publishing house of Secker & Warburg with his manuscript—they were enthusiastic, and *A Separate Peace* was published in England in 1959. The book received immediate critical acclaim; it was highly praised both for its insight and for the rich, evocative language that critics extolled as exceptional for a young author at the outset of his career. "Here is a first novel by a man already skilled in his craft and discerning in his perceptions," commented Edmund Fuller, reviewing *A Separate Peace* for the *New York Times Book Review*. "Knowles ... is sensitive without being delicate, subtle without being obscure." The novel was published in the United States early the following spring.

Set in the same picturesque region of New Hampshire where Knowles attended school as a young man, the events of *A Separate Peace* take place at Devon Academy, a fictional boy's preparatory school. The year is 1943. A close friendship between Gene Forester—a bright, introspective, athletic student–and his roommate, Phineas ("Finney"), provides the focus around which Knowles revolves questions of morality and the nature of war, of competition, of guilt, and of fair-play. Phineas, described by Forester—who narrates the story fifteen years after the events described occur—as "a student who combined a calm ignorance of the rules with a winning urge to be good," excels in athletics and possesses qualities of grace, charm, and physical prowess that his schoolmate both respects and envies. "Finney's great quality ... is his spontaneity," explained Granville Hicks in *Saturday Review*. "His unconventionality is not a form of protest against authority nor a way of self-assertion but the simple flowering of his nature. He is free from fear, free from hate, free from jealousy." The two sixteen-year-olds are enrolled in an academic summer program accelerated to allow them to go overseas and serve with U.S. troops fighting on the battleground of Europe during World War II. Although close friends, the competitive atmosphere of Devon Academy fosters an undercurrent of tension and rivalry between the two young men. This unseen animosity surfaces during a swimming excursion when, daring each other to jump from a high overhanging branch into the river below in a boyish test of courage, Phineas

becomes seriously injured. Schoolmates are suspicious that Gene may have somehow caused the fall because of the two boys' growing antagonism, and at times Gene himself questions whether he is responsible for Finny's crippling injury. Although he eventually comes to terms with his own guilt and makes peace with his friend, students at Devon stage a trial to determine Gene's culpability. In the meantime, Phineas returns to school but dies tragically on the eve of graduation.

Knowles intended *A Separate Peace* as an allegory of war. He strove in particular to explain the source of the war being waged in Europe during that summer in 1943 when he himself was a young man studying at Phillips Exeter Academy. He modeled his characters on the young men he knew during that period in his life: Gene was an extension of himself as a sixteen-year-old boy; Phineas was modeled after fellow student and consummate athlete David Hackett, who would become a member of the 1948 U.S. Olympic Ice Hockey Team; fellow author Gore Vidal provided the model for Brinker Hadley, a schoolmate at the fictional Devon Academy; other students Knowles remembered had fictional counterparts in his first novel. Knowles recalled his thoughts during that period of his life in *Esquire:* "It was just as World War II was turning in our favor, and were we boys going to be in it or not? And what was war, and what was aggression, and what were loyalty and rivalry, what were goodness and hate and fear and idealism, all of them swirling around us during that peculiar summer?" In his novel, Phineas's inner nature provides a counterpoint to the nature of war, to "something ignorant in the human heart" that fosters the hatred and fear prompting men into battle. From his position as narrator looking back on the summer of 1943 from a distance of fifteen years, Knowles has Gene Forester reflect on the natural spirit that Finney made manifest: "Phineas alone ... possessed an extra vigor, a heightened confidence in himself, a serene capacity for affection which saved him. Nothing as he was growing up at home, nothing at Devon, nothing even about the war had broken his harmonious and natural unity.... Only Phineas never was afraid, only Phineas never hated anyone." A reviewer for *Time* distilled a broader allegory from *A Separate Peace*, perceiving in Knowles's novel that "the enemy Gene killed, and loved, is the one that every man must kill; his own youth, the innocence that burns too hotly to be endured."

A sequel to his first published novel appeared in 1981. In *Peace Breaks Out* Knowles transports the reader back again to the state of New Hampshire, back to Devon Academy, the preparatory school where the events of *A Separate Peace* took place. The narrator of Knowles's seventh novel is Peter Hallam, a World War II veteran captured during the Italian Campaign who spent several years as a prisoner of war. Hallam returns from the war to find his family broken apart and his life a shambles; he arrives at Devon, his alma mater, in 1945 as a teacher of both physical education and American History. Expecting to find peaceful surroundings in which to recover from the emotional trauma of the war, Hallam instead finds Devon students disillusioned and bitter at their lost opportunity to participate in the War effort. The tension escalating among the students is condensed in a mounting conflict between two Devon students; Wexford, a Devon senior, and young Eric Hochschwender. Wexford, a manipulative young man, is the radical editor of the school newspaper, and he uses his position to incite racial tensions, causing the benign but outspoken German-American Hochschwender to come to the defense of the defeated Nazi regime. When Wexford's machinations result in the destruction of a stained glass window recently erected on campus as a memorial to Devon alumni killed in World War II, several overzealous students are tricked into blaming Hochschwender. Ultimately, as in *A Separate Peace*, the story's outcome is tragic.

Although critics have expressed some misgivings at the similarities between *A Separate Peace* and *Peace Breaks Out*, Knowles's later novel has been praised for the tight plotting and vivid prose characteristic of his work. Peter S. Prescott compared the two books and commented in *Newsweek*: "The particular strength of *A Separate Peace* lay in Knowles's inspired conception of his characters: of a victim who in no way resembles a victim and a murderer who does not know he is one until after the event." "By contrast," Prescott added, "in [*Peace Breaks Out*], the boys are neither likable nor believable." But reviewer Randolph Hogan commented in the *New York Times*, "In sentence after graceful sentence and page after seamless page, John Knowles builds a story as solid as the mahogany paneling of Devon."

Knowles Becomes a Full-Time Novelist

With the success of *A Separate Peace,* the then-thirty-five-year-old Knowles was able to resign from his job as editor of *Holiday* in 1960 and devote himself to writing fiction. He spent two years traveling throughout Great Britain, France,

Greece, and the Middle East before returning home to record the impressions of his trip in *Double Vision: American Thoughts Abroad,* published in 1964. Knowles's second work of fiction, *Morning in Antibes,* had been published the previous year while its author was still abroad. Dealing simultaneously with the contrasting worlds of the well-to-do residing on the French Riviera and the Algerians struggling for self-rule during the French-Algerian crisis of the late 1950s, the novel was perceived by critics as a flawed work containing hastily-drawn characters and clumsy metaphors. Knowles agreed, and in a 1986 interview with Mona Gable for the *Los Angeles Times* referred to *Morning in Antibes* as "really a rotten book." Undeterred by critical rejection of his second book, he published a third novel, *Indian Summer,* in 1966. Containing a dedication to Thornton Wilder, this work marked a return to the level of Knowles's usual craftsmanship and re-

Returning to the setting of *A Separate Peace* in this 1981 novel, Knowles focuses on a young teacher at Devon Academy as he searches for peace after being held as a prisoner of war.

ceived a much more favorable reception from reviewers.

Again set against the backdrop of World War II, *Indian Summer* introduces the reader to U.S. Air Force Sergeant Harold "Cleet" Kinsolving at the time of his return from the Pacific in 1946. A man of partial Native American heritage, twenty-three-year-old Kinsolving epitomizes Knowles's "American Character": a rugged non-conformist, he is full of optimism in the future while also sensing himself out of place in his present position within modern society. At one point in the novel, Kinsolving reflects on his country's past: "In those days a man who would take a dare and had the strength and fast reflexes and inner force would carve out a life to fit himself at sea or on the frontier or in a battle; in those days . . . . Well, that's when I ought to have lived, back then." Although desirous of creating a small cargo airline with routes extending from the state of Washington up to Alaska, Kinsolving has no money to finance his dream; traveling from his native Texas north to Missouri, he is content working as a pilot for a small crop-dusting outfit. He meets up with Neil Reardon, a boyhood friend who teaches at a nearby college. Reardon, who has become a best-selling author, is leaving his teaching position and convinces Kinsolving to return with him to his hometown of Wetherford, Connecticut, to become Reardon's secretary. Kinsolving is drawn to the job, not only because of his friendship with Reardon, but with the hope that Neil's family's wealth might possibly finance his dream of starting an air freight line at some point in the future.

Throughout the novel many characters are introduced—Reardon's parents; Gloria Sommers, a girl Neil chooses to marry because her common background so sharply contrasts with his own; the Sommers family—but Knowles solidly grounds his story in the complex relationship between Neil and Cleet. Reviewers have pointed up the structural similarities in the relationship existing between these two men and that of Gene and Phineas, the two young protagonists of *A Separate Peace*. "Like Finney, Cleet is a spontaneous person, a true individual," noted Hicks, "and that is why Neil looks up to him but at the same time has to try to dominate him." Peter Wolfe agreed in his analysis of the novel for *University Review*, taking as Knowles's major premise that "the condition of life is war. *A Separate Peace* describes the private battles of a prep school coterie boiling into the public fury of World War II. The individual and society are both at war again in Knowles's second

novel, *Morning in Antibes*. . . . [*Indian Summer*] not only presents the World War II period and its aftermath as a single conflict-ridden epoch, it also describes civilian life as more dangerous than combat."

Indian Summer, Knowles's third novel, also takes an in-depth look at the problems of the very wealthy and the strain that wealth places upon human relationships. The marriage between Georgia and Neil and the adult friendship between Neil and Cleet are both ultimately shattered under the weight of the Reardon fortune. While praising the author for his recreation of believable *nouveau riche*—upper middle-class—New England surroundings, Hicks found Knowles's third novel somewhat disappointing when compared to the literary triumph of *A Separate Peace*. "I can understand after a fashion what Neil sees in Cleet, but I cannot understand why Cleet is attracted to Neil," he commented. "In fact, Cleet is a mystery whatever way I look at him." However, Peter Buitenhuis praised *Indian Summer* in the *New York Times Book Review* as "a rich book, written with exuberance and an eccentric grace." While noting that at times the novel "seems unintegrated and uncertain of its own subject," Buitenhuis attributed this more to Knowles's choice of narrator than a deficiency of structure: he described Cleet as a "green-eyed half-primitive, who seems doomed to go on through life looking for a new frontier."

In Search of the Proper Setting

Although making his home since the early 1970s in Southampton, Long Island—sometime home to such literary figures as Truman Capote, Winston Groome, Willie Morris, and Irwin Shaw—Knowles has continued the traveling he views as an integral part of the process of writing a novel. His underlying examination of the many manifestations of the "American Character" in reaction to its environment gives a special significance to his choice of setting. Selection of a locale is Knowles's first step in writing; he once commented in *Something about the Author (SATA)*: "All of my books are based on places, places I know very well and feel very deeply about. I begin with that place and then the characters and the plot emerge from it." Knowles's gift for "describing local atmosphere, nurtured during his years with *Holiday*, has been frequently admired by his critics and is one of the mainstays of his appeal as a fiction writer," Nelson noted. Reviewer Ruel E. Foster found Knowles's fictional sphere to be "a cultivated, cosmopolitan, somewhat jaded world" and commented in *Contempo-*

rary Novelists that Knowles is "a fine craftsman, a fine stylist, alert to the infinite resources and nuances of language. Yet, as he says, he is one of the live-around-the-world people, rootless, nomadic, and making a virtue of that rootlessness." *Morning in Antibes* and the 1974 *Spreading Fires* both reflect Knowles' familiarity with the French Riviera, where he was a regular visitor for a period of eight years. *The Paragon* and *Indian Summer* recall youthful experiences at Yale University and the surrounding Connecticut countryside. "My way of increasing my understanding of these places is to set a novel there," Knowles added in *SATA*.

Knowles drew on his memories of the coal-mining regions of West Virginia, where he was born and raised, to write his sixth novel, published in 1978. Taking place during the coal boom of 1909-1924, *A Vein of Riches* is the saga of the wealthy Catherwood family of Middleburg. Lyle, the son of patriarchal coal baron Clarkston Catherwood, is disillusioned by his father's lack of confidence in his abilities to carry on the Clarkston Coal Company empire; he attempts to withdraw into university studies and strong whiskey. Lyle's disillusionment turns to rebellion as he secretly aligns himself with the mine workers and their families, people living in slum-like conditions on the outskirts of Middleburg as they eke out a meager living in the employment of the elder Catherwood, a shrewd businessman. The young man is finally drawn into the family business during a series of violent labor disputes culminating in the historic United Mine Workers strike in the summer of 1921. Events draw Lyle into in a love affair with the widow of a Catherwood employee, but the woman leaves him for his own father, whose power and money provide a greater attraction than Lyle's affections. Knowles carries the drama of the Catherwood family through the 1930s, where the family fortune is dissipated by both the Great Depression and America's shift from coal to oil as a primary energy source.

Knowles returns to Connecticut in setting the events of his 1983 novel, *A Stolen Past*, which revolve around the theft of a valuable gem. Alexei and Zinaida Trouvenskoy, members of the White Russian aristocracy forced to leave their homeland to avoid communist retribution after the 1917 abdication of Czar Nicholas II, flee to the United States. Alexei and his wife make their home in New Haven, living in relatively modest surroundings with only a few treasured possessions to remind them of the lavish lifestyle they once maintained in Russia. One of these valuable treasures, the Militsa

Knowles juxtaposes past and present in this 1983 tale of theft and loss.

Diamond, is stolen during a party at the couple's home. Noted author Allan Prieston, once a friend and college roommate of the Trouvenskoy's son, Greg, had learned of the Trouvenskoy family's tragedy during his college days; from it he found the inspiration for his first popular work of fiction and feels guilty over finding his fortune in their misfortune. A witness to the theft of the Militsa Diamond at the Trouvenskoy's New Haven home, Prieston's return to the city almost twenty years later on a speaking engagement at Yale University sparks memories of the past. Describing *A Stolen Past* as a "strange and compelling book," Brian Morton noted in the *Times Literary Supplement*: "Ultimately the diamond is only the fulcrum for an altogether more abstract fiction." Commenting on the complex juxtaposition of past and present, as well as the extreme literariness of Knowles's work, Morton added that "the novel's subjects are the act of remembering and the process of turning memory into literature, innocent, unliterary pastlessness seen against the dense, often malign, history of Europe."

The Private Life of Axie Reed

The Private Life of Axie Reed, Knowles's ninth novel, found its inspiration in an event in the author's own life. As he told Mona Gable of the *Los Angeles Times*, Knowles was at dinner with friends in Long Island. Driving home afterwards, he fell asleep behind the wheel of his car and was struck by oncoming traffic. Recalling the three weeks following the accident, during which time he was in the hospital suffering from severe injuries, Knowles explained to Gable: "It was very touch and go for four days whether I would live or not. And I knew that I sort of accepted it. I thought, 'If this is it, I've had a fascinating life.' Then they must have stopped the bleeding and I began to think there was a possibility to recover. I was determined to recover." *The Private Life of Axie Reed* grew out of that experience: "There were things I had to communicate I thought were valuable," said Knowles, "about the will to survive or the will not to survive."

The Private Life of Axie Reed was published in 1986. Amid the varied settings of Hollywood, California, Long Island, New York, and Paxos, a fictional island in Greece, Knowles tells the story of Alexandra Reed, a vital fifty-year-old woman who has enjoyed a successful career as an actress. While attending a party on Long Island, Reed is critically injured—during most of the length of the novel she lies comatose in her hospital room. Her story, then, is left to be told by the many friends and relatives who come to her bedside and reminisce about the events of her life. Knowles chooses Axie's cousin, Nick Reed, to serve as narrator: An unmarried academic, Reed's personal memories of his cousin are able to provide the reader a counterpoint to Axie's own hazy recollections during the times she slips into consciousness, and his proximity at her bedside allows him to participate in the conversations among her many friends. Reed's gradual return to consciousness and her sudden confrontation with mortality—questions about the quality of her life—comprise the subject of the novel. Although an entertaining novel reflecting the glamorous lives of Hollywood, *Axie Reed* received criticism for the somewhat stilted dialogue and overabundance of cliches. Although the novel's main character is a "tall, slender, glamorously beautiful woman," critic Michiko Kakutani expressed disappointment in the *New York Times* that "none of these aspects of Axie is ever drama-

tized—mostly, the characters just sit about her sickbed, reminiscing about what a great gal she used to be." Reviewer Elaine Kendall added in the *Los Angeles Times* that "the central figure is so idealized there's no room left for improvement or progress. The story is a star vehicle in which all the members of the cast are relegated to walk-on roles, gamely holding candles to illuminate their darling." However, the novel was popular with the reading public for its portrayal of the life of a dramatic, spirited personality, and Knowles's deft portrayal of his character through only her own feverish thoughts and the recollections of others brought praise from readers and critics alike.

Topping a Classic

Since the elevation of *A Separate Peace* to the status of a classic in the early 1960s, critics have consistently compared Knowles's subsequent works to his first novel. In many of his later novels, Knowles has returned to the themes underlying his first published novel: the exploration of man's inner character and its relation to social and cultural conventions. Most obviously in the sequel *Peace Breaks Out*, but also in such works as *A Stolen Past*, Knowles has attempted to duplicate both the academic setting and the retrospective narration of *A Separate Peace*. In comparing *A Stolen Past* to Knowles's first novel, Jim Moore of the *Los Angeles Times Book Review* commented that Knowles "has stolen ... from his own literary past (structure, length and manner are remarkably like those of 1959's *A Separate Peace*, not to mention title)." Moore sees in the novel "a lesson for authors too conscious of working in a Tradition," adding that *A Stolen Past* "argues sadly against the notion that being 57 and accepting is preferable to being 33 and startled." However, the popularity of Knowles's novels among the reading public and the praise of numerous critics place Knowles among those novelists possessing what James L. McDonald has termed "genuine stature." McDonald wrote of Knowles in *Arizona Quarterly*: "He has exhibited the courage to tackle large subjects and significant themes; and he has treated them with taste, understanding, and considerable technical skill. He certainly deserves more attention than he has received up until now."

Knowles himself perceives the mixed reception of his later works in a pragmatic light. The author commented in *Esquire* that he did not view the incredible success of *A Separate Peace* as a drawback, because "it freed me from having to teach school or be a journalist, enabling me to devote myself entirely to fiction writing." And regarding his first novel, the book that changed his life, Knowles said: "I feel about [*A Separate Peace*] the way a parent with a rather workaday existence must feel when he finds he has produced a world-beating child: a slight sense of wonder, pride, and a certain detachment."

■ **Works Cited**

Buitenhuis, Peter, "Hapless Hero," *New York Times Book Review*, August 14, 1966.

Foster, Ruel E., "John Knowles," *Contemporary Novelists*, 5th edition, St. James Press, 1991, pp. 534-535.

Fuller, Edmund, "Shadow of Mars," *New York Times Book Review*, February 7, 1960.

Gable, Mona, "Novelist Knowles Goes Hollywood with *Axie Reed*," *Los Angeles Times*, August 27, 1986, pp. 1, 10.

Hicks, Granville, "The Good Have a Quiet Heroism," *Saturday Review*, March 5, 1960, p. 15.

Hicks, Granville, "Blandishments of Wealth," *Saturday Review*, August 13, 1966, pp. 23-34.

Hogan, Randolph, "Books: Parable of Evil," *New York Times*, September 4, 1981.

Kakutani, Michiko, review of *The Private Life of Axie Reed*, *New York Times*, April 16, 1986.

Kendall, Elaine, "Axie Reed's Suffering Star Shines a Bit Too Brightly," *Los Angeles Times*, May 2, 1986.

Knowles, John, *Double Vision: American Thoughts Abroad*, Macmillan, 1964.

Knowles, John, *Indian Summer*, Random House, 1966.

Knowles, John, "My Separate Peace," *Esquire*, March, 1985, pp. 106-109.

"The Leap," *Time*, April 4, 1960, p. 98.

McDonald, James L., "The Novels of John Knowles," *Arizona Quarterly*, winter, 1967, p. 342.

Moore, Jim, "Innocence, Betrayal: A Gloss on Old Themes," *Los Angeles Times Book Review*, August 28, 1983.

Morton, Brian, "Recovering the Glow," *Times Literary Supplement*, August 31, 1984, p. 964.

Nelson, Robert M., "John Knowles," *Dictionary of Literary Biography*, Volume 6: *American Novelists since World War II, Second Series*, Gale, 1980, pp. 167-177.

Prescott, Peter S., review of *Peace Breaks Out*, *Newsweek*, April 20, 1981, p. 92.

Sipper, Ralph B., "Calculated Return to a School Setting," *Los Angeles Times*, April 2, 1981.

Something about the Author, Volume 8, Gale, 1976, pp. 101-103.

Wolfe, Peter, "The Impact of Knowles's *A Separate Peace*," *University of Missouri Review*, March, 1970, pp. 189-190.

■ **For More Information See**

BOOKS

Concise Dictionary of Literary Biography: Broadening Views, 1968-1988, Gale, 1989, pp. 120-135.

Contemporary Literary Criticism, Gale, Volume 1, 1973, p. 169; Volume 4, 1975, pp. 271-273; Volume 10, 1979, pp. 302-304; Volume 26, 1983, pp. 245-265.

PERIODICALS

Chicago Tribune, September 21, 1986.

English Journal, May, 1964, pp. 313-318.

Horn Book, August, 1981, pp. 461-462.

New York Times, February 3, 1978.

New York Times Book Review, February 7, 1960; October 30, 1983, p. 32; May 11, 1986, p. 19.

Time, April 6, 1981, p. 80.

Times Literary Supplement, May 1, 1959.

Voice of Youth Advocates, August, 1981, p. 26.°

—Sketch by Pamela L. Shelton

Gordon Korman

■ Personal

Full name, Gordon Richard Korman; born October 23, 1963, in Montreal, Quebec, Canada; son of C. I. (an accountant) and Bernice (a journalist; maiden name, Silverman) Korman. *Education:* New York University, B.F.A., 1985. *Hobbies and other interests:* Music, travel, sports.

■ Addresses

Home—20 Dersingham Cres., Thornhill, Ontario, Canada L3T 4E7. *Office*—c/o Scholastic Inc., 730 Broadway, New York, NY 10003. *Agent*—Curtis Brown Ltd., 10 Astor Place, New York, NY 10003.

■ Career

Writer, 1975—. *Member:* Writers Union of Canada, Canadian Society of Children's Authors, Illustrators, and Performers (CANSCAIP), Canadian Authors' Association, ACTRA, Society of Children's Book Writers.

■ Awards, Honors

Air Canada Award, Canadian Authors' Association, 1981, for "Most Promising Writer under Thirty-five"; Ontario Youth Award, International Year of the Youth Committee of the Ontario Government, 1985, for contributions to children's literature; Children's Choice Award, International Reading Association, 1986, for *I Want to Go Home!*, and 1987, for *Our Man Weston;* Markham Civic Award for the Arts, 1987; IRA Children's Choice Award for *Our Man Weston,* 1987; American Library Association (ALA) Editors' Choice and ALA Best Book List for *A Semester in the Life of a Garbage Bag,* 1988; ALA Best Book List for *Losing Joe's Place,* 1991; Manitoba Young Readers' Choice Award for *The Zucchini Warriors,* 1992; *The Twinkie Squad* was a Junior Library Guild selection, and was named an "Our Choice" book by the Canadian Children's Book Center, both 1992.

■ Writings

FOR CHILDREN AND YOUNG ADULTS

This Can't Be Happening at Macdonald Hall!, illustrated by Affie Mohammed, Scholastic, 1977.
Go Jump in the Pool!, illustrated by Lea Daniel, Scholastic, 1979.
Beware the Fish!, illustrated by Daniel, Scholastic, 1980.
Who Is Bugs Potter?, Scholastic, 1980.
I Want to Go Home!, Scholastic, 1981.
Our Man Weston, Scholastic, 1982.
The War with Mr. Wizzle, Scholastic, 1982.

Bugs Potter: Live at Nickaninny, Scholastic, 1983.
No Coins, Please, Scholastic, 1984.
Don't Care High, Scholastic, 1985.
Son of Interflux, Scholastic, 1986.
A Semester in the Life of a Garbage Bag, Scholastic, 1987.
The Zucchini Warriors, Scholastic, 1988.
Radio Fifth Grade, Scholastic, 1989.
Losing Joe's Place, Scholastic, 1990.
Macdonald Hall Goes Hollywood, Scholastic, 1991.
(With Bernice Korman) *The D-minus Poems of Jeremy Bloom*, Scholastic, 1992.
The Twinkie Squad, Scholastic, 1992.

Korman's books have been translated into French, Swedish, Danish, Norwegian, and Chinese.

■ Sidelights

Since publishing his first book when he was only fourteen years old, Canadian author Gordon Korman has written many best-selling novels for children and young adults. Korman's trademark

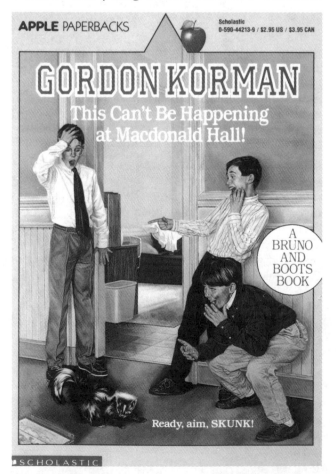

Korman creates the characters of Boots and Bruno, two trouble-causing boarding school roommates, in this 1977 bestseller.

storylines—featuring slapstick humor, madcap adventures, and high-spirited, rebellious characters—have helped make his books popular favorites with school-age readers across Canada and the United States. "Many of Mr. Korman's plots revolve around the frustrations of rambunctious boys forced to submit to stuffy academic authorities," noted Leslie Bennetts in the *New York Times*. Korman, whose books have sold over four million copies, strives to write stories that provide a healthy dose of humor for his young readers. "My books are the kind of stories I wanted to read and couldn't find when I was ten, eleven, and twelve," he was quoted as saying in *Something about the Author*. "I think that, no matter what the subject matter, kids' concerns are important, and being a kid isn't just waiting out the time between birth and the age of majority."

Korman was born in 1963 in Montreal, Quebec, where his father worked as an accountant and his mother wrote an "Erma Bombeck-type column" for a local newspaper, as he told Bennetts. In elementary and junior high school, Korman was always fond of writing—especially his own brand of zany stories and scenarios. "I wasn't a big reader for some reason," he remarked to Chris Ferns in *Canadian Children's Literature*. "But I always tried to put in creativity where I could: if we had a sentence with all the spelling words for that week, I would try to come up with the stupidest sentences, or the funniest sentences, or the craziest sentences I could think of."

Korman's professional writing career began at the age of twelve with a story assignment for his seventh-grade English class. "The big movies at the time were 'Jaws' and 'Airplane,' and everyone decided they were going to write action stories," he told Bennetts. "It was my mother who brought me down to earth. She told me to write about something a little closer to home." In response, Korman created the characters of Boots and Bruno, roommates in a private boarding school who are, according to Bennetts "best friends and incorrigible troublemakers." After such antics as replacing the Canadian flag at a school hockey game with a flag from their imaginary country of Malbonia, Boots and Bruno are separated by the headmaster. The two boys are forced to move in with new roommates and forbidden to see each other. In the boisterous tale that follows, Korman unfolds the boys' adventures as they reunite and stir up even more trouble together.

"I got kind of carried away . . . and I accidentally wrote the first book," Korman told Ferns. "The characters sort of became real people to me, and they more or less wrote the book for me. The class had to read all the assignments at the end of the whole business, and a lot of people were coming to me and saying how they really liked it. I suppose anyone who writes 120 pages for class is going to attract a certain amount of attention anyway—and I just got the idea of seeing if I could get the book published." Korman sent his manuscript to the publisher Scholastic, Inc., and two years later at the age of fourteen experienced the publication of both his first book and first best-seller, *This Can't Be Happening at Macdonald Hall.*

After his initial success, Korman published books at the rate of one per year, writing them during summers when he was on vacation from school. At the age of eighteen he was voted the "Most Promising Writer under Thirty-five" by the Canadian Author's Association, and was a popular author on school and reading tours across Canada and the United States. In addition to such Boots and Bruno novels as *Beware the Fish, The War with Mr. Wizzle,* and *Go Jump in the Pool,* his other best-selling books feature characters that similarly test boundaries of authority. Bugs Potter, in the 1980 novel *Who Is Bugs Potter?* and the 1983 novel *Bugs Potter Live at Nickaninny,* is a rock-and-roll drummer who lives for his music. Simon Irving in Korman's 1986 novel, *Son of Interflux,* organizes a high school campaign to save school land from being purchased by his father's corporation. Artie in the 1984 publication, *No Coins, Please,* to the frustration of his counselors, pulls off scams for money whenever his summer-camp group visits the city. The stories' far-fetched plots have in common the fact that their young characters succeed in areas that are usually considered adult domains. Korman commented to Ferns: "How many books have you read—and good books—about a kid who makes money: oh boy, isn't he cute, he raised sixty bucks, a hundred bucks, something like that? I mean, why can't an eleven-year-old make $150,000? If Bugs Potter is a good drummer, why can't he be the best drummer in the world?"

Korman acknowledges that his characters are something like he was as a child, but more active in their rebelliousness. He told Bennetts: "I was a gutless troublemaker; I probably did a lot more with my mouth than anything else. I talked back a lot; I was a pain in the neck. I'd be the type of guy who, if I caught a teacher in a mistake, would make a federal case out of it. I never really was a favorite with my teachers." But, while Korman's characters display a healthy disrespect for authority, part of

Tenth-graders Paul and Sheldon liven things up at their apathetic high school when they promote a strange student for Student Council President in this 1985 novel.

their wider appeal is that they draw the line between disrespect and anarchy. "I think the books are very respectful of people," Korman told Ferns. "I was writing at the time of [the 1978 *National Lampoon* film] *Animal House....* I think one of the things which makes the books fairly strong, so that they defy being compared to things like that, is that they don't cross that line. Considering how crazy the books are, I keep a firm foot in reality."

Not surprisingly for someone who began a writing career at the age of twelve, Korman's works changed in perspective and tone as he matured. His earlier children's books, relying more heavily on slapstick and farce, were known for their caricaturizations and their chaotic, high-paced plots. Korman described the approach he used in the 1982 *Our Man Weston* and the 1983 *Bugs Potter Live at Nickaninny* to Ferns: "What I was dealing with at the time was a lot of contrivance of events. So-and-so does this, and it just happens that at the same time this happens, and it happens at exactly the right moment. Those books tended to have an incredible number of contrived circumstances; they also had a large number of adult characters, many of whom were crazy and wild."

As Korman moved into adolescence, so did his characters, and he began to more fully develop their personalities and relationships with each other. His slapstick humor, although remaining a significant part of the action in his stories, began to share the stage with some realistic depictions of adolescent life. In his 1987 novel, *A Semester in the Life of a Garbage Bag*, Korman introduces Raymond Jardine, whose desire to win a school contest (and therefore spend the summer in Greece rather than at his uncle's New Jersey fish-gutting plant) stimulates a chain of events in the life of his English

It pays to be an underdog— when you end up a champ!

In this 1986 adventure, junior high school student Simon Irving rallies together a campaign to save school-owned land from his own father's corporation.

class partner, Sean Delancey. There is no shortage of absurdity in this novel. Among the characters who become involved in the plot are Sean's grandfather, a yo-yo prodigy, his younger sister (whom he calls "Genghis Khan in training"), and his rival in romance, the muscular but not-too-bright Steve "Cementhead" Semenski. The plot also includes a thirty-three million dollar experimental power plant that doesn't work. But along with the caricatures and absurdity there are real teenage emotions and interrelations. Ferns commented in his review of *A Semester in the Life of a Garbage Bag* that Korman's "lunatic comic inventiveness ... is accompanied by a perceptive eye for the quirks of adolescent behaviour." Ferns added that "the comedy and the observation almost seem to be pulling in different directions," and summarized that, although in this novel he is stretching into new, not yet mastered territory, "Gordon Korman's comic imagination is as fertile as ever."

Radio Fifth Grade, Korman's 1989 novel about a student-run radio show, contains Korman's customary zany elements—a stubborn parrot, a school bully who insists on radio air time to read his short stories about kittens, and an adviser who is too busy reading pulp science fiction to help the students with the show. The book was praised by Todd Morning in *School Library Journal* for its comic value. "This story works well on the level of sheer farce," Morning stated. "Korman is good at creating chaotic, if not always believable, situations." A *Publishers Weekly* critic, however, who found value beyond the book's humor, stated that *Radio Fifth Grade* is "feelingly written, and earns a place with the best middle-grade fiction; more than a romp, it has genuine charm."

Korman's 1990 book, *Losing Joe's Place*, is the story of Jason Cardone and two friends who, at the age of sixteen, sublet Jason's brother Joe's Toronto apartment while he is away in Europe. Everything that can go wrong does go wrong for the three boys while they strive to pay their rent each month, and the story is filled with the farcical characters and chaotic situations that Korman is known for. Again, the book offers more than its comic strain. Several critics noted the depth of characterization of Jason, who narrates the tale. Shirley Carmony commented in *Voice of Youth Advocates* that Jason "is a lovable adolescent whose hopes and fears are rather typical ones for a 16 year old boy. His humorous viewpoint is a pleasure." Jack Forman summarized in his *School Library Journal* review of *Losing Joe's Place*: "Surprisingly, it's not the quick twists and turns of the farcical plot that keep this

In this 1991 tale, Bruno decides to teach a lesson to a teen idol who is filming a movie at Macdonald Hall, only to be taught one himself.

very funny story moving. It's Jason's spirited narrative, his self-effacing sense of humor, and his finely tuned ear for the ridiculous that make these unbelievable antics work and create characters from these caricatures."

Korman attributes the popularity of his books to his portrayal of young characters that achieve power and success in an adult world—something a popular writer who began his career at the age of twelve knows about firsthand. "Whatever an adult can do, somewhere in the world there's one sixteen-year-old who can do it as well," he commented to Ferns. "The problem is with the age level where kids are starting to be able to do things, but it still seems unnatural. And I think that's one of the reasons why the books do well in that age bracket ... because they address that situation of kids being able to triumph over the adults, and in many cases with the adults coming to terms with it."

In 1985 Korman received a B.F.A. degree in dramatic and visual writing from New York Univer-

sity. His later books have been geared more towards young adult readers, and he has hopes to one day write an adult novel. "I'm torn between doing something totally different, and going back," he once told Ferns, "I'd like—and I don't know whether it's a romantic notion or not—I'd like to write, not necessarily the great Novel that's going to reshape the world, but a book that makes the sort of splash that [Joseph Heller's] *Catch-22* made.... What I see happening is that one day I'll set out to write about a seventeen-year-old character, and it'll just turn out that this guy isn't seventeen—he's twenty-three or so, and he's an adult. That's how I think the transition will come."

■ Works Cited

Bennetts, Leslie, "Gordon Korman: Old-Pro Author of 10 Books at 21," *New York Times Biographical Service*, July, 1985, pp. 862-863.

Carmony, Shirley, review of *Losing Joe's Place*, *Voice of Youth Advocates*, June, 1990, p. 106.

Ferns, Chris, "An Escape from New Jersey," *Canadian Children's Literature*, Number 52, 1988.

Ferns, Chris, "An Interview with Gordon Korman," *Canadian Children's Literature*, Number 38, 1985.

Forman, Jack, review of *Losing Joe's Place*, *School Library Journal*, May, 1990, p. 124.

Korman, Gordon, comments in *Something about the Author*, Volume 49, Gale, 1987, pp. 146-150.

Morning, Todd, review of *Radio Fifth Grade*, *School Library Journal*, September, 1989, p. 252.

Review of *Radio Fifth Grade*, *Publishers Weekly*, June 30, 1989.

■ For More Information See

PERIODICALS

Bulletin of the Center for Children's Books, November, 1985; December, 1985; November, 1986.

Canadian Children's Literature, Number 52, 1988.

Canadian Statesman, January 23, 1980.

Globe and Mail (Toronto), June 28, 1980; November 18, 1980; October 19, 1985; December 2, 1989.

Horn Book, March/April, 1986; November/ December, 1987.

Jam, spring, 1981.

Journal of Commonwealth Literature, February, 1982.

Publishers Weekly, July 24, 1987.

School Library Journal, October, 1987; September, 1988.

Toronto Star, July 29, 1978; December 14, 1982.

Voice of Youth Advocates, December, 1986; August-September, 1987; October, 1988, pp. 182-183.

David Letterman

■ Personal

Full name, David Michael Letterman; born April 12, 1947, in Indianapolis (one source says Broad Ripple), IN; son of Joseph (a florist) and Dorothy (a church secretary) Letterman; married Michelle Cook, c. 1969 (divorced, 1977). *Education:* Ball State University, B.A., 1970.

■ Addresses

Home—Connecticut. *Office*—NBC, 30 Rockefeller Plaza, New York, NY 10038.

■ Career

Television host, comedian, and writer. Radio announcer in Muncie, IN, in the 1960s; worked as a television announcer, weather reporter, and host of programs *Clover Power* and *Freeze-Dried Movies*, all for an American Broadcasting Companies (ABC-TV) affiliate in Indianapolis, IN, in the 1970s; radio talk show host in Indianapolis; appeared in television commercials in Indiana. Stand-up comedy performer, including regular at the Comedy Store, Los Angeles, CA, beginning in 1975. Appeared in television series, including announcer and regular performer, *The Starland Vocal Band Show*, Columbia Broadcasting System, Inc. (CBS-TV), 1977; regular, *Mary*, CBS-TV, 1978; guest host, *The Tonight Show*, National Broadcasting Company, Inc. (NBC-TV), 1979-80; host, *The David Letterman Show*, NBC-TV, 1980; host and executive producer, *Late Night with David Letterman*, NBC-TV, 1982–1993, CBS-TV, 1993—.

Appeared in television specials, including *The Peeping Times*, NBC-TV, 1978; *Battle of the Network Stars V*, ABC-TV, 1978; *Bob Hope Special: Bob Hope's Super Birthday Special*, NBC-TV, 1984; *The NBC All-Star Hour*, NBC-TV, 1985; host, *Late Night Film Festival*, NBC-TV, 1985; host and executive producer, *David Letterman's Second Annual Holiday Film Festival*, NBC-TV, 1986; *The Television Academy Hall of Fame*, NBC-TV, 1986; *The Jay Leno Show*, NBC-TV, 1986; cohost, *The Thirty-eighth Annual Emmy Awards*, NBC-TV, 1986; host and executive producer, *Late Night with David Letterman Fifth Anniversary Show*, NBC-TV, 1987; host and executive producer, *David Letterman's Old Fashioned Christmas*, NBC-TV, 1987; "Paul Shaffer: Viva Shaf Vegas," *Cinemax Comedy Experiment*, Cinemax, 1987; "Action Family," *Cinemax Comedy Experiment*, Cinemax, 1987; *The Thirty-ninth Annual Emmy Awards*, Fox, 1987; host and executive producer, *Late Night with David Letterman Sixth Anniversary Show*, NBC-TV, 1988; *The Tonight Show Starring Johnny Carson Twenty-sixth Anniversary Special*, NBC-TV, 1988; "Merrill Markoe's Guide to Glamorous Living," *Cinemax Comedy Experiment*, Cinemax, 1988; *The Comedy Store Fifteenth Class Reunion*, NBC-TV,

1988; host and executive producer, *Late Night with David Letterman Seventh Anniversary Show*, NBC-TV, 1989; host and executive producer, *Late Night with David Letterman Eighth Anniversary Special*, NBC-TV, 1990; *Two Years ... Later*, NBC-TV, 1990; *Sunday Night with Larry King*, NBC-TV, 1990; host and executive producer, *Late Night with David Letterman: Tenth Anniversary*, NBC-TV, 1992; *The Barbara Walters Special*, ABC-TV, 1992.

Appeared in television episodes, including *Celebrity Cooks*, syndicated, 1978; *Gong Show*, NBC-TV; *Mork and Mindy*, ABC-TV; *TV's Bloopers and Practical Jokes*, NBC-TV, 1984; and *Rock Concert*. Role as Matt Morgan in the television movie, *Fast Friends*, NBC-TV, 1979; appeared in the documentary *Skyscraper*, Public Broadcasting Service (PBS-TV), 1990. Executive producer, "Carol Doesn't Leifer Anymore," *Cinemax Comedy Experiment*, Cinemax, 1988.

■ Awards, Honors

Emmy awards, best host and best writing for a daytime variety series, both 1981, for *The David Letterman Show*; Jack Benny Award, University of Southern California, Los Angeles, 1984; Emmy awards (with others), best writing for a variety show, 1984, 1985, and 1986, for *Late Night with David Letterman*, and 1987, for *Late Night with David Letterman Fifth Anniversary Show*; American Comedy Award, funniest male performer in a television special, 1989, for *Late Night with David Letterman Sixth Anniversary Show*.

■ Writings

(With others) *The Late Night with David Letterman Book of Top Ten Lists*, edited by Leslie Wells, Pocket Books, 1990.
(With others) *An Altogether New Book of Top Ten Lists: From "Late Night with David Letterman*,*"* edited by Sally Peters, Pocket Books, 1991.

FOR TELEVISION

The Starland Vocal Band Show (series), NBC-TV, 1977.
The Paul Lynde Comedy Hour, ABC-TV, 1977.
Bob Hope Special: Bob Hope's All-Star Comedy Special from Australia, NBC-TV, 1978.
The David Letterman Show (series), NBC-TV, 1980.
Late Night with David Letterman (series), NBC-TV, 1982—.

David Letterman's Second Annual Holiday Film Festival, NBC-TV, 1986.
Late Night with David Letterman Fifth Anniversary Show, NBC-TV, 1987.
Late Night with David Letterman Sixth Anniversary Show, NBC-TV, 1988.
Late Night with David Letterman Seventh Anniversary Show, NBC-TV, 1989.
Late Night with David Letterman Eighth Anniversary Special, NBC-TV, 1990.
Late Night with David Letterman: Tenth Anniversary, NBC-TV, 1992.

Contributor of material for episodes of *Good Times*, CBS-TV; contributor of material to *The John Denver Special*.

■ Sidelights

David Letterman, host of the popular comedy-and-talk-show *Late Night with David Letterman*, has made a career out of making fun of television cliches and other quirky aspects of American culture, whether it be by mocking the verbal slips of Vice President Dan Quayle or devoting a portion of the show to a woman who dresses parrots to look like celebrities. The Indiana-born comedian enjoys taking the mundane and making it funny by exaggerating some aspect of an object or situation through the magic of television. Proudly displaying anomalies such as a giant doorknob or a custom-made suit covered in tortilla chips, Letterman has captured the imagination and late-night hours of millions of loyal viewers. His creative humor inspired *Time* contributor Richard Zoglin to term him television's "most inventive and influential comic."

Letterman was born in Indianapolis, Indiana, in 1947 and spent his childhood in the suburb of Broad Ripple, where his father owned a florist shop and his mother worked as a church secretary. It was a household that Letterman himself has described as "a solid *Father Knows Best* or *Leave It to Beaver* type of lower-middle-class family," as he is quoted by Caroline Latham in *The David Letterman Story*. Letterman fine-tuned his middle-American sensibilities by watching a lot of television programs that would later influence his own brand of comedy, as he observed in a *Time* interview with Zoglin: "When I was a kid I never really went to movies. In my house, going to movies was pretty much equated with as big a waste of time as you could come by as a human. When I got to an age where I could appreciate comedians, it was guys like Jonathan Winters; he used to really make me laugh hard. At about 16 or 17, on Friday nights I could stay up late and watch the *Steve Allen Show.* And sometimes after school I used to watch *Who Do You Trust?* with Johnny Carson." It was while watching Carson's early show that the young Letterman first developed an interest in a career in television. In a 1982 *Time* article, Letterman recalled his attraction to Carson's style of humor: "There was one guy who balanced a lawnmower on his chin—quite a booking coup—and Carson just made fun of him. I thought, 'What a great way to make a living!'"

Letterman's parents were not as enthusiastic about the medium that their son found so enthralling. "When I was growing up in Indianapolis, my parents, who regarded TV as the work of Satan, told me to go outside and do something real," Letterman told *People* contributor Jane Hall. Nevertheless, Letterman had set his sights on a career in television. "I always wanted to be in radio or television," he admitted in Hall's article. "I had to be a talk show host—I can't sing or act." Letterman's ideal of his own talk show had unique characteristics even at these early stages, as is noted in *The David Letterman Story:* "At first it was just vague vision of me on television with a few friends, drinking a warm eight-pack of beer and chatting about the week's events."

Broadcasting for Fun and Profit

With this lofty goal, at the age of eighteen Letterman headed to Ball State University in Muncie, Indiana, to pursue a degree in radio and television. Letterman credits his classroom and extracurricular experience in broadcasting during his college years with providing a workable knowledge of the field. Latham quotes Letterman asserting that "radio and TV were perfect for me.... It was just practical experience, and I was able to turn it into a career." Letterman always found ways to make the practical interesting, however. During his stint on the official college radio station, WBST, Letterman would liven up the mostly classical music format with some rather unofficial observations. This spontaneous commentary did not endear him to the station's management, who finally fired Letterman after he introduced composer Claude Debussy's piano composition *Clair de Lune* with the helpful note: "You know Mrs. Lune and all the little loonies," according to Bill Barol in *Newsweek.* Letterman, in a quote contained in *The David Letterman Story,* described his hours on the WBST airwaves as "my first outlet, my first place to just go and talk, and I loved it." Years later, after his

graduation and success as a television personality, Letterman provided Ball State with a fund to upgrade their telecommunications department and provide scholarships to students who are more adept at expressing their creativity than making perfect grades, much like his example. "What Ball State did was teach me that it is possible to make a living in broadcasting," he is quoted by Latham.

While attending Ball State, he met and married music major Michelle Cook. In order to support himself, Letterman secured a job at a radio station in Muncie, where he substituted for the host of a show. He then began a position as a fill-in announcer at an ABC-TV affiliate in Indianapolis. His temporary assignment continued after his 1970 graduation and became a permanent job by default—the station couldn't find anyone they wanted to hire to replace him. Letterman and his wife moved back to his hometown of Broad Ripple, and he worked in Indianapolis for the next five years. Letterman told Zoglin about these years in local television: "It was a great time.... I started as a voice-over announcer doing station identifications. Then gradually, through vacation schedules and attrition, I got to do morning news once; got to host a kids' show once; ended up doing the weather and a late-night movie show. You just do everything you can. It was great fun because there was no pressure. I could pretty much do whatever I

Letterman auspiciously began his quirky comedy-and-talk show, *Late Night with David Letterman,* in 1982 by walking through a virtual jungle of peacock feathers.

wanted, and nobody cared because I was always the fill-in guy."

While his assignments at the Indianapolis station were the type traditionally given to rookies, Letterman applied the same unpredictable creativity to his work that he had to his college projects—the same brand of humor that would later define his success as a television host. When assigned to host the Saturday morning show *Clover Power*, featuring 4-H Club members and their home-grown achievements, Letterman conducted his interviews with an ironic tone that he admits boiled down to making fun of the kids. Taking advantage of the little-watched time slot of his two o'clock in the morning late-movie show, he retitled the program *Freeze-Dried Movies* and signed off with a clip showing a miniature version of the station being blown up. Letterman discussed other unusual attractions of his movie show in *The David Letterman Story:* "In between movies, I'd goof around with a cast of regulars. We had a telethon to raise money for a washed-up fighter. We celebrated our tenth anniversary in the show's second week. One guy showed up at the station wearing a stupid suit, and we dragged him onto the show so people could see it."

Perhaps Letterman's most widely known role at the Indiana station was his job as the weekend weatherman. Many of his midwestern viewers may not have appreciated his reports of such meteorological whimsies as hailstones the size of canned hams, but Letterman didn't let that deter him. He expressed his forecasting technique in *The David Letterman Story:* "I used to like to make up cities and circumstances that didn't exist and describe devastation that didn't occur. I thought that was a high form of entertainment. Looking back on it, it probably wasn't funny, but I enjoyed using television for the purpose of disseminating false data."

After four years in local television and a stint as a local radio talk show host, Letterman realized that he needed a larger audience in order to find a place for his brand of comedy. With the support of his wife Michelle, he headed to Los Angeles in 1975 in the hope of working on a network level. He took with him several scripts on which he had been working, but was unable to get anyone in California to read them. He turned to stand-up comedy instead, a move about which he was not very confident. In Barol's *Newsweek* story, Letterman related his first appearance at the Comedy Store, a prominent club for new performers: "I got up and said from rote some stuff I had written that day. To dead silence." He quickly, however, found

an approach that worked by observing another Comedy Store performer, Jay Leno. Letterman stated in Barol's article that after watching Leno's successful show he realized "It wasn't two guys go into a bar, and it wasn't bathroom jokes. It was all smart, shrewd observations, and it could be anything—politics, television, education. The dynamic of it was, you and I both understand that this is stupid." In a quote in *The David Letterman Story*, Jay Leno asserted that Letterman's talent was apparent even in his first stage appearance in Los Angeles. After a number of unimpressive would-be comedians performed, said Leno, "All of a sudden, this new guy from the Midwest gets up and he has this really clever, hip material. He knocked everybody out. In fact, the only thing wrong with his act was that he had a big beard at the time. He looked

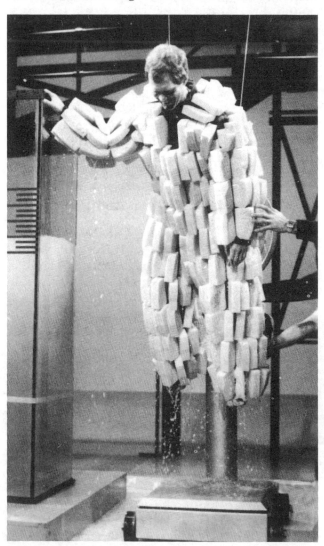

Answering one of his many "what if?" questions, Letterman covered himself with sponges and was lowered into a tank full of water during one of his shows—he weighed 500 pounds upon emerging.

like Dinty Moore." Letterman continued to work on his act and soon became a regular performer at the Comedy Store.

One of Letterman's first real breaks came when Jimmie Walker, a star of CBS-TV's popular show *Good Times,* hired him to write fifteen jokes a week for $150. Then in 1977, the talent agency of Rollins, Joffe, Morra & Brezna signed him and began to arrange small writing and acting jobs for him with the major television networks. As well as writing for comedy specials for entertainment figures such as Paul Lynde, John Denver, and Bob Hope, Letterman appeared as a regular on short-lived series such as *The Starland Vocal Band Show* and *Mary,* a variety program starring Mary Tyler Moore. While Letterman was excited about working on a major network series with a well-known actress, he was less than enthusiastic about the type of work that was required of him on *Mary.* He stated in Barol's *Newsweek* profile: "It was pretty exciting, having heard about Television City all my life, to be going to work there. I had a name badge with a picture on it and an ID number, and I could eat in the CBS commissary. I could talk to Mary Tyler Moore any time I wanted. I could do almost anything. I could share fruit with her if I wanted to. I, of course, wanted to. She never wanted any part of it. So that was great. But the hard part was that I had to sing and dance and dress up in costumes. That was tough. I knew my limitations, but this really brought 'em home."

Tonight Show Boosts Network Career

While his appearances on *Mary* may have provided Letterman with a few embarrassing moments, his work did get him noticed. Agents for Johnny Carson's late-night talk show, *The Tonight Show,* who had also seen Letterman perform at the Comedy Club, invited the young comic to appear on the program in November of 1978. This was the television opportunity for which Letterman had been waiting. Not only was Letterman's performance on the show well received, but after he finished his stand-up routine, Carson invited him to come over and talk with him and the other guests—a privilege rarely given to a first-time performer on the show. "It was the most fun I ever had. There I was holding my own with Johnny Carson. I knew then I could hit big league pitching," he noted in a 1980 *People* article. After only three *Tonight Show* appearances, Letterman was asked by the show's producer to serve as occasional guest host—a role that Letterman would fill more than twenty times in the next year. His frequent

spots on the show gave rise to speculation that he would be the next host when Carson retired and immediately catapulted Letterman to show business prominence. Latham quotes Letterman's reaction to these sudden and exciting changes: "In California, I was literally living in a one-room apartment on stilts in Laurel Canyon, and I had hosted *The Tonight Show* a couple of times, and then I went away. When I got back to my house in Laurel Canyon, I had mail from people all over the country, and they had all sent clippings carrying the same wire release saying I would be the next Johnny Carson.... The week before, I was having trouble getting enough money to have the clutch in my truck replaced, and the next week I'm getting clippings saying I'm the next Johnny Carson. It just made me laugh."

NBC-TV executives had much of the same confidence in Letterman's success that the comedian's agent, Jack Rollins, had felt when he signed a contract with the rising star in 1977. Rollins told Barol, "The format was hard to guess, but the medium wasn't. David has a readiness to have things bubble out of him. That's an enormous strength in television where everything is quick and short." Television was obviously where Letterman belonged, and NBC-TV was willing to help him find the right kind of show. In 1979, the company signed Letterman to a two-year contract. When it became apparent that Carson would not be leaving the *Tonight Show* early and Letterman would not be needed to fill his position, NBC-TV attempted to devise a show for Letterman, first creating the doomed *Leave It to Dave* show, which never aired.

In 1980, Letterman was given his own daytime talk show, *The David Letterman Show,* which was envisioned by NBC-TV executives as a family-oriented show filled with helpful household hints. What NBC-TV and its audience got, however, was a comedy style that television had never before experienced. Letterman's show, broadcast live from New York City, featured techniques that would become standard style in his later and more successful *Late Night* program. Comedian Merrill Markoe, Letterman's girlfriend since his 1977 divorce from his wife Michelle, was hired as headwriter for the show. Together Letterman and Markoe devised such memorable segments as "Stupid Pet Tricks," trips through the NBC halls in search of company president Fred Silverman or the nearest vending machine, and around-town reports on topics such as places that display signs for "The World's Best Coffee." Letterman utilized his audience as much as his small cast of regular performers for material in what *Newsweek* reviewer Harry F. Waters deemed "a laudable, if somewhat erratic, TV departure."

Reviews of the show were generally positive, but almost everyone agreed that the morning time slot of *The David Letterman Show* was inappropriate. Waters applauded the "inspired satirical mischief" of Letterman's program. *New York Times* contributor Tony Schwartz declared that "Letterman aficionados should be able to argue a case study in faulty scheduling. It is hard to imagine that there is not an audience, probably not housewives and perhaps late-night, for a talk-show host whom critics have called one of the cleverest, quickest, and least predictable comedians around." Letterman acknowledged the problem of selling his brand of humor to the mid-morning audience in a quote in *The David Letterman Story:* "In truth, I'm not sure that this show is something you want to watch at ten in the morning. But I decided I would try to do the things I like to do. It was always my feeling that if you do a show as interesting as you can make it, and as funny as you can make it, you could put it up anytime and people will watch it." Due to poor ratings the show was canceled after only four months. But by its final episode on October 24, 1980, Letterman had gained a loyal following and a promising reputation. Not only did Letterman earn two Emmys (for best host and writing) for his first show, but NBC-TV gave him a one-year holding contract, in which he promised not to sign with any other network.

It's Only Television: The *Late Night* Show

In just more than a year the company offered Letterman the 12:30 to 1:30 morning time slot formerly held by Tom Snyder's *The Tomorrow Show*. Entitled *Late Night with David Letterman*, the new show adapted the format and spirit of *The David Letterman Show* and added a few more elements of the traditional talk show, at least in appearances. Like his talk-show idol, Johnny Carson, Letterman begins his program with a short monologue, followed by an exchange of banter with band leader Paul Shaffer. Letterman then retires to his desk for a few regular routines such as presenting the evening's "Top Ten List," a list that *Late Night* writer Steve O'Donnell characterized in a 1990 *People* article as "10 different punch lines" to an opening line or category such as "Top Ten Campaign Pledges that George Bush Has Broken" or "Top Ten Fears of Snuggle, the Fabric Softening Bear." Once a week Letterman will also read

viewer mail and present the responses that he and his staff of writers have concocted. After preliminaries of this sort, the host welcomes a series of guests as well as a musical or comedy act. A basic outline of the show, however, reveals little of the energy that Letterman and his *Late Night* crew fill the show with four nights each week, causing amused, but somewhat baffled reviewers to consistently use terms such as "unpredictable" to describe the kind of comedy they witness there. Many critics have shared the opinion of Jane Hall, who declared, "*Late Night with David Letterman* may be the hippest show on network television." Within a few years of its 1982 debut, *Late Night* was in fact drawing top ratings across the country.

Letterman uses the talk-show model as only the most basic starting point and takes the program in any new direction he sees fit. The question "what if?" is frequently asked and indulged by the *Late Night* writing and production crew. Some evenings Letterman may come out for a special demonstration of one of his famous "suits," such as "The Suit of Suet," which he once wore while entering a pen of hungry barnyard animals, or "The Velcro Suit" in which he bounced off a trampoline and onto a Velcro wall (where he stuck). Other viewer favorites include the segment in which Letterman dropped an assortment of objects (a television, a watermelon, etc.) off a five-story building and another where he crushed items in a hydraulic press to see what they would look like afterward. Letterman makes no apologies for this type of primitive entertainment. As he likes to remind his audience, "It's only television, folks." He further describes the type of humor created for the show in *Newsweek:* "We do a lot of what we call 'found comedy.' Things you find in newspapers. Viewer mail. The fact that January actually *is* National Soup Month, so we're saluting soup all this month. I don't know if this stuff is more funny, but I do know that I feel more comfortable dealing with something that's actually there than with some lame premise we cook up."

Esquire contributor Tom Shales asserted that "David Letterman is the next step in the evolution of the talk-show host and is multidextrous at making something out of nothing, at making raving inconsequentiality terribly entertaining, by reeling in the essential evanescence of television." Letterman summarized his style of comedy-by-exaggeration in *Rolling Stone:* "You have to pretend that you're bigger than you are, that you're enjoying it more than you really are. It all has to be blown up, and you have to say and do things that you

Letterman talks with his guest, *Tonight Show* host Johnny Carson. *Late Night* is one of only a few talk shows to feature Carson as a guest.

wouldn't normally have the scantest opinion on. It's just show business, you know. We're just trying to sell Pintos here.''

Perhaps the people who get caught most frequently in Letterman's attempt to undermine typical TV protocol are his guests. *Late Night with David Letterman* books a wide assortment of people for its shows, both celebrities and more obscure oddities such as the curator of a nut museum and a man who collects old food in a drawer. No matter who the guest, Letterman is interested in combining elements that will lead to a spontaneous comic event. This may involve asking Mariel Hemingway to clean fish, introducing President Jimmy Carter to a bewildered stage technician, or convincing Teri Garr to take a shower off-camera while Letterman continues their conversation. Even without elaborate set-ups, the host finds a way to make the most of guests and situations. He reflected in Hall's *People* article: "When a guest is being strange, I have the feeling that I'm watching a live

grenade being rolled into a restaurant at brunch. Most TV is totally unsurprising. On our show we want viewers at home to look at each other and say, 'What the hell was that?' We want to pierce that flat TV screen.''

Many reviewers noted that in the early days of *Late Night,* Letterman's weak spot was interviewing. *TV Guide* critic Robert MacKenzie, who appreciated Letterman's ''restless, eccentric style,'' also declared outright that ''he is a rotten interviewer.'' James Wolcott in *New York* noted that Letterman seemed to prefer the comedy segments to interviews. ''Letterman has made it apparent that he's far happier with toys and stunts than with the cut and thrust of grown-up talk,'' observed Wolcott. Letterman conceded in a *Rolling Stone* article that his interviewing techniques have required some work. ''I'm not really suited for interviewing. . . . And then finally, someone just came out and said, 'He can't do interviews.'. . . then I started looking at tapes and I thought, 'Oh yeah. I can't. I'm not

Ted Koppel here.' So I worked really hard to do nice interviews. I spent a lot of time researching the guests, which I think overall helped, but when it comes right down to it, I wasn't hired to be a great interviewer.''

Late Night's host has also gained a reputation for provoking guests who arrive on the show expecting the usual easy questions about their career. Instead Letterman tends to ask questions that are just as likely to yield anger as a laugh, as in the case of actress Nastassja Kinski, who left the show in tears after Letterman repeatedly teased her about her gravity-defying hairstyle. In a similar situation, however, boxing promoter Don King (who also sports an unusual coiffure) responded good-naturedly to Letterman's rather blunt question: ''What's the deal with your hair?'' Many guests have learned, like *Late Night* favorite Jane Pauley told *People*, ''On this show I know I'm not going to be treated with the respect due my position. Most likely I'm going to be embarrassed within an inch of my life.'' But, as actress Teri Garr explained in *People*, ''David is 'mean' like my brother was. That's not really mean.''

Some celebrities note that their secret to a successful appearance on *Late Night* has been to join in the spirit of the show, as actress Cybill Sheperd demonstrated by once wearing a towel on stage rather than the dress she had sent to the studios—because Letterman had been displaying it all week on the show to promote her visit. Barry Sand, producer of *Late Night*, told *People* that the best guests are people who ''understand the show and come ready to play.'' Letterman asserts that it is the outrageous side of his guests that he finds funny. ''I want a guest to come in and derail me. Sometimes when I swarm a person, it's only because it's not going the way I hoped, and my instinct is to try to make it funny,'' he maintained in *People*.

Reviewers point to a host of reasons to explain the popularity of Letterman and *Late Night*. *Time* contributor Richard Corliss declared that Letterman is the kind of host that viewers are comfortable with: ''He seems to have been created for and by television, working within a narrow band of emotions, charming viewers with his unflappable attitude rather than with quick reaction, political satire, and confrontation comedy.'' MacKenzie dubbed him ''one of the more interesting talents to come along in a decade.'' A *People* reviewer declared that Letterman's show is fun to watch because he is a ''talk show host without fear'' who ''gleefully lets people make fools of themselves.''

Shales maintained that Letterman has tapped into a new source of humor: ''*Late Night with David Letterman* now hones the cutting edge of American humor (the way *Saturday Night Live* did in the Seventies).... Letterman is so far ahead of the pack that he's his own pack. He is that which wears best with daily exposure: a reluctant star but an instinctually ingratiating presence. He is ... attuned to the peculiar rhythms and textures and tonalities of television.'' Barol described the appeal Letterman has particularly with younger people, stating that ''in David Letterman, young adult TV viewers have found a comic temperament that matches their own—hip and ironic, at once silly and knowing.'' As a *People* contributor noted: ''The audience has to know what's out in order to be in.

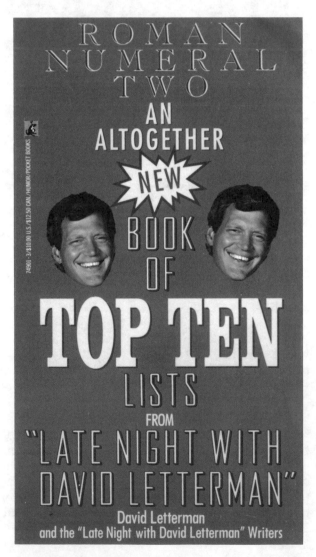

This 1991 book collects a number of Letterman's infamous ''Top Ten Lists,'' which cover everything from George Bush's broken campaign promises to the Snuggle Bear's greatest fears.

All his sight gags and references are acutely generational."

Letterman mocks television and its commercialism with jokes like presenting individually wrapped cornflakes as a great new consumer product or creating a list of the top ten soups that the Campbell's company opted against (Cream of Gristle and Sideburns and Barley were among the top contenders). These media and advertising parodies tap into the experiences of the generations of people that grew up watching television. Letterman's humor is so popular that his style and jokes have surfaced in a number of places in the media. Frequently his top ten lists can be read in newspapers and magazines; some of the lists have been compiled in the bestselling books *The Late Night with David Letterman Book of Top Ten Lists* and *An Altogether New Book of Top Ten Lists: From "Late Night with David Letterman."* Other talk show hosts have attempted to do *Late-Night*-like remote comedy segments or have used his roaming-the-hall techniques to get a laugh. While some critics have suggested that even talk-show king Johnny Carson tried to pick up some of the comic's tricks, Letterman feels just the opposite, telling *Rolling Stone* that many of his ideas come from earlier performers, particularly Carson. "I do things on the show every night, and I think I got this from Carson. Eighty percent of what we do, I can show you where it was done before. Steve Allen took the camera on the street. We do stupid pet tricks, Johnny Carson has a singing-dog contest once a year. It's the same kind of deal, and there are nights when I do something, and I almost hesitate to do it, because I know dead sure that's a gesture or a look or a kind of remark Carson might have made."

When *Time*'s Richard Corliss asked Letterman in 1989 what he would like to do in the future, the *Late Night* host replied, "Well, this is it. All I ever wanted to do is to have a television show. And I've got one. So from that standpoint I've succeeded. I also think the *Tonight* show is the only other show I would do. I think once this show is canceled or once I get fired, you'll never see me again in another TV show of my own. It's just too much work, too heartbreaking, and if you've done it once, congratulations." Letterman's desire to become the permanent host of the *Tonight Show* was thwarted when Johnny Carson finally retired in 1992 and Jay Leno was picked as the new host of the program. This turn of events led to a number of rumors that Letterman, in an attempt to get an earlier time slot, would leave NBC-TV for another network or go into syndication. Letterman, however, did not make a public statement that supported these claims. It is generally acknowledged by show business officials and observers that the huge success of the *Late Night* show has given Letterman the clout to design his own projects if he so desires, and other networks are eager to attract the bankable star. According to *Detroit Free Press* contributor Bill Carter, Letterman's iconoclastic humor on *Late Night* has made him "the most wanted man in television."

■ Works Cited

Barol, Bill, "A Fine Madness at the Midnight Hour," *Newsweek*, February 3, 1986, pp. 46-53.

Carter, Bill, "Letterman Gossip is Hot," *Detroit Free Press*, September 3, 1992, p. 5G.

Corliss, Richard, "And Now, Fernwood 4-Real," *Time*, March 22, 1982, p. 69.

"David Letterman," *People*, summer, 1989, p. 74.

Gilman, Tom, and Alan Carter, "And the No. 1 Reason David Letterman Keeps Reading the Top 10 List—Well, It's Funnier Than His Monologue," *People*, August 27, 1990, pp. 51-54.

Hall, Jane, "Late Night Letterman," *People*, July 14, 1986, pp. 88-92.

Hirschberg, Lynn, "David Letterman and the Gnat Who Sank the Love Boat," *Rolling Stone*, June 20, 1985, pp. 25-30, 82, 84.

Review of *Late Night with David Letterman*, *People*, June 4, 1984, p. 11.

Latham, Caroline, *The David Letterman Story*, F. Watts, 1987.

MacKenzie, Robert, review of *Late Night with David Letterman*, *TV Guide*, March 27, 1982, p. 46.

Schwartz, Tony, review of *The David Letterman Show*, *New York Times*, September 17, 1980.

Shales, Tom, "David Letterman and the Power of Babble," *Esquire*, November 11, 1986, pp. 144, 146, 148, 150-151.

Shaw, Bill, "David Letterman Could Succeed Johnny Carson, but He Frets That the Last Laugh Would Be on Him," *People*, February 4, 1980, pp. 45-46.

Waters, Harry F., "David in the Daytime," *Newsweek*, July 7, 1980, p. 62.

Wolcott, James, "Dead Letter," *New York*, May 30, 1983, pp. 69-70.

Zoglin, Richard, "He's No Johnny Carson," *Time*, February 6, 1989, pp. 66-68.

■ **For More Information See**

BOOKS

Breckman, Andy, and others, *Late Night with David Letterman: The Book*, edited by Merrill Markoe, Villard Books, 1985.

PERIODICALS

Esquire, September, 1991, pp. 141-146.

New York, January 19, 1987, pp. 36-45.
New York Times, July 27, 1986.
People, August 27, 1990, pp. 51-54.
Rolling Stone, November 3, 1988.
TV Guide, August 1, 1992, pp. 8-11.°

—Sketch by Marie Ellavich

Robert Ludlum

■ Personal

Previously wrote under pseudonyms Jonathan Ryder and Michael Shepherd; born May 25, 1927, in New York, NY; son of George Hartford (a businessman) and Margaret (Wadsworth) Ludlum; married Mary Ryducha (an actress), March 31, 1951; children: Michael, Jonathan, Glynis. *Education:* Wesleyan University, B.A., 1951. *Politics:* Independent.

■ Addresses

Home—Naples, FL. *Agent*—Henry Morrison, Box 235, Bedford Hills, NY 10507.

■ Career

Writer, 1971—. Actor on Broadway and on television, 1952-60; North Jersey Playhouse, Fort Lee, NJ, producer, 1957-60; producer in New York City, 1960-69; Playhouse-on-the-Mall, Paramus, NJ, producer, 1960-70. *Military service:* U.S. Marine Corps, 1944-46. *Member:* Authors League of America, American Federation of Television and Radio Artists, Screen Actors Guild.

■ Awards, Honors

New England Professor of Drama Award, 1951; awards and grants from American National Theatre and Academy, 1959, and from Actors' Equity Association and William C. Whitney Foundation, 1960; Scroll of Achievement, American National Theatre and Academy, 1960.

■ Writings

The Scarlatti Inheritance, World Publishing, 1971.
The Osterman Weekend, World Publishing, 1972.
The Matlock Paper, Dial, 1973.
(Under pseudonym Jonathan Ryder) *Trevayne*, Delacorte, 1973.
(Under pseudonym Jonathan Ryder) *The Cry of the Halidon*, Delacorte, 1974.
The Rhinemann Exchange, Dial, 1974.
(Under pseudonym Michael Shepherd) *The Road to Gandolfo*, Dial, 1975, reprinted under name Robert Ludlum, Bantam, 1982.
The Gemini Contenders, Dial, 1976.
The Chancellor Manuscript, Dial, 1977.
The Holcroft Covenant, Richard Marek, 1978.
The Matarese Circle, Richard Marek, 1979.
The Bourne Identity, Richard Marek, 1980.
The Parsifal Mosaic, Random House, 1982.
The Aquitaine Progression, Random House, 1984.
The Bourne Supremacy, Random House, 1986.
The Icarus Agenda, Random House, 1988.
The Bourne Ultimatum, Random House, 1990.
The Road to Omaha, Random House, 1992.

■ Adaptations

The Rhinemann Exchange was adapted as a television miniseries by NBC in March, 1977; *The Osterman Weekend* was filmed by EMI in 1980; *The Bourne Supremacy*, read by Michael Prichard, was released on cassette tape by Books on Tape, 1986; an abridged version of *The Bourne Identity*, read by Darren McGavin, was released on cassette tape by Bantam, 1987, and is also being adapted for television; *The Icarus Agenda*, read by Prichard, was released on cassette by Books on Tape, 1988; *The Bourne Identity* was adapted for television, c. 1989; *The Bourne Ultimatum*, read by Prichard, was released on cassette by Books on Tape, 1990; *The Road to Omaha*, read by Joseph Campanella, was released by Random House, 1992; *The Scarlatti Inheritance* was filmed by Universal Pictures.

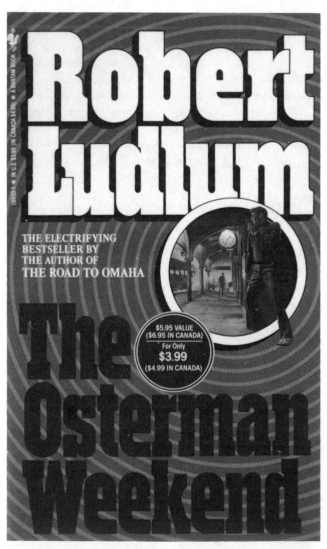

John Tanner, a television reporter, gets in over his head when he tries to help the CIA stop a possible conspiracy in this 1972 novel.

■ Sidelights

Suspense novelist Robert Ludlum "has his share of unkind critics who complain of implausible plots, leaden prose, and, as a caustic reviewer once sneered, an absence of 'redeeming literary values to balance the vulgar sensationalism,'" Susan Baxter and Mark Nichols noted in *Maclean's*. "But harsh critical words have not prevented Robert Ludlum . . . from becoming one of the most widely read and wealthiest authors in the world." In fact, with sales of his books averaging 5.5 million copies each, Ludlum is "one of the most popular living authors [writing] in the English language," Baxter and Nichols concluded.

Authorship came as a second career for Ludlum, who worked in the theater and found success as a producer before writing his first novel at age 42. As a schoolboy in 1941, Ludlum ran away to New York and won a part in a traveling production of *Junior Miss*. When the play arrived in Detroit, Ludlum saw his opportunity to fulfill another dream—to join combat in World War II—and crossed the border into Canada where he attempted to sign up with that country's air force under an assumed name. Although he was caught and returned to school, he later served with the Marines in the South Pacific. After completing his tour of duty, Ludlum enrolled at Wesleyan University, where he continued to act and met his wife-to-be, actress Mary Ryducha. The two were married the year he graduated; both embarked on acting careers.

After performing in New England repertory theaters, landing some small parts on Broadway and appearing in several 1950s television dramas, Ludlum made the switch from actor to producer. His most notable production, Bill Manhoff's *The Owl and the Pussycat*, featured then unknown actor Alan Alda, who later gained fame for his role in the television series, *M°A°S°H*. The play was performed at Playhouse-on-the-Mall in Paramus, New Jersey, the country's first theater in a shopping center, which Ludlum opened in 1960. After serving as producer at the Playhouse for ten years, Ludlum found himself bored and frustrated with the pressures of theater work. Finally, he gave in to his wife's admonition to give writing a try and fulfilled yet another of his life's ambitions.

The Scarlatti Inheritance, Ludlum's first novel, was written around an old story idea and outline, drafted years earlier and finally fleshed out when he left the theater. Based on Ludlum's curiosity at the wealth of one group of Germans during that

Suspected conspirators gather at their friend John Tanner's house for a suspenseful weekend in this 1980 movie adaptation of *The Osterman Weekend.*

country's economic collapse and skyrocketing inflation following World War I, *The Scarlatti Inheritance* follows a group of financiers, some American, who bankroll Hitler's Third Reich. The book set the pattern for Ludlum's career: its story was one of espionage and corruption, and it was a bestseller. Criticism of *The Scarlatti Inheritance* also foreshadowed that of future works. It was described by Patricia L. Skarda in *Dictionary of Literary Biography Yearbook: 1982* as having a "somewhat erratic pace and occasionally melodramatic characterizations" but nonetheless "a thrilling, compelling tale"—pronouncements typical of each of Ludlum's novels.

Career Gets Rolling with *Osterman Weekend*

In his next work, *The Osterman Weekend*, readers find danger much closer to home. A television reporter, John Tanner, is convinced by the CIA that his friends are involved in a conspiracy to control the world economy. As they gather for a weekend at his place, Tanner attempts to help the CIA gather evidence, but finds himself in over his head when his wife and children are threatened. Though the book's ending is considered disappointing by several reviewers, William B. Hill, writing in *Best Sellers*, noted, "If the ending is a bit weak, it is chiefly because it lets the rider down off a very high horse." Skarda pointed out that the story "exposes the inadequacies of American intelligence operations and our deepest fears that our friends cannot be trusted." Government agents again use a civilian as investigator in a situation beyond his expertise in *The Matlock Paper*. Professor Matlock is pushed "into an untenable and dangerous situation" while snooping around campus for information on a group of crime bosses, Kelly J. Fitzpatrick related in *Best Sellers*. "The climax is effective and leaves the reader wondering, 'Can it be so?'" Newgate Callendar countered in the *New York Times Book Review*, "The basic situation is unreal—indeed, it's unbelievable—but

#1

NEW YORK TIMES BESTSELLER

ROBERT

LUDLUM

$5.95 VALUE
($6.95 IN CANADA)
For Only
$3.99
($4.99 IN CANADA)

THE

BOURNE

IDENTITY

The first of a series of books featuring the spy character Jason Bourne, this 1980 bestseller has its protagonist running for his life as he searches for his identity.

a good writer can make the reader suspend his disbelief, and Ludlum is a good writer."

Trevayne and *The Cry of the Halidon,* both written under the pseudonym Jonathan Ryder, feature protagonists who discover they were hired not for their skills, but in hopes that they would be too dumb to realize the truth about their employers. Andrew Trevayne, appointed to investigate spending by the U.S. Defense Department, uncovers a company so powerful that even the president of the United States is controlled by it. "There is no doubt that big business exerts an inordinate amount of pressure," Callendar contended in a *New York Times Book Review.* "But how much pressure? Who is really running the country?" Reviewing *The Cry of the Halidon,* in which a

young geologist is sent to Jamaica to conduct an industrial survey and winds up in the cross fire of British Intelligence, the corporation that hired him, and various underground factions, Callendar disparaged Ludlum's "rather crude and obvious writing style," and commented, "[Ludlum] is not very good at suggesting real characters, and his hero is a cutout composite of a number of sources." A reviewer for *Publishers Weekly* found that, early on in *The Cry of the Halidon,* "cleverness ceases to look like a virtue and becomes an irritant. If the writing were as rich or subtle as the plot is involved the reader might more happily stay the course . . ., but the writing is in fact rather bare." Ludlum's final pseudonymous offering (this time writing as Michael Shepherd), *The Road to Gandolfo,* is "a strange, lurching amalgam of thriller and fantasy," Henri C. Veit contended in the *Library Journal.* Involving the Pope, the Mafia, and the U.S. Army, the book is intended to be funny, but falls short, Veit continued. A *Publishers Weekly* similarly noted that the book "comes crammed with zaniness and playful characters, but, unhappily, neither asset produces comedy or the black humor indictment of the military mind the author intended."

The Rhinemann Exchange contains "one extremely ingenious plot gimmick," according to Callendar in another *New York Times Book Review,* in which the United States and Germany arrange a trade—industrial diamonds for Germany, a weapons guidance system for the United States. Despite the author's "commonplace and vulgar style apparently much relished by his vast audience," Veit predicted in a *Library Journal* review that the book would be a success. In a review of the audio version of *The Rhinemann Exchange,* a *Publishers Weekly* contributor believed Ludlum fans "will find exactly what they're looking for—in a format already quite familiar."

A secret with devastating consequences, described by Irma Pascal Heldman in the *New York Times Book Review* as "absolutely within the realms of authenticity and fascinating to contemplate," is the key to *The Gemini Contenders.* Twin brothers, compelled by their father's deathbed wish to find the hidden vault containing a volatile document, unleash the secret on the world. Despite criticizing the plot, characters, and period detail of *The Gemini Contenders,* reviewer T. J. Binyon commented in the *Times Literary Supplement* that Ludlum "has the ability to tell a story in such a way as to keep even the fastidious reader unwillingly absorbed."

In *The Chancellor Manuscript* Ludlum returns to remaking history, as he did in *The Scarlatti Inheritance.* J. Edgar Hoover's death is found to be an assassination, not the result of natural causes as was previously believed. The murder was carried out to prevent Hoover from releasing his secret files, which, *Christian Science Monitor*'s Barbara Phillips noted, "contain enough damaging information to ruin the lives of every man, woman and child in the nation." A group of prominent citizens join forces to retrieve the files but find half have already been stolen. An unsuspecting decoy is deployed, as in many other Ludlum stories, to lead the group to the thieves. The message of *The Chancellor Manuscript* is familiar to Ludlum fans, as the book "seems to justify our worst nightmares of what really goes on in the so-called Intelligence Community in Washington," Richard Freedman maintained in the *New York Times Book Review*.

That Lucrative Ludlum Style

The key elements of Ludlum's books—corruption in high places, elaborate secret plans, and unsuspecting civilians drawn into the fray—are what keep Ludlum fans waiting for his next offering. His writing is characterized by the liberal use of exclamation points, italics, sentence fragments, and rhetorical questions, as in *The Matlock Paper*: "Where were you when men like myself—in *every institution*—faced the very real prospects of closing our doors! You were safe; we *sheltered* you. . . . And our appeals went unanswered. There wasn't room for our needs. . . . What was *left?* Endowments? Dwindling! There are other, more *viable tax incentives!* . . . Foundations? Small-minded tyrants—smaller allocations! . . . The Government? *Blind! Obscene!* Its priorities are bought! Or returned in kind at the ballot box! We had no funds; we bought no votes! For us, the system had collapsed! It was finished!" While some critics describe his writing style as crude, others acknowledge that the style is popular with millions of readers and has proven difficult to duplicate, leaving Ludlum with little copycat competition. Still, reviewers often point to Ludlum's use of mixed metaphors and illogical statements as serious flaws in his books. Horror novelist Stephen King, in a somewhat tongue-in-cheek review of *The Parsifal Mosaic* for the *Washington Post Book World*, highlighted some of Ludlum's "strange, wonderful, and almost Zen-like thoughts: 'We've got . . . a confluence of beneficial prerogatives.' 'What I know is still very operative.' 'I'll get you your cover. But not two men. I think a couple would be better.'"

As Ludlum gained a popular following, back-handed compliments for his work became common: critics often display frustration at their ineffectiveness in swaying public opinion of Ludlum's books. "Whether reviewers are universally savage or effusive seems irrelevant: the book is bound to be a best seller," Richard Harwood grumbled in the *Washington Post Book World*. "*The Bourne Identity* . . . is already on both the national and *Washington Post* best-seller lists and the damned thing won't officially be published [for three more days]. So much for the power of the press." The story of Bourne, a spy who awakens in a doctor's office with amnesia, is played out as a remarkable number of killers and organizations attempt to finish him off before he realizes his true identity. "Some of Mr. Ludlum's previous novels were so convoluted they should have been packaged with bags of

In this 1986 sequel to *The Bourne Identity*, Ludlum presents another intricately woven plot in which Bourne must face his past to save his kidnapped wife.

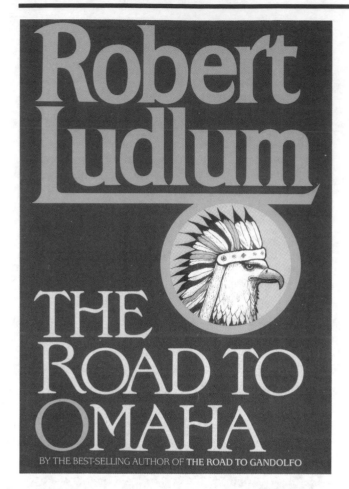

The heroes of *The Road to Gandolfo* return in this 1992 novel to fight the government for land that legally belongs to an Indian tribe.

bread crumbs to help readers keep track of the plot lines," Peter Andrews mused in the *New York Times Book Review*. "But *The Bourne Identity* is a Ludlum story at its most severely plotted, and for me its most effective." A sequel, *The Bourne Supremacy*, forces Bourne to face his past when his wife is kidnapped. The final story in the "Bourne" trilogy, *The Bourne Ultimatum*, finds Bourne drawn into one last battle with his arch-enemy, the Jackal. The *Los Angeles Times Book Review*'s Don G. Campbell praised the third "Bourne" book as an example of "how it *should* be done," concluding that "in the pulse-tingling style that began so many years ago with *The Scarlatti Inheritance*, we are caught up irretrievably."

"The Ludlum phenomenon continues to defeat me," yet another perplexed critic, Robin W. Winks, asserted in a *New Republic* review of *The Parsifal Mosaic*. As the now-familiar spy story unfolds, a woman comes back from the dead and a spy in the White House threatens humanity's continued existence. "Certainly, millions of en-

tranced readers tap their feet in time to his fiction, and I'm positive this new adventure will send his legions of fans dancing out into the streets," Evan Hunter remarked in the *New York Times Book Review*. "Me? I must be tone-deaf."

A world takeover is again imminent in *The Aquitaine Progression*, this time at the hands of five military figures. "Ludlum's hero, Joel Converse, learns of a plot by generals in the United States, Germany, France, Israel and South Africa to spawn violent demonstrations. Once the violence bursts out of hand, the generals plan to step in and take over," Charles P. Wallace wrote in the *Los Angeles Times Book Review*. *The Icarus Agenda* features a similar plot. This time, five wealthy, powerful figures arrange the election of the next United States president. "There is a sufficient amount of energy and suspense present in *The Icarus Agenda* to remind the reader why Mr. Ludlum's novels are best sellers," Julie Johnson commented in the *New York Times Book Review*. "Ludlum is light-years beyond his literary competition in piling plot twist upon plot twist," Peter L. Robertson commented in the *Tribune Books*, "until the mesmerized reader is held captive, willing to accept any wayward, if occasionally implausible, plotting device." In a more recent offering, *The Road to Omaha*, Ludlum departs from the seriousness of his espionage thrillers with a follow-up to *The Road to Gandolfo* that continues that novel's farcical tone. The Hawk and Sam, Ludlum's heroes in *Gandolfo*, return to fight the government for a plot of land legally belonging to an Indian tribe. In a review of the audio version of *The Road to Omaha*, a *Publishers Weekly* reviewer noted, "Hardcore Ludlum fans may be taken aback at first, but they stand to be won over in the listening."

Loyal Following for "Ludlums"

Journalist Bob Woodward, writing in the *Washington Post Book World*, summarized the media's view of Ludlum in a review of *The Icarus Agenda*: "Ludlum justifiably has a loyal following. Reviews of most of his previous books are critical but conclude, grudgingly, that he has another inevitable bestseller." In a review of *The Bourne Supremacy*, *New York Review of Books* contributor Thomas R. Edwards described the typical Ludlum novel, what he calls "a ludlum," as "a long, turgidly written, and frantically overplotted novel, the literary equivalent of seriously wielding a plumber's helper." Dick Lochte, reviewing *The Bourne Supremacy* for the *Los Angeles Times Book Review*, hoped for a savior to rescue Ludlum's readers from their hero: "Couldn't Random House find an editor with a slight tendency toward schizophrenia who, with the proper manipulation, would develop a suicidal alter ego to do battle with a powerful, best-selling author for the sake of readers the world over?"

With so many popular novels, even his most ardent critics cannot deny that Ludlum is doing something right, although they hasten to emphasize what they believe he does wrong. One *Washington Post* critic's comment, "It's a lousy book. So I stayed up until 3 a.m. to finish it," is a frequently heard refrain. Still, the bottom line is in Ludlum's favor: readers have voiced their approval in sales figures, despite the best efforts of reviewers who wield a mighty plumber's helper in Ludlum's direction. As Baxter and Nichols noted in *Maclean's*, "For all his imperfections, Ludlum manages—by pumping suspense into every twist and turn in his tangled plots and by demanding sympathy for well-meaning protagonists afflicted by outrageous adversity—to keep millions of readers frantically turning his pages."

■ Works Cited

Andrews, Peter, "Momentum Is Everything," *New York Times Book Review*, March 30, 1980, p. 7.

Baxter, Susan, and Mark Nichols, "Robert Ludlum and the Realm of Evil," *Maclean's*, April 9, 1984, pp. 50-52.

Binyon, T. J., review of *The Gemini Contenders*, *Times Literary Supplement*, October 1, 1976, p. 1260.

Callendar, Newgate, review of *Trevayne*, *New York Times Book Review*, January 28, 1973, p. 20.

Callendar, Newgate, review of *The Matlock Paper*, *New York Times Book Review*, May 6, 1973, p. 41.

Callendar, Newgate, review of *The Cry of the Halidon*, *New York Times Book Review*, August 4, 1974, p. 26.

Callendar, Newgate, review of *The Rhinemann Exchange*, *New York Times Book Review*, October 27, 1974, p. 56.

Campbell, Don G., "Storytellers: New in April," *Los Angeles Times Book Review*, March 18, 1990, p. 8.

Review of *The Cry of the Halidon*, *Publishers Weekly*, April 8, 1974, p. 76.

Edwards, Thomas R., "Boom at the Top," *New York Review of Books*, May 8, 1986, pp. 12-13.

Fitzpatrick, Kelly J., review of *The Matlock Paper*, *Best Sellers*, April 15, 1973, p. 41.

Freedman, Richard, review of *The Chancellor Manuscript*, *New York Times Book Review*, March 27, 1977, p. 8.

Harwood, Richard, "Hooked on the Lure of Ludlum," *Washington Post Book World*, March 23, 1980, p. 3.

Heldman, Irma Pascal, review of *The Gemini Contenders*, *New York Times Book Review*, March 28, 1976, p. 18.

Hill, William B., review of *The Osterman Weekend*, *Best Sellers*, April, 1972, p. 5.

Hunter, Evan, "Reincarnation and Annihilation," *New York Times Book Review*, March 21, 1982, p. 11.

King, Stephen, "The Ludlum Attraction," *Washington Post Book World*, March 7, 1982, p. 1.

Johnson, Julie, review of *The Icarus Agenda*, *New York Times Book Review*, March 27, 1988, p. 16.

Lochte, Dick, review of *The Bourne Supremacy*, *Los Angeles Times Book Review*, March 23, 1986, p. 3.

Ludlum, Robert, *The Matlock Paper*, Dial, 1973.

Phillips, Barbara, "'Chancellor Manuscript': New Ludlum Thriller," *Christian Science Monitor*, March 31, 1977, p. 31.

Review of *The Rhinemann Exchange*, *Publishers Weekly*, March 1, 1991, pp. 49-50.

Review of *The Road to Gandolfo*, *Publishers Weekly*, February 10, 1975, p. 52.

Review of *The Road to Omaha*, *Publishers Weekly*, March 2, 1992.

Robertson, Peter L., "Ludlum's Lightening Pace Keeps 'Icarus' Flying High," *Tribune Books* (Chicago), February 28, 1988, Section 14, p. 7.

Skarda, Patricia L., "Robert Ludlum," *Dictionary of Literary Biography Yearbook: 1982*, edited by Richard Ziegfeld, Gale, 1983, pp. 305-316.

Veit, Henri C., review of *The Rhinemann Exchange*, *Library Journal*, October 1, 1974, p. 2504.

Veit, Henri C., review of *The Road to Gandolfo*, *Library Journal*, April 1, 1975, pp. 694-695.

Wallace, Charles P., "The Military Minds and a World Obeys," *Los Angeles Times Book Review*, March 11, 1984, p. 3.

Winks, Robin W., review of *The Parsifal Mosaic*, *New Republic*, September 20, 1982, p. 43.

Woodward, Bob, review of *The Icarus Agenda*, *Washington Post Book World*, February 21, 1988, p. 1.

■ For More Information See

PERIODICALS

New Republic, November 25, 1981, p. 38.

New York, May 9, 1988, pp. 74-75.
New Yorker, June 20, 1988, pp. 90-92.
New York Times, March 13, 1978, p. C19.

New York Times Book Review, April 8, 1979, p. 14;
April 22, 1984, p. 14; March 9, 1986, p. 12.°

—*Sketch by Deborah A. Stanley*

Penny Marshall

■ Personal

Born October 15, 1943, in Bronx, NY; daughter of Anthony W. (an industrial film maker) and Marjorie Irene (a dance instructor; maiden name, Ward) Marshall; married Michael Henry (divorced); married Rob Reiner (an actor and director), April, 1971 (divorced, 1979); children: (first marriage) Tracy Lee. *Education:* Attended the University of New Mexico, 1961-64.

■ Career

Actress and director. Worked variously as a secretary and as a dance instructor; actress in summer stock, including an appearance in *Oklahoma!*, and choreographer at the Albuquerque Light Opera, mid-1960s. Television debut on *The Danny Thomas Hour*, National Broadcasting Company, Inc. (NBC-TV), 1967-68; played Myrna Turner on *The Odd Couple*, American Broadcasting Companies, Inc. (ABC-TV), 1971-75; played Janice Dreyfuss on *Friends and Lovers*, Columbia Broadcasting System, Inc. (CBS-TV), 1974-75; and played Laverne De Fazio on *Laverne and Shirley*, ABC-TV, 1976-83. Appeared in television pilots, including *Evil*

Roy Slade, NBC-TV, 1972, and *Wives*, CBS-TV, 1975. Director of episodes of television series, including *Working Stiffs*, CBS-TV, 1979; *Laverne and Shirley*, ABC-TV; and *The Tracey Ullman Show*, Fox, 1986. Appeared as a guest on numerous television series, including *The Super, The Bob Newhart Show, Happy Days, Saturday Night Live, The Comedy Zone, Chico and the Man, The Mary Tyler Moore Show, Blansky's Beauties, The Tonight Show, Dinah, The Mike Douglas Show, Danny Thomas Hour, The Merv Griffin Show, $20,000 Pyramid, Original Amateur Hour, Heaven Help Us,* and *The Simpsons*. Appeared on television specials, including *The Barry Manilow Special, Battle of the Network Stars, Circus of the Stars, General Electric's All-Star Anniversary, Celebrity Football Classic, Lily for President, Bugs Bunny-Looney Toons All Star Fiftieth Anniversary, Celebrity Challenge of the Sexes, Laverne and Shirley in the Army, The Sixth Annual American Comedy Awards, The 37th Annual Prime Time Emmy Awards, The 40th Annual Emmy Awards, Naked Hollywood,* and *Simpsons Roasting on an Open Fire*. Appeared on stage in *Eden Court*, produced Off-Broadway, 1985. Producer of the film *Calendar Girl*, 1992.

■ Films

ACTRESS

How Sweet It Is, National General, 1968.
The Savage Seven, American International, 1968.
The Grasshopper, National General, 1970.

The Feminist and the Fuzz (television), ABC-TV, 1971.
The Couple Takes a Wife (television), ABC-TV, 1972.
The Crooked Hearts (television), ABC-TV, 1972.
Love Thy Neighbor (television), ABC-TV, 1974.
Let's Switch (television), ABC-TV, 1975.
How Come Nobody's on Our Side?, American Films, 1975.
More Than Friends (television), ABC-TV, 1978.
1941, Universal, 1979.
Movers and Shakers, Metro-Goldwyn-Mayer/United Artists, 1985.
Challenge of a Lifetime (television), ABC-TV, 1985.
The Hard Way, Universal, 1991.

DIRECTOR

Jumpin' Jack Flash, Twentieth Century-Fox, 1986.
Big, Twentieth Century-Fox, 1988.
(And executive producer) *Awakenings*, Columbia, 1990.
(And executive producer) *A League of Their Own*, Columbia, 1992.

■ **Work in Progress**

Time Step (with brother, Garry Marshall), a film based on her mother's life.

■ **Sidelights**

Despite her enormous success as an actress and major motion picture director, Penny Marshall is still notoriously known for her incredibly low self-esteem. "Penny Marshall has been putting herself down too long to quit cold turkey," explains Joe Morgenstern in *Playboy*. "She still shrugs her self-deprecating shrug, still whines her self-doubting whine. Nevertheless, she has started sifting through evidence that she may actually be good at her new career." Marshall became a household name when she portrayed the wacky, wise-cracking, milk-and-Pepsi-drinking Laverne De Fazio on the popular prime-time sitcom *Laverne and Shirley* from 1976 to 1983. The switch from comedic actress to major motion picture director came unexpectedly in 1985, but Marshall's new career is progressing rapidly—her films include such box-office smash hits as *Big, Awakenings,* and *A League*

of *Their Own*. "Fifteen years after *Laverne and Shirley* made her a famous bottlecapper,... [Marshall] has evolved into a frazzled earth mama, with only a lingering hint of her daffy TV persona," comments Rachel Abramowitz in *Premiere*. "Slumped in her chair, beneath a mop of blond, unbrushed hair, Marshall offers a potent blend of vulnerability, honesty, and maternal vigor that makes one believe she can effectively cajole people into doing her bidding. You end up wanting to help her—her self-effacing shtick both cloaks and intimates her directing style."

Marshall was born October 15, 1943, the youngest of three children. Her introduction to the entertainment business came at an early age—her father, Tony Marscharelli, was an advertiser and industrial film maker, and her mother, Marjorie, ran an eccentric tap-dancing school which Marshall would later attend. In her *Playboy* interview, Marshall remembers her mother as "a funny lady. She was way ahead of her time. She was the only mother who wore slacks, the only mother who worked, and she had this sort of Harpo Marx style of humor. We all got our sense of humor from her." Marshall was also influenced by the Bronx neighborhood she grew up in; the block she lived on, Grand Concourse and Mosholu Parkway, was home to a number of other future celebrities, including Neil Simon, Calvin Klein, and Ralph Lauren. Marshall's older sister, Ronny Hallin (a television producer), tells Morgenstern that she remembers her younger sister as "a little devil kind of kid, always getting into trouble. She was a real good athlete, a tomboy. She rode a two-wheeler really young, and fast, always very fast, zip zip zip, testing people all the time."

Struggles through Adolescent Years

It was as early as her adolescent years that signs of Marshall's now infamous lack of self-confidence began appearing. "I made fun of myself before anyone did," reveals Marshall in an interview with Marty Friedman for *New York*, "because I looked like a coconut and had bucked teeth, braces, and a ponytail. I wore a Davy Crockett T-shirt. I guess because I couldn't get the guys on a romantic level I took the friendship level.... I don't remember myself as funny," continues Marshall. "I was heartbroken for most of those years, in love with everybody. But I was always the character. Today people tell me, 'You were always fun to be around,' but did I have a different view of what I was doing! Still I wouldn't trade that for anything.

Marshall found fame with her portrayal of wacky Laverne De Fazio on the long-running series *Laverne and Shirley*.

There was a place you belonged. You just went out to the Parkway and found all your friends.''

In addition to the difficulties she experienced socially, Marshall also had a hard time finding a role in her family while she was growing up. Her sister was the "pretty and bright" one, her brother Garry was the "sickly and bright" one, so Marshall finally chose to be the "rebellious and fun-loving" one. This sibling rivalry continued as she grew older; both her brother and her sister were able to attend the college of their choice, Northwestern, while Marshall had to attend the college of her mother's choice. By the time Marshall was ready for college her mother decided she wanted to keep one of her children close to home—so she sent her to the University of New Mexico. "My mother thought it was closer than Ohio," explains Marshall in her *Playboy* interview. "Because New York, New Jersey, New Hampshire, New Mexico—she figured all the News were together. I wanted to go to Ohio State because there was a guy there, but my mother said New Mexico. It didn't matter. I just wanted to get away."

During her first two years of college Marshall studied psychology, business, and anthropology, married Michael Henry (another student), and got pregnant. "He was on football scholarship, and one of us had to work, so I worked," relates Marshall in her interview with Morgenstern. "A man was supposed to finish college, a girl didn't have to. And I wasn't really dedicated, anyway; I felt it was no big sacrifice. I think I was just killing time." So, after her daughter Tracy was born, Marshall began working as a secretary, later becoming a dance teacher because of better pay and better hours. She also worked for a short time as a choreographer for the Albuquerque Light Opera and appeared in a production of *Oklahoma!* When her marriage broke up just a few years later, though, Marshall packed up her bags and headed out to Los Angeles, where her brother was working as a writer for *The Dick Van Dyke Show*.

Marshall's arrival in Hollywood began the stage of her life when she was known solely as "Garry's sister." And aside from being unknown, Marshall also had no idea what she wanted to do with her life. Garry tried to help her, but when he discovered that Marshall couldn't name one thing she liked, he sent her away until she could. A few days later she came back, remembering the pleasure acting had brought her—she liked the audience's laughter and their applause. It was decided; Marshall would be an actress. This was much easier said than accomplished, though. Marshall

"couldn't turn on the charm in interviews, because she didn't feel pretty enough," remarks Morgenstern, adding: "She couldn't get auditions, because she wasn't perky enough. In what became a painfully funny milestone in her life, she finally did get hired for a shampoo commercial, but as the girl with stringy hair; the girl with beautiful hair was Farrah Fawcett."

By this time Garry was a successful director and producer, and his sister's most promising hope for regular work. In 1971, despite possible charges of nepotism, he decided to cast Marshall as Jack Klugman's secretary in a show he was co-producing—*The Odd Couple*. Marshall played this role for three years, marrying Rob Reiner in the meantime. It was while auditioning for the role of Gloria on *All in the Family* that Marshall met Reiner (he was trying out for the part of Archie's Meathead son-in-law, which he got). The two were the first among a large circle of friends to marry and buy a house, which soon became a regular gathering spot. Among the group were a number of up-and-coming television personalities, including writer-producer Jim Brooks and actors Albert Brooks and Paul Sills. In his interview with Morgenstern, Jim Brooks fondly remembers the Marshall of this period. "This was a time when all her strengths and all her intelligence had no practical utilization in the world. She was sort of a housewife, and it was great for all of us who knew her then, because all her marvelous talents were available for your life. Any problems you had, you got this great force of energy from her. I enjoyed it while I had it, but I saw it slipping away, because she had to go out and be a whole person."

Brings Wise-Cracking Laverne to Life

After her small part in *The Odd Couple*, Marshall's acting career continued to forge ahead. Brooks helped her out by giving her a substantial role in the short-lived series *Friends and Lovers*. It was a year after this that *Laverne and Shirley*, the show that would make Marshall famous, came along. Produced and created by Garry, the show was a blue-collar comic spin-off from one of his other shows, *Happy Days*. Like other similar sitcoms, *Laverne and Shirley* was sarcastically criticized by reviewers and loved by its audience. Set in Milwaukee, Wisconsin, the show follows the often chaotic adventures of two mismatched roommates: Laverne De Fazio (played by Marshall) is a zany realist, while Shirley Feeny (played by Cindy Williams) is a naive romantic. Other characters include Lenny and Squiggy, Laverne and Shirley's

1986's *Jumpin' Jack Flash*, starring Whoopi Goldberg, marked Marshall's major motion picture directorial debut.

nerdy neighbors, Carmine Raguso, Shirley's ever-faithful fiancee, and Frank De Fazio, Laverne's father. During the show's nine-year-run, Laverne and Shirley leave their bottle-capping jobs, move to California, and finally separate when Shirley marries an Army doctor and joins him overseas. "Laverne was homely but lovable, gloomy about being a virgin but devilish in ways that Penny had been developing since her girlhood," describes Morgenstern. "Suddenly, Garry's sister and Rob's wife was a star in her own right, a heroine of working class America."

It was near the end of both *Laverne and Shirley* and *All in the Family*'s long runs that Marshall's marriage encountered problems. "We faced all the cliche things," recalls Marshall in a *People* interview with Lois Armstrong. "We could check all the boxes in the stress test. His success, my success, buying a house, building a house. There were never any fights or arguments, but we didn't seem to be connecting," continues Marshall. "We just asked each other, 'Is this it? Are we happy? I don't think so.' So we decided to try a separation." Reiner moved out and the couple eventually divorced, starting the beginning of what Marshall

now terms her "door-mat years. You could walk all over me and it was OK, 'cause that's what I thought of myself," she tells Morgenstern.

After the break-up Marshall tried the party scene for a while, dating such celebrities as singer/songwriter Art Garfunkel and actor David Dukes. She rented a number of houses before she finally convinced herself that she deserved an actual home of her own; but when she bought the large hillside house in which she still resides, she found the many rooms impossible to fill. This was when Marshall began taking in friends as house guests, who then became boarders, and eventually her surrogate family. "Marshall herself lived a strange, increasingly isolated life," relates Morgenstern. "In part, that grew out of her problems finding privacy as a celebrity. But mostly, it was an expression of her tastes and needs. . . . Her friends have always understood. They know her as a woman who doesn't go out, so they come to her. They also know her as a woman of extraordinary energy and stamina, when she isn't wallowing in lethargy, and a woman of extraordinary competence, when she isn't whining or playing helpless. That's the essential contradiction of Marshall's life:

She's a can-do person who often behaves as if she can't.''

In spite of this continuing low self-esteem, Marshall's career proceeded to grow during these years. She appeared as a guest on a number of television series, starred in a number of television movies, and was a cast member for an Off-Broadway production of *Eden Court*. It was in 1985 that Marshall's career took an unexpected turn—she became a major motion picture director. She had had some previous experience, directing a few episodes of *Laverne and Shirley* and the pilot episode of *Working Stiffs*, and it was on the basis of this work that the producer of *Jumpin' Jack Flash*, Lawrence Gordon, asked Marshall to take over as the movie's director.

Jumps into Directorial Debut

The production of *Jumpin' Jack Flash* was encountering a number of problems when Marshall entered into the project, making for a less than promising start to her feature film directorial debut. The movie had already begun shooting when Gordon called Marshall and asked her to replace the current director, Howard Zieff (he was having problems working with Whoopi Goldberg). "From Marshall's perspective," explains Morgenstern, "the prospect of plunging into someone else's movie after ten days of shooting was fearsome. The script was an amateurish, unpleasant mess, while the production was awash in panic and anger." But despite the difficulties Marshall encountered with *Jumpin' Jack Flash*, maintain Tom Cunneff and Jack Kelley in *People*, the end product proved to the film industry that she could make a movie. "I believed in her," asserts Jim Brooks (the producer of Marshall's next film, *Big*) in his interview with Cunneff and Kelley. "She came into *Jumpin' Jack Flash* under the most insane conditions imaginable and showed a lot of imagination."

Jumpin' Jack Flash stars Whoopi Goldberg as Terry Doolittle, a dissatisfied computer operator at a New York bank who begins to receive S.O.S. messages on her computer. The sender turns out to be a British agent, "Jumpin' Jack Flash," who is being held prisoner behind the Iron Curtain. Doolittle is the only one who can relay the information he needs to make his escape. Agreeing to help the agent, she suddenly finds her life filled with spies, killers, and traitors. It is only through the use of a number of disguises and her wit that Doolittle is able to deliver. During the course of helping Jack, though, Doolittle falls in love with

him and is heartbroken when faced with the prospect of never hearing from him again. But by the end of the movie he makes her dreams come true when he shows up in New York and charmingly asks her out to lunch.

"If judged as nothing more than a showcase for Whoopi Goldberg's comedic talent, then *Jumpin' Jack Flash* succeeds just fine, thank you," comments Jimmy Summers in *Boxoffice*. Other critics, however, such as Vincent Canby of the *New York Times*, found the movie to be a waste of Goldberg's talents. "She's a volatile natural resource that can't easily be contained by means as frail and soft-headed as those offered by *Jumpin' Jack Flash*, her first and—let's hope—her worst motion-picture comedy," relates Canby. Summers, on the other hand, is surprised at "just how funny the movie manages to be," concluding that "*Jumpin' Jack Flash* is fun, audience-pleasing fluff."

It was while filming *Jumpin' Jack Flash* that Marshall received the script for her next feature film—*Big*. One day Brooks came into her office, plopped an envelope down on her desk, and told her that it would be her next movie. *Big* differed from Marshall's first film in two very important ways: it was her project from the start, and it came with a much more appealing script. The production wasn't trouble free, though. Casting the lead, which Tom Hanks eventually took, was time-consuming, and this lost time was costly considering that three other movies with similar plots, *Vice Versa*, *Like Father Like Son*, and *18 Again!*, were getting ready for production at the same time. Such stars as Hanks (who was unavailable when first asked to do the movie), Kevin Costner, and Dennis Quaid turned the role down, and Marshall began to rethink the character as possibly someone older or stronger. This led her to show the script to Robert DeNiro, who agreed to play the part, but ended up withdrawing before shooting started because of studio and agent problems. By this time Hanks was available to do the part, and with his portrayal of Josh Baskin *Big* went on to become the smash hit its three competitors failed to be.

Makes It "Big" at the Box Office

Big begins on a normal weekday morning in modern-day suburbia. Twelve-year-old Josh Baskin makes his way through an average day of school with his best friend Billy before attending a traveling carnival later in the evening with his parents. Discouraged because he isn't tall enough to go on a ride with an older girl he likes, Josh

The success of *Big*, starring Tom Hanks as a kid whose wish to be bigger comes true, made Marshall one of the most sought-after women directors in Hollywood.

comes across a carnival wishing machine called Zoltar. Plunking in his quarter, he proceeds to wish to be big, then forgets all about it. The following morning Josh awakes, swings his legs over the side of his top bunk, and jumps down with an unexpected resounding thud—he has become big during the night and now possesses the body of thirty-year-old Hanks. Not understanding the transformation that has taken place, he stumbles around the room attempting to fit his thirty-year-old body into a twelve-year-old's pair of jeans before actually looking in the mirror. Realizing what's happened, Josh tries to tell his mother. All she sees is a strange man, though, and she drives him from the house with a knife as she accuses him of kidnapping her son.

Not knowing what else to do, Josh makes his way to school to find Billy. When he finally convinces Billy that it's really him, the two go off to New York in hopes of tracking down Zoltar so Josh can reverse his wish. While there, Josh decides he's going to have to support himself and applies for a job as a computer operator at a toy company. His knowledge of toys and games and of what kids really like brings him to the attention of his boss and moves him up the corporate ladder at an astounding pace. One of the people Josh meets while working at the toy company is Susan, played by Elizabeth Perkins, an ambitious executive who is attracted to his boyish innocence. At first Josh doesn't know what she wants from him, but once she takes him to bed a love affair blossoms and he begins to enjoy his "big" new life. Just as he is about to launch a new line of toys, though, Billy shows up to tell him that Zoltar has been located and to remind him that he is really just a kid. Josh decides he doesn't want to miss out on all the years between twelve and thirty—he wishes to be small again and returns home.

"*Big* is one of those seemingly effortless movies in which a comic style is sustained from beginning to end, and every detail along the way rings true," describes Morgenstern. A great deal of work went into presenting this appearance; Marshall made the movie using as much time as she deemed necessary and shot vast amounts of film in the process. She "has wonderful instincts, and the tenacity to follow them," remarks Morgenstern, adding: "*Big* was the product of an intricate collaboration: actors and technicians, writers and producers and director. But, like every good movie, it was shaped by the sensibility of its director." Gerald Clarke, writing in *Time*, maintains that "Marshall's directing style is one of understatement, and she sets a tone of instant nostalgia that only occasionally descends to the sentimental." Also praising Marshall's directing skills, David Ansen relates in *Newsweek*, "Former *Laverne & Shirley* star Penny Marshall has turned into an adroit director—the first two-thirds of *Big* are an utter delight, full of sharp things to say about men, boys and corporate life." "*Big* is big comedy news—that rare film that can tickle the funny bone and touch the heart," concludes a *People* contributor.

Big's enormous success made Marshall one of the most sought-after women directors in Hollywood. All the major studios were suddenly sending her scripts from their prized collections. "Mostly I got sent a lot of high-concept comedies, which were things like, someone sees the Madonna on the tennis court and it changes their life; or a frog turns into a prince, a dog turns into a human," remembers Marshall in an interview with Carol Caldwell for *Interview*. "And I didn't want to do that again," she continues. "So I read a massive number of scripts and came across *Awakenings*. All I know is the story was so fascinating and moving, and I didn't think I'd do it at the time, but it just wouldn't go away." Twentieth Century-Fox thought the script was too depressing, though, and wasn't very enthusiastic about Marshall doing it. By this time she had sent the script to DeNiro, and he had accepted once again. Originally unsure of which part she wanted him to play, Marshall left the choice up to DeNiro; and when he picked the part of the patient the difficult search to fill the role of the doctor began. It was while viewing *Dead Poets Society* that Marshall first considered Robin Williams for the part. DeNiro agreed with her choice, and after a few meetings Williams signed on. In the meantime, Columbia had decided to take the film, so the rest of the casting and production began soon after.

Delves into Drama with *Awakenings*

Awakenings is a fictionalized version of the clinical work Dr. Oliver Sacks describes in his 1973 book of the same title. Between the years of 1916 and 1927, a wave of sleeping sickness swept the nation, leaving its victims in a catatonic state. In 1969 Dr. Sacks administered a "miracle" drug, L-dopa, to a group of these living dead patients and recorded a number of their case histories in his book. In the movie version of the book, Dr. Malcolm Sayer (Williams) arrives at a psychiatric hospital in the Bronx in the late 1960s to be greeted by an often uncaring staff of doctors. The patients he finds most fascinating are a group of immobile postencephalitics who remain in a seemingly constant vegetative state. Dr. Sayer begins to notice, however, that they are able to react to things—when he throws a ball at one of them, it is reflexively caught, and almost all of the patients react to a particular type of music. Against the wishes of the other doctors, Sayer grudgingly receives permission to administer a new drug that has been successful in treating Parkinson's disease to one of the patients—Leonard Lowe (DeNiro).

With increased dosages of L-dopa, Lowe eventually "wakes" up and slowly begins to function as a normal person once again. The success with Lowe allows Dr. Sayer to administer the drug to the other victims of the disease, and they are soon all awake and as full of life as Lowe. The group attends a dance and goes on other field trips, and Lowe even experiences a short flirtation with a young woman who comes to the hospital to visit her father. The drug is only effective for a short period of time, though, and the patients begin slipping back into their original state. The first to go is Lowe, who begins to develop a tic, and then must deal with watching his body take control of his mind again. By the end of the film, all the patients are inert once again. Along with the patients, Dr. Sayer also experiences his own awakening. A shy and introverted man, he is slowly pulled out of his shell by the head nurse at the hospital, played by Julie Kavner. The movie ends with their budding romance and Sayer's realization of the preciousness of life.

"I think the common thread in *Awakenings* is, You should live every day because it could always be taken away from you," points out Marshall in her interview with Caldwell. "As well as, Treat people with illnesses like human beings. I think the theme is, A little bit of life is better than no life at all. That's not very difficult to follow. And if that hits the pulse of the nation, I guess we are in sync." The themes Marshall describes, the casts' performances, and the movie itself were favorably received by most critics. *Awakenings* is "a volatile mix of strength and weakness, intellectual boldness and commercial calculation," comments David Denby in *New York*, adding: "What it takes to unlock the energy inside [the patients], and then the exhilarations and tragedies of that unlocking, are the heart of this film, which, believe it or not, is an entertainment, and a smart one at that." Peter Travers, writing in *Rolling Stone*, sees the movie as a definite Oscar contender, concluding that "Marshall's direction shows the patients' situation, which the real Leonard once described as 'wonderful, terrible, dramatic and comic,' with pitiless clarity. In only her third film, Marshall joins the front ranks of directors. She draws exceptional performances."

Swings into Skirt-Flying Summer Hit

With her next film, 1992's summer hit *A League of Their Own*, Marshall returns to a familiar genre—comedy. Like *Awakenings*, *A League of Their Own* is based on historical fact. Back in the 1940s, during World War II, the All American Girls Professional Baseball League (AAGPBL) was formed to compensate for the loss of a number of major league baseball players to the war effort. The Chicago Cubs' owner, P. K. Wrigley, and the president of the new league, Ken Sells, hired recruiters in 1942 to start searching the women's softball leagues in the United States and Canada in hopes of creating an attraction to fill the void of the depleted men's league. Wrigley planned to sell the women ballplayers as attractive and ladylike, not as tomboys or women of questionable ethics. The uniform was a tunic worn over elasticized shorts, and the members of the league were required to attend charm school. The atmosphere changed on the field, though, where the women traded their high heels for spikes and, eventually, their softballs for hardballs. To the surprise of many, these women could *really* play baseball, and they kept the league going for eleven years because of this.

"You got a lot of people that liked to see the legs, and laugh, but they didn't expect to see you play good baseball. . . . We kept them there because we played damn good baseball," asserts Lavonne Paire Davis (one of the former league members and Marshall's technical advisor) in the documentary which the film is based on, quoted by Michael Sragow in the *New Yorker*. When Marshall saw this documentary, she recalls in a dual interview with her brother Garry conducted by Elvis Mitchell for *Lear's* that she thought to herself, "They did it. It was mainly about, Don't be ashamed of your talent.

Marshall ventures into the drama genre with *Awakenings*, a tale of a psychiatrist who brings a group of catatonic patients back to life.

So I thought that was what I had to say with this. These girls felt they were misfits, because they were good at something they weren't supposed to be good at. Then they bonded and found other girls like them, and they didn't feel so bad about themselves. From the experience of being in this league, they went on and accomplished things they never thought they could do."

A League of Their Own focuses on one particular team in the new league, the Rockford Peaches. The movie begins with the recruiter, played by Jon Lovitz, travelling across the midwest in search of appropriate players. He sees Dottie Hinson, played by Geena Davis, and decides that she fits the criteria—she's good-looking and she can play. When he approaches her, sarcasm flowing freely from his lips, she isn't interested, but her younger sister Kit, played by Lori Petty, is. Lovitz flat out tells her he doesn't want her, but finally agrees to let her try out if Dottie comes too. The try-outs ensue, introducing other future members of the Peaches, including a couple of bad girls from Brooklyn played by Madonna and Rosie O'Donnell.

It soon becomes clear that the members of the league are expected to be sex objects, not ballplayers; their uniforms consist of short skirts, they are required to take etiquette lessons, they are all given makeovers, and each team is assigned a chaperon to watch their behavior. The first big problem the Peaches encounter comes in the form of their new manager, Jimmy Duggan, played by Tom Hanks. A former baseball star who drank himself out of the league, Duggan is given the job as a last chance, and doesn't think much of coaching a bunch of "girls." He basically ignores the team for the first half of the movie, making it necessary for Dottie to take over. The next problem encountered comes in the form of empty stands—the league isn't catching on. So, when she finds out that a *Life* photographer is in the stands, Dottie decides to give him something to photograph; she goes back to get a pop-up, simultaneously doing the splits as she catches it. The picture generates some interest, and as more fans come to see the "sexy" girl ballplayers they realize they're seeing good baseball and come back for more.

As the league begins to catch on, Duggan finally begins to pay attention to his players. All seems to be going well until Dottie and Kit start encountering problems; Kit is jealous of Dottie, who always seems to do things better then her. The problem is resolved when Kit is traded to another team, but the two sisters fail to reconcile their differences.

Soon after, Dottie's husband unexpectedly returns from the war and she decides to go home with him just as the Peaches are getting ready to play the league's first World Series. Unable to stay away, though, she shows up for the final game, which comes down to Kit (who is on the other team) getting a hit. Kit leads her team to victory, and the movie ends with the members of the league reuniting a number of years later at the Baseball Hall of Fame for the opening of the AAGPBL exhibit.

Baseballs, Bruises, and Broken Noses

Aside from actors and actresses, *A League of Their Own* also features members of the original league (in the closing scenes at the Hall of Fame), and a number of extras who could already play baseball. "A lot of people in *A League of Their Own* hadn't done any acting," relates Marshall in her *Lear's* interview. "We looked at anyone who could play ball, then we read them. We picked as many as we could from the actual ballplayers. Then we had to go for some actresses who looked like they could be trained. And we took 'em all to baseball coaches to find out if there was any possibility that they could play the game. And if they said, 'No possibility,' then we couldn't use 'em. But if they said, 'Trainable' ... that's all we needed to hear. That word *trainable*. We'll take 'em!" Once the "trainable" actresses were cast, the actual training, done by USC baseball coaches, began in earnest. "I had bruises man, all over my legs, all over my arms," says Geena Davis in a group interview with Nancy Griffin for *Premiere*. "I had bruises that had stitches on them—you could see the imprint of a baseball on my forearms. Then I realized it was a lot easier to catch a ball with your glove than with other parts of your body." Another actress, Megan Cavanagh, relates Marshall's worries about the numerous injuries suffered by the cast. "Penny, God love her, was so worried; you know, people were breaking their noses—people were getting hurt," she tells Griffin. "We were having all kinds of little accidents with these '40s mitts, and Penny's reaction was 'Oh my God, keep them *healthy*.'"

The actual filming of the baseball sequences was also very difficult—to orchestrate a play as it was described in the script was next to impossible. "There was this one moment where Penny called everybody around and said, 'Okay, here's what happens: the first pitch is a ball, the second pitch you pop up over toward the Peaches' dugout, the third pitch you hit for a single that goes between

In her 1992 summer comedy *A League of Their Own*, Marshall humorously presents the historical story of the All American Girls Professional Baseball League.

Marshall and Hanks, who has appeared in two of her films, consult during the filming of *Big*.

the second baseman and the shortstop. Then Lori comes up,'" explains Tom Hanks in the group *Premiere* interview. "Now, you've got to understand," he continues, "it was very hard for whoever was pitching to actually get the ball from the pitcher's mound to home plate, because they were doing the full 60 feet. And Penny is insisting—she's screaming at us, 'The first pitch has to be a ball. The second pitch has to be popped up...' It's not going to *happen!* Who are you kidding? There were a couple of times when what was supposed to happen actually happened, but not too often. It was just ludicrous amounts of fun."

Critics also recognized the inherent fun of the movie, with Richard Schickel describing it as "energetic, full of goodwill and good feelings" in a review for *Time*. David Ansen asserts in *Newsweek* that *A League of Their Own* is "amiable entertainment" which offers "a mixture of shtik, schmaltz and feminism." *Entertainment Weekly* contributor Owen Gleiberman, though, maintains, "It's an odd

movie, at once bubbly and amorphous, with plenty of mild laugh lines but virtually nothing you could call dialogue. *League* is easy to watch, but there's no *there* there." Ansen, however, concludes that what Marshall ends up with is a "very likable pop historical comedy."

After this movie, or any movie for that matter, is completed, Marshall often struggles with an interior dialogue, which she reveals in her *Lear's* interview: "'This stinks. Why am I doing this?' There's a time after the movie's out, a couple of months later, when you have nothing to do.... Then you say, 'Well, I wonder if I should do another movie.' That's when all the pain has gone away. You forget that pain. Till you start in again and go, 'Ooh! This wasn't fun at all.'" Despite her trepidation and insecurities, though, Marshall continues to take on new projects. "Some part of me must be ambitious because I keep doing things," she concludes in her interview with Cunneff and Kelley.

■ Works Cited

Abramowitz, Rachel, "Shot by Shot," *Premiere*, January, 1991, pp. 93-95.

Ansen, David, "Big Laughs and Cheap Thrills," *Newsweek*, July 6, 1992, p. 54.

Ansen, David, "Man-Child in the Corporate Land," *Newsweek*, June 6, 1988, p. 72.

Armstrong, Lois, "It's Thumbs up—Sort of—as Penny Marshall Copes with Life without Meathead," *People*, April 28, 1980, pp. 98, 100, 102, 104, 106.

Review of *Big*, *People*, June 6, 1988, pp. 16-17.

Caldwell, Carol, "The Marshall Plan," *Interview*, January, 1991, pp. 16, 18-19.

Canby, Vincent, "Screen: Whoopi Goldberg in *Jumpin' Jack Flash*," *New York Times*, October 10, 1986, p. C7.

Clarke, Gerald, "Little Boy Lost and Found," *Time*, June 6, 1988, pp. 78-79.

Cunneff, Tom, and Jack Kelley, "Penny Marshall Finally Leaves *Laverne* behind and Scores *Big* as a Director—So Why the Long Face?," *People*, August 15, 1988, pp. 53-54.

Denby, David, "The Good Doctor," *New York*, December 17, 1990, pp. 68, 71.

Friedman, Marty, "The Parkway All-Stars," *New York*, October 26, 1981, pp. 74-75, 78-83.

Gleiberman, Owen, "Comedy of Errors," *Entertainment Weekly*, July 10, 1992, p. 39.

Griffin, Nancy, "Cleanup Women," *Premiere*, July, 1992, pp. 76-80, 82.

Mitchell, Elvis, "Sibling Revelry," *Lear's*, July, 1992, pp. 52-55.

Morgenstern, Joe, "Penny from Heaven," *Playboy*, January, 1991, pp. 144-145, 162, 170-176.

Schickel, Richard, "The Girls of Summer," *Time*, July 6, 1992, pp. 72-73.

Sragow, Michael, "The Current Cinema," *New Yorker*, July 13, 1992, pp. 66-68.

Summers, Jimmy, review of *Jumpin' Jack Flash*, *Boxoffice*, December, 1986, pp. R133-R134.

Travers, Peter, review of *Awakenings*, *Rolling Stone*, January 10, 1991, p. 59.

■ For More Information See

PERIODICALS

Boxoffice, August, 1988, pp. R62-R63.

New Republic, January 7-14, 1991, pp. 32-33.

Newsweek, December 24, 1990, p. 62.

New York, May 27, 1985, p. 101-102; June 13, 1988, p. 68.

New Yorker, May 27, 1985, p. 74; June 27, 1988, pp. 67-69; February 11, 1991, pp. 70-74; July 13, 1992, pp. 66-68.

New York Times, October 2, 1980, pp. D1, D14.

People, December 24, 1990, p. 13; spring, 1991, pp. 94-99; July 6, 1992, p. 13.

Time, December 24, 1990, p. 77.

Village Voice, October 21, 1986, p. 62.°

—Sketch by Susan M. Reicha

Pablo Picasso

Llonja Art School, 1896-97; attended Royal Academy of San Fernando, Madrid, 1897.

■ Career

Painter, illustrator, sculptor, lithographer, ceramist, and etcher. First exhibition of paintings in Paris, 1901. *Art Joven* (magazine), Madrid, publisher and illustrator, 1901; *Minotaure* (magazine), illustrator, 1933. Designer of sets, costumes, and curtains for Diaghilev Ballet Russes, including *Parade*, 1917, *Le Tricorne*, 1919, *Pulcinella*, 1920, and *Cuandro Flamenco*, 1921; designer of sets, costumes, and curtains for productions, including *Antigone* (play), 1922, *Mercure*, 1924, *Le Train bleu* (operetta), 1924, *Le Rendez-vous* (ballet), 1945, and *Chant funebre d'Ignacio Sanchez Mejias* (play), 1953. Painter of *Guernica*, mural representing second Spanish republic, at Paris World's Fair, 1937; painter of *The Fall of Icarus*, mural at Palais de l'UNESCO, Paris, 1958. Appeared in the films *La Vie commence demain (Life Begins Tomorrow)*, International Pictures, 1952; *Le Mystere Picasso (The Mystery of Picasso)*, 1956; and *Le Testament d'Orphee (Testament of Orpheus)*, Editions Cinegraphiques/Films around the World-Brandon, 1962. *Exhibitions:* Exhibitions of paintings held in numerous cities throughout the world, including Barcelona, Berlin, Buenos Aires, Chicago, Cologne, Jerusalem, London, Moscow, Munich, New York City, Paris, Prague, Rome, Tokyo, and Zurich. Works represented in permanent collections, including Museum of Modern Art, Art Institute of Chicago, Pushkin Museum of Fine Arts, Hermitage Museum, Musee Picasso (Paris), Picasso Museum

■ Personal

Given name, Pablo Diego Jose Francisco de Paula Juan Nepomuceno y Maria de los Remedios Crispin Cipriano de la Santissima Trinidad Ruiz; born October 25, 1881, in Malaga, Andalucia, Spain; died of pulmonary edema, April 8, 1973, in Mougins, France; son of Jose Ruiz Blasco (a painter and art instructor) and Maria Picasso Lopez Ruiz; companion of Fernande Olivier, 1905-11; companion of Marcelle Humbert (original name, Eva Gouel), 1912-15; married Olga Koklova (a dancer with the Ballet Russe), July 12, 1918 (separated in 1935, but officially married until Koklova's death in 1955); companion of Marie-Therese Walter, beginning in 1927; companion of Dora Maar (a photographer and painter), 1936-45; companion of Francoise Gilot (a painter), 1944-53; married Jacqueline Rocque (a sales clerk), March 2, 1961; children: (first marriage) Paulo (died, 1975); (with Marie-Therese Walter) Maria Concepcion; (with Francoise Gilot) Claude, Paloma. *Education:* Attended Provincial Fine Arts School of La Corona, 1892-95; attended Academy of Fine Arts of Barcelona, 1895-96; studied art under his father at La

(Barcelona), Tate Gallery, Centre Georges Pompidou, and Kunsthaus. *Member:* French Communist Party.

■ Awards, Honors

Honorable mention, Madrid Exhibition of Fine Arts, 1897, and gold medal, Customs of Aragon, Madrid and Malaga, 1898, for the painting *Science and Charity;* first prize, Carnegie International, 1930; named honorary curator of Prado Museum, 1936; Silver Medal of French Gratitude, France, 1948; Order of Polish Renascence commander's cross, Poland, 1948; Pennell Memorial Medal, Philadelphia Academy of Fine Arts, 1949, for lithograph *The Dove of Peace;* Lenin Peace prizes, Soviet Union, 1950 and 1962.

■ Writings

(And illustrator) *Sueno y mentira de Franco* (poetry; title means "Dreams and Lies of Franco"), [Paris], 1937.

Picasso: Poemas y declaraciones, Darro y Genil, 1944.

Le Desire attrape par la queue (play), Gallimard, 1945, translation by Bernard Frechtman published as *Desire: A Play,* Philosophical Library, 1948, revised edition published as *Desire Caught by the Tail,* Rider, 1950.

(With Paul Eluard) *Le Visage de la paix,* Editions Cerele d'art, 1951.

Picasso et a poesie, [Rome], 1953.

Tout le fatras immonde, [Paris], 1954.

Poems, translated by Richard Bowman and Charles Guenther, Bern Porter, 1956.

Les Quatre Petites Filles (play), Gallimard, 1968, translation by Roland Penrose published as *The Four Little Girls,* Calder & Boyars, 1970.

Hunk of Skin (poetry), translated by Paul Blackburn, City Lights Books, 1968.

El entierro del conde de Orgaz, Editorial G. Gili, 1970.

Picasso on Art: A Selection of Views, compiled by Dore Ashton, Viking, 1972.

(Contributor) *El tema del amor,* Ediciones Andromeda, 1975.

Picasso: Collected Writings, edited by Marie-Laure Bernadac and Christine Piot, translated by Carol Volk and Albert Bensoussan, Abbeville Press, 1989.

ILLUSTRATOR

Andre Salmon, *Poemes,* [Paris], 1905.
Max Jacob, *Saint Matorel,* [Paris], 1911.
Jacob, *Siege de Jerusalem,* [Paris], 1914.

Salmon, *Le Manuscrit trouve dans un chapeau,* [Paris], 1919.

Pierre Reverdy, *Cravates de chanvre,* [Paris], 1922.

Honore de Balzac, *Le Chef-d'oeuvre inconnu,* Vollard, 1931.

Ovid, *Metamorphoses,* Skira, 1931, translated by A. E. Watts, University of California Press, 1954.

Aristophanes, *Lysistrata,* Limited Editions Club, 1934.

Paul Eluard, *La Barre d'appui,* [Paris], 1936.

Iliazd, *Afat,* [Paris], 1940.

Georges Louis Leclerc de Buffon, *Histoire naturelle,* [Paris], 1942.

Guillaume Apollinaire, *Les Mamelles de Tiresias,* Edition du Belier, 1946.

Luis de Gongora y Argote, *Gongora,* [Paris], 1948, translation by Alan S. Trueblood, Braziller, 1985.

Andrien de Montluc, *La Maigre,* [Paris], 1952.

Erik Satie, *Memoires d'un amnesique,* Editions Dynamo, 1953.

Prosper Merimee, *Carmen,* Mermod, 1953.

Marc Sabathier-Leveque, *Oratoria pour la nuit de noel,* Editions de Minuit, 1955.

Genevieve Laporte, *Les Cavaliers d'ombre,* Dominique Viglino, 1956.

Jacob, *Chronique des temps heroiques,* Louis Broder, 1956.

Antonin Artaud, *Autre chose que de l'enfant beau,* Louis Broder, 1957.

Rene Char, *L'Escalier de Flore,* P. A. Benoit, 1958.

Tristan Tzara, *La Rose et le chien: Poeme perpetual,* Benoit, 1958.

Jean Tardieu, *L'Espace et la flute,* Gallimard, 1958.

Lucian Scheler, *Lucian Scheler: Sillage intangible,* [Paris], 1958.

Jose Delgado y Galvez, *La tauromaquia; o, Arte de torear,* Editorial G. Gili, 1959.

Char, *Pourquoi la journee vole,* Pierre Andre Benoit, 1960.

Camilo Jose Cela, *Gavilla de fabulas sin amor,* Ediciones de los Papeles de Son Armadans, 1962.

Iwan Goll, *Elegy of Ihpetonga,* translated by Babette Deutsch, Louise Bogan, and Claire Goll, Allen Press, 1962.

Pierre Reverdy, *Sable mousant,* Louis Broder, 1966.

■ Sidelights

Pablo Picasso's career as an artist covered a range of more than seventy years and several major periods. His iconoclastic style led to revolutions in painting and sculpture, most notably the founding of cubism, a style in which traditional concepts of perspective are undermined by presenting objects as a set of geometric components. Never settling into any one style for long, Picasso continually strived for new ways of capturing the emotional and psychological world in visual art. This mental energy was often represented by extreme contortions and exaggerations of physical forms in his work. Examples of this include the geometric, two-dimensional bodies found in his masterpiece *Les Demoiselles de Avignon* and the dislocated abstractions of heads and limbs as seen in the brightly colored *Three Dancers.* Picasso also received worldwide acclaim for *Guernica,* his representation of the horrors of war, prompted by the bombing of an undefended Spanish town by Germany in World War II. His ability to respond to the unique elements and tensions of the twentieth century caused American writer Gertrude Stein in *Picasso* to observe, "One must never forget that the reality of the twentieth century is not the reality of the nineteenth century, not at all and Picasso was the only one in painting who felt it, the only one." On the occasion of the Museum of Modern Art's 1980 retrospective of Picasso's career, *Harper's* contributor T. D. Allman stated, "If an artist's greatness lies in diversity of styles and volume of production, and above all in the monetary value society places on his work, then Picasso was undoubtedly the greatest artist of the twentieth century, perhaps the most 'successful' painter since [Peter Paul] Rubens."

Picasso enjoyed a great deal of celebrity during his lifetime. In every period of his work he associated with influential artists, authors, and members of the intelligentsia. These connections provided him with opportunities for a number of collaborations in painting, writing, illustrating, and contributing scenery or curtains for plays and ballets. His face became as well-known as his art; his Paris studio was a common stop for sight-seeing American soldiers at the end of World War II. According to *New York* contributor Pete Hamill, "For the last third of his life, his face, with its intense chestnut eyes, was more widely known than those of all but a few athletes, politicians, and actors." Such fame caused Picasso's work to bring in some of the highest prices for paintings by a living artist. Picasso himself occasionally scorned such acceptance, near the end of his life quipping, as quoted by Calvin Tomkins in the *New Yorker,* that he had painted many "fake Picassos" that the public hungrily bought up simply because the paintings bore his name.

Picasso was so impressed by the courage and agility of the members of the Medrano Circus that he went on to paint a number of portraits of them, including *The Family of Acrobats with Ape.*

The name Picasso, which came to be recognized around the world, was not the moniker first used by the artist. On October 25, 1881, in Malaga, Spain, Picasso was born to a struggling art instructor, Jose Ruiz Blasco, and his wife, Maria Picasso Lopez Ruiz. The Catalan parents, who had migrated to the Spanish province of Andalucia, christened their son after a number of relatives and patron saints. As a young artist, he used the shorter version of his mother's and father's names, signing his paintings Pablo Picasso y Ruiz, P. Ruiz Picasso, or P. R. Picasso before finally settling on Pablo Picasso around the end of the 1890s.

Early Artistic Abilities

Partly due to the artist's own tendency to exaggerate his early talents and signs of genius, there are many unsubstantiated stories that surround the childhood and development of Picasso. Picasso's mother is reported to have said that the boy's first word was "piz," babytalk for "lapiz" or pencil. John Richardson in *A Life of Picasso* related other instances of Picasso's alleged precocity: "When given a pencil, the infant would apparently draw spirals that represented a snail-shaped fritter called a *torruela*. None of the earliest drawings have survived, so these accounts have to be taken on faith. Picasso himself remembered that while other children played under the trees of the Plaza de la Merced, he would make drawings in the dust—a habit he recalled years later, when he would divert and at the same time dismay his companions (especially art dealers) by tracing elaborate compositions on a sandy beach and watch with sardonic glee as the sea washed away his handiwork."

As a child, Picasso disliked school, but was a competent student. His father, an amateur painter who specialized in portraits of doves, encouraged his son's interest in art. Picasso spent his youth constantly drawing and painting. He also trained at a number of art schools, first studying at the Provincial Fine Arts School of La Corona. When his father took a job at the Barcelona Academy of Fine Arts, Picasso enrolled there, finishing his entrance examination drawings in a fraction of the time allotted. The school officials were impressed by his speed, but also by the student's obvious technical ability. One legend that was perpetuated by Picasso himself was that Jose Ruiz Blasco once gave his son a section of one of his own paintings to complete, only to realize that Picasso's work was better than his own. Blasco was so convinced of his son's greatness that he gave Picasso his own paints and brushes, vowing never to paint again. In 1897, when Picasso was about sixteen, his painting *Science and Charity*, a portrait of a doctor and a nun attending a dying woman, received an honorable mention at the Exhibition of Fine Arts in Madrid.

The same year, Picasso enrolled at the Royal Academy of San Fernando in Madrid, with financial assistance from a successful uncle. Although he stopped attending his classes almost immediately, due to frustration with the rigid academic structure of the school, he spent many hours sketching in the Prado Museum. There he found inspiration in the works of Diego Velazquez, Titian, Rubens, and other artists. In a letter written by Picasso at this time, as quoted by Richardson, the artist expressed his disillusionment with the Academy: "[The teachers here] ... haven't a grain of common sense. They just go on and on, as I suspected they would, about the same old things: Velazquez for painting, Michelangelo for sculpture, etc., etc.... if I had a son who wanted to be a painter, I wouldn't keep him here in Spain for a moment. And I certainly wouldn't send him to Paris (though that's where I would gladly be myself) but to Muni[ch] ... for that is a city where painting is studied seriously without regard for dogmatic notions of pointillism and so on ... not that I think that sort of painting necessarily bad ... just because one painter has made a success of a certain style, all the others don't have to follow suit. I don't believe in following one particular school, all it leads to is mannerism and affectation in those who tag along."

No longer receiving financial support from his wealthy uncle, who was angry at Picasso's failure at the Royal Academy, the artist was forced to return to Barcelona, where he rented a small studio. The teenager spent his free hours with older artists, writers, and political radicals at the local cabaret, Els Quatre Gats (The Four Cats, a Catalan expression meaning "only a few people"). Arianna Stassinopoulos Huffington in *Atlantic* described the atmosphere of ideas that Picasso encountered there: "Talk of nihilism, Catalanism, anarchism, and modernism filled the smoky air of Els Quatre Gats.... Uneducated but quick to learn, [Picasso] devoured ideas and philosophies through his friends who had read and absorbed them." Picasso filled the cabaret with caricatures, portraits, and posters for the establishment and its frequent puppet plays.

Paris Provides Inspiration

In 1900 Picasso made his first trip to France, the country that he would make his home. When he arrived in Paris at the age of nineteen, he was unable to speak French and had no place to stay. Despite these factors, however, he was extremely productive, painting and sketching the type of street scenes and dance halls that had been portrayed in the work of Henri de Toulouse-Lautrec, an artist he admired. In these works, Picasso began to move away from conventionally realistic pictures to more modern styles. While in Paris he also became familiar with the work of contemporary artists such as Vincent van Gogh, Paul Gauguin, Hilaire Degas, Pierre Renoir, and other impressionists. These influences inspired him to work with many rich colors applied in the daubs of paint and noticeable brushstrokes of impressionist pieces. In the summer of 1901, the first exhibition of Picasso's works was held in Paris by Ambrose Vollard, the art dealer for such prominent artists as Paul Cezanne and Paul Gauguin.

Later in 1901, Picasso began painting in the first of his recognized styles which became known as his Blue Period. Using varying shades of blue (which Picasso would later say he used because it was cheaper than other colors) he presented solemn portraits and scenes of human struggle. Huffington stated that during this period, "Picasso, spurred by his inner turmoil, switched his focus to the solitude and pain of humanity and tried to express them by means of blue. So began the procession of beggars, lonely harlequins, tormented mothers, the sick, the hungry, and the lame. And in their midst was Picasso himself, his own suffering on display in a blue self-portrait." A French journalist at the time, according to Huffington, described the artist of these paintings as "a young god trying to remake the world. But a dark god." The journalist further acknowledged the importance of this new talent, stating, "Is this frighteningly precocious child not fated to bestow the consecration of a masterpiece on the negative sense of living, the illness from which he more than anyone else seems to be suffering?"

Around 1904, Picasso moved into a studio in a building nicknamed the "Bateau Lavoir," or "the boat wash-house," because of its run-down condition. There he entertained other young members of the avant-garde during the day, venturing out to cafes, cabarets, and brothels at night. He indulged in a bohemian lifestyle, dressing in brightly colored suits or period costumes, wearing his hair long, and smoking opium. His paintings began to sell among collectors such as Gertrude and Leo Stein and the Russian dealer Shchukine, but Picasso was still poor. At this time, he met Fernande Olivier, a woman with whom he was involved for seven years. Richardson quoted Olivier's recollection of Picasso's living conditions at the time she met him in 1904: "The studio was a furnace in summer, and it was not unusual for Picasso and his friends to strip completely.... In winter the studio was so cold that the dregs of tea left in cups from the day before were frozen by morning. But the cold did not prevent Picasso from working without respite."

Perhaps due to his burgeoning relationship with Olivier, Picasso's paintings began to focus on more lighthearted subjects and the tones of his works took on a corresponding rosy hue. Rather than looking flat and in poor health, the subjects of his pictures began to appear as healthier, more modeled figures. Due to the brighter color scheme and his frequent portrayals of circus performers, this time has been categorized as Picasso's Rose or Harlequin Period. Stein singled out *The Young Girl*

with a Basket of Flowers as representative of this period because it is "full of grace and delicacy and charm." She went on to say that "after that little by little his drawing hardened, his line became firmer, his color more vigorous, naturally he was no longer a boy he was a man, and then in 1905 he painted my portrait."

The Development of Cubism

Stein, a central personality of the Paris art circle, patiently sat for Picasso for a portrait that many were initially shocked by: although the rest of the picture was painted with conventional accuracy, the face, which gave the artist a great deal of trouble, was finally painted in a primitive manner incongruent with the rest of the portrait. The author related her experience in *Picasso*: "I posed for him all that winter, eighty times and in the end he painted out the head, he told me that he could not look at me any more and then he left ... for Spain.... Immediately upon his return from Spain he painted in the head without having seen me again." Picasso's portrait of Stein signalled his new interest with flat, ovoid African masks that he had observed in museums, as well as pre-Christian Iberian sculpture and the work of Cezanne. The

In this 1929 abstract, *Woman's Head with Self-Portrait,* Picasso hides his own portrait behind the grotesque, laughing face of his subject.

Picasso's attack on the female figure subsided in the early 1930s, and his interest in a new type of woman is evident in his 1932 painting, *The Dream*.

unique look of the African and Iberian artifacts would later influence his experiments with abstraction of bodies and objects.

This new turn in Picasso's style led him to abandon the sentimental themes of the Blue and Rose Periods and work with a more hardened, sculptural quality. The portrait of Stein was the first of a number of paintings in which faces appear flat and mask-like with empty eye sockets. Instead of light, linear forms, he filled his canvases with heavy, solid ones. Picasso's experiments with these qualities resulted in a painting that art critics have considered both a masterpiece and a major turning point in the development of modern art—*Les Demoiselles d'Avignon*. Painted in 1907, the break with tradition that the work represented had a profound effect on all aspects of the arts. The painting presents the figures of five prostitutes in a manner radically different from the traditional perspective of a fixed viewpoint. Instead, the artist explores the difficulty of making a two-dimensional canvas capture three-dimensional bodies. He used several different viewpoints at once, resulting in noses presented in profile in the middle of a full face, displaced eyes, and exaggerated and distorted limbs. The relationships of the bodies to each other and the rest of the space in the painting is made uncertain due to the geometric forms to which Picasso reduced everything. Reactions to Picasso's painting were as extreme as the work itself. Huffington related that many artists and critics were repulsed by the "five horrifying women, prostitutes who repel rather than attract and whose faces are primitive masks that challenge not only society but humanity itself." Artist George Braque compared the effect of the picture to "someone drinking gasoline and spitting fire," according to Huffington.

Braque, however, recognized the importance of Picasso's creation. He and Picasso began a partnership in which they would develop the principles of a new style. Often working on each other's paintings, they produced a number of pieces painted in monotones of brown or gray, in which the subject is realized by shifting patterns of lines and geometric planes. This new style of painting was named "cubism" by an art critic because of the artists' use of geometric figures. Huffington quoted Braque's comments on his historic collaboration with Picasso: "Picasso and I were engaged in what we felt was a search for the anonymous personality. We were inclined to efface our own personalities in order to find originality. Thus it often happened that amateurs mistook Picasso's painting for mine

and mine for Picasso's. This was a matter of indifference to us, because we were primarily interested in our work and in the new problem it presented."

Picasso collaborated with Braque in this style which became known as "analytical cubism" mainly during the years 1909 to 1911. As analytic cubism began to lose its original interest for him, Picasso continued to elaborate and enlarge the scope of his ideas. In 1912, he painted the first collage of the twentieth century, *Still-Life with Chair Caning*, by gluing a piece of oil cloth to the painted canvas and framing the entire work with a piece of rope. He began to use more vibrant colors and a greater freedom of expression, resulting in the development of a second phase of cubism known as "synthetic cubism." In these paintings, Picasso attempted to reduce objects to large, flat, simple shapes as opposed to the complex lines of analytical cubism.

Again, Picasso's change of mood in his painting reflected developments in his personal life. In 1912, he began living with Marcelle Humbert. When they first met, Humbert was the lover of one of Picasso's artist friends. Picasso soon changed all that, however, and Humbert's presence in his life resulted in a new lightheartedness in Picasso's work. In his paintings he would incorporate references to her, signing portraits of her as "Ma Jolie" ("My Pretty One") or inscribing their initials on the back of his paintings. After only three years together, however, this influence would come to an end with Humbert's death from consumption in 1915.

Marriage and Mistresses Affect Art

In 1917, Picasso traveled to Rome to work on the ballet *Parade*. A collaboration with author Jean Cocteau, composer Eric Satie, and Russian ballet director Sergei Diaghilev, the production was to feature sets, costumes, and curtains by the now well-known Picasso. He would work on a number of such productions in the late 1910s and early 1920s. At this time, Picasso met and married dancer Olga Koklova, the daughter of a Russian Imperial Army officer. Olga helped Picasso use his new wealth and prominence to enter some of the finest circles of European society. His growing interest in a more conservative and respectable lifestyle and his wife's dislike for his cubist works drew Picasso into a new appreciation of classical sculpture and realistic painting. Olga gave birth to a son, Paulo, in 1921, and Picasso painted a number of portraits of his wife and child in a tranquil and delicate manner that is markedly different from his earlier works.

Gertrude Stein characterized this period between 1919 and 1927 as a "second rose period." And like the first Rose Period, Stein saw the second ending with exaggerations of the female form. The "enormous and very robust women" that Stein noted are found in works such as Picasso's *The Race* or *Three Women at a Fountain*. Huffington describes the mid- to late-1920s as a time of turmoil in which Picasso's marriage was deteriorating and he was becoming increasingly dissatisfied with his aristocratic lifestyle. His anger with Olga, according to Huffington, resulted in the extreme dislocations of the limbs of the figures found in 1925's *Three Dancers*. Stein saw the painting as "the fact that naturalism for Picasso was dead, that he was no longer seeing as all the world thought they saw." In his move away from naturalism, Picasso worked with the ideas of the surrealist movement, which attempted to create a "super-reality" through the merging of the conscious and subconscious worlds. Although Picasso never described himself as a surrealist, the physical manifestations of emotional turmoil in his works made him an influential part of the movement.

Filled with rage and grief, Picasso's *Woman Weeping* was most likely inspired by the civil war in Spain.

In 1927, the violence of Picasso's female forms gave way to more organic, colorful, and sexual figures. The model for many of these canvases was his new lover, Marie-Therese Walter, a girl of seventeen. Picasso and Walter's relationship lasted for nearly twenty years, during which they had a daughter, Maria Concepcion (also called Maya). Besides a number of portraits, references to Walter appear in Picasso's powerful "minotaur" pictures. Huffington described the half-bull, half-man minotaur in the four etchings of *The Blind Minotaur* (1934) as an allegory for Picasso's frustration with his marriage and the comfort he found in Walter: "The minotaur, a symbol for himself, is being tenderly guided by a beautiful girl clutching a dove. There is an air of hopeless tragedy about the blinded beast, so strong but so vulnerable, as he struggles to find his way along the seashore. The girl looks like Marie-Therese, but there is something transcendent about her, beyond any physical personality." While Picasso apparently attempted to divorce his wife Olga at this time, she would not allow it, and they remained officially married until Olga's death in 1955.

Guernica Draws Worldwide Attention

Picasso was greatly moved by the outbreak of civil war in his native Spain in 1936. Although he had never been interested in politics before, he made strong statements opposing Nationalist leader Francisco Franco. He also financially supported the faltering Republican government. In return, the Republic named Picasso honorary curator of the Prado Museum in 1936. Picasso expressed his political beliefs in an address to the American Artists' Congress, as quoted in *Contemporary Authors (CA)*: "It is my wish at this time to remind you that I have always believed and still believe, that artists who live and work with spiritual values cannot and should not remain indifferent to a conflict in which the highest values of humanity and civilizations are at stake." Picasso continued his attacks on Franco and the Nationalists with a poem illustrated with nine etchings entitled *Sueno y mentira de Franco* or "Dreams and Lies of Franco." The etchings, which portrayed Franco as a centaur being gored by a bull, were mass produced and dropped over Nationalist territory in Spain for propaganda purposes.

Picasso's involvement with the events in Spain led to what is considered one of his greatest paintings—*Guernica*. In 1937 Picasso was commissioned by the Spanish government to paint a large mural for the Spanish pavilion at the Paris World's

Fair. The artist was slow to begin work on the project, but was suddenly and powerfully inspired when the small, undefended Spanish town of Guernica was bombed by German forces sympathetic to Franco. Voices from around the world protested the attack. Picasso threw himself into an intense period of creativity, turning out the eleven-by twenty-five-foot canvas in just over a month, completing it in June of 1937. The creation of the piece was recorded in the photographs of another of his mistresses, the Yugoslavian artist Dora Maar. The painting is done in stark tones of black, white, and grey and depicts the chaos and violence of the events at Guernica. In the picture are screaming women, a burning house, a mother carrying her dead child, a horse neighing in pain, and a distorted bull's head, reminiscent of the minotaur pictures. *Guernica* had an enormous impact on the public. Huffington quotes the surrealist poet Michel Leiris's reaction to the painting at the Paris exhibition: "In a rectangle of black and white such as that in which ancient tragedy appeared to us, Picasso sends us our announcement of our mourning: all that we love is going to die." A Russian correspondent of the time, Ilya Ehrenburg, was quoted in *CA* as declaring, "Picasso's canvas has all the horrors of the future, raising to infinity the atomic cataclysm, the world reduced to rubble, the triumph of hatred, despair, the absurd, nothingness."

After the exhibition in Paris, the painting traveled to Norway, England, and the United States, where it was shown at the Museum of Modern Art in New York City. When Franco's forces won the civil war in Spain, Picasso declared that the painting would not be returned to Spain until "public liberties" had been restored there. In 1981, six years after the death of Franco and eight years after the death of Picasso, *Guernica* was finally transferred from the Museum of Modern Art to the Prado in Madrid. A 1981 *Time* article asserted that *Guernica* was "Pablo Picasso's stark protest against the savagery of war, which had come to symbolize Spanish hopes for democracy."

Exhibitions Salute Picasso

Although Picasso joined the Communist party in 1944 and continued to paint until his death in 1973, his political and artistic consciousnesses would never again reach the heights they achieved in *Guernica*. His *Dove of Peace* lithograph, however, did gain popularity as a symbol of peace for the Communist party in the 1950s. He became romantically involved with the painter Francoise

Gilot in the 1940s and 1950s, and the couple had two children, Claude and Paloma. In 1961 Picasso was married to Jacqueline Rocque and became increasingly reclusive. In a number of elegant French villas, he lived surrounded by hundreds of his own works and rooms of odd objects that struck his fancy. In the last years of his life he produced an incredible number of works in several media including painting, engraving, sculpture, and pottery. Hamill noted in *New York,* "In one furious thirteen-month period from January 5, 1969 to February 2, 1970, he made 165 paintings and scores of drawings. Critics tend to dismiss the late works as badly conceived and sloppily executed, but as autobiography they are the triumphant shouts of a man who was not prepared to leave the world quietly." In 1971, Picasso achieved another milestone in the history of art when the Louvre art museum displayed a number of his works in honor of his ninetieth birthday, making him the first living artist to have works shown there.

Picasso died on April 8, 1973, at his villa in Mougins, France. He was remembered the world over as one of the most versatile and prolific artists of the twentieth century. As *New York* contributor John Ashbery noted, "There are almost as many different Picassos as there are critics." At the time of his death, according to Hamill, "Picasso had made more than 6,000 paintings, hundreds of sculptures, literally countless drawings, etchings, and lithographs, and thousands of ceramics." In a final tribute to the artist, New York City's Museum of Modern Art hosted a retrospective of Picasso's lengthy career. The huge display contained over one thousand Picasso works and in order to see the entire show a viewer had to walk a distance of approximately three miles. The size and scope of the show made it a unique cultural event. Mark Stevens, writing in *Newsweek,* observed that "such a show will almost never be staged again, making the ambition of the exhibit clear: to be the greatest show, of the greatest modernist, at the greatest museum of modern art."

Huffington summed up Picasso's importance to the world of art: "He brought to fullest expression the shattered vision of a century that perhaps could be understood in no other terms; and he brought to painting the vision of disintegrations that [composers Arnold] Schoenberg and [Bela] Bartok brought to music, [writers Franz] Kafka and [Samuel] Beckett to literature. He took to its uttermost conclusion the negative vision of the modernist world." Reflecting on his career, Picasso, quoted by Hamill in *New York,* described his work in similar terms:

Picasso surrounded by his work in his villa at Cannes on the French Riviera (photograph by Arnold Newman).

"In the old days, pictures went forward toward completion by stages. Every day brought something new. A picture used to be the sum of additions. In my case a picture is a sum of destructions." Stevens, in his assessment of the 1980 Picasso retrospective, declared, "Picasso, who was the pre-eminent modernist, also had old-world force. Seen together, his works suggest an ambition that dares compete with the power and variety of nature itself."

■ Works Cited

Allman, T. D., "Picasso, Inc.," *Harper's*, December, 1980, pp. 71-73.

Ashbery, John, "The Art," *New York*, May 12, 1980, pp. 28-31.

Contemporary Authors, Volumes 97-100, Gale, pp. 434-40.

Hamill, Pete, "The Man," *New York*, May 12, 1980, pp. 34-38.

Huffington, Arianna Stassinopoulos, "Creator and Destroyer," *Atlantic*, June, 1988, pp. 37-78.

"Return of the Last Exile," *Time*, September 21, 1981, p. 32.

Richardson, John, *A Life of Picasso*, Volume 1: *1881-1906*, Random House, 1991.

Stein, Gertrude, *Picasso*, Beacon Press, 1959.

Stevens, Mark, "Picasso's Imperial Eye," *Newsweek*, May 19, 1980, pp. 80, 85.

Tomkins, Calvin, "The Art World," *New Yorker*, June 30, 1980, p. 56.

■ For More Information See

BOOKS

Gilot, Francoise, and Carlton Lake, *Life with Picasso*, McGraw, 1964.

Picasso, Pablo, *Je suis le cahier: The Sketchbooks of Picasso*, edited by Arnold and Marc Glimcher, Atlantic Monthly, 1986.

Sabartes, Jaime, *Picasso: An Intimate Portrait*, translated by Angel Flores, Prentice-Hall, 1948.

PERIODICALS

Los Angeles Times Book Review, December 7, 1986.

Newsweek, October 2, 1989, p. 73.

New Yorker, December 15, 1986, p. 105.

New York Review of Books, December 19, 1985, p. 59; July 21, 1988, p. 19.°

Ayn Rand

■ Personal

First name rhymes with "pine"; born Alice Rosenbaum February 2, 1905, in St. Petersburg, Russia; immigrated to the United States, 1926; naturalized citizen, 1931; died March 6, 1982, in New York, NY; buried in Kensico Cemetery, Valahalla, NY; daughter of Fronz (a chemist) and Anna Rosenbaum; married Charles Francis "Frank" O'Connor (an actor and artist), April 15, 1929. *Education:* University of Petrograd, graduated with highest honors in history, 1924. *Politics:* "Radical for capitalism." *Religion:* Atheist.

■ Career

Peter and Paul Fortress, Leningrad (now St. Petersburg), Russia, tour guide, beginning in 1924; Cecil B. DeMille Studio, Hollywood, CA, movie extra and junior screenwriter, 1926-c. 1928; RKO Radio Pictures, Hollywood, 1929-32, began as filing clerk, became office head in wardrobe department; screenwriter for Universal Pictures, Paramount Pictures, and Metro-Goldwyn-Mayer (MGM), 1932-34; RKO Radio Pictures and MGM, New York City, free-lance script reader, 1934-35; Ely Jacques Kahn (architect), New York City, filing clerk, typist, and general assistant, 1937; Paramount Pictures, New York City, script reader, 1941-43; Hall Wallis Productions, Hollywood, screenwriter, 1944-49; full-time writer and lecturer, 1951-82. Visiting lecturer at Yale University, 1960, Princeton University, 1960, Columbia University, 1960 and 1962, University of Wisconsin, 1961, Johns Hopkins University, 1961, Harvard University, 1962, and Massachusetts Institute of Technology, 1962. Presenter of annual Ford Hall Forum, Boston, MA, beginning in 1963.

■ Awards, Honors

Doctor of Humane Letters, Lewis and Clark College, 1963.

■ Writings

NOVELS

We the Living, Macmillan, 1936.
Anthem, Cassell, 1938, revised edition, Pamphleteers, Inc., 1946.
The Fountainhead, Bobbs-Merrill, 1943, reprinted with special introduction by Rand, 1968.
Atlas Shrugged, Random House, 1957.

PHILOSOPHY

For the New Intellectual: The Philosophy of Ayn Rand, Random House, 1961.
The Virtue of Selfishness: A New Concept of Egoism, with additional articles by Nathaniel Branden, New American Library, 1964.

Capitalism: The Unknown Ideal, with additional articles by Branden and others, New American Library, 1966.

Introduction to Objectivist Epistemology, Objectivist, 1967.

The Romantic Manifesto: A Philosophy of Literature, World Library, 1969.

Philosophy: Who Needs It, introduction by Leonard Peikoff, Bobbs-Merrill, 1971.

The New Left: The Anti-Industrial Revolution, New American Library, 1982.

The Ayn Rand Lexicon: Objectivism from A to Z, introduction and notes by Peikoff, New American Library, 1984.

PLAYS

Night of January 16th (produced as *Woman on Trial* at Hollywood Playhouse, 1934; produced on Broadway, 1935; produced as *Penthouse Legend*, 1973), Longmans, Green, 1936.

The Unconquered (adaptation of *We the Living*), produced on Broadway, 1940.

OTHER

Love Letters (screenplay; adaptation of the novel by Chris Massie), Paramount, 1945.

You Came Along (screenplay), Paramount, 1945.

The Fountainhead (screenplay; adaptation of Rand's novel), Warner Bros., 1949.

The Early Ayn Rand: A Selection from Her Unpublished Fiction (includes *Red Pawn*, *Ideal*, and *Think Twice*), introduction and notes by Peikoff, New American Library, 1984.

The Ayn Rand Columns: A Collection of Her Weekly Newspaper Articles, Written for the Los Angeles Times, Second Renaissance Press, 1990.

The Ayn Rand Letter: 1971-1976, 5th edition, Second Renaissance Press, 1990.

Author of introduction, *The Ominous Parallels*, by Leonard Peikoff, NAL/Dutton, 1983. Coeditor and contributor, *The Objectivist Newsletter*, 1962-65, and its successor, *The Objectivist* (monthly journal), 1966-71; writer and publisher, *The Ayn Rand Letter*, 1971-76. Columnist for the *Los Angeles Times*.

■ Adaptations

Night of January 16th was filmed by Paramount and released in 1941; *We the Living* was filmed in Italy in 1942; and a revised and abridged version of the Italian film was released in the United States in 1988.

■ Sidelights

Ayn Rand has been both revered and disparaged as the author of controversial novels, essays, and other works that espouse her philosophy of Objectivism. A Russian-born American citizen, Rand celebrated laissez-faire capitalism in her writings, arguing that it is the only economic system that recognizes the sanctity of the individual. She described her philosophy as "the concept of man as a heroic being, with his own happiness as the moral purpose of his life, with productive achievement as his noblest activity, and reason his only absolute," according to Barbara Branden in *The Passion of Ayn Rand*. An atheist, Rand was a proponent of "rational selfishness" and regarded the Judeo-Christian ideal of self-sacrifice inconsistent with individualism. Her emphasis on capitalism and the freedom of the individual made her an influential figure among some political conservatives, especially Libertarians. Critical response to her work has ranged from the hostile to the enthusiastic, with common objections centering on her philosophy, which some critics considered too simplistic and self-centered. Nonetheless, Rand attracted an ardent following in the 1960s, and her enduring accomplishment, according to some critics, was her creation of popular novels of ideas, including *The Fountainhead* and *Atlas Shrugged*, that continue to sell well decades after their publication. "Objections to Rand's philosophy might seem to disparage her achievement," observed George Gilder in *Chicago Tribune Book World*. "But in fact, like every great thinker, she transcends her contradictions. In a world where most novelists lack any coherent philosophy at all, her work looms as a major triumph."

Rand was born Alice Rosenbaum in St. Petersburg, Russia, in 1905. During her early childhood her family was relatively affluent, living in a large apartment above her father's chemist shop. Rand's father was a self-made man; he had not been interested in becoming a chemist, but since one of the few Russian universities that enrolled Jews had an opening in that area, he took the opportunity to learn a profession. Rand recalled to Branden that she had little contact with her father as a young girl: "I felt a friendly respect for him in childhood, not a strong affection, a dutiful 'official' affection.... I liked him as a person, but in childhood I had very little to do with him. Children's education was totally in the hands of the mother in those days.... It was when he and I began discussing ideas when I was fourteen, when we became political allies, that I felt a real love, a love that meant something.''

Rand's mother ran the Rosenbaum household, which included a cook, a maid, and a governess, and loved to give parties and attend the theater and ballet. The relationship between mother and daughter was often strained, as Rand revealed to Branden: "I disliked her quite a lot. We really didn't get along. She was my exact opposite, and I thought so in childhood, and now. She was by principle and basic style, by sense of life, extremely social. She was not really interested in ideas, she was much more interested in the social aspect. Our clashes in childhood were that I was antisocial, I was insufficiently interested in other children, I didn't play with them, I didn't have girlfriends; this was a nagging refrain always. She disapproved of me in every respect except one: she was proud of my intelligence and proud to show me off to the rest of the family.''

A precocious child, Rand was often in the company of adults and constantly gathered information about the world around her. She taught herself to read and write about a year before she was to start school, an event that she eagerly anticipated. Once she began attending, however, she became bored by all her classes except arithmetic and, possibly because of her serious, shy nature, was unable to make friends with the other children.

Rand's mother, Anna, understood her child's boredom and searched for ways to keep her occupied. A governess gave Rand lessons in French and German, and Anna Rosenbaum provided the girl with French children's magazines. Rand was at first uninterested in the magazines, but then read a tale that intrigued her. The story was about a fearless detective who triumphed over a dangerous jewel thief, a good versus evil scenario that Rand found interesting. "The battle between good and evil was to engage her ever after," Branden commented. "It was to be the major element she sought in literature, it was to be the perspective from which she viewed the world.''

The stories she read in the French magazines inspired Rand to create her own, and writing became an enjoyable activity for her. "The ease with which I wrote has remained to this day as a kind of Atlantis behind me, a lost Garden of Eden," Rand told Branden. She continued to read magazine stories, and one particular adventure tale that she read when she was nine years old would have a lasting effect on her. Rand was impressed and excited by the story's hero, Cyrus. "Cyrus was a

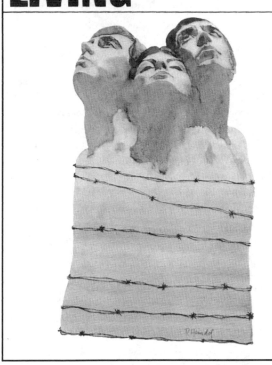

This 1936 book, Rand's first novel, relates the stifling effects of Communism on individuality.

personal inspiration," she revealed to Branden, "a concrete of what one should be like, and what a man should be like. He was a man of action who was totally self-confident, and no one could stand in his way. No matter what the circumstances, he'd always find a solution. He helped me concretize what I called 'my kind of man'—that expression, which I carried thereafter, began with that story. Intelligence, independence, courage. The heroic man." As an adult, Rand professed that every man had the potential to become a heroic being, and in her novels she attempted to create ideal men as her protagonists.

In 1914, the year she read about Cyrus, Rand spent the summer travelling abroad in Austria and Switzerland with her family. She decided at that time, while telling stories to her two younger sisters, that she would make writing her profession, a goal that she steadfastly held despite the difficulties she would later encounter. As the Rosenbaums vacationed in Europe, World War I began, sending them hurrying to find a ship to take them safely back to Russia. When they returned, Rand heard little about the war; her parents, in order to shield their children, did not discuss it or allow them to read about it in the newspapers. So Rand concentrated on her writing: "I was writing in every spare moment. I felt I was preparing for the future, for the world I would enter when I grew up," she told Branden.

Rand's Philosophy Reacts to Communism

By 1916, however, Rand could not help but notice the effects of the war on Russia, and she developed a strong interest in politics. St. Petersburg, the cosmopolitan city which had been renamed Petrograd in 1914, was disintegrating. More than one million Russians were killed in the war, and a million starving, ill-clothed soldiers deserted the front. That winter the city was filled with cold, hungry people and outbreaks of crime and violence. In February of 1917 the people of Petrograd ousted Czar Nicholas II, giving power to the Duma, a political assembly. Alexander Kerensky, a powerful orator whom Rand would come to admire, became prime minister. During that time, it seemed to Rand that "everybody was against the Czar," she explained to Branden. "What fascinated me was that it fit in with my own stage of development—it was the only time I was synchronized with history. It was almost like fiction taking place in reality. That was why I became so interested. I know that I romanticized it a great deal. It seemed the fight for freedom; since that's what they were talking about, I took it literally— by which I meant individualism: it's *man* who must be free." At that time, Rand noted, she "began to understand that politics was a *moral* issue," and that she was opposed to "the government or society or any authorities imposing anything on anyone."

A country in the midst of economic chaos, Russia did not fare much better as a fledgling democracy. The people remained disgruntled and many soldiers refused to continue fighting. The desperate conditions gave the exiled communist Bolsheviks, led by Lenin, a chance to return and seize power. Bolshevik tanks rolled into Petrograd in October of 1917, and ten days later the revolution was complete. Kerensky, the prime minister, was unable to hold his country together and escaped abroad, a move that disappointed Rand. As the Bolshevik

Revolution began, Rand's mother implored her husband to leave the country, but he would not consider it, saying that he could not leave his chemist shop. But after the revolution Communist soldiers seized private businesses throughout Russia, and Fronz Rosenbaum was forced to relinquish his shop to the government. Banks and other private properties were also nationalized, and the Rosenbaum family subsisted on Fronz's savings.

Conditions in Russia did not improve under the Communists. Starvation, disease, and crime were rampant. One man, rumored to have hoarded sour cream, was lynched by an angry, hungry mob. Rand was outraged not only by the hardships the Communists had imposed on her family, but also by the Communist ideology, and she was surprised that others seemed not to be bothered by collectivist principles. "Even at that age," Rand remarked to Branden, "I could see what was wrong with communism. It meant living for the State. I realized they were saying that the illiterate and poor had to be the rulers of the earth, *because* they were illiterate and poor."

In 1918 civil war broke out in Russia between the communist Red Army and the pro-czarist White Army. As conditions worsened in Petrograd, Anna Rosenbaum determined that her family must seek refuge in the Crimea region and with some difficulty obtained a travel permit. After arriving in the city of Odessa, which was not yet under Communist control, the Rosenbaum family secured a small house and Fronz Rosenbaum opened another chemist shop. For a short while the family was able to scrape by, but during the next three years the Crimea became contested territory. "It was like living on a battlefield," Rand told Branden. "Finally, we began to starve. Food was unobtainable. At last, we ate only millet. Except that Mother insisted on obtaining raw onions, which she fried in linseed oil; scurvy had become a terrible problem and Mother had read that onions prevented it."

While in the Crimea, Rand began attending high school, where "there was a tacit recognition of my superiority. I made no personal friends, I had no girlfriends, but I was recognized as the 'brain of the class,' which surprised me," she revealed to Branden. As an adolescent, Rand was outspoken about ideas and subjects that she found meaningful. "I argued at the slightest provocation, whether people did or did not want to hear," she recalled to Branden. "I criticized myself for this. I was very aware they didn't really want to talk, and I was forcing the conversation." Rand's favorite classes in high school were mathematics and logic. She also took courses in American history. "To me it was incredible. I saw America as the country of individualism, of strong men, of freedom and important purposes. I thought '*This* is the kind of government I approve of.'"

Rand gained other lifelong convictions as a teenager. She wrote in her diary, "Today, I decided to become an atheist." As Rand described later to Branden, "I had decided that the concept of God is degrading to men. Since they say God is perfect, and man can never be that perfect, then man is low and imperfect and there is something above him—which is wrong." She added that "no proof of the existence of God exists; the concept is an untenable invention." In addition, she disliked classic Russian literature and was greatly influenced by books by foreign authors such as Victor Hugo and Edmond-Eugene-Alexis Rostand. She also read, and was unimpressed with, the works of George Sand. "It was feminine, sentimental, romantic in a wishy-washy way; it was all love stories, studies of the relationship between men and women, which I considered totally unimportant subjects," she explained to Branden. "I had felt almost rivalistic in advance, because I thought she was the most famous woman writer in the world; but I felt nothing but contempt for her feminine preoccupation with romantic passions. Great romance is important, and all of my projected novels had great romances—but it is not the main concern. Love has to be part of a great cause, never the main focus for the man or the woman."

At sixteen then, "The essence of her value-system and her character were formed," commented Branden. That same year, Rand graduated from high school and the civil war ended, with the Communist forces victorious. Many Russians had escaped the country by way of the Black Sea, and Rand's mother thought the Rosenbaum family should as well. But Fronz Rosenbaum refused, and Rand and her family made their way back toward Petrograd. "Father's greatest mistake was that he didn't want to go," Rand told Branden. "He still hoped that communism would not last. He thought that Europe and the world at large would not allow it to last, and he would get his property—his business and his building—back."

Once in Petrograd, Rand attended college and graduated with a degree in history in 1924 (the same year Petrograd was renamed Leningrad). Though she intended to become a writer, she was not interested in pursuing a degree in literature because, as she told Branden, "I didn't want to study, as examples, writers who bored me and

whom I despised." Rand also had reservations about philosophy courses: "I was convinced a lot of it would be mystical chaos." Despite this opinion, she took a course in ancient philosophy, studying celebrated figures such as Aristotle and Plato. Rand was deeply influenced by Aristotle's laws of logic, but dismissed what she described to Branden as the "mysticism, and collectivism" of Plato. As it turned out, Rand's oral examination for the course focused on Plato. After she had answered her professor's questions, he asked, "You don't agree with Plato, do you?" Rand answered that she didn't, and when he asked her to explain she said, "My philosophical views are not part of the history of philosophy yet. But they will be." (Rand received a perfect score on her exam.)

During college, Rand met her first love, an engineering student named Leo. Their relationship lasted a few months, during which time Rand became enamored with the young man. "Of all the young people, he was the only one who seemed to value himself, who projected authentic self-esteem.... That was a top value for me," Rand explained to Branden. When their relationship ended, it "was the most prolonged period of pain in my life," Rand revealed. "You see—perhaps it's not easy to understand when one has known only the freedom of America—Leo was, to me, life in the present, and the only life I had there. The only human being who mattered to me in a personal way. Before Leo, I had regarded everything as something to get over with; life begins in the future, and all that matters is what I'm thinking and what books I will write; concrete reality doesn't matter. Now it mattered. He was my entry into life."

Although Rand was able to recover from Leo's rejection, she never forgot him. The hero of her first novel, *We the Living*, is named Leo, and the character fits the description of his real-life Russian counterpart. And as a middle-aged woman in 1961, Rand remarked, "I am not indifferent to Leo, to this day," according to Branden. "But you see, it was fortunate that he didn't ask me to marry him. I would have said yes, I would have stayed in Russia—and I would have died there."

From Petrograd to Hollywood

Rand was given the opportunity to leave Russia in 1925, when some American relatives agreed to have her visit them and to finance her trip. At that time it was difficult to secure a travel permit, since many Russians who journeyed abroad never returned to their native country. And though Rand told Branden that she "would no more have thought of returning [to Russia] than of jumping off a building," she was able to convince the American consul to give her a visa. She began her voyage in January of 1926, and before she left an acquaintance told her, "If they ask you, in America—tell them that Russia is a huge cemetery, and that we are all dying slowly," Branden reported. Rand remembered the man's entreaty when she wrote *We the Living,* which expresses how communism stifles the individual.

When Rand disembarked in New York City, she decided to change her first name to Ayn, the name of a Finnish writer. (She had not read any books by this author; she just liked the name.) She then traveled to Chicago, where she would stay with relatives. After her arrival Rand immersed herself in her writing and in perfecting her English, the language she would write her novels in. At the time, however, Rand was not working on novels; she instead aspired to write screenplays for a movie studio in Hollywood. Through a friend of her family, Rand was able to obtain a letter of introduction to a publicity agent of the Cecil B. DeMille Studio, which was named for Rand's favorite movie director. DeMille "did plot pictures," Rand recalled to Branden, "and most of them were glamorous and romantic.... he was famous in Russia for society glamour, sex, and adventure. He was my particular ideal of the American screen."

Having completed four screenplays in her shaky English, Rand departed for Los Angeles to begin what she hoped would be a career as a screenwriter. Before she left she changed her last name to Rand, getting the name from her Remington-Rand typewriter. She never told her family in Russia that Alice Rosenbaum had become Ayn Rand because, as Branden noted, "She had no doubt that she would one day be famous, and she feared that if it were known in Russia that she was Alice Rosenbaum, daughter of Fronz and Anna, her family's safety, even their lives, would be endangered by their relationship to a vocal anti-Communist."

Upon her arrival in Los Angeles, Rand was directed to the Hollywood Studio Club, a rooming house for women who hoped to break into the film industry as writers, dancers, actresses, costume designers, and in other positions. The next day she went to the DeMille Studio to speak with her contact from the publicity department, but discovered that the woman did not have the authority to place her in a screenwriting job. Dismayed and unsure of what to do next, Rand left the studio only to see Cecil B.

DeMille himself behind the wheel of a car at the curb. She had seen pictures of him in Russia, and could not help but stare. She continued walking, and as she reached the gate DeMille drove up to her and asked why she had been staring. "I just arrived from Russia," Rand said according to Branden, "and I'm very happy to see you." DeMille responded by opening his car door and saying, "Get in."

Rand and DeMille drove to where the movie *The King of Kings* was being filmed, and during the ride Rand expressed her interest in becoming a screenwriter and told him that he was her favorite director. That day, Rand watched the filming of *The King of Kings,* and at the end of the week DeMille hired her as an extra, a job that paid seven and a half dollars a day. While working on the movie set, Rand noticed an attractive young actor. "I spent the next three days just staring at him on the huge, crowded set, watching his every move, and trying to figure out how to meet him," she recalled to Branden, "I watched to see if anyone spoke to him whom I knew, but he was enormously anti-social—and of course I liked that. His manner suggested an aloof, confident, self-sufficiency."

Rand finally arranged to bump into the man during a crowd scene and learned that his name was Frank O'Connor. They happened to meet each other again in a library weeks later, and they eventually married. Frank explained to Branden what had first attracted him to Ayn Rand: "One of the most striking things about her was her complete openness.... The total honesty. You knew that it would be inconceivable for her ever to act against her own principles. Other people professed so many things that had no connection to what they actually did. But you knew that anything Ayn said, she *meant....* She had a tremendous capacity for enjoyment. Whether it was a piece of music she liked or a story or some present I bought her that cost a dollar—she was so expressively and radiantly delighted.... She constantly passed value judgements. If she liked something, she liked it violently. If she didn't like something, she would communicate *that* violently, too.... When we were with other people, she was reserved, even shy—until they began discussing ideas. Then all the shyness vanished."

Rand continued to work as a movie extra until the shooting of *The King of Kings* was finished, then DeMille offered her a job as a junior writer, which entailed summarizing works to be adapted for screen and making suggestions for the movie versions. Though she was excited at first to have found work as a screenwriter, she was quickly disillusioned. "The stories they gave me were impossible, and I didn't do well," she told Branden. "I had terrible 'squirms,' I felt blocked, and couldn't come up with ideas I really liked. The first story they gave me was entitled 'My Dog,' so you can just imagine how I felt."

We the Living

Rand was soon out of work, however, when Cecil B. DeMille sold his studio and began working as an independent producer at Metro-Goldwyn-Mayer. She then briefly tried various odd jobs, including waitressing, selling newspaper subscriptions, and stuffing envelopes. After her marriage to Frank, Rand found a position in the wardrobe department at RKO Radio Pictures, where she began as a filing clerk and was promoted to office head within a year. She told Branden that she had "loathed" her job, but was thankful to have money coming in when the Great Depression began and millions were unemployed. During her time at RKO, Rand began writing her first novel, *We the Living*, at night and on the weekends. Soon she found the combination of work and writing too taxing on weekdays, and limited her writing to Sundays and vacations.

With *We the Living*, Rand explained to Branden, "I did not really want to do a major novel—that is, a novel that would have *my* kind of hero and *my* philosophy; I felt more sure of myself writing about characters in their early twenties, about a major character who was a woman, and about a theme that was political rather than more widely philosophical." Frank and his brother Nick encouraged Rand to write about the horrors of Soviet Russia, and she remembered the acquaintance who had said, "Tell them that Russia is a huge cemetery and that we are all dying slowly."

So Rand began the slow process of writing *We the Living* and soon became frustrated that she could not devote herself full-time to her novel. She suspended work on the book in 1931, hoping to write a screenplay that, if sold, would allow her to quit her job. The result was *Red Pawn*, which Universal Studios bought for fifteen hundred dollars but was never able to produce. "I was enormously thrilled and proud," Rand told Branden, and with that success she was able to leave RKO and concentrate fully on her writing.

Before she returned to writing *We the Living*, however, Rand was inspired to create a play after seeing a courtroom drama entitled *The Trial of*

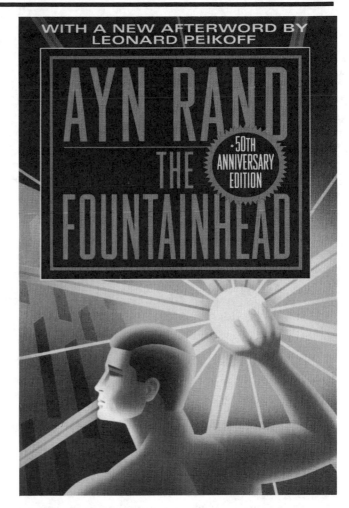

Rand considered this 1943 book, perhaps her best known work, to be her first "serious" piece.

Mary Dugan. The resulting stage production, originally titled *Penthouse Legend*, featured Bjorn Faulkner, an industrialist, and Karen Andre, who loved and worked with Faulkner and who was also on trial for his murder. Jurors were to be chosen from the audience, and the ending of the play depended on the jury's verdict. As she commented to Branden, Rand was quite satisfied with her work on *Penthouse Legend:* "I was more in control of technique then with *We the Living*, because it was simpler and involved no narration, only plot and dialogue. It was with narrative that I was not yet fully in control."

Penthouse Legend was produced as *Woman on Trial* in 1934 and as *Night of January 16th* on Broadway in 1935. Though Rand was pleased with her script, both productions dissatisfied her. She explained to Branden that the rehearsals of *Woman on Trial* were particularly unpleasant: "Instead of being glamorous, it was nerve-wracking day after day to hear people reading my lines and not really knowing what they were saying, and very few did it properly." Both runs of the play were relatively successful and received generally good reviews, but Rand objected to the changes that director Al Woods insisted on for *Night of January 16th*. "The entire history of the play has been the worst hell I ever lived through," Branden reported Rand's comment to Rex Reed in 1973. "It was produced in 1935 by Al Woods, a famous producer of melodramas, who . . . turned it into a junk heap of cliches that clashed with the style and confused the audience. . . . He was a faithful adherent to the school of thought that believes if a literary work is serious, it must bore people to death; if it's entertaining, it must not communicate anything of importance."

After *Night of January 16th* finished its Broadway run in 1936, Rand learned that *We the Living*, which she had completed in 1933, had been accepted for publication by the Macmillan Publishing Company. The manuscript had been rejected by a number of publishers, with common criticisms focusing on the book's intellectual nature and its condemnation of Soviet Russia. (Communist thought influenced many in America during the 1930s, and some publishers believed that an anti-communist book would not sell.) Upon publication, *We the Living* received little publicity and few reviews, and sales were lackluster. A year later, however, word-of-mouth recommendations caused the book to sell better than right after it was published. And by 1984, *We the Living* had sold more than two million copies.

We the Living, set in Soviet Russia following the Communist revolution, focuses on three main characters: Kira Argounova, Leo Kovalensky, and Andrei Taganov. Kira, daughter of middle-class parents, is in love with the aristocratic Leo. When Leo contracts tuberculosis, Kira must find a way to arrange medical care, which is not easily available to aristocrats and the middle class, groups considered "class enemies" by the Communists. Desperate to save Leo, Kira turns to a young Communist, Andrei, and the two become lovers. Andrei helps Kira by giving her monetary gifts, which she uses to pay for Leo's health care. Leo, who is involved in black market activities, is eventually arrested by Andrei, and the two discover that they both love Kira. Andrei comes to understand what communism did to Kira and, disillusioned, he sets Leo free before committing suicide. Leo, for his part, feels betrayed by Kira and leaves her for another woman. Believing that she no longer has anything

to bind her to Russia, Kira attempts to escape across the border into Latvia, but is shot and killed.

Though some reviewers found *We the Living* to be merely anti-Communist propaganda, others considered the work to have some merit. In the *New York Times Book Review*, for instance, Harold Strauss commented that "Rand can command a good deal of narrative skill, and her novel moves with alacrity and vigor upon occasion." Rand admitted to Branden that she was not completely satisfied with the book, noting some stylistic difficulties. But she remarked that "ideologically, I had said exactly what I wanted, and I had had no difficulty in expressing my ideas. I had wanted to write a novel about Man against the State. I had wanted to show, as the basic theme, the sanctity—the supreme value—of human life, and the immorality of treating men as sacrificial animals and ruling them by physical force. I did so." The author continued, "*We the Living* was only an exercise, it was not fully *my* novel yet. My first *serious* novel had to present my type of man."

The Fountainhead

Rand's first "serious" novel would be *The Fountainhead*, which she began outlining in 1936. The planning of the book proceeded at a frustratingly slow pace, however, and for several months Rand was at a loss for how to end her story. She decided to set the novel aside for awhile and write a novella, *Anthem*, which gave her "a rest from plotting," as she told Branden. *Anthem*, which was first published in England, is a futuristic work featuring a collectivist society where the word "I" is forbidden; an individual calls himself "we," and refers to another individual as "they." The society is primitive, as human accomplishments in art, science, and business have been forgotten. *Anthem*'s central idea is that humankind's greatest achievements are only possible if people are free, and that in a collectivist society ruled by force such achievement is not possible. The book was rejected by many American publishing houses but, like Rand's other work, it eventually became popular, especially among young readers. *Anthem* was "a surprising favorite among the high-school taste-makers," according to a 1966 *New York Times Book Review* article by Gerald Raftery. And in the words of *English Journal* contributor Tamara Stadnychenko, *Anthem* offers the young reader "exciting action, an appealing love story, and an interesting political philosophy."

After completing *Anthem*, Rand returned to her work on *The Fountainhead*, which required extensive research. The hero of the novel is architect Howard Roark, and to lend authenticity to the book Rand worked for six months in the office of renowned New York architect Ely Jacques Kahn as a filing clerk, typist, and general assistant. While employed by Kahn, Rand finally was able to work out a climax to *The Fountainhead*, and in 1938 she began actually writing the novel. More interruptions followed, however, as Rand wrote plays whose sale she hoped would alleviate her financial difficulties. *Ideal* and *Think Twice* were written during this period, but were never produced and only published posthumously in *The Early Ayn Rand*. A stage version of *We the Living*, entitled *The Unconquered*, was produced in New York City in 1940. The play, which Rand termed "a disaster," received negative reviews and closed after only five days. After her experiences with *Night of January 16th* and *The Unconquered*, Rand never wrote for the stage again.

By 1940 Rand had only finished the first few chapters of *The Fountainhead*, but was submitting them to publishers, hoping to land a contract and an advance payment. As with her other works, *The Fountainhead* was rejected by a number of publishing companies. But Archibald G. Ogden, a young editor at Bobbs-Merrill, loved the book and sought permission to sign a contract with Rand. Bobbs-Merrill head D. L. Chambers instructed Ogden to reject the novel, but Ogden sent him a telegram that said, "If this is not the book for you, then I am not the editor for you," according to Branden. Chambers wired this message to Ogden: "Far be it from me to dampen such enthusiasm. Sign the contract. But the book better be good."

Rand finished *The Fountainhead* in December of 1942, and it was published in May of the next year. The theme of the novel, as Rand described to Branden, was "individualism versus collectivism, not in politics, but in man's soul." The climax of *The Fountainhead* occurs when Howard Roark blows up a low-income housing project that he created, destroying it rather than see his design compromised. "The story is the story of Howard Roark's triumph," said Rand in her notes on the novel. She continued, according to Branden, noting that *The Fountainhead* "has to show every conceivable hardship and obstacle on his way—and how he triumphs over them, why he *has to* triumph. These obstacles, of course, can come from only one source; other men. It is *Society*, with all its boggled chaos of selflessness, compromise, servility, and

lies, that stands in the way of Howard Roark. As he goes on, it is every conceivable form of 'second-hand living' that comes to fight him, that tries to crush him in every possible manner . . . and fails in the attempt. To every second-hand creature he stands as a contrast, a reproach and a lesson."

In *The Fountainhead*, Rand presented Roark as her ideal man. She also used the novel to dramatize her philosophy—later to be named Objectivism—which championed freedom, the self, and reason. On trial for blowing up his building, Roark summarizes Rand's conviction: "It is said that I have destroyed the home of the destitute. It is forgotten that but for me the destitute could not have had this particular home.... It is believed that the poverty of the future tenants have them a right to my work.... That it was my duty to contribute anything demanded of me.... I came here to say that I do not recognize anyone's right to one minute of my life. Nor to any part of my energy. Nor to any achievement of mine. No matter who makes the claim, how large their number or how great their need. I wished to come here and say that I am a man who does not exist for others."

Reviews of *The Fountainhead* were mixed, with some critics not recognizing the theme of the novel, others condemning Rand's ideology, and still others calling the characters unrealistic. In a 1943 *New York Times Book Review* article, however, Lorine Pruette called Rand "a writer of great power. She has a subtle and ingenious mind and the capacity of writing brilliantly, beautifully, bitterly." Pruette added that "good novels of ideas are rare at any time. This is the only novel of ideas written by an American woman that I can recall."

Though sales were slow at first, the book that many publishers and critics considered to be too intellectual, controversial, and noncommercial sold more than 400,000 copies by 1948. By the mid-1980s, *The Fountainhead* had sold more than four million copies. Rand received bundles of mail from her diverse readers, from professionals to homemakers and from unskilled workers to artists. Branden reported that Rand's fans "wrote that they had found in Roark's moral intransigence a personal ideal—that the image of Roark had given them a greater courage to stand by their own convictions and to fight for their own achievements—that *The Fountainhead* had liberated them from the guilt they had experienced for their failure to live by altruist ethics–that it had taught them to feel proud of their work . . . that it had given them the sense of what is possible in life, what is possible to man, what is possible to *them*."

The success of *The Fountainhead* culminated in a movie deal with Warner Brothers that brought Rand fifty thousand dollars and an end to her financial troubles. Rand wrote the screenplay for *The Fountainhead* and fought for creative control but, as with her plays, she was ultimately dissatisfied with the final product. To her horror, Roark's line "I wished to come here and say that I am a man who does not exist for others," which summarized the book's theme, was cut from the film. When she saw the rough version of the movie, "I knew it was no good," she later told Branden. "And I never changed my mind. The people involved were not worthy of the assignment. I didn't even like the script; they wanted the movie to be under two hours, so the script was too short, it wasn't right. I was through with Hollywood."

Atlas Shrugged

While she was working on her next novel, *Atlas Shrugged*, Rand received a fan letter that particularly impressed her. The letter, which was from a young student named Nathaniel Branden, included literary and philosophical questions about *We the Living* and *The Fountainhead* that Rand found perceptive. Though she rarely took time to answer her mail, she responded to Nathaniel and eventually invited him to her home to further discuss her philosophy and books. Nathaniel and his future wife, Barbara (who wrote *The Passion of Ayn Rand*), began visiting Rand and her husband frequently, and the group became close friends. Rand even allowed Nathaniel and Barbara to read chapters of *Atlas Shrugged* as she wrote it, and when the book was published it was dedicated to both her husband and Nathaniel, whom she referred to as her "intellectual heir." Rand and Nathaniel eventually began a love affair—with the consent of their spouses—that lasted nearly fourteen years.

Rand finished writing *Atlas Shrugged* in the spring of 1957. With this novel, the author felt that she had accomplished her life work; she had dramatized her complete philosophy and created a character, John Galt, who embodied it. In *Atlas Shrugged* Rand presents a crumbling American welfare state where, in their frustration, the most creative and productive people in society—the artists, scientists, inventors, and others—go on strike. John Galt initiates the strike as a protest; he and his followers will no longer accept the burden of sustaining nonproductive citizens. They refuse to be like the Atlas of Greek mythology and hold the world on their shoulders. As the hero says, "I swear—by my life and my love of it—that I will never live for the sake of another man, nor ask another man to live for mine."

Atlas Shrugged, like Rand's other books, glorifies the individual, free will, capitalism, and reason as good while denouncing collectivism and altruism as evil. As Nathaniel Branden noted in *Who Is Ayn Rand? An Analysis of the Novels of Ayn Rand*, however, with *Atlas Shrugged* Rand expands upon her basic principles: "The novel presents the essentials of an entire philosophical system: epistemology, metaphysics, ethics, politics (and psychology). It shows the interrelation of these subjects in business, in a man's attitude toward his work, in love, in family relationships, in the press, in the universities, in economics, in art, in foreign relations, in science, in government, in sex. It presents a unified and comprehensive view of man and of man's relationship to existence."

As with Rand's other novels, critical response to *Atlas Shrugged* was mixed, with some reviewers objecting to her philosophy and literary technique. *Commonweal* contributor Patricia Donegan called the book "a cumbersome, lumbering vehicle in which characterization, plot and reality are subordinated to the author's expression of personal philosophy." Other critics, however, praised Rand for writing a book that is simultaneously intellectual and entertaining. Writing in the *New York Herald Tribune Book Review*, John Chamberlain characterized *Atlas Shrugged* as "so much more than a mere novel," and went on to describe the book as "a vibrant and powerful novel of ideas which happens to have all the qualities of a thunderously successful melodrama."

"Fiction, to me, *is Atlas Shrugged*," Rand explained to Branden in *The Passion of Ayn Rand*. "My mission was done.... Until *Atlas* was completed, I always felt an enormous tension, the drive of a central purpose. My loafing so much during the years after *Atlas* was malevolent in that I felt desperate about the state of the world, I could not decide what to do with my life nor how to bear going around despising everybody—yet often, alone in my study, it *was* Atlantis, I'd sit at my desk in happy contemplation, with the feeling of complete peace. While I was working on *Atlas*, I felt I didn't care if a bomb dropped, just so long as I could finish this book. But after *Atlas* I was no longer pressured, my lifelong assignment was over, and I felt as if my time from then on was a gift."

The popular success of *Atlas Shrugged*, which had sold more than five million copies by 1984, established Rand as a philosopher as well as a novelist and inspired a movement based on her ideas. Since the book's publication, Rand had received numerous requests for a detailed explication of her philosophy of Objectivism. Nathaniel Branden, responding to these requests, decided to set up the Nathaniel Branden Institute, which would present lectures on Rand's ideology. The lectures, which included topics such as "What is reason?," "The ethics of altruism," "The economics of a free society," and "The psychology of sex," were heavily attended during the 1960s. Rand also became a sought-after speaker on college campuses, wrote a weekly opinion column for the *Los Angeles Times,* and coedited and contributed to *The Objectivist Newsletter.* Though *Atlas Shrugged* was her last work of fiction, she continued to expound upon her philosophy in several nonfiction works, including *The Virtue of Selfishness: A New Concept of Egoism, Capitalism: The Unknown Ideal,* and *Philosophy: Who Needs It.*

During the last years of her life Rand was often ill—she lost a lung to cancer—but she continued to lecture and write until her death in 1982. She appeared on the *Phil Donahue Show* in 1979, had begun adapting *Atlas Shrugged* as a television miniseries in 1981, and at the age of seventy-six hired a tutor to teach her algebra, a subject that she enjoyed. Despite her often serious demeanor, Rand is remembered by those who were close to her as a brilliant, intense woman with a magnetic personality. She was also, according to Branden, something of an enigma. Though Rand extolled the virtues of reason, free will, and man-made inventions, she never learned to drive and was afraid of air travel; her phobic anxiety concerning germs caused her to boil her silverware; and she wore a good-luck watch. This outwardly formidable woman also liked it when her husband called her by her pet name, "Fluff," and she fed her cat expensive raw hamburger even when her early financial troubles forced her to skimp on meals for herself.

As she had predicted as a teenager in Russia, Rand became a well-known novelist and philosopher and her ideas continue to influence areas such as psychology, economics, and politics. Her philosophy of Objectivism inspired the creation of the Libertarian political party, which calls for both free markets and freedom of the individual. Many prominent figures acknowledge being inspired by Rand's novels, including U. S. Federal Reserve head Alan Greenspan, *Barron's* publisher Robert Bleiberg, former British prime minister Margaret Thatcher, and tennis champion Billie Jean King. Nathaniel Branden, now a psychologist and author

Set in a decomposing welfare state, this 1957 novel—like much of Rand's work—relates the author's philosophy and glorifies individual achievement.

of books on self-esteem, told Barbara Branden that "intellectually, I learned more from Ayn Rand than I could possibly summarize. . . . She had provocative and innovative ideas in virtually every sphere of philosophy, from epistemology to aesthetics. I think the creativity of her countless insights will go on being discovered and appreciated and new for a very long time."

■ Works Cited

Branden, Barbara, *The Passion of Ayn Rand,* Doubleday, 1986.

Branden, Nathaniel, *Who Is Ayn Rand? An Analysis of the Novels of Ayn Rand,* Random House, 1962.

Chamberlain, John, "Ayn Rand's Political Parable and Thundering Melodrama," *New York Herald Tribune Book Review,* October 6, 1957, pp. 1, 9.

Donegan, Patricia, "A Point of View," *Commonweal*, November 8, 1957, pp. 155-156.

Gilder, George, "Ayn Rand: Sex, Money, and Philosophy," *Chicago Tribune Book World*, June 29, 1986, pp. 1, 10.

Pruette, Lorine, "Battle against Evil," *New York Times Book Review*, May 16, 1943, pp. 7, 18.

Raftery, Gerald, "High-School Favorites," *New York Times Book Review*, February 27, 1966, pp. 14, 16.

Rand, Ayn, *The Fountainhead*, Bobbs-Merrill, 1943.

Rand, Ayn, *Atlas Shrugged*, Random House, 1957.

Stadnychenko, Tamara, "'Anthem': A Book for All Reasons," *English Journal*, February, 1983, pp. 77-78.

Strauss, Harold, "Soviet Triangle," *New York Times Book Review*, April 19, 1936, p. 7.

■ For More Information See

BOOKS

Branden, Nathaniel, *Judgement Day: My Years with Ayn Rand*, Avon, 1991.

Contemporary Literary Criticism, Gale, Volume 3, 1975, Volume 30, 1984, Volume 44, 1987.

PERIODICALS

Boston Review, December, 1984, p. 28.

Library Journal, May 1, 1979, p. 1062; January 1, 1983, p. 53.

Los Angeles Times Book Review, September 2, 1984; February 23, 1992, p. 10.

National Review, May 28, 1990, pp. 35-36.

New Republic, December 10, 1966, pp. 27-28; February 21, 1970, pp. 21-23.

Washington Post Book World, December 12, 1982.*

—*Sketch by Michelle M. Motowski*

Cynthia Rylant

■ Personal

Surname is pronounced "rye-*lunt*"; born June 6, 1954, in Hopewell, VA; daughter of John Tune (an army sergeant) and Leatrel (a nurse; maiden name, Rylant) Smith; married and divorced twice; children: Nathaniel. *Education:* Morris Harvey College (now University of Charleston), B.A., 1975; Marshall University, M.A., 1976; Kent State University, M.L.S., 1982. *Politics:* Democrat. *Religion:* "Christian, no denomination."

■ Career

Writer. Marshall University, Huntington, WV, part-time English instructor, 1979-80; Akron Public Library, Akron, OH, children's librarian, 1983; University of Akron, Akron, part-time English lecturer, 1983-84; Northeast Ohio Universities College of Medicine, Rootstown, OH, part-time lecturer, 1991—.

■ Awards, Honors

When I Was Young in the Mountains was named a *Booklist* reviewer's choice, 1982, Caldecott Honor Book, American Library Association (ALA) notable book, and Reading Rainbow selection, all 1983; American Book Award nomination, 1983, and English Speaking Union Book-across-the-Sea Ambassador of Honor Award, 1984, both for *When I Was Young in the Mountains; Waiting to Waltz . . . a Childhood* was named an ALA notable book, a *School Library Journal* best book of 1984, a National Council for Social Studies best book, 1984, and a Society of Midland Authors best children's book, 1985; *The Relatives Came* was named a *New York Times* best illustrated, a *Horn Book* honor book, a Child Study Association of America's children's book of the year, all 1985, and a Caldecott Honor Book, 1986; *A Blue-eyed Daisy* was named a Child Study Association of America's children's book of the year, 1985; *Every Living Thing* was named a *School Library Journal* best book, 1985; *A Fine White Dust* was named a *Parents' Choice* selection, 1986, and a Newbery Honor Book, 1987; *Boston Globe/Horn Book* Award, 1991, for *Appalachia: The Voices of Sleeping Birds*, 1992, for *Missing May*; Garden State Children's Book Award, Children's Services Section of the New Jersey Library Association, 1992, for *Henry and Mudge Get the Cold Shivers*; Newbery Medal, 1993, for *Missing May.*

■ Writings

PICTURE BOOKS

When I Was Young in the Mountains, illustrated by Diane Goode, Dutton, 1982.
Miss Maggie, illustrated by Thomas DiGrazia, Dutton, 1983.

This Year's Garden, illustrated by Mary Szilagyi, Bradbury, 1984.

The Relatives Came, illustrated by Stephen Gammell, Bradbury, 1985.

Night in the Country, illustrated by Szilagyi, Bradbury, 1986.

Birthday Presents, illustrated by Sucie Stevenson, Orchard Books, 1987.

All I See, illustrated by Peter Catalanotto, Orchard Books, 1988.

Mr. Griggs' Work, illustrated by Julie Downing, Orchard Books, 1989.

An Angel for Solomon Singer, illustrated by Catalanotto, Orchard Books, 1992.

The Everyday Books (board books; self-illustrated), Bradbury, in press.

"HENRY AND MUDGE" SERIES; ILLUSTRATED BY SUCIE STEVENSON; PUBLISHED BY BRADBURY

Henry and Mudge: The First Book of Their Adventures, 1987.

Henry and Mudge in Puddle Trouble: The Second Book of Their Adventures, 1987.

Henry and Mudge in the Green Time: The Third Book of Their Adventures, 1987.

Henry and Mudge under the Yellow Moon: The Fourth Book of Their Adventures, 1987.

Henry and Mudge in the Sparkle Days: The Fifth Book of Their Adventures, 1988.

Henry and Mudge and the Forever Sea: The Sixth Book of Their Adventures, 1989.

Henry and Mudge Get the Cold Shivers: The Seventh Book of Their Adventures, 1989.

Henry and Mudge and the Happy Cat, 1990.

Henry and Mudge and the Bedtime Thumps, 1991.

Henry and Mudge Take the Big Test, 1991.

Henry and Mudge and the Long Weekend, 1992.

Henry and Mudge and the Wild Wind, 1992.

OTHER

Waiting to Waltz ... a Childhood (poetry), illustrated by Stephen Gammell, Bradbury, 1984.

A Blue-eyed Daisy (novel), Bradbury, 1985, published in England as *Some Year for Ellie,* illustrated by Kate Rogers, Viking Kestrel, 1986.

Every Living Thing (stories), Bradbury, 1985.

A Fine White Dust (novel), Bradbury, 1986.

Children of Christmas: Stories for the Season, illustrated by S. D. Schindler, Orchard Books, 1987, published in England as *Silver Packages and Other Stories,* 1987.

A Kindness (novel), Orchard Books, 1989.

But I'll Be Back Again: An Album (autobiography), Orchard Books, 1989.

A Couple of Kooks: And Other Stories about Love, Orchard Books, 1990.

Soda Jerk (poetry), illustrated by Peter Catalanotto, Orchard Books, 1990.

Appalachia: The Voices of Sleeping Birds, illustrated by Barry Moser, Harcourt, 1991.

Missing May, Orchard Books, 1992.

I Had Seen Castles (novel), Harcourt, in press.

■ Adaptations

When I Was Young in the Mountains, 1983, *This Year's Garden,* 1983, and *The Relatives Came,* 1986, were adapted as filmstrips by Random House. Several of Rylant's books are available on film through American School Publishers.

■ Work in Progress

"Mr. Putter and Tabby," a series for beginning readers, Harcourt, 1994; "Blue Hill Meadows," a picture book series, Harcourt, 1994.

■ Sidelights

Cynthia Rylant is an award-winning children's and young adult author whose work includes picture books, poetry, short stories, and novels. With a writing style that has been described as unadorned, clear, and lyrical, the author presents young people's experiences with sensitivity and perceptiveness, branding her protagonists' concerns as legitimate and as important as those of adults. Rylant's characters tend to be contemplative and set apart from their peers by their situations. Explaining her leaning toward such subjects, the author remarked in *Horn Book,* "I get a lot of personal gratification thinking of those people who don't get any attention in the world and making them really valuable in my fiction—making them absolutely shine with their beauty." She continued, "... I don't ever quite write really happy novels; I don't want to deal with the people who have what they want. I want to deal with people who don't have what they want, to show their lives too."

Critics suggest that Rylant appears sympathetic to her characters' plights because she also faced uncommon hardships as a child. In her autobiography *But I'll Be Back Again: An Album,* the author stated, "They say that to be a writer you must first have an unhappy childhood. I don't know if unhappiness is necessary, but I think maybe some children who have suffered a loss too great for words grow up into writers who are always trying to find those words, trying to find a meaning for the way they have lived."

Rylant's parents had a stormy marriage and separated when the author was four years old; she admits that she naively blamed herself for their troubles. The author and her mother moved to West Virginia where Rylant was left in her grandparents' care while her mother earned a nursing degree. Her father wrote occasionally when she first moved, but the letters eventually stopped. Because none of her relatives spoke about her father, she was afraid to ask questions about him. After years of silence, however, he contacted Rylant. The author dreamed of their reunion, but before it could take place her father, a Korean War veteran who suffered from hepatitis and alcoholism, succumbed to these diseases. He died when she was thirteen. In *But I'll Be Back Again,* the author stated, "I did not have a chance to know him or to say goodbye to him, and that is all the loss I needed to become a writer."

An Appalachian Childhood

Unhappiness, however, did not dominate the author's childhood. Rylant enjoyed the rustic West Virginia environment while living with her grandparents in a mountain town where many houses had neither electricity nor running water. The lack of amenities did not bother young Rylant; she felt secure surrounded by equally poor yet friendly, church-going neighbors. When the author was eight years old, she and her mother moved to another West Virginia town named Beaver. Judging in retrospect for *Contempory Authors (CA)*, she called this new location "without a doubt a small, sparkling universe that gave me a lifetime's worth of material for my writing."

As an adolescent in this rural setting, though, Rylant began to recognize and become envious of the fact that other people had more material possessions than she and her mother did. In addition, Beaver—which had at first offered adventure—now appeared backward and dull compared to larger cities. Reflecting in her autobiography, *But I'll Be Back Again,* Rylant remarked, "As long as I stayed in Beaver, I felt I was somebody important.... But as soon as I left town to go anywhere else, my sense of being somebody special evaporated into nothing and I became dull and ugly and poor." She continued, "I wanted to be someone else, and that turned out to be the worst curse and the best gift of my life. I would finish out my childhood forgetting who I really was and what

This 1985 book, which deals with a young girl's maturation, was named book of the year by the Child Study Association of America.

I really thought, and I would listen to other people and repeat their ideas instead of finding my own. That was the curse. The gift was that I would be willing to try to write books when I grew up."

As an adolescent, Rylant claims she showed few signs of being a future writer. She was interested in boys, the Beatles, and *Archie* comic books. She remarked in the *Something about the Author Autobiography Series (SAAS)* that "it wasn't piles of poems or short stories which were the hints in my childhood that I might be a writer someday. The clues were much more subtle and had something to do with the way I grieved over stray animals, the heroes I chose (a presidential candidate, a symphony orchestra conductor), and the love I had of solitude. It is called sensitivity, this quality which sets creative people apart. If they have too much of it, they can be miserable and miserable to be around. But if they possess only a little-more-than-reasonable amount, they can see into things more deeply than other people and can write or paint or sing what they saw in a way that moves people profoundly."

In her first English class in college Rylant found a part of herself that she had not recognized before. She told *SAAS* that "after taking one college English class, I was hooked on great writing . . . I didn't know about this part of me until I went to college—didn't know I loved beautiful stories." But, thinking that great writers only wrote in the manner of Charles Dickens and William Shakespeare, Rylant did not attempt to write creatively while in college. After getting her master's degree in English, she eventually got a job in the children's room of a public library. In this job Rylant, who had never been exposed to children's literature before, absorbed herself in reading children's books and finally recognized that she was going to become a children's author.

Poetry and Picture Books

The first book Rylant produced was *When I Was Young in the Mountains,* a picture book reminiscing about her life in West Virginia's Appalachian Mountains during the time when she stayed with her grandparents as a child. "It's that time that seems to have sunk thickest into my brain and my heart and much of what I saw and heard then has come into my books," Rylant told *Sixth Book of Junior Authors.* A *Washington Post Book World* reviewer noted that Rylant has portrayed "a life swept clean both of clutter and of luxury. But there is a kind of poetry in it as well." *When I Was Young in the Mountains* was praised for its simple, yet evocative text and was named a Caldecott honor book.

With subsequent picture books, including *The Relatives Came, This Year's Garden,* and her "Henry and Mudge" series, Rylant has received considerable recognition and awards. Anne Tyler, who compared *The Relatives Came* to Garrison Keiller's *Lake Wobegon Days,* commented that Rylant's book has "the same air of fond, gentle amusement, the same ability to make readers bounce a little in their seats with the pleasure of recognition." A reviewer for *Booklist* applauded Rylant's capacity to relate "details that capture the essence of an experience. The excitement, fun, love, and joy of a good visit from faraway relatives is crystal clear in her wry text." In a review of Rylant's "Henry and Mudge" books, a *Bulletin of the Center for Children's Books* contributor commented that these adventures of a boy and his bull mastiff, "offer a perfect medium for Rylant's style of poetic com-

pression and repetition mixed with sensitive selection of detail." Rylant once said in the *Junior Literary Guild* that "of all the books I've written so far, the Henry and Mudge books were the most fun." The author told *CA:* "I like writing picture books because that medium gives me a chance to capture in a brief space what I consider life's profound experiences—grandmother crying at a swimming hole baptism, a family planting a garden together, relatives coming for a visit. There is a poignancy and beauty in these events, and I don't want to write adult poetry about them because then I'll have to layer it with some adult disillusionment."

Rylant continued her use of poetry in books for older readers. In *Waiting to Waltz . . . A Childhood,* the author offers an autobiographical collection of thirty free-verse poems which record her coming-of-age. These events include reckoning with the deaths of both an absent father and a beloved pet. One passage documents the surprising transforma-

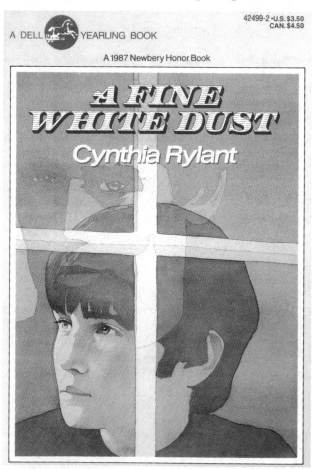

42499-2 ·U.S. $3.50
CAN. $4.50

A DELL YEARLING BOOK

A 1987 Newbery Honor Book

A FINE WHITE DUST
Cynthia Rylant

Published in 1986, this Newbery Honor Book tells the story of a religious boy who comes to believe he has found a human incarnation of God in a traveling preacher.

tion from child to young adult: "Forgetting when /I was last time/ a child./ Never knowing/ when it/ ended." *Waiting to Waltz* also weaves in events and symbols of the 1960s to produce what critics deemed a vivid re-creation of the era. "These are not easy poems," Margaret C. Howell said in a *School Library Journal* review, "but rather a quiet yet moving internalization of growing up. As such, they are a fine example for introspective readers of how poetry expresses intense feelings."

Another book of verse, *Soda Jerk*, combines illustrations by Peter Catalanotto with twenty-eight related poems by Rylant to present the thoughts of a nameless protagonist who works as an attendant at a soda fountain. The title of this work is the slang term for the job. The jerk, as the narrator calls himself, offers commentary on issues ranging from his customers' lives to his fears about the future. Valerie Sayers, writing in *New York Times Book Review*, remarked that with her short poems, "Rylant manages to shape enough action to fill several short stories and to create a protagonist who is not only likable but charming and engaging." *Soda Jerk*, the critic concluded, "is full of respect for a boy's powers of observation, and its images, both written and painted, are striking."

Rylant Moves to Fiction Writing

In 1985 Rylant published her first novel, *A Blue-eyed Daisy*. Set in Appalachia, the episodic work is told by eleven-year-old Ellie Farley during the course of a year. The youngest of five daughters, Ellie contends with her apprehensions and conflicting emotions about growing up. For example, she overcomes her fear of contracting epilepsy after witnessing a classmate's seizure; copes with her unemployed, alcoholic father's imperfections and the possibility of his death after an accident; and battles the nervous anticipation of her first co-ed party. A reviewer for *Publishers Weekly* proclaimed *A Blue-eyed Daisy* an "exquisite novel, written with love."

Rylant's 1986 novel, *A Fine White Dust*, was named a Newbery Honor Book. In this work, a deeply religious seventh-grader named Pete believes he has found a human incarnation of God in a roving preacher named Carson. When attending a revival meeting, Pete is mesmerized by Carson's charismatic presence and, after being "saved," agrees to become his disciple. Despite his reluctance to leave his family and friends, Pete reasons that such a sacrifice is needed to fully embrace the holy life. Pete's mission is never fulfilled, however, because

The poems in this 1990 collection are unified by a soda fountain attendant's perspective on his job, the future, and the lives of his customers.

the preacher unexpectedly runs off with a young woman. Although he initially feels betrayed, Pete develops a more mature understanding of love and faith. *Wilson Library Bulletin* contributor Frances Bradburn declared, "The careful crafting of delicate subjects is . . . beautifully illustrated" in *A Fine White Dust*.

Rylant's 1988 novel, *A Kindness*, tackles a similarly complex set of circumstances when Anne, the single mother of fifteen-year-old Chip, becomes pregnant. Anne does not tell Chip who the father of the new baby is, nor will she consider having an abortion. After the birth of a baby girl, despite Chip's anger and resentment, the family of three adapts to its new life, learning about the responsibilities and sacrifices inherent in real love and kindness. Frances Bradburn concluded in her *Wilson Library Bulletin* review that although the subject matter of *A Kindness* is "excruciatingly difficult," it is a valuable book for young adults to read: " . . . it is during the early teen years that people need to begin to confront the true meaning of the word 'kind'. . . . And there is no better way to begin to think about these difficult choices than by reading such a beautiful, superbly crafted book as Cynthia Rylant's *A Kindness*."

Rylant's 1990 collection, *A Couple of Kooks: And Other Stories about Love*, offers various examples of the emotion of love. In "A Crush," a mentally handicapped man secretly leaves flowers for a

The short stories collected in this 1990 book explore the aspects of love through a variety of characters.

female hardware store worker. An older woman finds love with a man ten years her junior in "Clematis." And in the title story, a teenage couple uses the nine months of the girl's pregnancy to try to instill their hopes, love, and food preferences on the baby that they will be forced to give up for adoption. Critics commended Rylant for her honest, compassionate portrayal of her subjects' feelings.

With her works for children and young adults, Rylant has earned a loyal readership as well as positive critical response. Yet, when facing the future of her career, Rylant admits to insecurities. In *Horn Book* she explained, "I get afraid of what I am going to do for the next fifty years. Surely, I think to myself, I can't keep this up. I am just going to run dry—or worse, get boring and predictable." Nonetheless, the author does feel a sense of accomplishment beyond the recognition and awards her works have received. In *Horn Book*

Rylant confided that writing "has given me a sense of self-worth that I didn't have my whole childhood. I am really proud of that. The [books] have carried me through some troubled times and have made me feel that I am worthy of having a place on this earth."

■ Works Cited

Review of *A Blue-eyed Daisy, Publishers Weekly,* March 8, 1985, p. 91.

Bradburn, Frances, review of *A Fine White Dust, Wilson Library Bulletin,* April, 1987, p. 49.

Bradburn, Frances, review of *A Kindness, Wilson Library Bulletin,* February, 1989, pp. 84-85.

Review of *Henry and Mudge: The First Books of Their Adventures* and *Henry and Mudge in Puddle Trouble, Bulletin of the Center for Children's Books,* April, 1987.

Review of *Henry and Mudge in the Green Time, Junior Literary Guild,* October, 1987-March, 1988.

Howell, Margaret C., review of *Waiting to Waltz, School Library Journal,* November, 1984, p. 138.

Rylant, Cynthia, *Waiting to Waltz . . . a Childhood,* Bradbury, 1984.

Rylant, Cynthia, *But I'll Be Back Again: An Album,* Orchard Books, 1989, pp. 7, 32-34.

Rylant, Cynthia, article for *Something about the Author Autobiography Series,* Volume 13, Gale, 1991, pp. 155-163.

Sayers, Valerie, review of *Soda Jerk, New York Times Book Review,* June 3, 1990, p. 24.

Silvey, Anita, "An Interview with Cynthia Rylant," *Horn Book,* November/December, 1987, pp. 695-703.

Sixth Book of Junior Authors, H. W. Wilson, 1989, pp. 255-256.

Tyler, Anne, "Disorder at 4 A.M.," *New York Times Book Review,* November 10, 1985, p. 37.

■ For More Information See

BOOKS

Best Wishes, Richard C. Owen Publishers, 1992.
Children's Literature Review, Volume 15, Gale, 1988, pp. 167-174.

PERIODICALS

New York Times Book Review, June 30, 1990, p. 24.
Washington Post, December 24, 1990.

John Saul

Personal

Born February 25, 1942, in Pasadena, CA; son of John W., Jr., and Elizabeth (Lee) Saul. *Education:* Attended Antioch College, 1959-60, Montana State University, 1961-62, and San Francisco State College (now University), 1963-65. *Politics:* "Mostly Democrat." *Religion:* "Sort of Swedenborgian."

Addresses

Home—Bellevue, WA. *Agent*—Jane Rotrosen, 318 East 51st St., New York, NY 10022.

Career

Writer. Spent several years traveling about the United States, writing and supporting himself by odd jobs; worked for a drug and alcohol program in Seattle, WA; director of Tellurian Communities, Inc., 1976-78; Seattle Theater Arts, Seattle, director, 1978—. *Member:* Authors Guild, Authors League of America.

Writings

NOVELS

Suffer the Children, Dell, 1977.
Punish the Sinners, Dell, 1978.
Cry for the Strangers, Dell, 1979.
Comes the Blind Fury, Dell, 1980.
When the Wind Blows, Dell, 1981.
The God Project, Bantam, 1982.
Nathaniel, Bantam, 1984.
Brainchild, Bantam, 1985.
Hellfire, Bantam, 1986.
The Unwanted, Bantam, 1987.
The Unloved, Bantam, 1988.
The Fear Factor, Bantam, 1988.
Creature, Bantam, 1989.
Sleepwalk, Bantam, 1990.
Second Child, Bantam, 1990.
Darkness, Bantam, 1991.
Shadows, Bantam, 1992.

Also author of other novels under pseudonyms.

Sidelights

Best-selling horror novelist John Saul has produced a suspenseful thriller every year since 1977, but there is nothing mysterious about his rise to success. Saul, best known for eerie tales set in isolated locales and high-tech novels bordering on science fiction, has become especially popular among young adults who relish the author's adolescent characters as much as his frightening narratives. Today, with over twenty-three million copies of his novels in print, Saul continues to please his

THE *NEW YORK TIMES* BESTSELLER BY
JOHN SAUL
AUTHOR OF *SECOND CHILD* AND *DARKNESS*

THE GOD PROJECT

This 1982 thriller about a secret government experiment marked a departure in Saul's narrative technique and was also his first book to be published in hardcover.

legion of fans with the successful formula he created early in his career.

As a youngster growing up in Whittier, California, Saul enjoyed a normal childhood. Whenever the question comes up, the author has denied having lived through anything as bizarre as the experiences his young characters confront. Instead, Saul directed his youthful energies towards school and recalled that, even as a youth, he was very focused on writing to please his audience. "If you had to write 300 words on a subject," he told Andrea Chambers in a *People* magazine interview, "300 words was exactly what they got. I sat there and counted them." Although Saul continued to diligently hone his writing skills while in college by penning a "technically correct" twenty-line poem

every day, after five years he left school without a degree.

College was followed by a series of odd jobs, including stints as a technical writer and temporary office helper. Whatever he did by day, at night the aspiring author continued working on his unpublished books and stories. "Between the ages of 30 and 35 you really start to lose your dignity badly when you say you've been trying to be a writer for fifteen years," he admitted to Chambers. "I finally thought that by the time I was 35, I would no longer be a struggling writer, I'd be a failed writer."

Finds Niche in Horror Genre

After a number of works had been rejected by publishers, including comic murder mysteries and one novel about the citizen band radio craze of the 1970s, Saul finally received a suggestion that paid off. When a New York literary agent mentioned the tremendous popularity of horror novels, Saul visited a drugstore paperback rack for ideas, wrote an outline for *Suffer the Children*, signed a contract for the book and produced it in less than a month. "I'd never really tried writing horror before," Saul recalled in a *Publishers Weekly* interview with Robert Dahlin, "but when I began, I found it fascinating. There were times I was writing certain scenes that I had to stop because I even scared myself, but I'm convinced that it helps to be a total coward when it comes to writing a book like this. If you can't scare yourself, how can you scare anyone else?"

Saul's first novel, about a dysfunctional family in a small New England town whose disturbed daughter becomes a suspect in the gruesome and mysterious disappearance of several of the town's children, became an instant bestseller. *Suffer the Children* introduces the themes which have dominated almost all of the works that followed, including the use of children and teenagers as victims or perpetrators of crime and a marked ambiguity which leaves the reader uncertain "whether spooks are at work or merely morbid psychology," as a *Detroit News* reviewer observed. Despite the book's popularity, reviewers lambasted Saul's exceedingly violent tale. Upon the book's release, a *Publishers Weekly* reviewer criticized the novel for its "graphically violent scenes against children which are markedly tasteless."

The brutality of Saul's first novel was not matched in his later work. The author made a concentrated effort to focus less on violent acts and instead depended on mood to frighten readers. "After [*Suffer the Children*], my books got progressively less violent because I really saw no reason for gore for gore's sake . . .," Saul explained in *Publishers Weekly.* "It seems to me that what makes a book good is the tension in wondering what's going to happen next." Saul did not, however, stray too far from the formula which propelled him to the top of the bestseller lists. His next novel, *Punish the Sinners,* involves bizarre sex rites within an order of priests. Once again, Saul was criticized by a *Publishers Weekly* reviewer for opening "the proceedings with a dual meat-cleaver slaying" and then writing "with cleaver in hand throughout." But once again, despite negative reviews, Saul's book enjoyed tremendous success and was followed by three more books with similar themes, all of which enjoyed equal success. In a typical plot, the ghost of a blind girl who was taunted and killed by classmates one hundred years earlier returns to seek revenge on the young descendants of her tormenters in *Comes the Blind Fury.*

Explaining his reasons for featuring children in his novels, Saul told *Publishers Weekly:* "Children are very imaginative. They share a lot of fear based on the unknown, or what might happen in the dark. I can remember everything that ever happened to me since I was three, and that certainly helps me write from a children's point of view. Also, children are very appealing, both as villains and as victims. It's hard to stay mad at a kid, no matter what he does."

Techno-Thrillers Offer Futuristic Fright

Saul ventured into a new realm with his sixth book, *The God Project,* his first hardcover publication. "I'd begun to feel I was repeating myself, and I needed something new," he told Dahlin. Instead of focusing on ghosts from the past as he had in his previous novels, Saul looked toward the future and produced a "techno-thriller" about a secret government project called CHILD. The project involves the genetic engineering of unsuspecting women's fetuses. Once born, the children have amazing powers of regeneration, but when the project backfires they begin to die. Discussing the plot with a *Detroit News* writer, Saul said: "I feel that the experiments in genetic engineering ought to be going on . . . but I'm also convinced that it can't be done with too much care. There is talk now about adjusting human beings genetically to fit certain job slots. Do you have to go any further than that for a scary idea?"

At the time it was released, Saul described *The God Project* as his most ambitious undertaking. "It seems as though I'm starting all over again," he told Dahlin. "I feel just like a first novelist waiting around and wondering how my book will do, but I'm looking forward to reading the professional criticism—constructive criticism, I hope—that will be written about it." The book, which Saul described in *Publishers Weekly* as containing "very little overt violence," did not achieve quite the same level of popularity as some of his earlier books, but it did mark an expansion in the author's scope of themes and topics.

In 1985's *Brainchild,* Saul combined the centuries-old revenge plot formulas of his earlier works with the futuristic slant of *The God Project.* The result is the story of Alex Lonsdale, a teenager who suffers

In 1990, Saul published this book, which uses themes of Native American folklore to relate its tale of a mysterious experiment being carried out on teenagers.

THE TERRIFYING *NEW YORK TIMES* BESTSELLER
BY THE AUTHOR OF *SLEEP WALK* AND *CREATURE*

JOHN SAUL

SECOND CHILD

An evil young girl comes to live with her estranged father and half sister in this 1990 novel. Little does she know that her half sister is under the influence of a ghost.

brain damage in a car accident and is operated on by renowned surgeon Raymond Torres, a fourth-generation Mexican-American whose ancestors were murdered when America acquired California in 1850. Although young Alex's recovery seems complete, his strange behavior disturbs his friends and family, who begin to suspect Alex's involvement when a series of brutal murders takes place. When Torres' hatred for *gringos* is revealed, the plot's revenge elements come into play. A *Kliatt* reviewer found *Brainchild* to be a fast-paced, "intriguing story with fascinating implications."

Not deviating from the successful premise of a ghost seeking revenge for the deeds of years past, Saul wrote *Hellfire* in 1986. Set in an isolated Massachusetts town, the story revolves around a wealthy family's plans to transform their empty mill into a shopping mall. When their renovations go awry, the family matriarch fears they have roused the spirit of a girl who died there in a fire one hundred years ago. True to his formula, Saul includes several young characters, including an amiable girl named Beth and her spoiled, snobby cousin, Tracy. A *Publishers Weekly* reviewer found "an inevitability about much of the novel," but conceded that "the bloody, tantalizing plot rushes forward, the setting and historical background are well-drawn and Tracy is memorably, startlingly nasty."

A wealthy family stirring old resentments is also at the center of *The Unloved*. The plot centers around elderly Helena Devereaux, who lures her estranged son and his family to her estate on a South Carolina island, where her sweet-natured daughter, Marguerite, cares for the cantankerous old woman. Helena finally dies, but her control extends beyond the grave in the form of a malicious will which ties her children to her estate. When frequent sightings of her ghost occur and the formerly pleasant Marguerite begins behaving more and more like her mother, the plot takes an expected turn into the supernatural. "Saul plays out the expected Southern gothic but does so with empathy for the lives caught in the Devereaux web, from the relatives and friends to the dispirited townspeople who are dependent on the family for their very homes," remarked a *Publishers Weekly* reviewer.

Saul's twelfth novel, *Creature*, mixes modern-day headlines about steroid abuse with the mad scientist motif of classic horror novels such as *Frankenstein*. In Saul's modern twist, the mad scientist is Dr. Marty Ames, an employee of the TarrenTech conglomerate, who poses as a high-tech athletic trainer at a local high school in order to conduct clandestine experiments upon unsuspecting jocks. In his attempt to create the perfect physical specimen, Ames accidentally turns his subjects into unmanageable, violent freaks. Critics were not especially impressed with Saul's adaptation of the classic horror novel premise. "While Saul's storytelling is energetic and atmospheric, it can not mask the direction of this thinly drawn and predictable plot," commented Marc Shapiro in *Inside Books*. A *Publishers Weekly* reviewer also found the story formulaic, but added "it should please the author's fans as it continues Saul's focus on children as the vehicles and victims of unnatural forces."

Saul's next novel, *Sleepwalk*, contains themes and a plot line similar to *Creature*. Once again, a sleepy town is the setting for a mysterious experiment on teenagers, but this time Saul includes an extra dimension through the use of Native American folklore. The characters include Judith Sheffield, the math teacher who first suspects that the students in her New Mexican hometown are in danger, teenaged Jed, and his Native American grandfather, Brown Eagle. A *Publishers Weekly* critic praised the book for its "compelling scenes in which Brown Eagle introduces Jed to Native American mysticism" and its climax, which includes "a spectacular display of man restoring nature to its rightful place—after having almost destroyed everything in the process."

Successful Formula Continues to Produce Bestsellers

Saul's novel *Second Child* appeared on the *New York Times* bestseller list just one month after publication, proving once again the author's bankable popularity. The story, featuring a teenage villain, centers around fifteen-year-old Teri MacIver, who finds herself living with her biological father after a fire kills her mother and stepfather. What Teri's father does not know is that Teri was responsible for the blaze which killed her mother and that she has come to live with him for the express purpose of propagating more evil. She finds the perfect victim in her shy, unstable half-sister, Melissa. An element of the supernatural is added when Melissa appears to become unknowingly manipulated by the ghost of D'Arcy, a young maidservant who committed hideous acts of violence one hundred years ago. Critics gave *Second Child* a reception typical of a Saul novel: "With a tired plot and boring dialogue, John Saul never deviates from the predictable in his new novel," wrote a *Detroit News and Free Press* reviewer.

Reviews were no better, but sales were just as good, for Saul's 1991 effort, *Darkness*. The story focuses this time on a group of teenagers suffering from disturbing nightmares about a menacing old man. The prologue, described by a *Publishers Weekly* reviewer as "wonderfully scary," features the sacrifice of a newborn baby performed by none other than the Dark Man of the teens' dreams. Despite the novel's promising start, the mystery of the Dark Man is "revealed halfway through the book," continued the reviewer, who found Saul's ending "cozily sentimental."

In his 1992 novel, *Shadows,* Saul again features school-age children prominently. At the center of the story is a school for gifted children called The Academy, where a diabolical experiment is being carried out without anyone's knowledge. When strange things begin to happen, the bright students realize they are in danger of being destroyed by the evil presence behind the experiment and must join forces to escape the terror of The Academy. With all the elements of a successful Saul novel, *Shadows* quickly became a bestseller.

Saul's astounding popularity continues to grow in the face of sometimes harsh criticism. One point about which critics are especially contentious is Saul's tendency to feature young victims and villains, thereby making his novels especially attractive to young readers. Because of the disturb-

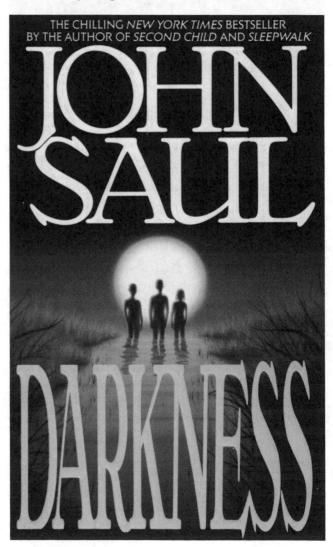

THE CHILLING *NEW YORK TIMES* BESTSELLER BY THE AUTHOR OF *SECOND CHILD* AND *SLEEPWALK*

JOHN SAUL

DARKNESS

Published in 1991, this book tells the story of a group of teenagers who are haunted by a common dream of a menacing "Dark Man."

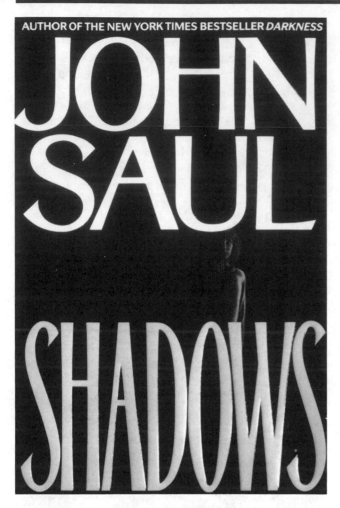

AUTHOR OF THE NEW YORK TIMES BESTSELLER *DARKNESS*

JOHN SAUL

SHADOWS

Students at a school for the gifted discover a bizarre experiment run by an evil presence and must fight for their very survival in this 1992 story.

ing subject matter he deals with, Saul has said he was reluctant, at first, to recommend them to a young audience. "Originally, I though they were a bit strong for children, for anyone under 15," Saul said in a *Publishers Weekly* interview, "but since then, I've talked to school librarians who are happy with them. Young people like my books, and as it turns out, in this way I've introduced many of them to the act of reading. Librarians aren't concerned that any of my violence is going to affect children. They would rather have them reading, and these kids have told me they don't read the books for the violence. They read them for the plot."

With little regard for critical appraisal, Saul's fans continue to make each successive novel a bestseller. The author himself never denigrates his books or the people who enjoy them. "Hopefully," as he told Dahlin, "each of my books is better than the last. Each gets rewritten more." Saul certainly plans to continue writing in the genre which has

made him so successful. Topics for future novels are unlimited in scope, since Saul has the ability to "find horror in the commonplace," as he related to Chambers. "In my books everything looks perfectly normal and wonderful at the beginning," he continued, "but there's some little thing that's wrong, and it gets out of control."

■ Works Cited

Review of *Brainchild, Kliatt Young Adult Paperback Book Guide*, fall, 1985, p. 20.

Review of *Brainchild, Publishers Weekly*, June 28, 1985, p. 71.

Review of *Comes the Blind Fury, Publishers Weekly*, April 11, 1980, p. 75.

Review of *Creature, Publishers Weekly*, March 10, 1989, p. 74.

Review of *Cry for the Strangers, Publishers Weekly*, April 23, 1979, p. 79.

Review of *Darkness, Publishers Weekly*, April 12, 1991, p. 45.

Review of *The God Project, Publishers Weekly*, June 25, 1982, p. 104.

Review of *Hellfire, Publishers Weekly*, June 27, 1980, p. 82.

Review of *Punish the Sinners, Publishers Weekly*, April 10, 1978, p. 70.

Saul, John, interview with Robert Dahlin in *Publishers Weekly*, August 13, 1982.

Saul, John, interview with Andrea Chambers in *People*, June 26, 1989.

Review of *Second Child, Detroit News and Free Press*, July 1, 1990.

Shapiro, Marc, review of *Creature, Inside Books*, August, 1989, p. 80.

Review of *Sleepwalk, Publishers Weekly*, December 14, 1990.

Review of *Suffer the Children, Publishers Weekly*, April 25, 1977, p. 73.

Review of *The Unloved, Publishers Weekly*, April 29, 1988, p. 72.

■ For More Information See

BOOKS

Contemporary Literary Criticism, Volume 46, Gale, 1988.

PERIODICALS

Fantasy Review, October, 1985, p. 20.

Kirkus Reviews, March 1, 1989, p. 329.

Los Angeles Times Book Review, October 10, 1982; August 10, 1986, p. 6.*

—*Sketch by Cornelia A. Pernik*

Gary Soto

◼ Personal

Born April 12, 1952, in Fresno, CA; son of Manuel and Angie (Trevino) Soto; married Carolyn Sadako Oda, May 24, 1975; children: Mariko Heidi. *Education:* California State University, Fresno, B.A. (magna cum laude), 1974; University of California, Irvine, M.F.A., 1976. *Hobbies and other interests:* Karate, reading, and traveling.

◼ Addresses

Home—43 The Crescent, Berkeley, CA 94708. *Office*—Department of English, University of California at Berkeley, Berkeley, CA 94720.

◼ Career

University of California at Berkeley, lecturer in Chicano studies, 1977-81, assistant professor, 1981-85, associate professor of English and Chicano studies, 1985—, senior lecturer of English, 1992—. San Diego State University, writer-in-residence.

◼ Awards, Honors

Academy of American Poets prize and *Discovery/The Nation* prize, both 1975; United States Award, International Poetry Forum, 1977, for *The Elements of San Joaquin;* Bess Hokin Prize for poetry, 1978; Guggenheim fellowship, 1980; fellowship, National Endowment for the Arts, 1981, 1990; Levinson Art Award for poetry, 1984; American Book Award, Before Columbus Foundation, 1985, for *Living Up the Street;* Best Book for Young Adults designation, American Library Association, and Beatty Award, California Library Association, both 1990, both for *Baseball in April, and Other Stories;* fellowship from California Arts Council.

◼ Writings

POETRY

The Elements of San Joaquin, University of Pittsburgh Press, 1977.
The Tale of Sunlight, University of Pittsburgh Press, 1978.
Father is a Pillow Tied to a Broom (chapbook), Slow Loris Press, 1980.
Where Sparrows Work Hard, University of Pittsburgh Press, 1981.
Black Hair, University of Pittsburgh Press, 1985.
Who Will Know Us?; New Poems, Chronicle Books, 1990.
Home Course in Religion; New Poems, Chronicle Books, 1991.

A Fire in My Hands: A Book of Poems (juvenile), illustrations by James M. Cardillo, Scholastic Inc., 1991.

Neighborhood Odes (juvenile), illustrations by David Diaz, Harcourt, 1992.

PROSE

Living Up the Street: Narrative Recollections (autobiography), Strawberry Hill Press, 1985.

Small Faces (memoirs), Arte Publico Press, 1986.

(Editor) *California Childhood: Recollections and Stories of the Golden State*, Creative Arts, 1988.

Lesser Evils: Ten Quartets (autobiography), Arte Publico Press/University of Houston, 1988.

A Summer Life (essays), University Press of New England, 1990.

(Editor) *Pieces of the Heart: New Chicano Fiction*, Chronicle Books, 1993.

PROSE; FOR YOUNG READERS

The Cat's Meow, illustrations by wife, Carolyn Soto, Strawberry Hill Press, 1987.

Baseball in April, and Other Stories, Harcourt, 1990.

Taking Sides, Harcourt, 1991.

Pacific Crossing, Harcourt, 1992.

The Skirt, illustrations by Eric Velasquez, Delacorte, 1992.

Too Many Tamales, illustrations by Ed Martinez, Putnam, 1993.

The Pool Party, Delacorte, 1993.

Local News, Harcourt, 1993.

OTHER

Contributor of poetry to periodicals, including *American Poetry Review, Antaeus, Nation, New Chicano Writing, New Republic, New Yorker, Nation, North American Review, Paris Review, Partisan Review, Poetry,* and *Ploughshares.* Contributor of articles to *Bloomsbury Review, Image, Los Angles Times, MELUS, Parnassus, San Francisco Review of Books, Washington Post,* and *Zyzzyvz.*

■ Work in Progress

Jesse, a novel; *A Mean Weekend,* a young adult novel; *Where We Left Off,* a book of poems. Also working on films, including *The Bike,* a ten-minute short for young viewers, and *The Pool Party,* a thirty-minute family feature.

■ Sidelights

Gary Soto has been called "one of the finest natural talents to emerge" from among today's Chicano writers by Alan Cheuse in the *New York Times Book Review.* An award-winning author best known for his poetry, short stories, and novels for young adults, Soto brings the sights and sounds of the barrio, the urban Spanish-speaking neighborhood where he was raised, vividly to life within the pages of his books. The shrill whistle of a nearby factory piercing the gleeful screams of playing children, the coarse oaths of playground brawls, picking grapes in the fields beneath a harsh sun that turns the air to dust, the taste of Kool-Aid in the summer—the reader experiences an abundance of small details characteristic of growing up in a Mexican American tradition. Soto recreates telling, intimate vignettes from his own childhood and adolescence: He allows us to stand beside him in his mother's kitchen amid the aroma of warm butter and tortillas browning in a black, cast-iron pan and shares with us the strong sense of love and loyalty characteristic of his working-class Hispanic heritage.

Growing up in Fresno

Soto was born on April 12, 1952, in Fresno, California. Although his parents were both American-born, their Mexican heritage figured strongly in his upbringing. Like many Mexican Americans, both Soto's parents and his grandparents labored in the fields picking grapes, oranges, and cotton, worked in the packing houses of the Sunmaid Raisin Company, or found jobs as factory or warehouse workers; their lives were typical of the Mexican American employed in the areas around Fresno, the industrial center of the agriculture-based San Joaquin Valley. Soto and his family moved to a Mexican American community on the outskirts of the city when he was five. Shortly after the move to their new house, the family was struck by tragedy when Soto's father died as the result of an accident at Sunmaid Raisin where he worked. His mother was left to raise her three children, Gary, his older brother Rick, and his younger sister, Debra, with the help of the children's grandparents.

Memories of a childhood spent in the barrio, including recollections of growing up in impoverished surroundings as his mother, step-father, and grandparents struggled to provide the children with a secure home, of neighbors and friends, and of the ethnic cultural traditions he experienced throughout his youth, serve as a basis for Soto's writing. In *Living up the Street,* a collection of narratives first published in 1985, he vividly recreates incidents of his youth. "There were eight children on the block that year, ranging from

G A R Y   S O T O

LIVING
UP THE STREET

By the author of
A Summer Life

Winner of an American Book Award, Soto's 1985
autobiography is a collection of stories that recall the
sights, sounds, and sensations of his youth.

twelve down to one," he recalls of the year 1957 in
the short story "Being Mean," "so there was much
to do; Wrestle, eat raw bacon, jump from the
couch, sword fight with rolled-up newspapers,
steal from neighbors, kick chickens, throw rocks at
passing cars.... While we played in the house,
Mother Molina just watched us run around, a baby
in her arms crying like a small piece of machinery
turning at great speed. Now and then she would
warn us with a smile, 'Now you kids, you're going
to hurt yourselves.' We ignored her and went on
pushing one another from an opened window,
yelling wildly when we hit the ground because we
imagined that there was a school of sharks ready to
snack on our skinny legs."

"I don't think I had any literary aspirations when I
was a kid," Soto told Jean W. Ross in an interview
for *Contemporary Authors,* looking back on his
childhood in Fresno. "In fact we were pretty much
an illiterate family. We didn't have books, and no

one encouraged us to read. So my wanting to write
poetry was a sort of fluke." He graduated from
high school in 1970 and enrolled at Fresno City
College with the intention of majoring in geogra-
phy, but his interests soon shifted to literature. "I
know the day the change began, because it was
when I discovered in the library a collection of
poems edited by Donald Allen called *The New
American Poetry.* I discovered this poetry and
thought, This is terrific: I'd like to do something
like this. So I proceeded to write my own poetry,
first alone, with no one's help, and then moving on
to take classes at [California State, Fresno] and
meeting other writers." Soto was greatly influenced by what he calls "very rambunctious, lively,
irreverent writers" such as Gregory Corso, Edward
Field, Kenneth Koch, and, later, Weldon Kees,
Theodore Roethke, Gabriel Garcia Marquez, and
W. S. Merwin, writers whom Soto considers more
sophisticated. Another major influence on Soto was
the noted poet Philip Levine, his instructor in
creative writing from 1972 to 1973. Soto graduated magna cum laude from California State University, Fresno, in 1974. The following year he
married Carolyn Oda, the daughter of Japanese-
American farmers. In 1976, he received his master's degree in creative writing from the University
of California, Irvine, and became writer-in-residence at San Diego State University. Soto went on
to become a lecturer in Chicano studies at the
University of California, Berkeley, in 1977, received associate professorships in both Chicano
studies and English, and since 1992 has become a
senior lecturer in the English department there.

The Elements of San Joaquin

It was in 1977, the same year he received his
position at the University of California at Berkeley,
that Soto published his first volume of poetry. *The
Elements of San Joaquin,* which garnered several
literary awards, paints a grim portrait of the lives of
Mexican Americans living amid the urban violence,
disillusionment, and poverty characteristic of rural
migrant farmworker communities. Resounding in
emotive metaphors recalling anger, filth, and despair, Soto's verses engage the reader in an unsettling observation of life within America's Latino
neighborhoods. Even so, critics have praised Soto's
first work for its radiance. "Within this seemingly
hopeless, profoundly grey world of Soto's poems,
however, occasional affirmative images introduce
muted, contrapuntal notes of something akin to
hope," comments Patricia de la Fuente in *Revista
Chicano-Riquena.* And Juan Bruce-Novoa lauds

Soto's ability to draw a non-Hispanic audience into poor ethnic neighborhoods where they would otherwise be unwilling to venture. *The Elements of San Joaquin* "convinces because of its well-wrought structure, the craft, the coherence of its totality— because of its overall beauty," notes Bruce-Novoa in *Chicano Poetry: A Response to Chaos.* Soto's verse "forces the reader to travel a route not usually chosen by the literate public," continues the critic. "This is a social as well as a literary achievement."

The Elements of San Joaquin was the first of several volumes of verse, including Soto's *Tales of Sunlight* and *Where Sparrows Work Hard,* the latter published in 1981. The year 1985 marked a turning point for Soto—he published his fourth poetry collection, *Black Hair,* as well as his first prose work. "I think it felt a little awkward at first, because I'd never considered myself a prose writer," Soto remarked, describing the process of writing *Living up the Street* to Ross. "But I wanted to do something different, and I'm glad I did. It was a testing ground to see if I could write prose. I didn't tire of poetry, but I wanted to move on into a thicker forest." Soto intended *Living up the Street* as a series of narrative recollections without the addition of an author's commentary. He told interviewer Hector Avalos Torres in *Dictionary of Literary Biography:* "I would rather show and not tell about certain levels of poverty, of childhood; I made a conscious effort not to tell anything but just present the stories and let the reader come up with assumptions about the book—just show and tell, which is what my poetry has been doing for years and years."

Living up the Street was followed by *Small Faces,* a selection of prose memoirs published in 1986, and *Lesser Evils: Ten Quartets,* a collection of autobiographical essays about growing up near Fresno, California, that Soto published in 1988. In each of these works, the element of youthful fantasy figures largely, and vivid details and Soto's obvious fondness for people and places from his youth effectively recreate his own childhood for the reader. As a *Publishers Weekly* reviewer noted, Soto has an ability to make "the personal universal, and readers will feel privileged to share the vision of this man who finds life perplexing but a joy." His work may be imbued with his personal optimism and a sometimes poignant nostalgia, but it is poverty that serves as the thread binding the author, his friends, and his family together within Soto's narratives. Critic Alicia Fields notes in *Bloomsbury Review:* "Poverty teases and haunts

Soto's memories in many forms. A new jacket 'the color of day-old guacamole' made him cry when he was eleven 'because it was so ugly and so big that I knew I'd have to wear it a long time.' He tells about the desperately impoverished—a hitchhiking bum who was once a successful brick mason and a ragged old married couple who foraged in garbage cans and lived a life 'that scared even the poor.'" Soto has organized *Lesser Evils* in such a way that it can be divided into quartets—four sections that distill a broader meaning from the work taken as a whole.

Baseball in April

Soto has gone on to write several collections of short stories and novels specifically geared for younger readers. *Baseball in April, and Other Stories,* published in 1990, received both the American Library Association's "Best Book for Young Adults" designation and the Beatty Award. A collection of eleven short stories about everyday events in a modern-day Mexican American neighborhood, *Baseball in April* is praised by a *Horn Book* reviewer as "an acute [observation] of the desires, fears, and foibles of children and teenagers going about the business of daily living." The ethnic flavor of the barrio setting is intensified by the Spanish vocabulary that Soto scatters throughout the text—many of his books contain a glossary of Spanish terms at the back to aid non-Spanish speaking readers. Soto focuses on a different young person as the subject of each of his stories. Alfonso wants to transform himself from an awkward young man to an Aztec warrior in "Broken Chain": "Last week he did fifty sit ups a day, thinking that he would burn those already apparent ripples on his stomach to even deeper ripples, dark ones, so when he went swimming at the canal next summer, girls in cut-offs would notice. And the guys would think he was tough, someone who could take a punch and give it back." But Alfonso finds that the girl he likes accepts him just the way he is. In "Mother and Daughter," Yollie is looking forward to the eighth-grade dance, but has no dress to wear. Her mother dyes Yollie's white summer dress black, but the night of the school dance turns into a disaster when Yollie gets caught in a cloudburst and the rain causes the black dye to run. Michael and his younger brother Jesse try out for Little League in "Baseball in April," but the two boys don't make the team for the third year in a row. They end up playing with the Hobos, a community team, and are content playing ball even through a losing season that causes their teammate's interest to fade. And in "La Bamba," Manuel impresses his classmates with his lip-sync/dance performance to a Richie Valens song at the school talent show until a scratch in the record throws his act into chaos: Manuel "was stuck dancing and moving his lips to the same words over and over. He had never been so embarrassed. He would have to ask his parents to move the family out of town."

As is characteristic of all of Soto's work, *Baseball in April, and Other Stories* is written in a spare style that brings to life his young characters and the loving families in which they are raised. Reviewer Kevin Kenny remarks in *Voice of Youth Advocates* that the story's characters are realistic, that Soto's "knowledge of, and affection for, their shared Mexican-American heritage is obvious and infectious." Roberto Gonzalez Echevarria reviews the book for the *New York Times Book Review* and comments on the sophistication of Soto's stories. Echevarria describes "Two Dreamers," where Hector's grandfather, Luis, puts his grandson's mastery of English to use on the telephone as he tries to work a real estate deal which will make the old man rich and enable him to return to his hometown of Jalapa, Mexico, a respected man: "Hector, both skeptical and embarrassed, demurs. . . . As Hector grows older, the situation is reversed. With his command of English, Hector is now a probe into the future, and into the alien yet alluring world that surrounds him." The critic examines the subtle meaning underlying Soto's deceptively simple text: "The story is about this swap of roles. . . . The grandfather is unwaveringly Mexican; Hector is on his way to becoming something still undefined, but certainly not Mexican anymore."

Soto's depiction of the Americanization of a generation of Latino teenagers is one of the themes unifying his writing for young adults. Media pressures figure strongly in the lives of his characters: Alfonso wants his hair to look like that of the rock singer, Prince. Young Veronica covets a Barbie doll after watching numerous Barbie commercials, and a pretend one won't do. Fausto covets a guitar so that he can accomplish his mission in life: "to play guitar in his own band; to sweat out his songs and prance around the stage; to make money and dress weird." Unconscious of the threat of poverty weighing upon the shoulders of their parents— hard-working men and women trying to support their families as night watchmen, warehousemen, auto mechanics, and teacher's aides—the young people in Soto's stories are caught up in the

ODYSSEY

BASEBALL IN APRIL
AND OTHER STORIES

GARY SOTO

Soto strives to capture the flavor of a Mexican American neighborhood through the eyes of its children in this 1990 Beatty Award winner.

commercialism aimed at a more affluent, primarily white culture. As Echevarria notes, the young generation of Mexican Americans that inhabit Soto's stories "are transforming themselves awkwardly into facsimiles of adults; the world of adults is turning into an anxious copy of the Anglo world."

While Soto's writing takes place in the ethnic neighborhoods that are familiar to him, the conflicts faced by his young protagonists are universal. One example is Soto's 1991 novel, *Taking Sides*, about an eighth-grade Mexican American boy named Lincoln Mendoza. One of the best basketball players on his school team, Lincoln's loyalties become divided after he and his mother move from the Mission District barrio in San Francisco, where he grew up, to the wealthier white suburb of Sycamore, California. Although he has problems fitting in at his new school, Lincoln joins the basketball team in his new junior high school. As a crucial basketball game between his old team and his new team approaches, Lincoln finds himself involved in confrontations with his coach and teammates, as well as with himself, as he wrestles with the fear that he is somehow a traitor to his old neighborhood. Soto's study of sportsmanship and loyalty ends on a positive note as the young man adapts to his circumstances in a mature way, makes peace with both his old and new friends, and learns a valuable lesson about maintaining his individuality and trusting in himself.

Soto Returns to Poetry

In the writing that Soto has done since the publication of his first volume of poetry, *The Elements of San Joaquin,* he has begun to express more of the wonder and joy of his youth, things hidden by the poverty and violence expressed so overtly in his early poems. "I think it's a matter of maturity," he explained to Ross during a discussion of his evolution as a writer. "The initial books may be very, very painful books. The ones that follow, at least for me, are less painful." He commented: "When I write I like the youth in my poetry, sort of a craziness. For me that's really important. I don't want to take a dreary look at the world and then start writing. I left that somewhere along the line." Characteristic of this more positive perspective are two volumes of poetry written for young readers. *A Fire in My Hands* and *Neighborhood Odes,* both published in 1992, describe growing up in the Mexican neighborhoods of California's Central Valley where commonplace events of life—feeding the birds, running through a lawn sprinkler on a sultry summer afternoon, lifting weights, going on one's first date, discovering the ancient civilizations of the Incas and Aztecs in the still of the local library, selling oranges door to door—become something special when imbued with Soto's poetic skill. Maeve Visser Knoth describes Soto's verse as "simple poems of childhood, adolescence, and adulthood . . . about ordinary events and emotions made remarkable by Soto's skilled use of words and images," in her review for *Horn Book.* In *A Fire in My Hands,* the poet prefaces each selection with a brief paragraph providing background information on both the events described in the poem and the process by which it was written, thus aiding younger readers' comprehension of his work. *Neighborhood Odes* glorifies the small celebrations in a child's life. "Ode to Las Raspados" tells of the arrival of the snow-cone truck: "Strawberry and root beer,/ Grape that stains/ The mouth with laughter,/ Orange that's a tennis ball/ Of snow/ You could stab/ With a red-striped straw." In another selection, "Ode to Mi Perrito," Soto

lovingly recalls a pet from his youth: "When one cow dared/ To moo, *mi perrito* barked/ And showed his flashing teeth./ *Mi perrito* is a chihuahua—/ Smaller than a cat,/ Bigger than a rubber mouse./ Like mouse and cat,/ He goes running/ When the real dogs/ come into the yard." While Soto's setting remains the barrios of Fresno, as a *Horn Book* reviewer noted, "other than the small details of daily life—peoples' names or the foods they eat—these poems could be about any neighborhood."

While much of his inspiration comes from the events of his Mexican American upbringing, Soto has expressed concern that limitations might be placed upon him because of his ethnic background. Rather than remain in a separate category and be judged solely against other Chicano writers, Soto wants his work to be considered on its own merits: "One of the things I would like to do is make that leap from being a Chicano writer to being simply a writer," he told Ross. Chicanos—Americans of Mexican descent—are among the oldest immigrants to the North American continent, but, notes Cheuse, "only in the past 20 years have Chicano writers emerged to add their pieces to the puzzle we call American literature." Soto worries that the ethnic label of Chicano writer can be very damaging to an author, commenting that "it can mean that libraries will look at the writer's book and feel they should have it for their collections *because* of the label."

Soto does not feel that his more recent work is necessarily geared towards a specifically Chicano audience. "The fact of the matter is, except for two books, mine are not heavily concerned with Mexican themes," he commented. "*Living up the Street* is, but not the poetry after *The Tale of Sunlight.*" Attesting to the fact that his work speaks to an audience that crosses many ethnic boundaries, Soto's verses have been published in periodicals as diverse as *The New Yorker* and *New Chicano Writing.* However, by broadening the audience and his experience of life, Soto has also received criticism—he was once chastised by a radio personality for leaving the Hispanic neighborhood he grew up in to live a "cosmopolitan life" with his wife and daughter. "Some critics want to keep Mexicans in the barrio and once they get out of there they point the finger and say 'Shame, shame,'" Soto remarked. Indeed, the fear of returning to the poverty of his childhood still haunts Soto, and its spectre appears throughout his later works. In her review of *Small Faces,* Fields notes Soto's insecurity with the comfortable lifestyle he is now able to maintain through an active career as both author and educator: "In 'To Be a Man,' he recounts his childhood fear of following in his stepfather's weary footsteps as a factory laborer. 'Now I am living this other life that seems like a dream,' Soto writes, and he notes that it is accompanied by a lingering nightmare about becoming a bum to avoid the grind of the assembly line."

As a successful writer in the genres of both poetry and prose, Soto finds one of the major differences between narrative fiction and verse to be the extent to which impressions are involved in the writing process. "In poetry you have lyric, and lyrics are not necessarily logical progressions, not even of time or character of space. In fiction writing, I think you have to have that logical progression of time and space and character. In poetry, I don't think that exists—unless it's a narrative poem, and even then I don't think you have characters who deepen and develop; they simply happen."

Writing, for Soto, is a daily activity. A prolific author, he finds that constant work keeps his outlook fresh and his imagination active. Soto discussed with Ross the process whereby he composed his works: "If I'm writing a book, as opposed to working on a collection of miscellany, I like to think in terms of the overall structure of the book," he noted. "I get up and write from about nine to twelve daily, and I will think about an area that I want to delve into.... I sit there and just mull it over. When I've been thinking about this for some time, I will start to write, and the words will come out on the theme ... whatever that many mean on that given day. But I don't know until I sit down to write. I may have a slight suspicion that it's going to be on marriage, or it's going to be a childhood piece, or its going to be on a friend, or a place. But I don't know exactly what the ultimate subject will be until I start writing." Soto writes in a relaxed, casual voice reflective of both childhood and the attitude he takes towards his craft. "I think I'm very childlike, and I often write youthful poems," Soto commented to Ross, adding humorously: "It's sort of a silly act, writing itself. I don't know why anyone would pay attention to these half-schooled, half-illiterate poets." Soto takes a realistic attitude towards his craft: he believes that writers should not take their vocation too seriously. Remarking on his ability to write a poem a day, Soto quips "if I can do that, I figure it can't be *that* good! You've got to take it at that."

In addition to a prolific writing career, Soto teaches at the University of California at Berkeley.

He feels that teaching and writing simultaneously is beneficial in that the two areas mesh together. "You should take whatever sensitivity you have in writing and carry it over into teaching," he commented to Ross, adding that "you're trying to spread the gospel of literature and make students interested in writing and what it takes to be a writer." As well as introducing students to a broad variety of written works—James Baldwin, Richard Wright, John Williams, Bernard Malamud, and Philip Roth—Soto believes that young writers should be well-grounded in the mechanics of writing: "I stress mechanics–how a piece is put together, characterization, dialogue, pace, symbolism—so that students can take what they've learned from reading one novel and apply it to other literature to see how it works and to deepen their understanding of writing. I show them how to spot cliches, for example when Mexicans are stereotyped, and things that are too contrived to be believable. I want them to be able to go on from this to appreciate other things and to understand

This 1992 collection of poems portrays facets of Mexican American life, including vivid descriptions of a youngster's cat and a mother's spicy cooking.

how a writer puts things together, to see that it's not simply a mishmash of feelings."

Soto's ability to tell a story, to recreate moments of his own past in a manner that transcends the boundaries of race or age, to transport his reader to the world of his own childhood is felt within each of his written works. "Soto's remembrances are as sharply defined and appealing as bright new coins," writes Fields. "His language is spare and simple yet vivid." But it is his joyful outlook, strong enough to transcend the poverty of the barrio, that makes his work so popular. The optimism with which he views his own life radiates from each of his young characters–Soto views life as a gift and his talent for expression is his gift to his readers. As he told Torres: "[Writing] is my one talent. There are a lot of people who never discover what their talent is . . . I am very lucky to have found mine."

■ Works Cited

Review of *Baseball in April, and Other Stories*, *Horn Book*, July, 1990.

Bruce-Novoa, Juan, "Patricide and Resurrection: Gary Soto," in his *Chicano Poetry: A Response to Chaos*, University of Texas Press, 1982, p. 207.

Cheuse, Alan, "The Voice of the Chicano," *New York Times Book Review*, October 11, 1981, pp. 15, 36-37.

de la Fuente, Patricia, "Ambiguity in the Poetry of Gary Soto," *Revista Chicano-Riquena*, summer, 1983, pp. 35-36.

Echevarria, Roberto Gonzalez, "Growing up North of the Border," *New York Times Book Review*, May 20, 1990.

Fields, Alicia, "Small but Telling Moments," *Bloomsbury Review*, January, 1987, p. 10.

Review of *A Fire in My Hands: A Book of Poems*, *Horn Book*, March, 1992, p. 216.

Kenny, Kevin, review of *Baseball in April, and Other Stories*, *Voice of Youth Advocates*, August, 1990, p. 163.

Review of *Lesser Evils: Ten Quartets*, *Publishers Weekly*, March 4, 1988, p. 102.

Review of *Neighborhood Odes*, *Horn Book*, May, 1992.

Soto, Gary, *Living up the Street: Narrative Recollections*, Strawberry Hill Press, 1985, p. 2.

Soto, Gary, interview with Jean W. Ross, *Contemporary Authors*, Volume 124, Gale, 1989, pp. 424-427.

Soto, Gary, *Baseball in April, and Other Stories*, Harcourt, 1990.

Soto, Gary, *Neighborhood Odes*, illustrations by David Diaz, Harcourt, 1992, pp. 1, 16.

Torres, Hector Avalos, "Gary Soto," *Dictionary of Literary Biography*, Volume 82: *Chicano Writers*, Gale, 1989, pp. 246-252.

■ For More Information See

BOOKS

Contemporary Literary Criticism, Volume 32, Gale, 1985, pp. 401-405.

PERIODICALS

Five Owls, July, 1990, p. 115.

Publishers Weekly, April 22, 1988, p. 77; June 8, 1990; September 6, 1991, p. 104.

Voice of Youth Advocates, December, 1991, p. 318.

—*Sketch by Pamela L. Shelton*

Art Spiegelman

■ Personal

Born February 15, 1948, in Stockholm, Sweden; emigrated to United States; naturalized citizen; son of Vladek (in sales) and Anja (Zylberberg) Spiegelman; married Francoise Mouly (a publisher), July 12, 1977; children: Nadja Rachel, Dashiel Alan. *Education:* Attended Harpur College (now State University of New York at Binghamton), 1965-68.

■ Addresses

Home—New York, NY. *Office*—Raw Books and Graphics, 27 Greene St., New York, NY 10013; Galerie St. Etienne, 24 West 57th St., New York, NY 10019. *Agent*—Wylie, Aitken, & Stone, 250 West 57th St., Suite 2106, New York, NY 10107.

■ Career

Free-lance artist and writer, 1965—; Topps Chewing Gum, Inc., Brooklyn, NY, creative consultant, artist, designer, editor, and writer for novelty packaging and bubble gum cards and stickers, including "Wacky Packages" and "Garbage Pail Kids," 1966-89. Instructor in studio class on comics, San Francisco Academy of Art, 1974-75; instructor in history and aesthetics of comics at New York School of Visual Arts, 1979-87. Advisory board member of the Swann Foundation. *Exhibitions:* Artwork exhibited in numerous gallery and museum shows in the United States and abroad, including the Museum of Modern Art, New York City, 1991; "The Road to Maus," at Galerie St. Etienne, New York City, 1992; and shows at the New York Cultural Center, the Institute of Contemporary Art in London, England, and the Seibu Gallery in Tokyo, Japan. *Member:* P.E.N.

■ Awards, Honors

Annual *Playboy* Editorial Award for best comic strip and Yellow Kid Award (Italy) for best comic strip author, both 1982; Regional Design Award, *Print* magazine, 1983, 1984, and 1985; Joel M. Cavior Award for Jewish Writing, and National Book Critics Circle nomination, both 1986, both for *Maus: A Survivor's Tale, My Father Bleeds History;* Inkpot Award, San Diego Comics Convention, and Stripschappenning Award (Netherlands) for best foreign comics album, both 1987; Special Pulitzer Prize, National Book Critics Circle award, *Los Angeles Times* book prize, and Before Columbus Foundation Award, all 1992, all for *Maus: A Survivor's Tale II, and Here My Troubles Began;* Speigelman also received a Guggenheim fellowship for his work on *Maus.*

■ Writings

COMICS

The Complete Mr. Infinity, S. F. Book Co., 1970.

The Viper Vicar of Vice, Villainy, and Vickedness, privately printed, 1972.

Zip-a-Tune and More Melodies, S. F. Book Co., 1972.

(Compiling editor with Bob Schneider) *Whole Grains: A Book of Quotations*, D. Links, 1972.

Ace Hole, Midget Detective, Apex Novelties, 1974.

Language of Comics, State University of New York at Binghamton, 1974.

(Contributor) Don Donahue and Susan Goodrich, editors, *The Apex Treasury of Underground Comics*, D. Links, 1974.

Breakdowns: From Maus to Now, an Anthology of Strips, Belier Press, 1977.

Work and Turn, Raw Books, 1979.

Every Day Has Its Dog, Raw Books, 1979.

Two-Fisted Painters Action Adventure, Raw Books, 1980.

(Contributor) Nicole Hollander, Skip Morrow, and Ron Wolin, editors, *Drawn Together: Relationships Lampooned, Harpooned, and Cartooned*, Crown, 1983.

Maus: A Survivor's Tale, My Father Bleeds History, Pantheon, 1986.

(Editor with wife, Francoise Mouly, and contributor) *Read Yourself Raw: Comix Anthology for Damned Intellectuals*, Pantheon, 1987.

Maus: A Survivor's Tale II, and Here My Troubles Began, Pantheon, 1991.

Contributor to numerous underground comics. Editor of *Douglas Comix*, 1972; editor, with Bill Griffith, and contributor, *Arcade, the Comics Revue*, 1975-76; founding editor, with Mouly, and contributor, *Raw*, 1980—. *Maus* has been translated into sixteen languages, including Japanese and Hungarian.

■ Work in Progress

"Profusely illustrating" *The Wild Party* by Joseph March; editing *The Raw and the Restless*.

■ Sidelights

"Art Spiegelman's *Maus* is among the remarkable achievements in comics," wrote Dale Luciano in *The Comics Journal*. The comic, an epic parable of the Holocaust that substitutes mice and cats for human Jews and Nazis, marks a zenith in Spiegelman's artistic career. Prior to the *Maus* books, Spiegelman made a name for himself on the underground comics scene. He has been a significant presence in graphic art since his teen years, when he wrote, printed, and distributed his own

comics magazine. By the end of his first year in college Spiegelman was employed by Topps Chewing Gum as a creative consultant, artist, and writer. His affiliation with the company has wrought such pop culture artifacts as "Wacky-Packs" and the "Garbage Pail Kids." In the early 1980s Spiegelman and his wife, Francoise Mouly, produced the first issue of *Raw*, an underground comics (or as Spiegelman and Mouly refer to them, "comix") anthology that grew into a highly respected alternative press by the middle of the decade. It was not until the publication of the first *Maus* collection in 1986, however, that a wide range of readers became aware of Spiegelman's visionary talent and his considerable impact on the realm of comics.

Spiegelman was born in Stockholm, Sweden, to Vladek and Anja, two survivors of the Holocaust, Nazi Germany's massacre of six million Jews during World War II. As a young child, his family moved to the United States, where he grew up in Rego Park, New York. Spiegelman recalls an early affinity for cartoons and comics. "I think . . . that I learned to read from looking at comics," he told Joey Cavalieri in *Comics Journal*, citing early exposure to the likes of *Mad* magazine and various superhero books. By the age of twelve, Spiegelman was emulating the artists whose creations had captured his imagination and funnybone. As a hobby he began to draw his own cartoons, but as he told Cavalieri, "it was a pastime only for a brief period. It became an obsession very quickly." At the age of thirteen, Spiegelman was illustrating for his school newspaper, and by his fourteenth year he had already made his first professional sale, a cover for the *Long Island Post*—for which he was paid fifteen dollars.

Spiegelman continued his interest in drawing when he entered the High School of Art and Design in New York, where, as part of a cartoon course assignment, he wrote and illustrated a comic strip. The strip attracted the interest of a New York publishing syndicate. The experience made Spiegelman aware that the parameters for conventional comics were too narrowly defined for his ideas. He sought and found a creative outlet with the burgeoning underground comics scene, including printing and distributing his own magazine, *Blase* (the title is French for 'apathetic' or 'world-weary'). Spiegelman was still unclear as to what kind of career he would forge out of his artistic activity, as he told Cavalieri, "I just knew I wanted to do lines on paper and write at the same time."

Spiegelman began work on the *Maus* series with a three page strip in 1972 and eventually expanded the tale into this award-winning 1986 book.

Topps and the "Wacky Packs" Revolution

Spiegelman was influenced by a number of artists working in the comics field, among them *Mad* magazine creator Harvey Kurtzman, *Mad* artist John Severin, and Jack Davis, who drew baseball cards for Topps Chewing Gum. Eager to get his hands on cards with original Davis art on them, Spiegelman sent a copy of *Blase* to Topps, hoping that they would send him some cards in return. The company's response complimented his work and invited him out to Topps headquarters for lunch. Spiegelman visited the production studios and returned home with a handful of Jack Davis originals. A few years later, during his first year at Harpur College, Spiegelman received a phone call from Topps asking him if he would like a summer job with the company. He did and accepted their offer. Spiegelman assumed the duties of "resident tinkerer" at Topps, creating various novelty items. He also streamlined Topps's production process from an inefficient circuit between conception and

realization to a smooth idea-to-artist procedure. "I sort of created a job that hadn't been there before because I was able to both write a bit and draw a bit," Spiegelman told Cavalieri. By the summer's end Spiegelman was an integral part of Topps's production, and the company asked him to continue working with them. He maintained his affiliation with the company for twenty-five years.

Spiegelman's employment with Topps included writing and drawing various card series and humorous other items. His biggest contribution, however, came about in response to another product that the company was planning. An executive at Topps was interested in issuing a series of cards featuring the miniaturized labels of supermarket products. Spiegelman, seeing little curiosity value in commercial artwork that was not antiquated enough to be charming, decided to poke fun at the project. He drew up a parody version of a company's package art. Spiegelman's loopy version of the product label was a hit with Topps, and "Wacky Packages" were born. Marketed with a stick of gum like baseball cards, "Wacky Packages" soon became a fixture of the 1970s alongside such items as the lava lamp, the hula-hoop, and black light posters. "Wacky Packages" offered a humorous alternative to the ever increasing onslaught of advertised products. The small sticker-cards depicted such skewed and vaguely familiar products as "Fright Guard" deodorant, "Bustedfinger" candy bars, and "Koduck" film—"for ducks." Some adults found "Wacky Packages" crude and remotely offensive. Children, however, were delighted with a product that appealed to their sense of humor, and they gleefully displayed the stickers on their bedroom doors, lunchboxes, and school books. In the 1980s Spiegelman mounted a second wave of humorous stickers with the creation of the "Garbage Pail Kids," which featured drawings of slovenly children accompanied by information that cited the children's more unsavory attributes.

While Spiegelman was devoting time to Topps, he never lost touch with the comics scene. By the mid-1970s the influx of new underground products was staggering. With so many new titles being produced, many readers, fearing low quality, would only purchase their tried and true favorites. This was distressing news to Spiegelman, who was a proponent of new material. So along with fellow artist Bill Griffith, author of the popular *Zippy the Pinhead* strip, Spiegelman formed *Arcade,* a comics anthology that would highlight the new work of some of the best underground artists and writers. *Arcade* debuted in 1975 and featured work by such esteemed artists as Kim Deitch, Robert Crumb, and Spiegelman himself.

Comics as Art and Academics

Spiegelman's work with *Arcade* lasted a short time, owing in large part to his desire to work at a more deliberate pace rather than worry about making deadlines for the magazine's frequent publication. Following his departure from *Arcade*, Spiegelman began to publish books that compiled his own comics. One such book, 1977's *Breakdowns*, featured numerous short works that he had written over the years. Among the stories is a "comics noir" piece titled "Ace Hole, Midget Detective," which recounts the exploits of a diminutive detective on the case of an art theft ring. Among the characters Ace encounters is a young woman drawn in mock-Picasso style whose profile lines become darker and more defined as Ace follows her, until she proclaims, "I'm being shadowed!" The humor is the double play on the word "shad-

With the 1991 publication of *Maus II*, Spiegelman completed the tale of his father's harrowing experience as a prisoner of a Nazi concentration camp.

ow," which is both an artistic technique and a detective's term for trailing a suspect. Inside jokes regarding art and outright references to artistic technique such as this are a trademark of Spiegelman's, and many of his strips offer glimpses into his creative procedure. *Two-Fisted Painters Action Adventure*, a 1980 work, uses artistic process as a centerpiece. The book is essentially a satire, with Spiegelman mixing and comparing comics and fine art. As Michael Dooley wrote in *Comics Journal*: "'Painters' is an elaborate study of contrasts and conflicts: fine art vs. commercial art; originality vs. cliche; color vs. black and white; even creativity vs. impotence, and life vs. death." Not only is *Painters* considered intelligent and funny—Dooley called the book a *"tour de force"*—it also displays Spiegelman's extensive and esoteric knowledge of both classic and comics art.

"We've all gone through a phase of treating comics as art instead of comics—then after a certain phase, you know they're art and treat them like comics again," Spiegelman said to *Cavalier* in 1969. A decade later he would stand in front of a classroom and expand upon those words. In 1979 Spiegelman began teaching a course on the history and aesthetics of comics at the New York School of Visual Arts. His primary challenge is widening his students perceptions of comics and showing them that comics have a place in the world of art. Whereas Spiegelman lives and works in the realm of the offbeat underground, many of his students perceive comics in the context of superhero books like *Batman, Superman,* and *The Incredible Hulk*—all highly commercial mainstream comics. As a teacher Spiegelman strives to show his students the entire scope of comics. He also gives them background that delineates the evolution of comics and their kinship to fine art. Spiegelman discontinued his regular teaching in 1987. As he told *Authors and Artists for Young Adults (AAYA)*, "Since time pressures haven't allowed me to continue teaching on a regular basis, I now lecture at various colleges and universities and give shorter seminar courses."

The Magazine for Damned Intellectuals

When he was editing the *Arcade* anthologies, Spiegelman found that, due to the magazine's publication schedule, he was spending more time as an editor than as a contributor. Considering himself an artist by vocation and an editor by necessity, Spiegelman reasoned that his next venture into publishing would have to allow for his creativity. Thus in 1980 he and his wife and partner, Francoise Mouly, published the first issue of *Raw*, an anthology magazine that would come out once or twice a year and feature adult comics work from around the world. From the start Spiegelman and Mouly sought to differentiate *Raw* from other comics anthologies. The magazine is printed on high quality paper and cut a size larger than conventional magazines, giving it a distinct visual appeal. For the content Spiegelman and Mouly made their own contributions and solicited work from some of the world's finest comics purveyors, including France's Jacques Tardi and Holland's Joost Swarte. The first issue of *Raw* debuted under the subtitle *"The Graphix Magazine of Postponed Suicides."* Explaining the reason for the title, Spiegelman told Cavalieri, "Every moment that you don't commit suicide is an affirmation. It's deciding to live some more." He continued that a postponed suicide "implies an act of faith has been committed. Which is, to create a work of art, a book, a painting, a poem, a magazine, a comic strip, whatever, and that the work is in itself a justification for remaining alive."

Spiegelman and Mouly's ambitions for *Raw* were modest: they expected to only print three thousand copies of the first issue. As Spiegelman described *Raw* to Aron Hirt-Manheimer in *Reform Judaism*, "When we began we weren't thinking of it as an ongoing magazine. We just wanted to do the ultimate prototype and hoped some other publisher would get the idea." Opposite of their expectations, *Raw* sold out the entire print run for its first two issues, and by the third issue Spiegelman and Mouly were printing ten thousand copies. The magazine took hold among mature comics readers, providing a graphics haven for those whose tastes had outgrown superheroes and pulp fiction. The material in *Raw* often centers on the confusion and pathos of modern life and reflects these emotions in its structural style. Conventions such as linear narrative and simplistic imagery are often eschewed in favor of elliptical jumps and oblique text that challenge the reader to search for deeper meanings. Whereas underground comics were once perceived as a wellspring of scatological and graphic sexual humor, *Raw* demonstrated a different facet of graphic art. *Raw*'s willingness to make its readers think earned it a devoted following of educated readers, as well as one of its many nicknames, "the magazine for damned intellectuals."

Raw's popularity increased with each new issue. Public demand for the original magazines prompted Spiegelman and Mouly to compile the first three issues into a book titled *Read Yourself Raw*. The

This chapter heading from *Maus II* depicts the graphic deaths that were an everyday occurrence in the Auschwitz camp.

magazine's success not only vindicated Spiegelman's comics ethic but reflected a flowering of his own artistic output. Beginning with the second issue of *Raw*, Spiegelman began serializing *Maus*, the work that would change both his and the comics world's perception of graphic art.

Of Mice and Men

Spiegelman has described *Maus* as "the point where my work starts." As he told Cavalieri: "Up to that point, I feel like I'd been floundering. . . . All of a sudden, I found my own voice, my own needs, things that I wanted to do in comics." Although his work on *Maus* began in earnest in the 1980s, the comic actually had its genesis as a three page strip back in 1972. In that year Spiegelman was approached to contribute to a compilation titled *Funny Aminals* (sic), whose only dictum required the strips to feature animals exhibiting human characteristics. Spiegelman contemplated several ideas and finally hit upon his theme while watching old cartoons. Viewing cartoons that featured cats and mice, Spiegelman related to Cavalieri that he was struck with the epiphany that "this cat and mouse thing was just a metaphor for some kind of oppression." Initially he thought of using cats and mice for a strip dealing with slavery, but being a white Jewish man, he reasoned that he could not be true to what was, regardless the form, a black man's story. He decided to explore a theme that was much closer to him, his mother and father's experience in, and survival of, a Nazi concentration camp.

Maus starts with Spiegelman, representing himself as a humanoid mouse, going to his father, Vladek, for information about the Holocaust. As Vladek's tale begins, he and his wife, Anja, are living in Poland with their young child, Richieu, at the outset of World War II. The Nazis, as cats, have overrun much of Eastern Europe, and their oppression is felt by everyone, especially the Jews/mice. The story recalls Vladek's service in the Polish army and subsequent incarceration in a German war prison. As he returns to Anja and his home, the Nazi "Final Solution"—to exterminate the entire Jewish race—is well under way. There is much talk of Jews being rounded up and shipped off to the camps, where they are either put to strenuous work or put to death. Vladek and Anja's attempt to flee is thwarted and they are sent to Auschwitz, Poland, site of one of the most notorious camps. As the first book of *Maus* concludes, Richieu has been taken from his parents by the Nazis—never to be seen again—and Vladek and Anja are separated and put in crowded train cars for shipment to Auschwitz.

As the second volume, *And Here My Troubles Began*, opens, Art and his wife, Francoise, are visiting Vladek at his summer home in the Catskills. During the visit Art and his father resume their discussion. Vladek recounts how he and Anja were put in separate camps, he in the Auschwitz facility, she in the neighboring Birkenau. The horrors and inhumanity of concentration camp life are related in graphic detail. Vladek recalls the discomfort of cramming three or four men into a bunk that is only a few feet wide and the ignominy of scrounging for any scrap of food to sate his unending hunger. His existence at Auschwitz is marked by agonizing physical labor, severe abuse from the Nazis, and the ever present fear that he—or Anja—may be among the next Jews sent to the gas chambers. Despite these overwhelming incentives to abandon hope, Vladek is bolstered by his clandestine meetings with Anja and the discovery of supportive allies among his fellow prisoners. In an encounter with a former priest, Vladek is told that the numerals in his serial identification, which the Nazis tattooed upon their victims, add up to eighteen, a number signifying life.

Vladek manages to hold on through several harrowing incidents, including a bout with typhus. As the war ends and the Allied troops make their way toward Auschwitz, Vladek and some fellow prisoners flee the camp and eventually make their way to safety. In the haste of his escape, however, Vladek loses contact with Anja and does not know if she is alive. Their reunion marks a happy point in Vladek's tale. As the book continues Vladek and Anja desperately search orphanages in Europe for Richieu, to no avail. They eventually emigrate to Sweden where Art is born, and from there the family moves to America. The horrors of the war have scarred Anja permanently however, and in 1968 she commits suicide. The book concludes with Art visiting Vladek just before his death in 1982.

Although *Maus* is essentially the story of Vladek and Anja's ordeal, the two books also serve in an autobiographical sense for Spiegelman, who appears at intervals throughout the narrative. He has stated that *Maus* is, in part, a meditation on "my own awareness of myself as a Jew." There are deeply personal passages depicting conversations between Art and his psychiatrist, Pavel, who, like Vladek, survived the Nazi's attempted purge. Their conversation ranges from Anja's suicide to the guilt that Art feels for being successful in light of his father's tribulation. As much as *Maus* serves as a piece of edifying literature, it also provided its creator with an opportunity to confront his personal demons. As Spiegelman wrote in an article in the *Voice, Maus* was motivated "by an impulse to look dead-on at the root cause of my own deepest fears and nightmares."

A good deal of discussion has arisen since the publication of the *Maus* books, much of it regarding Spiegelman's use of animals in the place of humans. When the story originated in *Funny Aminals*, Spiegelman made no mention of Jews or Nazis. The protagonists were mice, persecuted because they were "Maus." Likewise, the antagonists were cats, or "Die Katzen," and they chased the mice, although "chasing" the mice meant rounding them up in camps for work, torture, and extermination. The closest the strip comes to an outright identification with the Holocaust is in the name of the concentration camp, "Mauschwitz." As Spiegelman began the expanded version however, he found that he had to write in terms of "Jews" and "Nazis" when going into detail. As he told Cavalieri: "One can't keep changing it to metaphor. It would come out like some clumsy version of *Animal Farm* or something. It wouldn't ring true." Spiegelman decided to maintain his characters as animals however, citing a fear that using human characters would turn the work into a "corny" plea for sympathy. As he explained to Cavalieri, "To use these ciphers, the cats and mice, is actually a way to allow you past the cipher at the people who are experiencing it. So it's really a much more direct way of dealing with the material." As Lawrence Weschler described *Maus* in *Rolling Stone:* "Spiegelman's draftsmanship is clean and direct, his characterizations are charming and disarming—the imagery leads us on, invitingly, reassuringly, until suddenly the horrible story has us gripped and pinioned. Midway through, we hardly notice how strange it is for us to be having such strong reactions to these animal doings." Dale Luciano also agreed with Spiegelman's reasoning, as he described *Maus* in *The Comics Journal:* "By making the characters cats and mice, the result is that the characters' *human* qualities are highlighted all the more, to an inexplicably poignant effect." Luciano continued, "The situations recalled and acted-out in *Maus* place the characters in a variety of delicate situations: they express themselves with a simplicity and candor that is unsettling because it is so accurately *human.*"

Prior to *Maus*, the idea of a comic book that dealt with serious, realistic issues was considered a commercially unsound project. Comic books were not viewed as an outlet for sober or reflective writing. Spiegelman began to change that perception with *Raw*, and with the first collection of *Maus* in 1986, he demonstrated the extent to which comics literature could be taken. Both volumes of *Maus* became bestsellers and firmly established their author in the pantheon of great graphic artists. In addition, *Maus* made readers aware of other graphic works that forsook superheroes and wackiness for realistic situations. Books like the Hernandez brothers' *Love and Rockets* and Harvey Pekar's *American Splendor* received greater recognition due to *Maus*'s popularity. Luciano summed up the book's impact, stating that "after *Maus*, nobody will ever be able to say that the graphic story medium isn't well-suited to convey the complexity and delicacy of human emotion. The Goddamn thing is brilliant."

Th- th- that's All, Folks!

"There's something that I like about the fact that comics are such a gritty medium. That they're so ignored. There's something to be said for that," Spiegelman stated in *Comics Journal.* While some might disagree that comics are ignored, Spiegel-

This self-portrait shows Spiegelman turning to three of his well-known comics creations—and Ernie Bushmiller's character Nancy—for inspiration.

man's implication that the format is sufficiently removed from mainstream literature to serve as a proving ground for new techniques is evident in his work. Critics such as Luciano have commented on the artist's groundbreaking work, citing *Maus* as a defining plateau for comics. In graphic art, Spiegelman not only sees a potential for exploration, but also a medium through which ideas can be disseminated. Spiegelman has, in fact, stated that comics are his primary mode for communication. When Hirt-Manheimer asked Spiegelman if *Maus* could have appeared in a form other than comics, the author replied: "No. It's my voice. It's the way I speak and understand things."

Spiegelman's exploration of social issues in his work has led him to realizations about the modern world. *Maus* raised his comprehension of humanity's dark capabilities. In an article he wrote for the *Voice,* Spiegelman states that while there is a certain level of awareness and moral outrage toward the events of the Holocaust, society at large still operates on a level of denial. As he wrote: "It's like the old Looney Tunes cartoons where the character runs past the edge of a cliff and keeps running through midair. It takes a while to notice there's no ground left to run on. Finally he notices and plummets earthward with a crash. So, Western Civilization ended at Auschwitz. And we still haven't noticed." His comprehension of this condition in the Western psyche has led Spiegelman to view his responsibility as an artist in a new light. As he concluded in the *Voice*, "After the Holocaust, we *are* all Jews ... *all* of us ... including George Bush, J. Danforth Quayle, [leader of the PLO] Yassir Arafat, and even [Israeli prime minister] Yitzhak Shamir. Now our job is to convince them of that ... and th- th- that's all, *Volk*."

■ Works Cited

Cavalier, April, 1969.

Cavalieri, Joey, "An Interview with Art Spiegelman and Francoise Mouly," *Comics Journal*, August, 1981, pp. 98-125.

Dooley, Michael, "Art for Art's Sake," *Comics Journal*, April, 1989, pp. 110-117.

Hirt-Manheimer, Aron, "The Art of Art Spiegelman," *Reform Judaism*, spring, 1987, pp. 22-23, 32.

Luciano, Dale, "Trapped by Life," *Comics Journal*, December, 1986, pp. 43-45.

Spiegelman, Art, "Maus and Man," *Voice*, June 6, 1989, pp. 21-22.

Weschler, Lawrence, "Mighty 'Maus,'" *Rolling Stone*, November 20, 1986, pp. 103-106, 146-148.

■ For More Information See

BOOKS

Contemporary Authors, Volume 125, Gale, 1989.

Contemporary Graphic Artists, Volume 3, Gale, 1988.

PERIODICALS

New York Times Book Review, November 3, 1991, pp. 1, 35-36.

Publishers Weekly, April 26, 1991.

—*Sketch by David Galens*

Rosemary Sutcliff

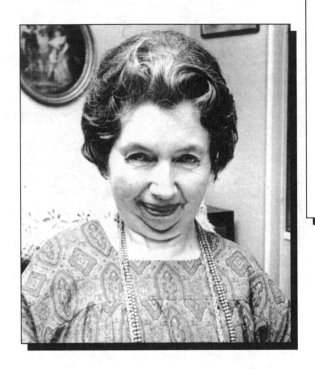

■ Personal

Born December 14, 1920, in East Clanden, Surrey, England; died July 23, 1992; daughter of George Ernest (an officer in the Royal Navy) and Nessie Elizabeth (Lawton) Sutcliff. *Education:* Educated privately and at Bideford School of Art, 1935-39. *Politics:* "Vaguely Conservative." *Religion:* "Unorthodox Church of England." *Hobbies and other interests:* Archaeology, anthropology, primitive religion, making collages and costume jewelry.

■ Addresses

Home—Swallowshaw, Walberton, Arundel, West Sussex BN18 0PQ, England.

■ Career

Writer, 1945—. *Member:* PEN, National Book League, Society of Authors, Royal Society of Miniature Painters.

■ Awards, Honors

Carnegie Medal commendation, 1955, and American Library Association (ALA) Notable Book, both

for *The Eagle of the Ninth;* Carnegie Medal commendation and *New York Herald Tribune*'s Children's Spring Book Festival honor book, both 1957, and ALA Notable Book, all for *The Shield Ring;* Carnegie Medal commendation and *New York Herald Tribune*'s Children's Spring Book Festival honor book, both 1958, both for *The Silver Branch;* Carnegie Medal commendation and Hans Christian Andersen Award honor book, both 1959, International Board on Books for Young People honor list, 1960, Highly Commended Author, 1974, and ALA Notable Book, all for *Warrior Scarlet;* Carnegie Medal, 1960, and ALA Notable Book, both for *The Lantern Bearers;* ALA Notable Book, 1960, for *Knight's Fee; New York Herald Tribune*'s Children's Spring Book Festival Award, 1962, ALA Notable Book, and *Horn Book* honor list, all for *Dawn Wind;* ALA Notable Book and *Horn Book* honor list, both 1962, both for *Beowulf;* ALA Notable Book and *Horn Book* honor list, both 1963, both for *The Hound of Ulster;* ALA Notable Book and *Horn Book* honor list, both 1965, and Children's Literature Association Phoenix Award, 1985, all for *The Mark of the Horse Lord; Horn Book* honor list, 1967, for *The High Deeds of Finn MacCool;* Lewis Carroll Shelf Award, 1971, ALA Notable Book, and *Horn Book* honor list, all for *The Witch's Brat; Boston Globe-Horn Book* Award for outstanding text and Carnegie Medal runner-up, both 1972, ALA Notable Book, and *Horn Book* honor list, all for *Tristan and Iseult; Heather, Oak, and Olive: Three Stories* was selected one of Child Study Association's "Children's Books of the Year," 1972, and *The Capricorn Bracelet* was selected, 1973; Officer, Order of the British Empire, 1975; *Boston Globe-*

Horn Book honor book for fiction, 1977, and *Horn Book* honor list, both for *Blood Feud; Children's Book Bulletin* Other Award, 1978, for *Song for a Dark Queen; Horn Book* honor list, 1978, for *Sun Horse, Moon Horse;* Children's Rights Workshop Award, 1978; ALA Notable Book, 1982, for *The Road to Camlann: The Death of King Arthur;* Royal Society of Literature fellow, 1982; Commander, Order of the British Empire, 1992.

■ Writings

"ROMAN BRITAIN" TRILOGY

The Eagle of the Ninth (also see below), illustrated by C. Walter Hodges, Oxford University Press, 1954, Walck, 1961.

The Silver Branch (also see below), illustrated by Charles Keeping, Oxford University Press, 1957, Walck, 1959.

The Lantern Bearers (also see below), illustrated by Keeping, Walck, 1959, revised edition, Oxford University Press, 1965.

Three Legions: A Trilogy (contains *The Eagle of the Ninth, The Silver Branch,* and *The Lantern Bearers*), Oxford University Press, 1980.

"ARTHURIAN KNIGHTS" TRILOGY

The Light beyond the Forest: The Quest for the Holy Grail, illustrated by Shirley Felts, Bodley Head, 1979, Dutton, 1980.

The Sword and the Circle: King Arthur and the Knights of the Round Table, illustrated by Felts, Dutton, 1981.

The Road to Camlann: The Death of King Arthur, illustrated by Felts, Bodley Head, 1981, Dutton Children's Books, 1982.

CHILDREN'S BOOKS

The Chronicles of Robin Hood, illustrated by C. Walter Hodges, Walck, 1950.

The Queen Elizabeth Story, illustrated by Hodges, Walck, 1950.

The Armourer's House, illustrated by Hodges, Walck, 1951.

Brother Dusty-Feet, illustrated by Hodges, Walck, 1952.

Simon, illustrated by Richard Kennedy, Walck, 1953.

Outcast, illustrated by Kennedy, Walck, 1955.

The Shield Ring, illustrated by Hodges, Walck, 1956.

Warrior Scarlet, illustrated by Charles Keeping, Walck, 1958, 2nd edition, 1966.

The Bridge-Builders, Blackwell, 1959.

Knight's Fee, illustrated by Keeping, Walck, 1960.

Houses and History, illustrated by William Stobbs, Batsford, 1960, Putnam, 1965.

Dawn Wind, illustrated by Keeping, Oxford University Press, 1961, Walck, 1962.

Dragon Slayer, illustrated by Keeping, Bodley Head, 1961, published as *Beowulf,* Dutton, 1962, published as *Dragon Slayer: The Story of Beowulf,* Macmillan, 1980.

The Hound of Ulster, illustrated by Victor Ambrus, Dutton, 1963.

Heroes and History, illustrated by Keeping, Putnam, 1965.

A Saxon Settler, illustrated by John Lawrence, Oxford University Press, 1965.

The Mark of the Horse Lord, illustrated by Keeping, Walck, 1965.

The High Deeds of Finn MacCool, illustrated by Michael Charlton, Dutton, 1967.

The Chief's Daughter (also see below), illustrated by Ambrus, Hamish Hamilton, 1967.

A Circlet of Oak Leaves (also see below), illustrated by Ambrus, Hamish Hamilton, 1968.

The Witch's Brat, illustrated by Richard Lebenson, Walck, 1970, illustrated by Robert Micklewright, Oxford University Press, 1970.

Tristan and Iseult, illustrated by Ambrus, Dutton, 1971.

The Truce of the Games, illustrated by Ambrus, Hamish Hamilton, 1971.

Heather, Oak, and Olive: Three Stories (contains *The Chief's Daughter, A Circlet of Oak Leaves,* and "A Crown of Wild Olive"), illustrated by Ambrus, Dutton, 1972.

The Capricorn Bracelet (based on BBC scripts for a series on Roman Scotland), illustrated by Richard Cuffari, Walck, 1973, illustrated by Keeping, Oxford University Press, 1973.

The Changeling, illustrated by Ambrus, Hamish Hamilton, 1974.

(With Margaret Lyford-Pike) *We Lived in Drumfyvie,* Blackie, 1975.

Blood Feud, illustrated by Keeping, Oxford University Press, 1976, Dutton, 1977.

Shifting Sands, illustrated by Laszlo Acs, Hamish Hamilton, 1977.

Sun Horse, Moon Horse, illustrated by Shirley Felts, Bodley Head, 1977, Dutton, 1978.

(Editor with Monica Dickens) *Is Anyone There?,* Penguin, 1978.

Song for a Dark Queen, Pelham Books, 1978, Crowell, 1979.

Frontier Wolf, Oxford University Press, 1980.

Eagle's Egg, illustrated by Ambrus, Hamish Hamilton, 1981.

Bonnie Dundee, Bodley Head, 1983, Dutton, 1984.

Flame-Coloured Taffeta, Oxford University Press, 1985, published in the United States as *Flame-Colored Taffeta*, Farrar, Straus, 1986.

The Roundabout Horse, illustrated by Alan Marks, Hamilton Children's, 1986.

The Best of Rosemary Sutcliff, Chancellor, 1987, Peter Bedrick, 1989.

Little Hound Found, Hamilton Children's, 1989.

A Little Dog Like You, illustrated by Jane Johnson, Simon & Schuster, 1990.

The Shining Company, Farrar, Straus, 1990.

OTHER

Lady in Waiting (novel), Hodder & Stoughton, 1956, Coward, 1957.

The Rider of the White Horse (novel), Hodder & Stoughton, 1959, abridged edition, Penguin, 1964, published in the United States as *Rider on a White Horse*, Coward, 1960.

Rudyard Kipling, Bodley Head, 1960, Walck, 1961, bound with *Arthur Ransome*, by Hugh Shelley, and *Walter de la Mare*, by Leonard Clark, Bodley Head, 1968.

Sword at Sunset (novel; Literary Guild selection), illustrated by John Vernon Lord, Coward, 1963, abridged edition, Longmans, 1967.

The Flowers of Adonis (novel), Hodder & Stoughton, 1969, Coward, 1970.

Blue Remembered Hills: A Recollection (autobiography), Bodley Head, 1983, Morrow, 1984.

Mary Bedell (play), produced in Chichester, England, 1986.

Blood and Sand, Hodder & Stoughton, 1987.

Also co-author with Stephen Weeks of a screenplay, *Ghost Story*, 1975, and author of radio scripts for BBC Scotland. A collection of Sutcliff's manuscripts is housed at the Kerlan Collection, University of Minnesota.

■ Adaptations

Song for a Dark Queen was adapted for stage by Nigel Bryant, Heinemann, 1984; *Dragon Slayer: The Story of Beowulf* has been recorded onto audio cassette (read by Sean Barrett), G. K. Hall Audio, 1986.

■ Sidelights

"For Rosemary Sutcliff the past is not something to be taken down from the shelf and dusted. It comes out of her pages alive and breathing and now," maintained John Rowe Townsend in his *A Sense of Story: Essays on Contemporary Writers*. A Carnegie

Medal-winning author, Sutcliff was essentially a storyteller, bringing history to life through her heroes, the atmospheres she created, and the sense of continuity found in her works. She presented English history from the late Bronze Age through the coming of the Roman legions, the Dark Age invasions of the Angles and the Saxons, and the Norman conquest, focusing on the experiences of young men and women who overcome the unrest of their times to find a measure of peace, despite their personal or physical limitations. Sutcliff also explored history through her many retellings of old legends or stories, such as those of King Arthur and the Knights of the Round Table and Beowulf. In these works, she presented well-known heroes, often adding a new dimension to their tales. "Most critics," contended May Hill Arbuthnot and Zena Sutherland in their *Children and Books*, "would say

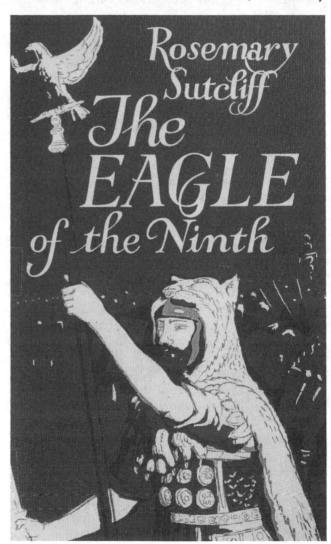

This 1954 historical novel begins Sutcliff's popular "Roman Britain" trilogy, and it also won the Carnegie Medal in 1955.

that at the present time the greatest writer of historical fiction for children and youth is unquestionably Rosemary Sutcliff."

Although she spent most of her time writing about the history of others, Sutcliff recounted her own history in *Blue Remembered Hills: A Recollection*. She described her isolated childhood caused by a severe case of rheumatoid arthritis, her father's career as a naval officer, and her mother's obsessive personality. She was constantly moved about, and because her mother was a storyteller, Sutcliff did not learn to read until she was nine. Unfortunately, Sutcliff's mother was also manic-depressive and became very overprotective during her daughter's illness. The author wrote, "My mother was one of those people, generally, I think, women, capable of great love and great self-sacrifice, but not capable of giving these things without demanding a return. During those years, she devoted herself to me to an extent which I sometimes think must have come hard on my father.... She was wonderful, no mother could have been more wonderful. But ever after, she demanded that I should not forget it, nor cease to be grateful, nor hold an opinion different from her own, nor even, as I grew older, feel the need for any companionship but hers."

When she was eleven years old, Sutcliff's father retired from the navy and the family settled in a somewhat isolated moorland house in north Devon. Despite her illness, Sutcliff was able to attend a normal school for a few years. "Miss Amelia Beck," she wrote, "had no teaching qualifications whatsoever, save the qualifications of long experience and love. She was the daughter of a colonel of Marines, in her eighty-sixth year when I became one of her pupils; and for more than sixty years, in her narrow house overlooking the Lines at Chatham, she had taught the children of the dockyard and the barracks.... When I went to Miss Beck's Academy I could not read, and ... by the end of my first term, without any apparent transition period, I was reading, without too much trouble, anything that came my way."

Sutcliff's father returned to the navy at the onset of World War II, leaving mother and daughter alone again. Their isolation was broken when their house became a Home Guard signals post, and Sutcliff's interest in battles and the military can be traced back to this time. Leaving school at the age of fourteen, Sutcliff began training as a miniature painter, a profession that was chosen for her because of her disability. Even though she had no inclination for the work, she made it through three

years at Bideford Art School and became a professional. "I was quite a good one," she explained. "Technically I was a very good one; but technique is not everything.... I painted children for the most part ... but as the war went on, I began to get more and more work to do at home from photographs; husbands and sons in the uniform of one or other of the services. And then, sadly, more and more often, photographs of husbands and sons who would not be coming home again."

"I suppose it must have been around the middle of the war that I began to get the itch to write," Sutcliff continued. "Almost from the beginning I felt cramped as a miniature painter and I think my first urge to break out into writing was the result of this. One can write as big as one needs; no canvas is too large to be unmanageable." Soon she began writing stories on paper she kept under her blotting pad. It was the pain of an early love that drove her to write her first published works, *The Chronicles of Robin Hood* and *The Queen Elizabeth Story*, which she later saw as "too cosy and sweet." These early works were only a beginning—it was not until such later works as *Warrior Scarlet* and *The Lantern Bearers* that Sutcliff found her true voice. Joan Aiken, reviewing *Blue Remembered Hills* in the *Times Educational Supplement*, observed: "Told with robust candour and fond photographic memory for detail, especially for outdoor places and gardens, it is an engrossing record of close family relationships, and also of quite unusually adverse conditions not so much overcome as cheerfully ignored and set on one side."

Fiction about Prehistoric and Roman Britain

Warrior Scarlet relates a tale of Bronze Age England, focusing on a boy and his coming to manhood. In order to become a full warrior in this heroic age, young Drem—crippled by a withered arm—must kill a wolf in single combat. When he fails, he becomes an outcast and flees the tribe to keep sheep with the Little Dark People on the open downs. "Sutcliff has widened her range to cover the hinterland of history and realized," Meek explained, "with the clarity we have come to expect, every aspect of the people of the Bronze Age, from hunting spears and cooking pots to king-making and burial customs, from childhood to old age. The book is coloured throughout with sunset bronze."

Sutcliff's "Roman Britain" trilogy begins with *The Eagle of the Ninth*, the story of a young Roman centurion during his first few years spent in second-century Britain, around the year 127 A.D. It is based on two historical events, Sutcliff states in her foreword to the book: the disappearance of the ill-omened Ninth Legion around 117 A.D. on its way to quell an uprising among the Caledonian tribes in the north, and the discovery in the twentieth century of a battered Legion's Eagle— its banner and pride of its fighting men—in the ruins of Calleva Atrebatum (modern Silchester).

Marcus Aquila is about to begin what he hopes will be a lengthy and magnificent military career and is at the same time resolved to discover the fate of the Ninth, in which his father served. His career is cut short, however, by a disabling wound suffered in his first battle, but his quest for his father and the fate of the Ninth continues. With his friend Esca, a native Briton and formerly a gladiator and slave, Marcus heads north into the former Roman province of Valencia (modern lowland Scotland), disguised as an eye-doctor. Together Marcus and Esca find the Eagle in the hands of a Highland tribe, steal it from the place where the priests have stowed it, and flee back to Britain, pursued by the angry natives. *The Eagle of the Ninth,* maintained Ruth M. McEvoy in *Junior Libraries,* "is one of the few good stories" covering the period of Roman rule in Britain.

The Silver Branch, the second book in the "Roman Britain" trilogy, takes place during the latter part of the third century. It tells the story of Justin, a junior surgeon newly arrived in Britain, and his cousin Centurion Flavius, both descendants of Marcus Aquila, the hero of *The Eagle of the Ninth.* Like the earlier book, some of the events of *The Silver Branch* were inspired by archaeological discoveries and historical events: the uncovering of the remains of a Saxon warrior at Rutupiae (Richborough Castle), and the burning of the basilica at Calleva (Silchester) in the late Roman period. Historical characters such as Marcus Aurelius Carausius, the Emperor of Britain, Allectus, his advisor and assassin, and the Legate Asklepiodotus also figure in the story.

Justin and Flavius are supporters of Carausius, a self-made man whose battle fleets based in southeastern Britain are holding back the Saxon invaders and pirates. On a hunting expedition, they overhear a meeting between a Saxon warrior and Allectus, who is plotting to become Emperor himself with the assistance of the Saxons. They prove unable to convince Carausius, however, and are sent north to take service at Hadrian's Wall. When the emperor is killed, the two young men are forced into hiding, realizing that the unity of

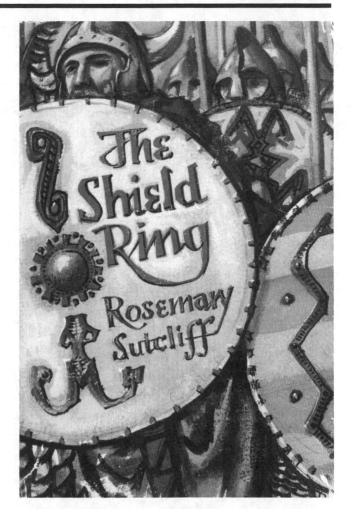

Published in 1956, this ALA Notable Book tells the tale of a small band of Norse settlers who resist a Norman invasion.

Britain is at risk. They become members of a resistance movement, preserving a hope that Roman forces will overthrow Allectus and his Saxon mercenaries. When the Roman forces arrive, Justin and Flavius form their supporters into a legion— under the standard of the Eagle recovered many years before by Marcus and Esca—and fight for Rome. "All the characters . . . are entirely credible," remarked Lavinia R. Davis in the *New York Times Book Review,* adding that the meticulous details "create a brilliant background for a vigorous and unusually moving narrative."

"*The Lantern Bearers* is the most closely-woven novel of the trilogy," claimed Margaret Meek in her *Rosemary Sutcliff,* adding that "in it the hero bears within himself the conflict of dark and light, the burden of his time and of himself." In this book, Sutcliff depicts the decline of Roman Britain through the adventures of another Aquila, only a few generations removed from Justin and Flavius, who deserts his legion in order to remain in Britain as the last of the Roman fighting forces are pulled out. Torn at having abandoned his soldiers, Aquila lights the beacon of Rutupiae port as the last legions set sail across the narrow seas to Gaul. He then returns to his family, just in time to see his home destroyed, his father killed, and his beloved sister Flavia borne off by marauding Saxons.

Aquila himself is taken as a serf to Juteland, on the opposite shore of the North Sea; but two years later, when the Jutes return to Britain, he finds Flavia and escapes. Flavia, however, chooses to remain with her Saxon husband and sends Aquila westward without her. Aquila joins the British who still resist the invaders in the west and becomes, as years go by, a leader in the host of Ambrosius Aurelianus and the friend of Ambrosius' nephew Artor. He eventually comes to accept Flavia's choice and to find peace within himself.

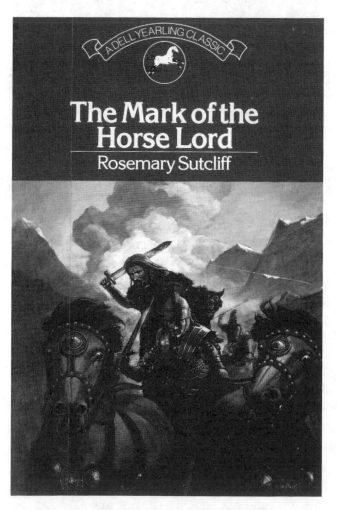

A DELL YEARLING CLASSIC

The Mark of the Horse Lord
Rosemary Sutcliff

Winner of a Phoenix Award, this 1965 book is the story of an ex-gladiator who becomes embroiled in a plan to return a deposed Scottish king to power.

Britain in the Post-Roman Period

Chronologically *Dawn Wind* follows *The Lantern Bearers*, for it deals with sixth-century Britain at the time of the Saxon invasion. The fourteen-year-old British hero, Owain, is the only survivor of a brutal battle with the Saxons that demolished his people. In the destroyed city of Viroconium Owain finds Regina, a lost and half-starved girl. The two are bound first by misery, then by mutual respect, so that when Regina becomes ill Owain takes her to a Saxon settlement. The Saxons care for Regina, but Owain pays the price for her life with his freedom: he sells himself as a slave. As time passes, however, he becomes a trusted thrall of a kindly master, witnesses the arrival of St. Augustine at Canterbury, gains his freedom and returns for Regina after eleven years. "So life is not snuffed out by the night," concluded Arbuthnot and Sutherland. "Sutcliff gives children and youth historical fiction that builds courage and faith that life will go on and is well worth the struggle."

The events of *The Shield Ring* come many years after those of *Dawn Wind*. Set in Northern England in the late eleventh and early twelfth centuries, during the reigns of William Rufus and Henry I, it tells of the resistance of a small band of Norse settlers against the incursions of the Normans under Ranulf Le Meschin. Young Frytha, her home burned and parent killed by the Normans, is taken by her father's serving-man, Grim, to the hall of Jarl Buthar. There she meets Bjorn, orphaned son of a settler of the nearby dales, who has come to the Jarl's house to live with his foster-father, Haethcyn the harper. Under the leadership of Aikin the Beloved, Frytha and Bjorn and the other men and women fight a long, slow war to break the Norman power in the Lake District and to maintain their freedom.

Similar themes and images connect many of Sutcliff's books. Margaret Sherwood Libby, writing in the *New York Herald Tribune Book Review* about *The Lantern Bearers*, declared that "the plot, both interesting and plausible, has its significance heightened by the recurring symbolism of light in dark days." For example, Aquila's lighting of the Rutupiae beacon becomes not only a personal symbol of his choice to remain in Britain but also a symbol of hope for those who fight on with him, a sign that the light of civilization will not die forever. Meek recognized this theme of light and dark in all three of the books: "The conflict of the light and dark is the stuff of legend in all ages.... Sutcliff's artistry is a blend of this realization in her own terms and an instructive personal identification with problems which beset the young, problems of identity, of self-realization.''

Another of the threads that run through Sutcliff's works is the great oath of loyalty, found in titles from *Warrior Scarlet* to *The Shield Ring*: "If we break faith ... may the green earth open and swallow us, may the grey seas roll in and overwhelm us, may the sky of stars fall on us and crush us out of life for ever.'' The shamanistic ritual of the spear that marks Drem's entrance into manhood in *Warrior Scarlet* is echoed many years later in a similar scene in *The Eagle of the Ninth*, which Marcus observes in a village on the western coast of modern Scotland. Still another connection lies in the continuity of Aquila's family from one generation to the next, symbolized by the massive golden ring, inset with a flawed emerald and carved with the figure of a dolphin, which is the emblem of Aquila's house. The ring reappears at intervals throughout Sutcliff's history: Marcus first sees it on a thong around the neck of an ancient warrior in the Scottish highlands; it is a sign of recognition between Flavius and Justin when they first serve together in Britain; it comes to Aquila from his sister Flavia when he escapes from the Jutish camp; it comes to Owain more than a hundred years later from the hand of his dead father as he flees the battlefield; and it comes to Bjorn from his foster-father Haethcyn six hundred years later still when he marches with Aikin Jarlson's war-band to fight the Normans as a token that he has come into his father's estate.

A Retelling of Arthurian Legend

The medieval stories of King Arthur and the Knights of the Round Table are the subjects of Sutcliff's "Arthurian Knights" trilogy. "Many people believe, as I do," Sutcliff wrote in her introduction to *The Sword and the Circle*, "that behind the legends of King Arthur as we know them today, there stands a real man. No king in shining armour, no fairy-tale palace at Camelot, but a Romano-British war leader, who when the dark tide of the barbarians came flooding in, did all that a great leader could do to hold them back and save something of civilisation. In *The Lantern Bearers* and *Sword at Sunset*, I have written about this war leader, trying to get back through the hero-tale and the high romance to the real man and the world he lived in.''

The "Arthurian Knights" stories, however, are Sutcliff's retellings of these legends, rather than

Should Damaris risk helping the mysterious stranger?

In eighteenth-century England, two young boys come to the aid of a wounded messenger and eventually become involved with the courier's cause in this 1985 book.

historical reconstructions of the men and the times they celebrated. *The Light beyond the Forest: The Quest for the Holy Grail* deals with the mystical search that Bors, Perceval, Galahad, and Lancelot conduct in an attempt to liberate the Wasteland from a religious curse. Although Donald K. Fry, writing in *School Library Journal*, found Sutcliff's retelling to be "sentimental and overexplained," a *Horn Book* contributor asserted that "a few archaic words unobtrusively add color to a narrative noteworthy for the grace and clarity of its prose." *The Sword and the Circle: King Arthur and the Knights of the Round Table* brings together thirteen Arthurian stories that are clarified by the allusions to the movements of other characters such as Merlin, Morgan le Fay, and Sir Lancelot, wrote a *Horn Book* contributor. "As in her other retellings," continued the contributor, Sutcliff "is constantly sensitive to the pageantry of color and rejoices in echoing the sounds and scents of nature." And Ann Evans declared in a *Times Literary Supplement* review that the collection "stands far above" any other.

The final book in the trilogy, *The Road to Camlann: The Death of King Arthur*, centers on Mordred's destruction of the round table, Lancelot's love of Guenevere, and the wars and the final battle, ending with Lancelot's death. Sutcliff was able to relate the penetrating sadness of the story, Marcus Crouch pointed out in a *Junior Bookshelf* review: "Here, young readers and their parents may be assured, is the best of a great and lasting story matched with the best of one of this age's great writers." Sutcliff's trilogy stands as "a valiant attempt to bring the often tragic, violent and sensual tales within the compass of children's understanding without cutting the heart from them," concluded *Times Educational Supplement* contributor Neil Philip.

From *Beowulf* to Bonnie Prince Charlie

As she did in her Arthurian trilogy, Sutcliff retold tales from early Celtic and Anglo-Saxon times in such works as *Beowulf*, *The Hound of Ulster*, *The High Deeds of Finn MacCool*, and *Tristan and Iseult*. "The well-read will revel" in the splendid language and in "the generous use of historical detail" found in *Beowulf*, asserted Mary Louise Hector in the *New York Times Book Review*. In *The Hound of Ulster*, Sutcliff tells the early Irish story of Cuchulain, the Champion of Ulster. Using various techniques, Sutcliff interpreted the seasoned tales, noted *Book Week* contributor Margaret Sherwood Libby, achieving the sensation of increasing excitement. "Rarely are young readers confronted with such exultant joy, such fierce hatred and such stark tragedy," added Libby. *The High Deeds of Finn MacCool* also retells an Irish legend—that of the famous captain of the *Fianna* and his many adventures. Sutcliff's "style is flowingly beautiful," described a *Times Literary Supplement* reviewer. And Paul Heins stated in *Horn Book* that the stories are told in such a way that they "fairly cry out for listeners." The famous Celtic love story of Tristan and Iseult is narrated in Sutcliff's work of the same title. *Tristan and Iseult* "moves along with epic cadence and grandeur" asserted Heins; and a *Times Literary Supplement* contributor maintained that the narrative is "superbly managed."

Sutcliff returned to Roman Britain for *The Mark of the Horse Lord*, but Phaedrus, the book's main character, is not a member of the Aquila family. He is an ex-gladiator of mixed Latin and British parentage, honorably discharged from the arena,

This 1990 historical novel is based on a Welsh epic poem and recounts the tale of a prince who unites Celtic tribes against a Saxon threat.

who becomes involved in a plan to restore a king to the Dalriadain tribe of the western Scottish coast. Both religious and political issues are involved: the throne was seized when the former king died by his half-sister Liadham. To prevent an uprising in the name of Midir, the young heir to the throne, she mutilated him and sent him into exile. Liadham represents the powers and beliefs of the Caledones, the ancient people who inhabited Scotland before the arrival of the Dalriadain: worshippers of dark forces, who practiced human sacrifice. Because of his resemblance to Midir, Phaedrus becomes the new Horse Lord, representing the powers of light, and leads the Dalriadain against Liadham and the Caledones.

The setting of *The Shining Company* will also be familiar to many of the author's readers. "Fans of Sutcliff's historical fiction will welcome her return to the post-Roman British setting of some of her finest novels as she tells a stirring tale," pointed out *School Library Journal* contributor Christine Behrmann. The plot itself is adapted from the Welsh epic *Y Gododdin*, the earliest surviving poem set in North Britain, and is told by Prosper, who joins Prince Gorthyn as a shield-bearer when the prince enlists in a company formed by the High Chief Mynyddog Mwynfawr to unite the Celtic tribes against the Saxon threat. For over a year the company trains outside of Edinburgh, but it is destroyed at the battle of Catterick, cut off without reinforcements; and only one man of the company—in addition to Prosper—returns to the court of Mynyddog alive. Much of the story, relates Behrmann, is concerned with the coming together of men from diverse parts of Britain, combining under a common cause. "Sutcliff has called all of her considerable talents into play here," said Behrmann, adding that readers who are willing to succumb to Sutcliff's "hypnotic language will be drawn into a truly splendid adventure."

Flame-Coloured Taffeta leaves the battlefields of ancient England behind, turning to the Sussex Downs in the eighteenth century. Twelve-year-old Damaris Crocker of Carthagena Farm and Peter Ballard from the vicarage know the woods near their home very well. While exploring the countryside one afternoon after a nighttime smuggling run, Damaris finds Tom, a wounded messenger for the lost cause of the disinherited Charles Stuart and the Jacobite court. The two children are not concerned with the rights and wrongs of the situation, but feel they must protect and help the wounded man. Many adventures ensue, including a fox hunt, a midnight rescue of Tom, and an exciting escape through the woods. "A beautifully written and intricately woven tale, this novel should appeal to any lover of historical fiction," claimed *Voice of Youth Advocates* contributor Ellen Gulick. Joanna Motion concluded in the *Times Literary Supplement* that *Flame-Coloured Taffeta* "succeeds as an enjoyable, soundly-crafted short novel where no whisker of plot or detail of character is wasted. And the sense of history under the lanes, the past seeped into the landscape, as Damaris looks out to sea from her farm house built of wrecked Armada timbers, will be familiar and satisfying to Sutcliff's many admirers."

Sutcliff's numerous historical adventures have been described by Sheila A. Egoff in her *Thursday's Child: Trends and Patterns in Contemporary Children's Literature* as "a virtually perfect mesh of history and fiction." Sutcliff "seems to work from no recipe for mixing fact and imagination and thus, like fantasy, which it also resembles in its magic qualities, her writing defies neat categorization." Similarly, Neil Philip contended in the *Times Educational Supplement* that "to call the books historical novels is to limit them disgracefully." Sutcliff "does not bring 'history' to the reader," continued Philip, "but involves the reader in the past—not just for the duration of a book, but for ever. She can animate the past, bring it to life inside the reader in a most personal and lasting way." Sutcliff immerses herself and the reader in the time period that she is relating, and "her method of settling on the felt details that remain in the mind, driven along the nerves of the hero, is even more convincing than the historian's account," Meek declared. "Sutcliff's name," stated Ann Evans in the *Times Literary Supplement*, "will be remembered and revered long after others have been forgotten."

■ Works Cited

Aiken, Joan, "Rosemary and Time," *Times Educational Supplement*, January 14, 1983, p. 24.

Arbuthnot, May Hill, and Zena Sutherland, *Children and Books*, 4th edition, Scott, Foresman, 1972, pp. 508-509.

Davis, Lavinia R., "Turmoil in Britain," *New York Times Book Review*, June 29, 1958, p. 18.

Egoff, Sheila A., *Thursday's Child: Trends and Patterns in Contemporary Children's Literature*, American Library Association, 1981, pp. 159-192.

Evans, Ann, "The Real Thing," *Times Literary Supplement*, March 27, 1981, p. 341.

Gulick, Ellen, review of *Flame-Colored Taffeta*, *Voice of Youth Advocates*, February, 1987, p. 287.

Libby, Margaret Sherwood, review of *The Lantern Bearers*, *New York Herald Tribune Book World*, February 14, 1960, p. 11.

McEvoy, Ruth M., review of *The Eagle of the Ninth*, *Junior Libraries*, January, 1955, p. 33.

Meek, Margaret, *Rosemary Sutcliff*, Walck, 1962.

Motion, Joanna, "Helping Out," *Times Literary Supplement*, September 19, 1986, p. 1042.

Philip, Neil, "Romance, Sentiment, Adventure," *Times Educational Supplement*, February 19, 1982, p. 23.

"The Search for Selfhood: The Historical Novels of Rosemary Sutcliff," *Times Literary Supplement*, June 17, 1965.

Sutcliff, Rosemary, author's note to *The Sword and the Circle: King Arthur and the Knights of the Round Table*, Dutton, 1981, pp. 7-8.

Sutcliff, Rosemary, *Blue Remembered Hills: A Recollection*, Bodley Head, 1983, Morrow, 1984.

Townsend, John Rowe, *A Sense of Story: Essays on Contemporary Writers for Children*, Lippincott, 1971, pp. 193-199.

■ For More Information See

BOOKS

Children's Literature Review, Volume 1, Gale, 1976.

Contemporary Literary Criticism, Volume 26, Gale, 1983.

Crouch, Marcus, *Treasure Seekers and Borrowers: Children's Books in Britain 1900-1960*, Library Association, 1962.

Crouch, Marcus, *The Nesbit Tradition: The Children's Novel in England 1945-1970*, Benn, 1972.

Townsend, John Rowe, *Written for Children: An Outline of English Language Children's Literature*, Lippincott, 1974.

PERIODICALS

Booklist, February 1, 1955, p. 251.

Horn Book, June, 1958, pp. 209-210; February, 1968; April, 1970; December, 1971; August, 1980; February, 1982.

Junior Bookshelf, December, 1981.

New Yorker, October 22, 1984.

New York Times Book Review, October 26, 1952; January 9, 1955; March 17, 1957; January 4, 1959; April 22, 1962; November 11, 1962; May 26, 1963; May 3, 1964; November 7, 1965; January 30, 1966; February 15, 1970; September 30, 1973; April 5, 1987.

Observer, February 6, 1983.

Publishers Weekly, December 1, 1969; November 1, 1971; January 7, 1983; October 6, 1989; June 8, 1990.

School Library Journal, August, 1980; July, 1990.

Times (London), January 26, 1983; June 9, 1990.

Times Educational Supplement, October 23, 1981; January 13, 1984.

Times Literary Supplement, November 27, 1953; November 19, 1954; November 21, 1958; December 4, 1959; November 25, 1960; June 14, 1963; December 9, 1965; May 25, 1967; October 30, 1970; July 2, 1971; September 28, 1973; April 4, 1975; December 10, 1976; July 15, 1977; December 2, 1977; July 7, 1978; November 21, 1980; April 22, 1983; September 30, 1983.

Tribune Books (Chicago), March 8, 1987.

Washington Post Book World, November 5, 1967; September 9, 1990.°

Mildred D. Taylor

■ Personal

Born September 13, 1943, in Jackson, MS; daughter of Wilbert Lee and Deletha Marie (Davis) Taylor; married Errol Zea-Daly, August, 1972 (divorced, 1975). *Education:* University of Toledo, B.Ed., 1965; University of Colorado, M.A., 1969.

■ Career

Writer. English and history teacher with the Peace Corps, Tuba City, AZ, 1965, and Yirgalem, Ethiopia, 1965-67, recruiter, 1967-68, instructor in Maine, 1968; University of Colorado, Boulder, study skills coordinator, 1969-71; proofreader and editor in Los Angeles, CA, 1971-73.

■ Awards, Honors

First prize (African-American category), Council on Interracial Books for Children, 1973, outstanding book of the year citation, *New York Times,* 1975, and Jane Addams Honor citation, 1976, all for *Song of the Trees;* notable book citation, American Library Association, 1976, National Book Award (finalist), honor book citation, *Boston Globe-Horn Book,* Jane Addams Honor citation, and

Newbery Medal, all 1977, and Buxtehuder Bulle Award, 1985, all for *Roll of Thunder, Hear My Cry;* outstanding book of the year citation, *New York Times,* 1981, Jane Addams Honor citation, 1982, American Book Award nomination, 1982, and Coretta Scott King Award, 1982, all for *Let the Circle be Unbroken;* Coretta Scott King Award, and fiction award, *Boston Globe-Horn Book,* both 1988, both for *The Friendship;* notable book citation, *New York Times,* 1987, and Christopher Award, 1988, both for *The Gold Cadillac;* Coretta Scott King Award, 1990, for *The Road to Memphis.*

■ Writings

Song of the Trees, illustrated by Jerry Pinkney, Dial, 1975.
Roll of Thunder, Hear My Cry, Dial, 1976.
Let the Circle Be Unbroken, Dial, 1981.
The Friendship, illustrated by Max Ginsburg, Dial, 1987.
The Gold Cadillac, illustrated by Michael Hays, Dial, 1987.
The Road to Memphis, Dial, 1990.
Mississippi Bridge, Dial, 1990.

■ Adaptations

Roll of Thunder, Hear My Cry was recorded by Newbery Awards Records, 1978, and adapted as a three-part television miniseries of the same title, American Broadcasting Companies, Inc. (ABC-TV), 1978.

■ Sidelights

Inspired in large part by the oral history of her family, Mildred D. Taylor has written a series of novels that help redefine literary representations of black family life. Many of Taylor's works are set in the rural South of the 1930s, where racial discrimination, segregation, and fear were part of the everyday experience of many black families. Taylor brings a unique perspective to her work; although born in Mississippi, she spent most of her youth in Ohio. "I grew to know the South—to feel the South—through the yearly trips we took there and through the stories told.... In those days, before the civil rights movement, I remember the South and how it was. I remember the racism, the segregation.... But I also remember the other South—the South of family and community," Taylor relates in her 1988 *Boston Globe-Horn Book* acceptance speech. Taylor's ability to mix the events of everyday life with volatile issues and complex characters has gained the author both wide critical acclaim and popular appeal. "Mildred's words flow smoothly, effortlessly ... and they abound in richness, harmony, and rhythm.... Her ability to bring her characters to life and to involve her readers is remarkable," sums up Phyllis D. Taylor in *Horn Book*. "This woman was born to write."

Some Painful Lessons

Taylor's exposure to segregation and discrimination began at an early age. In an essay for *Something about the Author Autobiography Series* (*SAAS*), the author recounts that she "was born in a segregated city, in a segregated state, in a segregated America." Three weeks after Taylor's birth, her father, angry over a number of ugly racial incidents, decided to seek a new life for his family in the North. The Taylors eventually relocated to Toledo, Ohio, where an extended network of family and friends helped make the transition easier. Taylor tells *SAAS*: "As aunts and uncles were able to rent other places or buy their own houses, we continued to do many things together as a family."

One tradition the Taylors maintained after their move was that of taking long car trips back to the South. These trips were often bittersweet experiences, largely because the family had to deal once again with the realities of segregation. "Each trip down reminded us that the South into which we had been born ... still remained," Taylor notes in her essay. "As soon as we crossed over the Ohio River into Kentucky, lest we forget, the signs reminded us that they remained. On the restrooms of gasoline stations were the signs: WHITE ONLY, COLORED NOT ALLOWED. Over water fountains were the signs: WHITE ONLY. In restaurant windows, in motel windows, there were always the signs: WHITE ONLY, COLORED NOT ALLOWED. Every sign we saw proclaimed our second-class citizenship."

Despite the difficulties of these trips—which often required traveling in a caravan with other family members for protection from police and white locals—Taylor was still able to enjoy part of the experience. "Life was good then," she recalls in her 1977 Newbery Medal acceptance speech. "Running barefoot in the heat of the summer sun, my skin darkening to a soft, umber hue; chasing

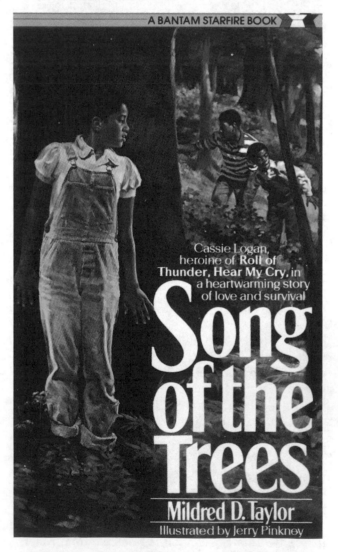

A BANTAM STARFIRE BOOK

Cassie Logan, heroine of **Roll of Thunder, Hear My Cry,** in a heartwarming story of love and survival

Song of the Trees

Mildred D. Taylor

Illustrated by Jerry Pinkney

This 1975 book introduces readers to the Logan family and depicts a struggle the family encounters as land-owners.

butterflies in the day, fireflies at night; riding an old mule named Jack and a beautiful mare named Lady; even picking a puff of cotton or two—there seemed no better world." Taylor was also entranced by the stories her relatives told about the family's past. Some of the stories were funny, some sad, but all featured the distinctive personalities of Taylor's ancestors. As Taylor grew older, however, her understanding of the stories changed: "I do not remember how old I was when the stories became more than tales of faraway people, but rather, reality. I do not remember when the twenty-four hour picnic was no longer a picnic, the adventure no longer an adventure. I only remember that one summer I suddenly felt a climbing nausea as we crossed the Ohio River into Kentucky."

One of the things that helped Taylor understand and cope with the more difficult aspects of her childhood was the love and support of her father, who tried to instill in Taylor and her sister Wilma an understanding of both the past and their role in the future. "He wanted us to appreciate the good of the South as well as to be thankful for the privileges and freedoms of our life in the North," Taylor notes for SAAS. "He said that without understanding the loss of liberty in the South, we couldn't appreciate the liberty of the North." He also encouraged his daughters to strive to be the best people possible. In her Newbery speech, Taylor remembers that she was "blessed with a special father, a man who had unyielding faith in himself and his abilities.... A highly principled, complex man ... he impressed upon my sister and me that we were somebody, that we were important, and could do or be anything we set our minds to do or be.... He was more concerned about how we carried ourselves, how we respected ourselves and others, and how we pursued the principles upon which he hoped we would build our lives."

When the author was ten years old, her family moved into a newly integrated Ohio town; as a result, Taylor was the only black child in her class. She felt burdened by the realization that her actions would be judged—by whites unfamiliar with blacks—as representative of her entire race. "I remember the pressure of being 'the only one,'" she remarks for SAAS. "I felt that what I did reflected not only upon me, but upon my family and upon my race." Taylor was also uncomfortable because her understanding of black history contrasted sharply with that presented in textbooks. In her Newbery speech, Taylor comments that such publications contained only a "lackluster history of Black people ... a history of a docile, subservient people happy with their fate who did little or nothing to shatter the chains that bound them, both before and after slavery." Taylor's efforts to tell her classmates what she knew about black history were met with general disbelief. "Most of the students thought I was making the stories up," she reminisces in SAAS. "Some even laughed at me. I couldn't explain things to them. Even the teacher seemed not to believe me. They all believed what was in the history book."

By the time Taylor entered high school, the civil rights movement had begun to gain momentum. A number of incidents—including the murder of a young black boy named Emmett Till, the Montgomery bus boycott, and the Supreme Court decision in Brown v. Board of Education of Topeka—had raised awareness of racial discrimination to new levels. Despite the publicity surrounding these and other incidents, Taylor felt somewhat removed from the problem. "I was in Toledo after all, in the North, and though there certainly was discrimination, certainly prejudice, and certainly open violation of civil rights, I had seldom felt open hostility," she writes in her essay. One incident, however, helped draw Taylor into the fray. In 1957, a black senior was chosen as homecoming queen at Taylor's high school. The student body reaction ranged from happiness (especially on the part of minority students) to anger which exploded into violence. The author recollects: "Though things returned to normal ... those days of my freshman year hammered home to all of us that racism was not only part of the South, but of the North as well."

Inspiration and Adventure

A visit to Toledo by then-senator John F. Kennedy further stimulated Taylor's interest in civil rights. Elected to report on the senator's visit, Taylor was impressed by both Kennedy's charisma and his interest in the civil rights movement. "I loved the promise of the future he offered, and hearing him I very much intended to be a part of it," she notes in SAAS. Inspired by Kennedy's speech, Taylor began making plans for her own future, plans that included faraway places and people. "Before John F. Kennedy, I had never known I could achieve this," she records in SAAS, "It was something I intended to do, but until John F. Kennedy it was only a dream."

Part of Taylor's plans included college. When not preparing for classes, she wrote stories (some of which were later submitted to various writing contests). In many ways, Taylor found writing difficult. At first, she tried to pattern her efforts after writers that she admired, such as Charles Dickens and Jane Austen: "I was trying to emulate a literary form that left my work stiff and unconvincing. It was an unnatural style for me," she comments in *SAAS*. Taylor wrote her first novel at age nineteen; told using a first-person narrator, "Dark People, Dark World" explores the retreat of a young, blind, white man into Chicago's black ghetto. Although a publishing house expressed some interest in the work in a shorter, edited format, Taylor abandoned the project, largely because she was "very naive and full of artistic self-righteousness."

After graduating from college, the author was invited to join the Peace Corps. While Taylor was elated over the prospect of going to Ethiopia to teach, her family was unsettled by the prospect. Taylor's father was worried about the distance and potential danger; Taylor's mother, although resigned to her daughter's decision, was sad about the amount of time she would be gone. Eventually, Taylor's enthusiasm overrode her parents' concerns. During her Peace Corps service, Taylor taught English as a second language on a Navajo reservation in Arizona and later traveled to Ethiopia, where she taught at a small school.

Taylor enrolled in graduate school after her stint with the Peace Corps. Inspired by another graduate student, she became involved with the Black Student Alliance and other organizations established by the Alliance, such as the Black Education Program. "In addition to putting together plans to force the university into meeting our demands for black enrollment and black programs, we studied black culture, black history and black politics," Taylor notes in her essay. At one point, Taylor was approached by *Life* magazine about writing an article describing the Black Studies movement. Unfortunately, the magazine felt that the final product did not capture the spirit of the organization and the article was never published; Taylor's ensuing disappointment made her question the direction her life was taking. She writes in her essay: "I began to question whether or not individual goals must be suppressed to the will of the group in order for the group's goals to flourish." Eventually, Taylor returned to Ethiopia to regroup.

After returning from Africa, Taylor moved to Los Angeles. There, she worked at a number of temporary jobs to help make ends meet, all the while applying for positions more in keeping with her

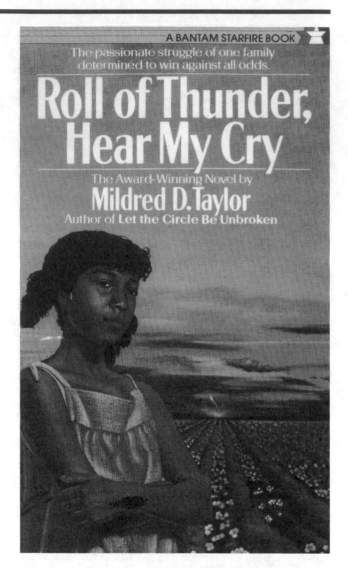

Winner of the Buxtehuder Bulle Award, this 1976 book continues the story of the Logan family and expands upon themes of everyday discrimination against African Americans.

work experience and education. At one point, Taylor was offered a job as a reporter for CBS; after much self-analysis, she turned the position down in favor of concentrating on her writing. Taylor's first success in the latter area came about when she entered a contest sponsored by the Council on Interracial Books for Children. Much to her surprise, Taylor's revision of an old manuscript won in the African-American category.

The Logan Cycle

The revised manuscript formed the basis for *Song of the Trees*, Taylor's first book featuring the Logan family. Based on an actual incident and narrated by eight-year-old Cassie Logan, *Song of the Trees* highlights the conflict between a group of money-hungry white men and Papa Logan over some trees on Logan's land. In a standoff, Logan forces the interlopers out by threatening to blow up both himself and the remaining trees. A reviewer for the *Bulletin of the Center for Children's Books* calls the novel's style "fairly brisk, verging on the poetic," adding that "the plot is nicely constructed." "The simple story has been written with great conviction and strength," concurs a *Horn Book* reviewer, "Cassie's descriptions of the trees add a poetic touch."

Taylor's next book, *Roll of Thunder, Hear My Cry,* continues the story of the Logan family. Covering a brief time period between 1933 and 1934, the book explores how discrimination can be an everyday occurrence. While Papa is away working on the railroad, the rest of the family struggles with

This 1981 novel, winner of a Coretta Scott King Book Award, finds the Logan family struggling through the Depression.

the cruelty and bigotry of their hometown. The Logan children are targeted for splashing by the driver of the whites-only school bus, while at school they receive the cast-off, ragged school texts that white students will no longer use. Mama Logan loses her teaching job after she defies school district officials by including a discussion of slavery in a history lesson. After an incident in which several black men are set on fire, the Logans help orchestrate a boycott of the suspected culprit's store. This act sets off a series of events, including a foreclosure threat on the Logan's land and a suspicious fire. "The events and settings of the powerful novel are presented with such verisimilitude and the characters are so carefully drawn that one might assume the book to be autobiographical, if the author were not so young," concludes a *Bookbird* reviewer.

In the next addition to the Logan chronicle, *Let the Circle be Unbroken*, Cassie narrates the story of her town and how its people cope with the devastating effects of the Depression. *Circle* examines how hard times can bring out both the best and worst in people. In the novel, white and black sharecroppers band together to give each other food and moral support, while an elderly black woman is ridiculed for memorizing the state constitution in order to vote and a young man is denied justice in a rigged trial. *New York Times Book Review* contributor June Jordan praises the book for its "dramatic tension and virtuoso characterization," while Holly Eley of the *Times Literary Supplement* notes that Taylor "gives us a historical perspective on racial issues which she insists can only be successfully resolved by recognizing the fundamental equality of all human beings."

In *The Road to Memphis*, Taylor concludes the Logan cycle. Cassie is now a high school senior, attending school in Jackson, Mississippi, and dreaming of becoming a lawyer. Cassie's brother Stacey and his friend Moe are also living in Jackson where they have found work in a factory. Away from family and friends for the first time, the trio must deal with certain ugly realities without benefit of familial support. Several racial incidents and the outbreak of World War II put a heavy strain on the three young people, especially Moe, who is forced to flee the city after defending himself in a racially-motivated attack. While allowing that Taylor loses a little narrative power in the novel, Susan Sculler of *School Library Journal* concludes that *Road* "is a dramatic, painful book."

Mississippi Bridge is connected to the Logan stories in that it is told from the viewpoint of Jeremy

MILDRED D. TAYLOR

The Road to Memphis

By the Newbery Award–winning author of *Roll of Thunder, Hear My Cry*

Fed up with racial prejudice, Cassie Logan attempts to forge a career in the white-dominated legal system in this 1990 book.

Simms, a ten-year-old white boy who befriends the Logan family. The novel chronicles Jeremy's reaction to the forcible removal of Grandma Logan and other black passengers from a bus during a severe storm so that white latecomers can ride in comfort. A few minutes later, the bus and its new riders crashes into a creek. A *Publishers Weekly* reviewer states that "the ironies and injustices presented in [Taylor's] story will be strongly felt and remembered."

Difficult Issues

The Friendship presents a racial confrontation between two men in 1930s Mississippi. Tom Bee, a black man, saves the life of John Wallace, a white storekeeper, when the two are young men. In gratitude, John insists that he and Tom always remain friends. Years later, however, John forgets this bond when he shoots Tom for addressing him by his first name in public—an act considered socially unacceptable. A *Bulletin of the Center for Children's Books* reviewer claims that the novel "elicits a naturally powerful response in depicting cruel injustice," with writing that is "concentrated to heighten that effect."

Taylor turns to rural family life again in *The Gold Cadillac*. Set in the 1950s, the novel chronicles a black family's car trip to the South (a trip much like those Taylor took with her own family). Along the way, Wilma, 'lois, and their parents are confronted with "whites only" signs and suffer harassment from white police officers who are both jealous and suspicious of the family's car and the prosperity it represents. Through these and other ugly encounters, the two sisters are eventually able to better appreciate the greater freedom and opportunity they enjoy in their Ohio hometown. Helen E. Williams, writing in *School Library Journal*, remarks: "Clear language and logical, dramatic sequencing of story events make this story bittersweet for adult readers but important for the social development of beginning readers."

Taylor gives her father much of the credit for her literary success, both because of his storytelling legacy and his refusal to be cowed by racism and segregation. The author accepted her Newbery medal for *Roll of Thunder, Hear My Cry* on behalf of her father, remarking that "without his teachings, without his words, my words would not have been." Taylor adds that she hopes her books about the Logan family "will one day be instrumental in teaching children of all colors the tremendous influence that Cassie's generation . . . had in bringing about the great Civil Rights movement of the fifties and sixties."

■ Works Cited

Eley, Holly, "Cotton Pickin' Blues," *Times Literary Supplement*, March 26, 1982, p. 343.

Fogelman, Phyllis J., "Mildred D. Taylor," *Horn Book*, August, 1977, pp. 410-414.

Review of *The Friendship, Bulletin of the Center for Children's Books*, December, 1987.

Jordan, June, "Mississippi in the Thirties," *New York Times Book Review*, November 15, 1981, pp. 55, 58.

Review of *Mississippi Bridge, Publishers Weekly*, July 27, 1990, p. 234.

Review of *Roll of Thunder, Hear My Cry, Horn Book*, April, 1982, p. 174.

Schuller, Susan, review of *The Road to Memphis*, *School Library Journal*, June, 1990, p. 138.

Review of *Song of the Trees*, *Bulletin of the Center for Children's Books*, October, 1975.

Review of *Song of the Trees*, *Horn Book*, August, 1975.

Taylor, Mildred D., Newbery Award acceptance speech, *Horn Book*, August, 1977, pp. 401-409.

Taylor, Mildred D., essay in *Something about the Author Autobiography Series*, Gale, 1988, pp. 267-286.

Williams, Helen E., review of *The Gold Cadillac*, *School Library Journal*, September, 1987, pp. 171-172.

■ **For More Information See**

BOOKS

Children's Literature Review, Volume 9, Gale, 1985.

Contemporary Literary Criticism, Volume 21, Gale, 1982.

Dictionary of Literary Biography, Volume 52: *American Writers for Children since 1960: Fiction*, Gale, 1986, pp. 365-367.

Holtze, Sally Holmes, editor, *Fifth Book of Junior Authors and Illustrators*, H. W. Wilson, 1983, pp. 307-308.

Kirkpatrick, D. L., editor, *Twentieth Century Children's Writers*, St. James Press, 1989, pp. 951-952.

PERIODICALS

Bookbird, March, 1977.

New York Times Book Review, May 20, 1990, p. 48.

School Library Journal, November, 1990, p. 119-120.

Wilson Library Bulletin, March, 1988, p. 37.°

—Sketch by Elizabeth A. Des Chenes

J. R. R. Tolkien

■ Personal

Full name, John Ronald Reuel Tolkien; surname is pronounced "*Tohl*-keen"; born January 3, 1892, in Bloemfontein, South Africa; brought to England in April, 1895; died of complications resulting from a bleeding gastric ulcer and a chest infection, September 2, 1973, in Bournemouth, England; buried in Wolvercote Cemetery, Oxford; son of Arthur Reuel (a bank manager) and Mabel (Suffield) Tolkien; married Edith Mary Bratt (a pianist), March 22, 1916 (died November 29, 1971); children: John, Michael, Christopher, Priscilla. *Education:* Exeter College, Oxford, B.A., 1915, M.A., 1919. *Religion:* Roman Catholic.

■ Career

Author and scholar. Assistant on *Oxford English Dictionary*, 1918-20; University of Leeds, Leeds, England, reader in English, 1920-24, professor of English language, 1924-25; Oxford University, Oxford, England, Rawlinson and Bosworth Professor of Anglo-Saxon, 1925-45, Merton Professor of English Language and Literature, 1945-59, fellow of Pembroke College, 1926-45, honorary resident fellow of Merton College, 1972-73. Free-lance tutor, 1919; Leverhulme research fellow, 1934-36; Sir Israel Gollancz Memorial Lecturer, British Academy, 1936; Andrew Lang Lecturer, St. Andrews University, 1939; W. P. Ker Lecturer, University of Glasgow, 1953; O'Donnell Lecturer, Oxford University, 1955. *Military service:* Lancashire Fusiliers, 1915-18. *Member:* Royal Society of Literature (fellow), Philological Society (vice president), Science Fiction Writers of America (honorary), Hid Islenzka Bokmenntafelag (honorary).

■ Awards, Honors

New York Herald Tribune Children's Spring Book Festival award, 1938, for *The Hobbit;* Dr. en Phil. et Lettres, Liege, 1954; D.Litt., University College, Dublin, 1954, and Oxford University, 1972; International Fantasy Award, 1957, for *The Lord of the Rings;* Benson Medal, 1966; Commander, Order of the British Empire, 1972; *Locus* Award for best fantasy novel, 1978, for *The Silmarillion.*

■ Writings

(Editor with C. L. Wiseman, and author of introductory note) Geoffrey Bache Smith, *A Spring Harvest* (poems), Erskine Macdonald, 1918.

A Middle English Vocabulary, Clarendon Press, 1922.

(Editor with Eric V. Gordon) *Sir Gawain and the Green Knight,* Clarendon Press, 1925, 2nd edition, revised by Norman Davis, 1967.

(With Gordon and others) *Songs for the Philologists* (verse), Department of English, University College, Oxford, 1936.

Beowulf: The Monsters and the Critics (originally published in *Proceedings of the British Academy*, 1936; also see below), Oxford University Press, 1937, reprinted, 1958.

(Self-illustrated) *The Hobbit; or, There and Back Again*, Allen & Unwin, 1937, Houghton, 1938, 2nd edition, 1951, 3rd edition, 1966, 4th edition, 1978.

Chaucer as a Philologist, Oxford University Press, 1943.

Farmer Giles of Ham (also see below), Allen & Unwin, 1949, Houghton, 1950, 2nd edition, Allen & Unwin, 1975, Houghton, 1978.

The Lord of the Rings, Houghton, Volume 1: *The Fellowship of the Ring*, 1954, Volume 2: *The Two Towers*, 1954, Volume 3: *The Return of the King*, 1955, with new foreword by the author, Ballantine, 1966, 2nd edition, Allen & Unwin, 1966, Houghton, 1967.

The Adventures of Tom Bombadil and Other Verses from the Red Book (also see below), Allen & Unwin, 1962, Houghton, 1963, 2nd edition, Houghton, 1978.

(Editor) *Ancrene Wisse: The English Text of the Ancrene Riwle*, Oxford University Press, 1962.

Tree and Leaf (includes "On Fairy-Stories" and "Leaf By Niggle" [originally published in *Dublin Review*, 1945]; also see below), Allen & Unwin, 1964, Houghton, 1965, reprinted, 1989, 2nd edition, Allen & Unwin, 1975.

The Tolkien Reader (includes "The Homecoming of Beorhtnoth" [originally published in *Essays and Studies*, English Association, 1953; also see below], *Tree and Leaf*, *Farmer Giles of Ham*, and *The Adventures of Tom Bombadil*), introduction by Peter S. Beagle, Ballantine, 1966.

The Road Goes Ever On: A Song Cycle, music by Donald Swann, Houghton, 1967.

Smith of Wootton Major (also see below), Houghton, 1967, 2nd edition, Allen & Unwin, 1975, Houghton, 1978.

Smith of Wootton Major [and] *Farmer Giles of Ham*, Ballantine, 1969.

(Translator) *Sir Gawain and the Green Knight*, *Pearl*, [and] *Sir Orfeo*, edited by Christopher Tolkien, Houghton, 1975.

Tree and Leaf, Smith of Wootton Major, The Homecoming of Beorhtnoth, Unwin Books, 1975.

Farmer Giles of Ham, The Adventures of Tom Bombadil, Unwin Books, 1975.

The Father Christmas Letters, edited by Baillie Tolkien, Houghton, 1976.

The Silmarillion, edited by Christopher Tolkien, Houghton, 1977.

Pictures by J. R. R. Tolkien, foreword and notes by Christopher Tolkien, Houghton, 1979.

Unfinished Tales of Numenor and Middle-Earth, edited by Christopher Tolkien, Houghton, 1980.

Poems and Stories, Allen & Unwin, 1980.

The Letters of J. R. R. Tolkien, selected and edited by Humphrey Carpenter and Christopher Tolkien, Houghton, 1981.

(Author of text and commentary, and translator) *The Old English Exodus*, edited by Joan Turville-Petre, Oxford University Press, 1981.

Mr. Bliss (reproduced from Tolkien's illustrated manuscript), Allen & Unwin, 1982, Houghton, 1983.

Finn and Hengest: The Fragment and the Episode, edited by Alan Bliss, Allen & Unwin, 1982, Houghton, 1983.

The Monsters and the Critics and Other Essays, edited by Christopher Tolkien, Allen & Unwin, 1983, Houghton, 1984.

Bilbo's Last Song (verse), illustrated by Pauline Baynes, Riverwood Publishers, 1990.

"HISTORY OF MIDDLE EARTH" SERIES; EDITED BY CHRISTOPHER TOLKIEN

The Book of Lost Tales, Part 1, Allen & Unwin, 1983, Houghton, 1984.

The Book of Lost Tales, Part 2, Houghton, 1984.

The Lays of Beleriand, Houghton, 1985.

The Shaping of Middle-Earth: The Quenta, the Ambarkanta, and the Annals, Houghton, 1986.

The Lost Road and Other Writings: Language and Legend before The Lord of the Rings, Houghton, 1987.

The Return of the Shadow: The History of The Lord of the Rings, Part 1, Houghton, 1988.

The Treason of Isengard: The History of The Lord of the Rings, Part 2, Houghton, 1989.

The War of the Ring: The History of The Lord of the Rings, Part 3, Houghton, 1990.

Sauron Defeated: The History of The Lord of the Rings, Part 4, Houghton, 1992.

OTHER

(Contributor) G. D. H. Cole and T. W. Earp, editors, *Oxford Poetry, 1915*, B. H. Blackwell, 1915.

(Contributor) *A Northern Venture: Verses by Members of the Leeds University English School Association*, Swan Press, 1923.

(Contributor) G. S. Tancred, editor, *Realities: An Anthology of Verse*, Gay & Hancock, 1927.

(Contributor) *Report on the Excavation of the Prehistoric, Roman, and Post-Roman Sites in Lydney Park*, Gloucestershire, Reports of the Research Committee of the Society of Antiquaries of London, Oxford University Press, 1932.

(Author of foreword) Walter E. Haigh, *A New Glossary of the Dialect of the Huddersfield District*, Oxford University Press, 1928.

(Author of preface) John R. Clark Hall, *Beowulf and the Finnesburg Fragment: A Translation into Modern English Prose*, edited by C. L. Wrenn, Allen & Unwin, 1940.

(Contributor) *Essays Presented to Charles Williams*, Oxford University Press, 1947.

(Author of preface) *The Ancrene Riwle*, translated by M. Salu, Burns & Oates, 1955.

(Contributor) *Angles and Britons: O'Donnell Lectures*, University of Wales Press, 1963.

(Contributor) Caroline Hillier, editor, *Winter's Tales for Children: 1*, St. Martin's, 1965.

(Contributor) William Luther White, *The Image of Man in C. S. Lewis*, Abingdon Press, 1969.

(Contributor) Roger Lancelyn Green, *The Hamish Hamilton Book of Dragons*, Hamish Hamilton, 1970.

(Contributor) Jared Lobdell, editor, *A Tolkien Compass*, Open Court, 1975.

(Contributor) Mary Salu and Robert T. Farrell, *J. R. R. Tolkien: Scholar and Storyteller*, Cornell University Press, 1979.

Contributor of translations to *The Jerusalem Bible*, Doubleday, 1966. Contributor to *The Year's Work in English Studies*, 1924 and 1925, *Transactions of the Philological Society*, 1934, *English Studies*, 1947, *Studia Neophilologica*, 1948, and *Essais de philologie moderne*, 1951. Contributor to periodicals, including *The King Edward's School Chronicle, Oxford Magazine, Medium Aevum, Dublin Review, Welsh Review*, and *Shenandoah: The Washington and Lee University Review*.

The greater part of the manuscripts of *The Hobbit, The Lord of the Rings, Farmer Giles of Ham*, and *Mr. Bliss* are in the collection of the Memorial Archives Library of Marquette University, Milwaukee, WI. Various of Tolkien's letters are in the collections of the BBC Written Archives, the Bodleian Library of Oxford University, the Oxford University Press and its Dictionary Department, the Humanities Research Center of the University of Texas at Austin, and the Marion E. Wade Collection of Wheaton College, Wheaton, IL.

■ Adaptations

Recordings of J. R. R. Tolkien reading from his own works, including "Poems and Songs of Middle-earth," "The Hobbit and The Fellowship of the Ring," and "The Lord of the Rings," have all been released by Caedmon. Christopher Tolkien reads "The Silmarillion: Of Beren and Luthien," also for Caedmon. Tolkien's illustrations from *Pictures by J. R. R. Tolkien* have been published in various editions of his books and have appeared on calendars, posters, and postcards. Rankin-Bass animated a version of *The Hobbit* for television, which aired in 1977. Ralph Bakshi directed a theater film based on *The Fellowship of the Ring* and bits and pieces of *The Two Towers*, which was released as *The Lord of the Rings* in 1978. A Bunraku-style puppet version of *The Hobbit* was produced in Los Angeles in 1984 by Theatre Sans Fil of Montreal.

■ Sidelights

J. R. R. Tolkien was best known to most readers as the author of *The Hobbit* and *The Lord of the Rings*. These books are regarded, stated Augustus M. Kolich in the *Dictionary of Literary Biography*, as "the most important fantasy stories of the modern period." From 1914 until his death in 1973, Tolkien drew on his familiarity with Northern European and other ancient literatures and his own invented languages to create not just his own story, but his own world: Middle-earth, a world complete with its own history, myths, legends, epics and heroes—"an imagined world," said Kolich, "that includes a vast gallery of strange beings: hobbits, elves, dwarfs, orcs, and, finally, the men of Westernesse." His works—especially *The Lord of the Rings*—have pleased countless readers and fascinated critics who recognize their literary depth.

However, Tolkien held another reputation not as well known to readers of his fantasies: he "was in fact one of the leading philologists of his day," Kolich reported. Philology—literally the love of words or language—is the study of the construction of languages and their relationship to one another. His academic work, teaching English language and literature at Leeds and later at Oxford, heavily influenced his fiction. Tolkien himself wrote in a letter to his American publishers in 1955 that "a primary 'fact' about my work [is] that it is all of a piece, and *fundamentally linguistic* in inspiration." Humphrey Carpenter declared in *Tolkien: A Biography*, "There were not two Tolkiens, one an academic and the other a writer. They were the same man, and the two sides of him

overlapped so that they were indistinguishable—
or rather they were not two sides at all, but
different expressions of the same mind, the same
imagination.''

Tolkien's Early Life

Tolkien was born early in 1892 in Bloemfontein,
South Africa, where his father, Arthur Reuel
Tolkien, worked as a bank manager. In 1894,
however, the child's health began to fail. His
mother, Mabel Suffield Tolkien, took him and his
younger brother Hilary back to England early the
next year, where they settled near Birmingham.
Arthur Tolkien, who had stayed behind in Africa,
planned to join his family in a year or so, but he
contracted rheumatic fever and died early in 1896.
Mabel Tolkien introduced her eldest son to two of
his strongest loves—the Catholic church and the
study of language—before she succumbed to dia-
betes in November, 1904. She left her orphaned

First published in 1937, this classic work introduces
readers to the mythical land of Middle-earth and
serves as a prequel to the ''Lord of the Rings'' trilogy.

sons under the guardianship of her close friend and
confessor, Father Francis Xavier Morgan. "I first
learned charity and forgiveness from him," Tolkien
recalled in a letter to his son Michael, published in
The Letters of J. R. R. Tolkien, many years later,
"and in the light of it pierced even the 'liberal'
darkness out of which I came." Morgan provided
Tolkien with a father figure and helped finance his
studies at King Edward's School in Birmingham
and at Oxford University.

Tolkien's passion for languages expanded while he
attended King Edward's School. It was an ardor he
developed early and kept throughout his life,
exploring tongues that were no longer spoken and
creating languages of his own. Latin and Greek
were important parts of the curriculum, and Tolkien excelled at both. Not satisfied with studying
just these, he also taught himself some Welsh, Old
and Middle English, and Old Norse, with the
encouragement and assistance of several of his
teachers. Carpenter explained, "It was a deep *love*
for the look and sound of words [that motivated
him], springing from the days when his mother had
given him his first Latin lesson." He went on to
write the only poem known to exist in Gothic, a
language related to English and German, but with
no modern descendant. Later he added Finnish to
his list of beloved tongues; the Finnish epic *The
Kalevala* had a great impact on his *Silmarillion,* and
the language itself, said Carpenter, inspired the
creation of "Quenya," the High-elven speech of
his stories.

It was also while attending King Edward's that
Tolkien met the third of his great loves: Edith
Bratt, a pianist who lived in the boarding house in
which the Tolkien brothers stayed from 1908 until
1910. Like the Tolkiens, Edith was an orphan, and
she was drawn toward the older brother, "with his
serious face and perfect manners," wrote Carpenter. Their friendship gradually deepened into love.
However, she was three years older than her
admirer and she was not a Catholic; and when
Tolkien's guardian Father Francis found out that
his ward had been conducting a clandestine love
affair he forbade Tolkien to see or write Edith
again. Dutifully, Tolkien gave her up; but three
years later, on the day he turned twenty-one, he
wrote and proposed to Edith. They were formally
engaged the following year and married in 1916.

Philology and Tolkien's Early Mythology

Throughout these years Tolkien became a philologist in the most literal sense of the word—a lover

Taken from a 1986 calendar, this illustration is artist Michael Haig's interpretation of a climactic scene from *The Hobbit*.

of language. When he entered Exeter College of Oxford University on a scholarship in the autumn of 1911, he intended to study Classics: Greek and Latin and the works of writers such as Cicero and Demosthenes. As he progressed, however, he found that his interests lay more in the study of comparative philology, which he learned from the dynamic teacher Joseph Wright, and in 1913 he switched from Classics to the Honour School of English Language and Literature.

In the Honour School Tolkien expanded his grasp of Germanic languages and literatures. He studied the Old Norse historical poems (sagas) and the stories from Nordic mythologies, collected in the *Elder Edda,* which includes the *Voluspa,* the prophecies forecasting the end of the world and the death of the gods. He also explored many more works in Old English, including a religious poem called *Crist.* These had a profound effect on Tolkien's imagination. According to Carpenter, Tolkien said upon reading it, "I felt a curious thrill, as if something had stirred in me, half wakened from sleep. There was something very remote and strange and beautiful behind those words, if I could grasp it, far beyond ancient English." In 1914, Tolkien wrote a poem inspired by a line from *Crist.* Entitled "The Voyage of Earendel, the Evening Star," it marked the first appearance in his work of the mariner who sails across the heavens through the night, and, stated Carpenter, was "the beginning of Tolkien's own mythology."

Tolkien served in the army throughout World War I, although illness kept him out of combat most of the time. After the Armistice was signed in 1918, he took a position with the Oxford English Dictionary for a couple of years, then joined the staff of Leeds University. His job there lay chiefly in the teaching of the science of philology, or linguistics: the reconstruction of ancient languages by observing how they differed from related ancient forms of modern tongues. Philologists can sometimes, on examination of surviving fragments of ancient literature, discover facets of the writer's culture and can find remnants of still older tales. One example of this in Tolkien's own work is *Finn and Hengest: The Fragment and the Episode,* based on Tolkien's teaching lectures. In these essays, wrote E. Christian Kopff in *Chronicles of Culture,* "Tolkien takes a brief and fragmentary tale sung by a bard in *Beowulf* and a fragment of a separate version of the same story that survives on a single manuscript page and tries to reconstruct the history that lies behind the two sources."

In the scattered stories that Tolkien composed throughout these years, he exercised his philological talents and training to create a sort of "inferred history" based on elements of the Northern (and especially the English) literature he loved. "Like Walter Scott or William Morris before him," T. A. Shippey declared in *The Road to Middle-Earth,* "he felt the perilous charm of the archaic world of the North, recovered from bits and scraps by generations of inquiry. He wanted to tell a story about it simply, one feels, because there were hardly any complete ones left." "J. R. R. Tolkien," said Jessica Yates in *British Book News,* "... felt that the English people, as opposed to the Greeks or the Celts for example, had no 'body of ... connected legend' of their own. All we had was *Beowulf* (imported from Denmark) and our native fairy stories. So partly with the sense of mission and partly as an escape from the horrors of the First World War, he wrote a series of tales." Tolkien called the first collection of these stories *The Book of Lost Tales.* "It is the starting point," wrote Christopher Tolkien in his foreword to *The Book of Lost Tales, Part 1,* "at least in fully-formed narrative, of the history of Valinor and Middle-earth."

Although these stories form the background for much of Tolkien's fiction, they only reached their final form with the publication of *The Silmarillion,* after the author's death. Earendel's story was joined by other tales, including "The Music of the Ainur," an account of the creation of the world; "The Silmarillion," the history of the return of the High-Elves to Middle-earth and their wars with Morgoth, the Great Enemy; "The Fall of Gondolin," Morgoth's assault on the last Elven fortress; "The Story of Turin Turambar," the tragedy of the son of Hurin Thalion, a mortal man counted among the greatest of Morgoth's foes, recounting how fate twisted his life so that although he slew the great dragon Glaurung he destroyed himself and those he loved; and "The Tale of Beren and Luthien," an epic story describing the love of Beren, a mortal man, for Luthien Tinuviel, the immortal daughter of a king of Elves, who together penetrated the fortress of Morgoth and took back from him a Silmaril, one of the great Jewels of Light he stole before the first Rising of the Sun. But in the process of bringing the Jewel to her father as Luthien's bride-price Beren was slain, and Luthien, pleading for love of him in the Halls of Mandos, chose to forsake immortality and die as well.

In *The Book of Lost Tales,* however, these stories sometimes originally had quite different forms and were more explicitly related to English legends and traditions. For instance, in the tale of Beren and Luthien, Beren was originally an elf, and before he and Tinuviel could retake the Silmaril he was captured by Morgoth and held in slavery by a giant cat named Tevildo. The structure Tolkien chose for *The Book of Lost Tales* resembled Chaucer's *Canterbury Tales*, with stories about the creation of the world and the ancient deeds of Elves and Men told by the Elves to a man, a traveler called Eriol or Aelfwine. Eriol/Aelfwine himself was closely connected to early English legends: Tolkien made him the father of Hengist and Horsa, traditionally considered the leaders of the Saxons who successfully invaded Britain in the fifth century A.D.

Some time after developing the legends, however, Tolkien abandoned the structure of *The Book of Lost Tales.* Such periodic abandonment of work was characteristic of him: he often dropped ideas, only to pick them up later on and change them. "Before the *Tales* were complete," Christopher Tolkien explained, "he turned to the composition of long poems, the *Lay of Leithian* in rhyming couplets (the story of Beren and Luthien) and *The Children of Hurin* in alliterative verse." He developed a prose version of his mythology, which "began again from a new starting-point in a quite brief synopsis, or 'Sketch' as he called it, written in 1926 and expressly intended to provide the necessary background of knowledge for the understanding of the alliterative poem." He also changed jobs; in 1925 he was elected Rawlinson and Bosworth Professor of Anglo-Saxon at Oxford University, a post that he held for twenty years.

Tolkien produced some of his most important philological work while at Oxford. He published "Beowulf: The Monsters and the Critics," one of the most influential pieces of criticism on the Old English epic, in 1936. He also made the acquaintance of C. S. Lewis, a fellow member of the English staff, who became a close personal friend. Tolkien regularly met with Lewis and a group of friends who called themselves "The Inklings" to discuss literature and to read and criticize each other's work. Lewis and Tolkien inspired each other to write fiction: Lewis's space-travel trilogy *Out of the Silent Planet, Perelandra,* and *That Hideous Strength,* features many of Tolkien's ideas. Tolkien himself began *The Lost Road,* a time-travel novel with an Atlantis-style fate, which was unrelated to his earlier mythological work. Although he never completed the book, it represented the first appearance of Numenor and the Men of Westernesse in his writing.

This Tolkien-drawn depiction of the Middle-earth village of Hobbiton was used as a cover for an edition of *The Fellowship of the Ring,* the first book of the "Lord of the Rings" trilogy.

The Hobbit

It was also while teaching at Oxford that Tolkien began to compose his children's book, *The Hobbit.* "Tolkien often recorded how he began the story," wrote Douglas A. Anderson in his introduction to *The Annotated Hobbit.* "One hot summer day he was sitting at his desk, correcting students' examination papers . . . on English literature. He told an interviewer, 'One of the candidates had mercifully left one of the pages with no writing on it, which is the best thing that can possibly happen to an examiner, and I wrote on it, "In a hole in the ground there lived a hobbit." Names always generate a story in my mind: eventually I thought I'd better find out what hobbits were like.'" Around the end of the 1920s or beginning of the 1930s, Tolkien began using the hobbit—now named Bilbo Baggins—as the basis for stories. "I had the habit while my children were still young of inventing and telling orally, sometimes of writing down, 'children's stories' for their private amusement," he stated in a 1964 letter published in *The Letters*

Artist Michael Whelan's depiction of Sam and Frodo's escape from Mount Doom from *The Return of the King,* the final book in the immensely popular "Lord of the Rings" epic.

of J. R. R. Tolkien. "The Hobbit was intended to be one of them."

Now regarded as a classic of children's literature, *The Hobbit* had at first no connection with Tolkien's legendary histories. It was simply the story of one hobbit's travels and adventures from his comfortable everyday life into terrible danger— represented by a dragon—and back again into security. It owed its inspiration more to sources such as the Anglo-Saxon epic *Beowulf* and Victorian fairy tales such as the collections of Andrew Lang and George MacDonald's *The Princess and Curdie.* Gradually, however, Tolkien worked references to his own mythos into the story. Tolkien remarked in a letter to his publishers Allen &

Unwin that "Mr. Baggins began as a comic tale among conventional and inconsistent Grimm's fairy-tale dwarves, and got drawn into the edge of it—so that even Sauron the Terrible peeped over the edge."

Tolkien drew on ancient languages and literature for inspiration while writing *The Hobbit.* "The dwarf-names of 'Thorin and Company,' as well as Gandalf's," declared Shippey, "come from a section of the Eddic poem *Voluspa,* often known as the *Dvergatal* or 'Dwarves' Roster.'" The names that Tolkien chose for his characters also serve as descriptions of the people that bear them. "Gandalf," for instance, is made up of two Norse words: *gandr,* a magical implement (probably a staff), and *alfr,* an elf. Tolkien's Gandalf, therefore, is an elf with a staff, or a wizard. Shippey explained, "Accordingly when Gandalf first appears, 'All that the unsuspecting Bilbo saw that morning *was an old man with a staff.*'" The character Gollum continually refers to himself and to the Ring throughout *The Hobbit* and *The Lord of the Ring* as "my precious"; Douglas A. Anderson, in his notes to *The Annotated Hobbit,* cited Constance B. Hieatt, who declared that "Old Norse gull/goll, of which one inflected form would be *gollum,* means 'gold, treasure, something precious' and can also mean 'ring,' a point which may have occurred to Tolkien."

A Sequel to *The Hobbit*

The Hobbit was a great success when it was published in September of 1937, and late that year Tolkien began work on a sequel. He hoped to publish his legends, stated Christopher Tolkien, further developed from the prose "Sketch" into a more coherent form called *The Silmarillion,* "which was nearing completion towards the end of 1937, when my father broke off to send it as it stood to Allen and Unwin in November of that year." However, *The Silmarillion* was not really suitable as a sequel to *The Hobbit,* and Tolkien had no clear idea what such a sequel should be about. As months went by, Tolkien evolved an alternate plot centered on the magic ring Bilbo found and on the references to the Necromancer in *The Hobbit.* By the end of August, 1938, Tolkien had begun to call the new story *The Lord of the Rings.* He wrote to his publisher that the new book "is more grown up—but the audience for which *The Hobbit* was written has done that also. The readers young and old who clamoured for 'more about the Necromancer' are to blame, for the N[ecromancer] is not child's play."

It took Tolkien another eleven years to finish the story. Part of the reason for this delay was because of his teaching schedule: in 1945 he became Merton Professor of English Language and Literature. But he was seldom satisfied with his original ideas, and he rewrote sections of the book many times. For some time he toyed with a plot that told how Bilbo, having lost all his money, left home again in search of treasure. This proved unworkable. Many other elements were worked into the plot, developed, then dropped, as the story progressed. Later revisions introduced Bilbo's son Bingo as the major character in place of Bilbo. The part first played by Aragorn, or Strider—a major character in the finished work—was originally given to a hobbit nicknamed "Trotter," who was a relative of Bilbo's. Characters changed names and functions many times before Tolkien settled on Frodo Baggins, Sam Gamgee, Pippin Took and Merry Brandybuck as major players in the drama. And, as elements of *The Silmarillion* crept into the new story, it moved into the realm of legend until it became the chronicle of the last days of the Third Age of Middle-earth.

Tolkien returned to his love for ancient languages and literature, as well as his original stories and his created languages, for inspiration and to clarify points in the plot that became important. "In the case of the 'ents,'" stated A. N. Wilson in the *Spectator,* quoting Tolkien, "... 'as usual with me they grew rather out of their name than the other way about. I always felt that something ought to be done about the peculiar Anglo-Saxon word *ent* for a "giant" or a mighty person of long ago—to whom all old works are ascribed.' He was not content to leave the ents as they appear on the page of *Beowulf,* shadowy, unknown figures of an almost forgotten past." "Tolkien's attitude to language," explained Janet Adam Smith in the *New York Review of Books,* "is part of his attitude to history ... to recapture and reanimate the words of the past is to recapture something of ourselves; for we carry the past in us, and our existence, like Frodo's quest, is only an episode in an age-long and continuing drama."

Pauline Baynes created illustrations like this one for *Bilbo's Last Song,* **Tolkien's verse book—published in 1990—describing a final episode from the "Lord of the Rings."**

Shippey traces the origins of the Balrog—the evil creature Gandalf faces on the bridge in Moria—to an article Tolkien published in two parts in the journal *Medium Aevum* on the Anglo-Saxon word *Sigelhearwan,* used to translate Latin biblical references to natives of Ethiopia. Tolkien suggested that the element *sigel* meant both "sun" and "jewel," and that the element *hearwa* was related to the Latin *carbo,* meaning soot. He further conjectured that when an Anglo-Saxon used the word, he did not picture a dark-skinned man but a creature like the fire-giants of Northern myth. "What was the point of the speculation," asked Shippey, "admittedly 'guess-work,' admittedly 'inconclusive'? It offers some glimpses of a lost mythology, suggested Tolkien with academic caution, something 'which has coloured the verse-treatment of Scripture and determined the diction of poems.' A good deal less boringly, one might say, it had helped to naturalise the 'Balrog' in the traditions of the North, and it had helped to create (or corroborate) the image of the *silmaril,* that fusion of 'sun' and 'jewel' in physical form." "That is lovely," wrote Ursula Le Guin in *The Language of the Night: Essays on Fantasy and Science Fiction;* "that is the Creator Spirit working absolutely unhindered—making the word flesh."

The Lord of the Rings

The Lord of the Rings was completed in 1949. Because of disagreements Tolkien had with Allen & Unwin, it did not see publication until 1954. Tolkien was convinced that *The Silmarillion* had to appear with *The Lord of the Rings,* and he negotiated with a representative of the British publisher Collins, who suggested that they might be willing to publish the two works together. Several problems intervened, however: Tolkien had not completed *The Silmarillion,* and his estimate that it would run about 600,000 words when complete—greater than *The Lord of the Rings*—proved too much for Collins to handle. Tolkien returned to Allen & Unwin, dropping his demand that the two works be published together. The first two sections, *The Fellowship of the Ring* and *The Two Towers,* were released in 1954. The final volume, *The Return of the King,* was published very late in 1955, because the indexes that Tolkien had promised were not finished.

The work was a financial success, and over the next few years it was published in the United States and translated into many foreign languages. Its greatest popularity, however, came in the mid-1960s when it was discovered by American university students.

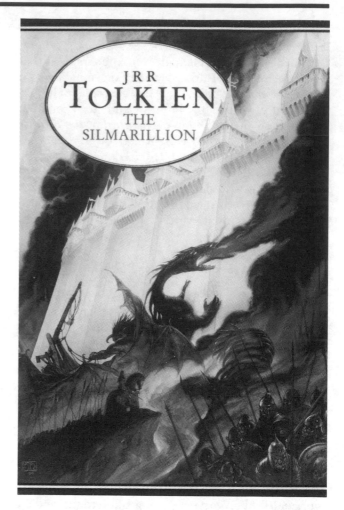

Published posthumously, this 1977 *Locus* Award-winning work not only provides background to the events in the "Lord of the Rings," but is also the fulfillment of Tolkien's great ambition to provide the English people with a legendary tradition they lacked.

Part of the reason for this was due to a dispute over publishing rights that attracted much attention. By 1965, the international copyright on the book had lapsed. In that year Ace Books, a prominent science fiction publisher, announced plans for a paperback edition of the work—an edition that would not pay the author any royalties. To prevent this, Tolkien revised the book and copyrighted it as a second edition, and his American publishers produced their own "authorized" paperback which soon sold more than a million copies. Ace Books later wrote and apologized to Tolkien, offering him a royalty on all the books they had sold and agreeing not to reprint the book after the stocks were exhausted. However, "Ace had unwittingly done a service to Tolkien," declared Carpenter, "for they had helped to lift his book from the 'respectable' hard-cover status in which it had languished for some years and had put it at the top of the popular best-sellers." "By the end of 1968," Carpenter continued, "approximately three million copies of *The Lord of the Rings* had been sold around the world."

Criticism

Although many readers have viewed *The Lord of the Rings* as an allegory of modern history—especially of World War II—Tolkien explicitly rejected such an interpretation; in the foreword to the American paperback edition of *The Lord of the Rings*, he stated, "As for any inner meaning or 'message,' it has in the intention of the author none. It is neither allegorical nor topical." "I cordially dislike allegory in all its manifestations," he continued, "and have always done so since I grew old and wary enough to detect its presence. I much prefer history, true or feigned, with its varied applicability to the thought and experience of readers. I think that many confuse 'applicability' with 'allegory'; but the one resides in the freedom of the reader, and the other in the purposed dominations of the author." He expanded on these comments in a letter to his publisher Stanley Unwin in *The Letters of J. R. R. Tolkien:* "There is a 'moral,' I suppose, in any tale worth telling. But that is not the same thing. Even the struggle between light and darkness (as [Rayner Unwin] calls it, not me) is for me just a particular phase of history, one example of its pattern, perhaps, but not The Pattern; and the actors are individuals—they each, of course, contain universals or they would not live at all, but they never represent them as such." "You can make the Ring into an allegory of our own time, if you like," he concluded: "an allegory of the inevitable fate that waits for all attempts to defeat evil power by power. But that is only because all power magical or mechanical does always so work. You cannot write a story about an apparently simple magic ring without that bursting in, if you really take the ring seriously, and make things happen that would happen, if such a thing existed."

Tolkien did, however, suggest that his work had an underlying theme. "*The Lord of the Rings,*" he wrote in a letter to the Jesuit Father Robert Murray published in *The Letters of J. R. R. Tolkien,* "is of course a fundamentally religious and Catholic work; unconsciously so at first, but consciously in the revision." Shippey pointed out that the rejoicing of the forces of the West after the downfall of Sauron in *The Return of the King* is an example of what Tolkien called a "eucatastrophe." Tolkien wrote to his son Christopher that in his

essay "On Fairy Stories" "I coined the word 'eucatastrophe': the sudden happy turn in a story which pierces you with a joy that brings tears (which I argued it is the highest function of fairy-stories to produce). And I was there led to the view that it produces its peculiar effects because it is a sudden glimpse of Truth." "It perceives," he explained, "... that this is indeed how things really do work in the Great World for which our nature is made. And I concluded by saying that the Resurrection was the greatest 'eucatastrophe' possible in the greatest Fairy Story—and produces that essential emotion: Christian joy which produces tears because it is qualitatively so like sorrow, because it comes from those places where Joy and Sorrow are at one." "Of course," he added, "I do not mean that the Gospels tell what is *only* a fairy-story; but I do mean very strongly that they do tell a fairy-story: the greatest. Man the story-teller would have to be redeemed in a manner consonant with his nature: by a moving story."

"A good way to understand *The Lord of the Rings* in its full complexity," said Shippey, "is to see it as an attempt to reconcile two views of evil, both old, both authoritative, each seemingly contradicted by the other." To the orthodox Christian, Evil does not exist by itself but springs from an attempt to separate one's self from God—an opinion expressed most clearly in *The Consolation of Philosophy,* a work by the early medieval thinker Boethius, a Roman senator imprisoned and later executed for his views. Tolkien was probably most familiar with it through King Alfred's Old English translation, made in the ninth century A.D. An alternate view—labelled Manichaean, and considered heretical by the church—is that Good and Evil are separate forces, equal and opposite, and the world is their battleground. King Alfred's own career, campaigning against marauding Norsemen, wrote Shippey, emphasizes the "strong point of a 'heroic' view of evil, the weak point of a Boethian one: if you regard evil as something internal, to be pitied, more harmful to the malefactor than the victim, you may be philosophically consistent but you may also be exposing others to sacrifices to which they have not consented (like being murdered by Viking ravagers or, as *The Lord of the Rings* was being written, being herded into gas-chambers)."

In *The Lord of the Rings,* Shippey stated, Tolkien strikes a balance between these two views of evil, using the symbol of the shadow: "Shadows are the absence of light and so don't exist in themselves, but they are still visible and palpable just as if they did." Tolkien's attitude "implies the dual nature of wickedness," which can also be found in the Lord's Prayer: "'And lead us not into temptation; but deliver us from evil.' Succumbing to temptation is our business, one might paraphrase, but delivering us from evil is God's." "At any rate," Shippey concluded, "on the level of narrative one can say that *The Lord of the Rings* is neither a saint's life, all about temptation, nor a complicated wargame, all about tactics. It would be a much lesser work if it had swerved towards either extreme."

Final Years

Sales from revised editions of *The Lord of the Rings* and *The Hobbit* made Tolkien a moderately wealthy man. He had retired from teaching in 1959 but, even though a considerable proportion of his income went to pay his taxes, he was perhaps better off financially than he had ever been before. He was also able to devote his time to finishing *The Silmarillion.* At times, however, the sheer quantity of work that remained to be done on *The Silmarillion* made him wonder if he could ever complete it. "I do not really know what to make of it," he wrote to Professor Clyde Kirby. "It began in hospital and sick-leave (1916-1917) and has been with me ever since, and is now in a confused state having been altered, enlarged, and worked at, at intervals between then and now. If I had the assistance of a scholar at once sympathetic and yet critical, such as yourself, I feel I might make some of it publishable."

Personal problems added to Tolkien's burden. Edith's health was failing, and late in 1971 she died of complications from an inflamed gall-bladder. He wrote his eldest son Michael, "Since I came of age, and our 3 years separation was ended, we had shared all joys and griefs, and all opinions (in agreement or otherwise), so that I still often find myself thinking 'I must tell E. about this'—and then suddenly I feel like a castaway left on a barren island under a heedless sky after the loss of a great ship." Her headstone read simply, "Edith Mary Tolkien, Luthien, 1889-1971." "I never called Edith *Luthien*," Tolkien recalled in a letter to his son Christopher, "—but she was the source of the story that in time became the chief part of the *Silmarillion.*" "But the story has gone crooked, & I am left," he continued, "and *I* cannot plead before the inexorable Mandos." He explained to Michael, "Now she has gone before Beren, leaving him indeed one-handed, but he has no power to move the inexorable Mandos, and there is no *Dor Gyrth i chuinar*, the Land of the Dead that Live, in this Fallen Kingdom of Arda. . . ." He followed her less than two years later. They were buried side by side. To Edith's headstone was added the caption, "John Ronald Reuel Tolkien, Beren, 1892-1973."

In the last two years of his life, Tolkien received many honors, including receiving an honorary Doctorate of Letters from Oxford University for his contributions to philology, and being made a Commander of the Order of the British Empire. *The Silmarillion* was never published in his lifetime, but in 1977 his son Christopher completed the work and released it to great critical acclaim. Since then, many volumes of Tolkien's works—both fictional and philological—have been edited and published by family, friends or former students. The great body of Tolkien's writing has only recently begun to be appreciated with the release of Christopher Tolkien's "History of Middle Earth" series. Tolkien remains a potent force in literature: *The Silmarillion, The Lord of the Rings* and *The Hobbit* remain popular the world over, and they constitute his true memorial.

■ Works Cited

Anderson, Douglas A., introduction and notes to *The Annotated Hobbit*, Houghton, 1988.

Carpenter, Humphrey, *J. R. R. Tolkien: A Biography*, Allen & Unwin, 1977, published as *Tolkien: A Biography*, Houghton, 1978.

Kolich, Augustus M., "J. R. R. Tolkien," *Dictionary of Literary Biography*, Volume 15: *British Novelists, 1930-1959*, Gale, 1983, pp. 520-530.

Kopff, E. Christian, "Inventing Lost Worlds," *Chronicles of Culture*, April, 1985, pp. 6-8.

Le Guin, Ursula K., *The Language of the Night: Essays on Fantasy and Science Fiction*, edited and with an introduction by Susan Wood, Putnam, 1979.

Shippey, T. A., *The Road to Middle-Earth*, Allen & Unwin, 1982, Houghton, 1983.

Smith, Janet Adam, "Does Frodo Live?," *New York Review of Books*, December 14, 1972, pp. 19-21.

Tolkien, Christopher, foreword to *The Book of Lost Tales, Part 1* by J. R. R. Tolkien, Allen & Unwin, 1983, Houghton, 1984, pp. vii-xxi.

Tolkien, J. R. R., foreword to *The Lord of the Rings*, Volume 1: *The Fellowship of the Ring*, 2nd edition, Houghton, 1966.

Tolkien, J. R. R., *The Letters of J. R. R. Tolkien*, selected and edited by Humphrey Carpenter and Christopher Tolkien, Houghton, 1981.

Wilson, A. N., "Beyond the Misty Mountains," *The Spectator*, September 12, 1981, pp. 17-18.

Yates, Jessica, review of *The Book of Lost Tales, Part 2*, *British Book News*, December, 1984, p. 751.

■ For More Information See

BOOKS

Authors in the News, Volume 1, Gale, 1976.

Bingham, Jane, editor, *Writers for Children*, Scribner's, 1988.

Carpenter, Humphrey, *The Inklings: C. S. Lewis, J. R. R. Tolkien, Charles Williams and Their Friends*, Allen & Unwin, 1978, Houghton, 1979.

Carter, Lin, *Tolkien: A Look behind The Lord of the Rings*, Houghton, 1969.

Contemporary Literary Criticism, Gale, Volume 1, 1973; Volume 2, 1974; Volume 3, 1975; Volume 8, 1978; Volume 12, 1980; Volume 38, 1986.

Day, David, *A Tolkien Bestiary*, Ballantine, 1979.

Ellwood, Gracia F., *Good News from Tolkien's Middle Earth: Two Essays on the Applicability of The Lord of Rings*, Eerdmans, 1970.

Fonstad, Karen Wynn, *The Atlas of Middle-Earth*, Houghton, 1981.

Foster, Robert, *A Guide to Middle-Earth*, Mirage Press, 1971, revised edition published as *The Complete Guide to Middle-Earth*, Del Rey, 1981.

Fuller, Edmund, and others, *Myth, Allegory and Gospel: An Interpretation; J. R. R. Tolkien, C. S. Lewis, G. K. Chesterton, Charles Williams*, Bethany Fellowship, 1974.

Harvey, David, *Song of Middle Earth*, Allen & Unwin, 1985.

Isaacs, Neil D., and Rose A. Zimbardo, editors, *Tolkien and the Critics*, University of Notre Dame Press, 1968.

Johnson, Judith A., *J. R. R. Tolkien: Six Decades of Criticism*, Greenwood Press, 1986.

Kocher, Paul H., *Master of Middle-Earth: The Fiction of J. R. R. Tolkien*, Houghton, 1972.

Lobdell, Jared, editor, *A Tolkien Compass*, Open Court, 1975.

Noel, Ruth S., *The Languages of Tolkien's Middle-Earth*, Houghton, 1980.

Purtill, Richard L., *Lord of the Elves and Eldils: Fantasy and Philosophy in C. S. Lewis and J. R. R. Tolkien*, Zondervan, 1974.

Ready, William B., *The Tolkien Relation: A Personal Inquiry*, Regnery, 1968.

Stimpson, Catherine R., *J. R. R. Tolkien*, Columbia University Press, 1969.

Strachey, Barbara, *Journeys of Frodo: An Atlas of J. R. R. Tolkien's The Lord of the Rings*, Ballantine, 1981.

West, Richard C., compiler, *Tolkien Criticism: An Annotated Checklist*, Kent State University Press, 1970, revised edition, 1981.

PERIODICALS

Atlantic, March, 1965.

Book Week, February 26, 1967.

Chicago Tribune Book World, March 22, 1981.

Commentary, February, 1967.

Commonweal, December 3, 1965.

Criticism, winter, 1971.

Critique, spring-fall, 1959.

Encounter, November, 1954.

Esquire, September, 1966.

Hudson Review, Number 9, 1956-57.

Kenyon Review, summer, 1965.

Los Angeles Times Book Review, January 4, 1981; February 10, 1985.

Nation, April 14, 1956.

New Republic, January 16, 1956.

New York Times Book Review, March 14, 1965; October 31, 1965; November 16, 1980; May 27, 1984; June 17, 1984.

New York Times Magazine, January 15, 1967.

Saturday Evening Post, July 2, 1966.

Sewanee Review, fall, 1961.

South Atlantic Quarterly, summer, 1959; spring, 1970.

Spectator, November, 1954.

Sunday Times (London), September 19, 1982.

Thought, spring, 1963.

Time and Tide, August 14, 1954; October 22, 1955.

Times Literary Supplement, July 8, 1983; July 19, 1985; December 23, 1988.

Washington Post Book World, September 4, 1977; December 9, 1980; February 13, 1983.

OBITUARIES

Newsweek, September 17, 1973.

New York Times, September 3, 1973.

Publishers Weekly, September 17, 1973.

Time, September 17, 1973.

Washington Post, September 3, 1973.°

—*Sketch by Kenneth R. Shepherd*

Garry Trudeau

nominations for book and lyrics, 1983, and Grammy Award nomination for cast show album, 1984, for the musical *Doonesbury*; National Endowment for the Arts grant; several honorary degrees from colleges and universities.

■ Writings

"DOONESBURY" BOOKS; UNDER NAME G. B. TRUDEAU, EXCEPT AS NOTED

Doonesbury, American Heritage Press, 1971.
Still a Few Bugs in the System, Holt, 1972, sections published as *Even Revolutionaries Like Chocolate Chip Cookies* and *Just a French Major from the Bronx*, both Popular Library, 1974.
The President Is a Lot Smarter Than You Think, Holt, 1973.
But This War Had Such Promise, Holt, 1973, sections published as *Bravo for Life's Little Ironies*, Popular Library, 1975.
(Under name Garry Trudeau) *Doonesbury: The Original Yale Cartoons*, Sheed, 1973.
Call Me When You Find America, Holt, 1973.
(With Nicholas von Hoffman) *The Fireside Watergate*, Sheed, 1973.
(Under name Garry Trudeau) *Joanie*, Sheed, 1974.
(Under name Garry Trudeau) *Don't Ever Change, Boopsie*, Popular Library, 1974.
Guilty, Guilty, Guilty!, Holt, 1974.
The Doonesbury Chronicles, Holt, 1975.
Dare to Be Great, Ms. Caucus, Holt, 1975.
What Do We Have for the Witnesses, Johnnie?, Holt, 1975.

■ Personal

Full name, Garretson Beekman Trudeau; also writes under name G. B. Trudeau; born in 1948, in New York, NY; son of Francis (a physician) Trudeau and Jean Amory; married Jane Pauley (a television journalist), June 14, 1980; children: Rachel, Ross (twins), Tom. *Education:* Yale University, B.A., 1970, M.F.A., c. 1972.

■ Addresses

Home—New York, NY.

■ Career

Cartoonist and writer. Cartoonist for *Yale Daily News*, 1969-70; operator of a graphic arts studio in New Haven, CT; writer and illustrator of syndicated comic strip *Doonesbury*, 1970—.

■ Awards, Honors

Pulitzer Prize for editorial cartooning, 1975; Oscar Award nomination for animated short film, 1977, for *A Doonesbury Special*; Special Jury Prize, Cannes Film Festival, 1977; Drama Desk Award

(Under name Garry Trudeau) *We'll Take It from Here, Sarge*, Sheed, 1975.

(Under name Garry Trudeau) *I Have No Son*, Popular Library, 1975.

Wouldn't a Gremlin Have Been More Sensible?, Holt, 1975.

(With von Hoffman) *Tales from the Margaret Mead Taproom: The Compleat Gonzo Governorship of Doonesbury's Uncle Duke*, Sheed, 1976.

"Speaking of Inalienable Rights, Amy...", Holt, 1976.

You're Never Too Old for Nuts and Berries, Holt, 1976.

An Especially Tricky People, Holt, 1977.

(Under name Garry Trudeau) *As the Kid Goes for Broke*, Holt, 1977.

Stalking the Perfect Tan, Holt, 1978.

Doonesbury's Greatest Hits, Holt, 1978.

(Under name Garry Trudeau) *Any Grooming Hints for Your Fans, Rollie?*, Holt, 1978.

(Under name Garry Trudeau) *A Doonesbury Special: A Director's Notebook* (book version of animated special; also see below), Sheed Andrews & McMeel, 1978.

We're Not out of the Woods Yet, Holt, 1979.

But the Pension Fund Was Just Sitting There, Holt, 1979.

And That's My Final Offer!, Holt, 1980.

A Tad Overweight, but Violet Eyes to Die For, Holt, 1980.

Guess Who, Fish-Face!, Fawcett, 1981.

(With von Hoffman) *The People's Doonesbury: Notes from Underfoot*, Holt, 1981.

In Search of Reagan's Brain, Holt, 1981.

He's Never Heard of You Either, Holt, 1981.

Do All Birders Have Bedroom Eyes, Dear?, Fawcett, 1981.

Ask for May, Settle for June, Holt, 1982.

Gotta Run, My Government Is Collapsing, Fawcett, 1982.

Unfortunately She Was Also Wired for Sound, Holt, 1982.

We Who Are about to Fry, Salute You: Selected Cartoons from "In Search of Reagan's Brain," Volume 1, Fawcett, 1982.

Is This Your First Purge, Miss?: Selected Cartoons from "In Search of Reagan's Brain," Volume 2, Fawcett, 1982.

You Give Great Meeting, Sid, Holt, 1983.

The Wreck of the Rusty Nail, Holt, 1983.

It's Supposed to Be Yellow, Pinhead: Selected Cartoons from "Ask for May, Settle for June," Volume I, Fawcett, 1983,

The Thrill Is Gone, Bernie, Fawcett, 1983.

Sir, I'm Worried about Your Mood Swings, Fawcett, 1984.

Confirmed Bachelors Are Just So Fascinating, Fawcett, 1984.

Dressing for Failure, I See, Fawcett, 1984.

Doonesbury Dossier: The Reagan Years, Holt, 1984.

Check Your Egos at the Door, Holt, 1985.

That's Doctor Sinatra, You Little Bimbo!, Holt, 1986.

Death of a Party Animal, Holt, 1986.

Calling Dr. Whoopee, Holt, 1987.

Downtown Doonesbury, Holt, 1987.

Doonesbury Deluxe: Selected Glances Askance, Holt, 1987.

We're Eating More Beets!, Holt, 1988.

Talking about My G-G-Generation, Holt, 1988.

Give Those Nymphs Some Hooters!, Holt, 1989.

Read My Lips, Make My Day, Eat Quiche and Die!, Andrews & McMeel, 1989.

Recycled Doonesbury: Second Thoughts on a Gilded Age, Andrews & McMeel, 1990.

You're Smokin' Now, Mr. Butts!, Andrews & McMeel, 1990.

The Doonesbury Stamp Album, Viking Penguin, 1990.

I'd Go for the Helmet, Ray, Andrews & McMeel, 1991.

Welcome to Club Scud, Andrews & McMeel, 1991.

What Is It, Tink, Is Pan in Trouble?, Andrews & McMeel, 1992.

OTHER

(With David Levinthal) *Hitler Moves East: A Graphic Chronicle, 1941-43*, Sheed, 1977.

A Doonesbury Special (animated film), National Broadcasting Co. (NBC-TV), 1977.

Doonesbury (musical; produced in Boston, 1983, produced on Broadway, 1983), Holt, 1984.

Rap Master Ronnie (musical; produced Off-Broadway, 1984; broadcast on Cinemax, 1988), Lord John, 1986.

(Contributor) *Comic Relief: Drawings from the Cartoonists' Thanksgiving Day Hunger Project*, Holt, 1986.

Tanner '88 (television series), Home Box Office, 1988.

Also lyricist for musical *Doonesbury* cast show album.

■ Sidelights

Known for his acerbic humor and political acumen, Garry Trudeau is the creator of *Doonesbury*, a ground-breaking comic strip that has satirized a variety of social and political issues for more than

These strips from the 1989 collection *Read My Lips, Make My Day, Eat Quiche and Die!* depict Elvis Presley's return to the performing stage after being found alive, overweight, and bald by Donald Trump's yacht.

twenty years. Appearing in about 900 newspapers throughout the United States, *Doonesbury* has sustained its popularity since its debut in 1970. The strip, which is found on the editorial rather than the comics page in some newspapers, is often hard hitting and controversial. Trudeau's commentary on the current political scene often rankles his targets—among his favorites are President George Bush and Vice President Dan Quayle—and elicits cheers from his readers. The cartoonist also explores charged topics such as the Persian Gulf War, acquired immunodeficiency syndrome (AIDS), and abortion, thereby creating strips that are thought-provoking as well as entertaining. "He is as much journalist as artist—an investigative cartoonist," Jonathan Alter wrote in *Newsweek*. "Trudeau," Alter continued, "is the premier American political and social satirist of his time."

Trudeau was born in New York City and raised in the resort town of Saranac Lake in upstate New York. Several generations of the Trudeau family also lived in the area. Trudeau's great-grandfather, Dr. Edward Trudeau, moved to Saranac Lake when he developed tuberculosis—a disease affecting the lungs—around the turn of the century. The doctor expected to die from his illness, but the fresh country air alleviated his symptoms and he was credited with discovering the "rest cure," which became the first therapy for the tubercular. Trudeau's great-great-grandfather, James Trudeau, also a doctor, was chased out of New York City after his caricatures of his colleagues created an outrage. "That's where Garry got his genes [from James Trudeau], and he looks just like him," Trudeau's father told Alter. Prominent family members on Trudeau's mother's side include a treasurer of the United States under President Abraham Lincoln and one of the founders of International Business Machines (IBM).

Despite his privileged background, Trudeau "avoided the life of a pampered rich kid," according to Alter. The cartoonist's early love was theater; as a young boy Trudeau was producing plays in his basement and was careful to include such details as scripts, tickets, and programs. "Theater was my earliest life's passion," he told Rick Kogan in *Chicago Tribune Book World.* "I formed a theater group at the ripe old age of seven. At first, I wrote the shows. Then at ten I decided it was time to stop doing amateurish pieces and get on with the real business of theater. I sent away for the catalog of Samuel French plays, and I'll never forget the rush when my first package of plays arrived. I devoured them."

At age thirteen, Trudeau enrolled in St. Paul's boarding school in New Hampshire. His parents had divorced the year before, making this a particularly difficult time for him. (Trudeau developed an ulcer that year, a condition often brought on by stress and one that is unusual in teenagers.) More interested in art than in football, Trudeau was unhappy at St. Paul's, where the popular kids were jocks and where he was teased for his lack of athletic prowess. And though he is now known for his wit, "I was not the class clown," Trudeau revealed to Alter. "In fact, I was pretty shy. One of the reasons that adolescence was such a tortured time for me was that I was the second or third smallest in my class." Trudeau did gain some positive attention from his peers when his first cartoon character, "Weenie Man," appeared on advertisements for hot dogs at school football games. He was also coeditor of the school yearbook, president of the Art Association, and winner of the senior-class art prize.

The Birth of *Doonesbury*

Trudeau's talents were more highly valued at Yale University, where he was editor of the campus humor magazine and a columnist for the Yale *Daily News.* During his junior year, Trudeau developed the comic strip *Bull Tales,* which centered around Yale star quarterback Brian Dowling (whose cartoon alter ego is B. D.) and lampooned aspects of college life from campus radicals to Yale President Kingman Brewster. *Bull Tales* appeared in the *Daily News* and soon caught the attention of Jim Andrews, who was then launching the Universal Press Syndicate with his partner, John McMeel. Andrews was impressed by *Bull Tales* and convinced Trudeau to syndicate his work nationally. To give *Bull Tales* widespread appeal, Trudeau omitted expletives and the "Y" from B. D.'s helmet, clothed the strip's nude coeds, and redrew a year's worth of panels. He also rechristened the cartoon *Doonesbury,* after another character, Mike

Doonesbury. The name is a combination of "doone" (which Trudeau defined for Alter as "well-meaning fool") and "Pillsbury," the last name of one of Trudeau's former roommates, a flour-fortune heir on whom Mike is loosely based.

Several of *Doonesbury*'s regular characters were also inspired by real people. The Reverend Scot Sloan, for example, is based on both a roommate of Trudeau's who became a lawyer and minister and on former Yale chaplain William Sloane Coffin, Jr. Mark Zanger, a Yale activist, inspired *Doonesbury*'s "Megaphone" Mark Slackmeyer, and journalist Hunter S. Thompson, who wrote *Fear and Loathing in Las Vegas,* appears in the cartoon as the amoral opportunist Uncle Duke. "The closest correspondence between a character and a real person," Trudeau told Alter, is feminist Joanie Caucus, who was modeled after the cartoonist's cousin who left her husband and children to create a new life for herself. *Doonesbury*'s Joanie separated from her own husband after he put his arm around her one day and said, "My wife. I think I'll keep her." Joanie explained, "I broke his nose."

Debuting nationally in the fall of 1970, *Doonesbury* appeared in nearly thirty newspapers and was an immediate success. The strip mostly centered around the Walden Puddle commune, where *Doonesbury*'s regular characters lived while attending the fictional Walden College. The experiences of Trudeau's characters often reflected current social and political events. "Megaphone" Mark Slackmeyer, for instance, found his background as a campus activist helpful when he organized a trucker's strike during the energy crisis of the early 1970s. B. D. traded his football uniform for fatigues when he served in Vietnam, where he befriended Phred, the Vietcong terrorist. And Joanie Caucus served as an inspiration to many women when she enrolled in law school at the University of California at Berkeley after students there sent Trudeau an application for her. Joanie's popularity prompted Trudeau to remark in a 1976 *Time* profile, "I've received so much mail addressed to Joanie . . . that my mother thinks I'm living with her."

Cartoon Controversy

In the early years *Doonesbury* also addressed hot topics such as the Watergate scandal, when members of the Committee to Re-elect President Nixon (CRP) were found to be behind a break-in at the Democratic National Committee headquarters at the Watergate Hotel in Washington, D.C. Top

Trudeau satirizes leadership in America on such fronts as education, AIDS, and the homeless in this strip from 1990's *Recycled Doonesbury.*

White House officials were eventually found to be behind a cover-up of the operation, and Nixon himself was also suspected and eventually resigned in 1974. Trudeau developed a series of strips about the scandal and created his own controversy in the process. In one installation, Mark Slackmeyer (now a radio host) ends a balanced profile of former CRP head John Mitchell with "everything known to date could lead one to conclude that he's guilty. That's guilty, guilty, guilty!" Since Mitchell had not yet been pronounced guilty in court, several papers refused to run *Doonesbury*—even though Trudeau explained that he was simply trying to satirize over-zealous Nixon opponents. In a 1973 *Washington Post* editorial, Robert C. Maynard wrote, "The reason the Tuesday [*Doonesbury*] was dropped is that it was, in the opinion of the editors of the *Washington Post*, entirely too pointed and overstepped the bounds of decency, fairness and good judgement."

Trudeau's brushes with controversy and censorship have not dulled his sharp satire nor have they suppressed his sometimes daring story lines. In 1976, for instance, the cartoonist attracted atten-

tion by having Joanie Caucus and her boyfriend, Rick Redfern, engage in sexual relations before marriage. That same year President Gerald Ford's son was called a "pothead" in the strip. In 1985 entertainer Frank Sinatra received the Medal of Freedom from President Reagan, a tribute that Trudeau questioned in *Doonesbury* by pointing out that Sinatra had associated with members of organized crime. Fearing a libel suit, many newspapers dropped the strip. Earlier that year, Trudeau's syndicate refused to distribute another controversial *Doonesbury* series, this time about abortion. The strips parodied the antiabortion film *Silent Scream* by introducing *Silent Scream II: The Prequel*, which presents the short life of "Timmy," a twelve-minute-old dividing cell. The sequence was only published in the *New Republic*, *Ms.*, and a few newspapers—an arrangement that did not upset Trudeau. Unlike some of his loyal fans, the cartoonist is nonplussed when editors occasionally refuse to run *Doonesbury*. He remarked to Alter, "That's not censorship, it's editing. Each [editor] makes a daily judgment about community standards."

Inciting both praise and controversy, Trudeau introduces AIDS sufferer Andy Lippincott as a strong, humorous character in a series of strips that openly deal with the disease.

Though Trudeau's forthright portrayal of issues and public figures in *Doonesbury* has won him numerous devotees and a Pulitzer Prize for editorial cartooning in 1975, some of his targets are less enthusiastic about the cartoonist's sardonic pen. President George Bush, whom Trudeau depicts as a void in *Doonesbury* (indicating the chief executive's perceived lack of image), told the *Miami Herald* in 1987, "My first reaction was anger, testiness, getting upset. I thought, what the hell? Who is this elitist who never ran for sheriff, never [took] his case to the people? Who is this little guy that comes out of some of the same background as me? So I had that personal feeling that I wanted to go up and kick the hell out of him, frankly." Hunter S. Thompson (who inspired Uncle Duke) said, "If I ever catch that little bastard [Trudeau], I'll tear his lungs out," according to *Time*. And quoted by the *New York Times Book Review*, Frank Sinatra opined that Trudeau is "about as funny as a tumor."

Trudeau answered his detractors by telling Alter, "Criticizing a political satirist for being unfair is like criticizing a nose guard for being physical." In a separate *Newsweek* article, Alter noted, "One could argue that the whole point of political cartoons and strips is to be biting—and occasional tastelessness and even unfairness go with the territory." Regarding the Sinatra strips, Alter wrote, "Sinatra is fair game. His association over the years with reputed mob bosses is beyond dispute, and Trudeau had every right to question the propriety of his being honored at the White House and elsewhere."

Despite the widespread attention that *Doonesbury* often receives, Trudeau is known for guarding his privacy and rarely gives interviews. To evade a Baltimore *Sun* reporter, he once hid in a bathroom for four hours. "I don't like celebrification," the cartoonist told *Time* in 1976. "Everything I have to share I share in the strip." And he admitted to Alter, "I would have been more comfortable being a 19th-century famous person, at a time when a president of the United States could walk down the street without being recognized... Nobody cared 200 years ago what Thomas Jefferson's living room looked like or whether he was kind to his children or whether he worked late."

Though Trudeau usually avoids talking to the press, he has been known to appear at public events, such as political conventions and Congressional hearings, in order to gather material for *Doonesbury*. He also scans numerous newspapers and magazines and keeps two to three hundred files of clipped articles. And when President Ford visited China in 1975, Trudeau went along (he and NBC-TV news correspondent Tom Brokaw reportedly played Frisbee on top of the Great Wall). Trudeau's experience in China cropped up in *Doonesbury* when Uncle Duke was appointed that country's U.S. envoy. Because of his thorough research and timeliness, Trudeau is, according to *Time*, "more than any of his comic-page contemporaries,... a true journalist."

Indeed, Trudeau has been lauded more for his writing than his artwork. In 1976 *Time* described him as "an indifferent draftsman," who "is usually just good enough to strike an attitude or sink a platitude." Critics have observed, however, that Trudeau's drawing has greatly improved through the years. Trudeau told Alter that he became tired of the strip's "static" look in 1987, commenting that "this is when the cartoonist decided to wake up." With a series that took *Doonesbury* correspondent Roland Hedley on a tour of President Reagan's brain (the former chief executive's "memory vault" was described as "shrunken and calcified from chronic disuse"), Trudeau, according to Alter, "dramatically" improved his art.

Trudeau first draws *Doonesbury* strips in pencil, which gives him the freedom to make changes. "I don't laugh when I'm writing. I don't even smile. It's very serious," he told Alter. Working from his studio in New York City, he then faxes the panels to Kansas City, the home of his "inker" Don Carlton and his syndicate. (Many cartoonists employ an inker as a time-saving measure.) Carlton redraws the cartoon in ink, and the final product is virtually identical to Trudeau's pencil originals. These ink versions, complete with Carlton's reproduction of Trudeau's signature, sell for about $600, with the proceeds going to the National Coalition for the Homeless. Trudeau must send out his daily strips about ten days before publication and Sunday panels must be finished five weeks in advance. To keep *Doonesbury* as current as possible, Trudeau often works right up to his Friday deadlines. "If I'm lucky there will be two or three ideas that kind of jockey for position in my mind through the week, which I will bone up on," he explained to Alter. "Somewhere around Wednesday or Thursday, I'll start making the final cuts and commit to one story line. The process for me is very much sitting down and holding a casting call to marry an idea with the right characters and the right story."

Broadway *Doonesbury* and the Ronnie Revue

After thirteen years of deadlines, Trudeau decided to take a break from writing *Doonesbury* in 1983. The cartoonist's sabbatical, an unusual move in his profession, lasted about twenty-one months. "Editors across the nation were outraged that I could be so presumptuous as to take control of my own career," Trudeau told Kogan in *Chicago Tribune Book World*. "People regard their comics pages as sacrosanct. Stopping them is like an interruption of a public utility. I knew editors would think I was being frivolous, that I was being a dilettante that I would want to try my hand at other endeavors."

During his leave of absence from cartooning, Trudeau pursued his long-time interest in theater. He and composer Elizabeth Swados staged a musical version of *Doonesbury* on Broadway in 1983 that garnered Trudeau two Drama Desk nominations for the book and lyrics. In the production, hippie and perpetual student Zonker Harris finally graduates from Walden College, Uncle Duke schemes to develop pristine Walden Puddle for condominiums, and Joanie's daughter J.J., an artist, is romanced by Mike Doonesbury. The show also features White House news breaks read by an actor portraying President Reagan. Trudeau told Kogan that the stage version of *Doonesbury* "was about transitions, about people caught at a crossroads, who were no longer sheltered by collegiate life, who were forced to challenge their belief systems in order to survive the '80s."

Though the musical *Doonesbury* received mixed reviews, with some critics observing that the writing seemed more suited to comic strips than theater, Trudeau continued to write for the stage and produced *Rap Master Ronnie* with Swados in 1984. A cabaret, *Rap Master Ronnie* lampoons Reagan and his policies by tackling a variety of subjects, including the President's forgetfulness, his light working schedule, the environment, poverty, racism, sexism, bureaucrats, religion, and Yuppies (young urban professionals). "The total effect," remarked Kogan, "is a wickedly clever entertainment, a carefully crafted bit of theater with a considerable bite." Trudeau disclosed to Kogan that "what we did not want was 'The First Family Rides Again.' We did not want safe humor. . . . Many of Ronald Reagan's policies outrage us in a very direct manner, and the trick was always to put through the filter of our art and make it palatable and accessible to people who may not share our outrage."

Rap Master Ronnie, staged Off-Broadway in New York, also played in several other cities, including Los Angeles, Boston, Chicago, and Washington, D.C. The musical revue ran for four years, with Trudeau and Swados continually adding and updating material. Despite *Rap Master Ronnie's* humorous slant, Trudeau intended the show to be a thought-provoking experience. "I want people to think about events during the Reagan years that we tend to forget, to look at this national amnesia of ours," Trudeau told William A. Henry III in *Time*. "Ronald Reagan has presided over a transformation of America from a country that wanted to *be* good to one that wanted to *feel* good—which I have a suspicion should not be the highest priority of a community."

Back to the Drawing Board

As *Rap Master Ronnie* was debuting in the fall of 1984, Trudeau returned to cartooning and maintained his reputation as a bold, provocative satirist who "manages to combine editorial-page gravity and funny-paper levity," according to *Time*. After thirteen years of drawing the *Doonesbury* gang as a group of college students living in sheltered Walden Puddle, Trudeau decided to allow his characters to grow up and venture out into the world. Mike Doonesbury and J. J. marry and have children; B. D. (who never removes his football helmet) moves to California and becomes his girlfriend Boopsie's talent agent; Mark Slackmeyer works for National Public Radio; and Joanie Caucus, now married to Rick Redfern, juggles the demands of family and career. In one series, Mike Doonesbury compromises his values in order to work on a tobacco company's advertising account and is haunted by an imaginary humanized cigarette, "Mr. Butts." Subsequent strips show J. J. painting murals on the ceilings of billionaire Donald Trump's bathrooms, Elvis performing a comeback concert at Trump's Las Vegas casino, Boopsie posing for the *Sports Illustrated* swimsuit issue, condom sales representative Dr. Whoopee bringing his safe-sex message to college campuses, and B. D. in Saudi Arabia awaiting the beginning of 1991's Persian Gulf War. The war provided plenty of material for Trudeau: *Doonesbury* news correspondent Roland Hedley got lost in the desert, Uncle Duke became the proprietor of Saudi Arabia's "Club Scud," and Boopsie learned to be more self-reliant in B. D.'s absence.

Trudeau also continued to poke fun at political figures of all persuasions. He depicts Vice President Dan Quayle as a feather in the strip, unders-

WELCOME TO CLUB SCUD!

"THE BEST COVERAGE FROM THE GULF SO FAR HAS BEEN IN DOONESBURY."
—HERB CAEN
San Francisco Chronicle

THINK I'LL MAKE CNN?

HOW DO YOU THINK WE FOUND YOU?

A DOONESBURY BOOK by G. B. TRUDEAU

Trudeau's strips lampooning the Persian Gulf War are collected in this 1991 book.

coring Quayle's reputation in the media as a political and intellectual lightweight. He mocked Democratic presidential candidate Bill Clinton for admitting that he tried marijuana but "didn't inhale." And Trudeau couldn't resist ridiculing the Bush administration's concept of "family values," an issue that drew widespread attention during the 1992 presidential campaign. "Trudeau's dislikes are ambidextrous," a *Time* writer noted. "Neither radicals nor reactionaries are safe from his artillery. Stuffed shirts of Oxford broadcloth or frayed denim receive the same impudent deflation."

Perhaps some of Trudeau's most challenging and controversial *Doonesbury* strips have involved fictional AIDS patient Andy Lippincott. Written after three years of contemplating the issue, the series shows Andy coming to terms with his disease as well as the reactions of his family and friends. Despite his fatal illness, Andy displays a wry sense of humor. When friend Joanie Caucus asks how a person in his condition can joke, Andy replies, "How can you not?" Trudeau was praised for presenting the reality of AIDS (Andy eventually dies) with sensitivity and wit, which some critics found especially impressive since he drew the strips without personally knowing a victim of the disease. Appreciative AIDS patients sent the cartoonist bundles of letters, which were "the most moving I've ever received," he told Alter. "In order to understand and come to terms with [AIDS], I had to strip it of its taboos, to attack the

fear and ignorance by laughing in its face," *Newsmakers 91* quoted Trudeau's comment to the *St. Paul Pioneer Press*. "It's an outlet for despair, a means to quell the terror. As a satirist, I am trying to make it easier to look into the abyss as all of us will have to do. These [AIDS patients] are fellow human beings with mothers, fathers, friends. It's time to come to terms with that."

Trudeau affirmed in the interview with Alter that "if you bring a certain amount of taste and judgement there's *nothing* that can't be addressed in comic strips." One subject that does not crop up in *Doonesbury*, however, is Trudeau's personal life. He married popular television journalist Jane Pauley in 1980, and the couple shares in the care of their three children. Trudeau doesn't want "readers to feel I'm reporting on my own family, which is a violation [as well as] infinitely banal," he remarked to Alter. The cartoonist extends the ban to Pauley's colleagues and incidents involving Pauley's job at NBC. When Pauley was replaced on the *Today* show by the younger, blonder Deborah Norville, for instance, *Doonesbury* was silent on the issue even though it would have been easy to satirize.

Because his satire reflects the rapidly changing current scene, however, Trudeau is virtually never at a loss for ideas. Political events often provide unlimited material: the 1988 presidential campaign, for example, inspired Trudeau to create *Tanner '88*, a television show focusing on fictional Democratic candidate Jack Tanner from Michigan. On the program, Tanner appears at real news events and interacts with actual candidates such as Gary Hart, Bob Dole, and Pat Robertson. Maureen Dowd commented in the *New Republic* that Trudeau and director Robert Altman "wanted to tell the classic story of a decent, intelligent man struggling to keep his ideals through the corrupting, trivializing, media-dominated, image-fixated process of politics." The reviewer added that Trudeau "writes the show with his usual deft sense of the hip and the hypocritical." Though she felt that *Tanner '88* might hold little interest for the average American television viewer, Dowd noted that "the film has become a cult favorite among those who have watched it being filmed," and called it a "fantastic voyage into the inner arteries of politics." And Harry F. Waters described *Tanner '88* in *Newsweek* as "a study of campaign madness that's almost as hilarious as the real thing."

In addition to his work in theater and television, Trudeau has written a few screenplays, but has been unable to get them produced in Hollywood.

Significantly more successful are the dozens of soft-cover *Doonesbury* cartoon collections that he has published, compilations that have been welcomed by critics and readers alike. In a *Nation* review of *Doonesbury Dossier: The Reagan Years* (1984), for instance, Robert Grossman noted that the book "may be the most entertaining and lucid chronicle of the present era we have." The critic added that *Doonesbury Dossier* "reads as smoothly as a novel, and its characters exhibit far greater realism than we have come to expect from the funnies."

Whether as the creator of comic strips, plays, or television shows, Trudeau is recognized as a wry and insightful observer of American society and politics. "I think all the cartoonists admire Garry's originality," *Peanuts* creator Charles Schulz told *Time.* "He's gone into areas that haven't been touched before." A *Time* writer surmised that "Trudeau's greatest gift is the ability to present . . . satire without bile, to put strong statements in the mouths of gentle characters—to demonstrate, as Mike Doonesbury says, that 'even revolutionaries like chocolate-chip cookies.'" And though the cartoonist downplays his contribution to American culture, the *Time* reviewer added that "for most readers, to be tired of *Doonesbury* is to be tired of life." His forays into television and theater notwithstanding, Trudeau plans to continue drawing *Doonesbury.* As he commented to Alter, he feels "some serene sense of job satisfaction." And he revealed to Kogan, "I would be very happy if someone gave me permission to do the strip for the rest of my life."

■ Works Cited

Alter, Jonathan, "Doonesbury Contra Sinatra," *Newsweek,* June 24, 1985, p. 82.

Alter, Jonathan, "Real Life with Garry Trudeau," *Newsweek,* October 15, 1990, pp. 60-66.

"Doonesbury: Drawing and Quartering for Fun and Profit," *Time,* February 9, 1976, pp. 57-60, 65-66.

Dowd, Maureen, "Eighty-Eightsomething," *New Republic,* August 1, 1988, p. 37.

Grossman, Robert, "Zonker's Reagan," *Nation,* October 27, 1984, p. 427.

Henry, William A. III, "Attacking a 'National Amnesia': Garry Trudeau Breaks His Vow of Silence to Skewer Reagan," *Time,* December 8, 1986, p. 107.

Kogan, Rick, "Why Would a Popular Cartoonist Turn to Theater? Listen to Rap Master Garry," *Chicago Tribune Book World,* November 24, 1985, pp. 4-6.

Macnow, Glen, "Garry Trudeau," *Newsmakers 91: The People behind Today's Headlines, Cumulation,* Gale, 1991, pp. 435-438.

Maynard, Robert C., "The Comic Strip Isn't a Court," *Washington Post,* May 31, 1973, p. A18.

Richler, Mordecai, "Batman at Midlife: Or, the Funnies Grow Up," *New York Times Book Review,* May 3, 1987, p. 35.

Waters, Harry F., "A Presidential Pretender: Garry Trudeau and Robert Altman Parody Politics," *Newsweek,* February 15, 1988, p. 82.

■ For More Information See

BOOKS

Contemporary Literary Criticism, Volume 12, Gale, 1980, pp. 588-591.

PERIODICALS

Booklist, June 15, 1986, p. 1492; September 1, 1988, p. 25; October 1, 1990, p. 241.

Los Angeles Times Book Review, May 15, 1983; September 11, 1983; December 3, 1989; July 8, 1990; December 23, 1990, p. 10.

Ms., November, 1985, pp. 101-102.

New Republic, April 27, 1992, p. 14.

New York Times Book Review, December 7, 1975, p. 7; May 4, 1980.

People, August 29, 1988.

Time, June 24, 1985, p. 66.

Voice of Youth Advocates, August, 1981, p. 42; December, 1981, p. 46; December, 1982, p. 46; April, 1985, pp. 69-70; April, 1988, p. 49; February, 1989, p. 307.

Washington Post Book World, December 2, 1973, p. 4.*

—*Sketch by Michelle M. Motowski*

Acknowledgments

Acknowledgments

Grateful acknowledgment is made to the following publishers,
authors, and artists for their kind permission to reproduce copyrighted material.

WOODY ALLEN. Mia Farrow and Jeff Daniels, photograph by Brian Hamill./ Alvy, in a fantasy sequence, photograph by Jonathan Munk./ Movie still from "Allen's All-Stars," photograph by Brian Hamill/PMK.

AVI. Cover of *Captain Grey*, by Avi Worti. Scholastic Book Service, 1977. Copyright © 1977 by Avi Wortis. Cover illustration by George Gaadt. Reprinted by permission of Random House, Inc./ Cover of *Night Journeys*, by Avi. Scholastic Book Service, 1979. Copyright © 1979 by Avi Wortis. Cover illustration by Ted Hanke. Reprinted by permission of Random House, Inc./ Cover of *S.O.R. Losers*, by Avi. Avon Books, 1984. Copyright © 1984 by Avi Wortis. Cover illustration by Tom Newsom. Reprinted by permission of Avon Books, New York./ Cover of *The Fighting Ground*, by Avi. Harper Trophy, 1987. Copyright © 1984 by Avi Wortis. Cover art © 1987 by Michael Garland. Cover © 1987 by Harper & Row, Publishers, Inc. Reprinted by permission of HarperCollins Publishers./ Jacket of *The Man Who Was Poe*, by Avi. Orchard Books, 1989. Copyright © 1989 by Avi Wortis. Jacket painting copyright © 1989 by Ted Lewin. Reprinted by permission of Orchard Books, a division of Franklin Watts, Inc./ Photograph © by Steve Adams.

CLIVE BARKER. Cover of *Clive Barker's Books of Blood Volume Three*, by Clive Barker. Berkley, 1986. Copyright © 1984 by Clive Barker. Reprinted by permission of The Berkley Publishing Group./ Jacket of *Cabal*, by Clive Barker. Copyright © 1985, 1988 by Clive Barker. Jacket painting and design copyright © 1988 by Wendell Minor. Copyright © 1988 by Simon & Schuster, Inc. Reprinted by permission of Poseidon Press, a division of Simon & Schuster, Inc./ Cover of *The Damnation Game*, by Clive Barker. Charter, 1988. Copyright © 1985 by Clive Barker. Reprinted by permission of The Berkley Publishing Group./ Cover of *Tapping the Vein Book Two*, by Clive Barker. Cover artwork copyright © 1989 by Scott Hampton. Reprinted by permission of Eclipse Books./ Jacket of *Imajica*, by Clive Barker. Jacket design by Gene Mydlowski. Jacket illustration copyright © 1991 by Kirk Reinert. Reprinted by permission of HarperCollins Publishers./ Photograph by Geoff Shields./ Illustration copyright © 1987 by New World.

JAY BENNETT. Cover of *The Dangling Witness*, by Jay Bennett. Copyright © 1974 by Jay Bennett. Reprinted by permission of Dell Publishing, a division of Bantam Doubleday Dell Publishing Group, Inc./ Jacket of *The Pigeon*, by Jay Bennett. Copyright © 1980 by Jay Bennett. Jacket illustration by Tony Sella./ Cover of *Sing Me a Death Song*, by Jay Bennett. Ballantine Books, 1991. Copyright © 1990 by Jay Bennett. Reprinted by permission Ballantine Books, a division of Random House, Inc./ Jacket of *Coverup*, by Jay Bennett. Franklin Watts, 1991. Copyright © 1991 by Jay Bennett. Jacket Art by Cris Cocozza. Reprinted by permission of Franklin Watts./ Photograph courtesy of Jay Bennett.

MARY HIGGINS CLARK. Cover of *A Stranger Is Watching*, by Mary Higgins Clark. Dell, 1988. Copyright © 1977 by Mary Higgins Clark. Reprinted by permission of Dell Publishing, a division of Bantam Doubleday Dell Publishing Group, Inc./ Cover of *Where Are the Children?*, by Mary Higgins Clark. Dell, 1988. Copyright © 1975 by Mary Higgins Clark. Reprinted by permission of Dell Publishing, a division of Bantam Doubleday Dell Publishing Group, Inc./ Cover of *While My Pretty One Sleeps*, by Mary Higgins Clark. Pocket Books, 1990. Copyright © 1989 by Mary Higgins Clark. Cover illustration by Sonja Lamut and Nenad Jakesevic. Reprinted by permission of Pocket Books, a division of Simon & Schuster, Inc./ Cover of *Loves Music, Loves to Dance*, by Mary Higgins Clark. Copyright © 1991 by Mary Higgins Clark. Jacket design by Paul Bacon. Jacket illustration by Wendi Schneider. Copyright © 1991 by Simon & Schuster. Reprinted by permission of Simon & Schuster, Inc./ Photograph © 1984 by Helen Marcus.

ELLEN CONFORD. Jacket of *Hail, Hail Camp Timberwood*, by Ellen Conford. Copyright © 1978 by Ellen Conford. Illustrations by Gail Owens. Reprinted by permission of Little, Brown and Company./ Cover of *If This Is Love, I'll Take Spaghetti*, Ellen Conford. Copyright © 1983 by Ellen Conford. Reprinted by permission of Scholastic Inc./ Jacket of *Why Me?*, by Ellen Conford. Copyright © 1985 by Conford Enterprises Ltd. Jacket painting by Carol Newsom. Reprinted by permission of Little, Brown and Company./ Cover of *Genie with the Light Blue Hair*, by Ellen Conford. Bantam, 1990. Copyright © 1989 by Conford Enterprises Ltd. Cover art copyright © 1990 by Garin Baker. Reprinted by permission of Bantam Books, a division of Bantam Doubleday Dell Publishing Group, Inc./ Cover of *Loving Someone Else*, by Ellen Conford. Bantam, 1991. Copyright © 1991 by Conford Enterprises Ltd. Book design by Terry Karydes Reprinted by permission of Bantam Books, a division of Bantam Doubleday Dell Publishing Group, Inc./ Photograph by Richard Haynes.

MICHAEL CRICHTON. Cover of *The Andromeda Strain*, by Michael Crichton. Copyright © 1969 by Centesis Corporation, Reprinted by permission of Dell Publishing, a division of Bantam Doubleday Dell Publishing Group, Inc./ Cover of *Westworld*, by Michael Crichton. Bantam, 1974. Copyright © 1974 by Michael Crichton. Photo insert and cover art courtesy of Metro-Goldwyn-Mayer, Inc. Copyright © 1973. Reprinted by permission of Bantam Books, a division of Bantam Doubleday Dell Publishing Group, Inc./ Cover of *Jurassic Park,* by Michael Crichton. Ballantine Books, 1991. Copyright © 1990 Michael Crichton. Cover illustration by Chip Kidd. Reprinted by permission of Ballantine Books, a division of Random House, Inc./ Jacket of *Rising Sun,* by Michael Crichton. Alfred A. Knopf, 1992. Copyright © 1992 by Michael Crichton. Front-of-jacket photograph by Melissa Hayden. Reprinted by permission of Alfred A. Knopf, a division of Random House, Inc./ Photograph © Joyce Ravid./ Illustrations from ''Frankenstein,'' National Film Archive/Stills Library./ Illustration from ''Coma,'' National Film Archive/Stills Library.

LOUISE ERDRICH. Cover of *Love Medicine,* by Louise Erdrich. Bantam, 1989. Copyright © 1984 by Louise Erdrich. Cover art copyright © 1989 by Glen Harrington. Reprinted by permission of Bantam Books, a division of Bantam Doubleday Dell Publishing Group, Inc./ Cover of *Tracks,* by Louise Erdrich. Copyright © 1988 by Louise Erdrich. Cover illustration copyright © 1989 by Glen Harrington. Reprinted by permission of HarperCollins Publishers./ Cover of *The Beet Queen,* by Louise Erdrich. Bantam, 1989. Copyright © 1986 by Louise Erdrich. Cover art copyright © 1989 by Wendel Minor. Reprinted by permission of Bantam Books, a division of Bantam Doubleday Dell Publishing Group, Inc./ Cover of *The Crown of Columbus,* by Louise Erdrich and Michael Dorris. HarperPaperbacks, 1992. Copyright © 1991 by Michael Dorris and Louise Erdrich. Cover illustration by Greg Harlin/Stansbury, Ronsaville, Wood Inc. Reprinted by permission of HarperCollins Publishers./ Photograph © 1989 by Michael Dorris.

ESTHER FRIESNER. Cover of *Here Be Demons,* by Esther Friesner. Ace, 1988. Copyright © 1988 by Esther Friesner. Cover art by Walter Velez. Reprinted by permission of Berkley Publishing Group./ Cover of *Demon Blues,* by Esther Friesner. Ace Books, 1989. Copyright © 1989 by Esther Friesner. Cover art by Walter Velez. Reprinted by permission of The Berkley Publishing Group./ Cover of *Hooray for Hellywood,* by Esther Friesner. Ace, 1990. Copyright © 1990 by Esther Friesner. Cover art by Walter Velez. Reprinted by permission of The Berkley Publishing Group./ Cover of *Gnome Man's Land,* by Esther Friesner. Ace, 1991. Copyright © 1991 by Esther Friesner. Cover art by James Warhola. Reprinted by permission of The Berkley Publishing Group./ Cover of *Harpy High,* by Esther Friesner. Ace Books, 1991. Copyright © 1991 by Esther Friesner. Cover art by David Mattingly. Reprinted by permission of The Berkley Publishing Group./ Cover of *Unicorn U.,* by Esther Friesner. Ace Books, 1992. Copyright © 1992 by Esther Friesner. Cover art by David Mattingly. Reprinted by permission of The Berkley Publishing Group./ Photograph by Beth Gwynn.

JOHN KNOWLES. Cover of *A Separate Peace,* by John Knowles. Copyright © 1959 by John Knowles. Reprinted by permission of Bantam Books, a division of Bantam Doubleday Dell Publishing Group, Inc./ Jacket of *Peace Breaks Out,* by John Knowles. Copyright © 1981 by John Knowles. Jacket design by Paul Bacon. Reprinted by permission of Henry Holt and Company./ Jacket of *A Stolen Past,* by John Knowles. Copyright © 1983 by John Knowles. Jacket design and illustration by Paul Bacon. Reprinted by permission of Henry Holt and Company, Inc./ Photograph by Jerry Bauer./ Illustration copyright © 1972 by Paramount Pictures Corporation.

GORDON KORMAN. Cover of *This Can't Be Happening at Macdonald Hall,* by Gordon Korman. Copyright © 1978 by Gordon Korman. Reprinted by permission of Scholastic Inc./ Cover of *Don't Care High,* by Gordon Korman. Scholastic Inc., 1985. Copyright © 1985 by Gordon Korman. Reprinted by permission of Scholastic Inc./ Cover of *Son of Interflux,* by Gordon Korman. Copyright © 1988 by Gordon Korman. Reprinted by permission of Scholastic Inc./ Cover of *Macdonald Hall Goes Hollywood,* by Gordon Korman. Scholastic, 1991. Copyright © 1991 by Gordon Korman Enterprises, Inc. Jacket painting copyright © 1991 by Richard Lauter. Reprinted by permission of Scholastic Inc./ Photograph by Daniels & Glionna Photography, courtesy of Gordon Korman.

DAVID LETTERMAN. Cover of *An Altogether New Book of Top Ten Lists,* by David Letterman, Steve O'Donnell, Rob Burnett, Randy Cohen, Spike Feresten, Joe Furey, Larry Jacobson, Gerard Mulligan, Maria Pope, Adam Resnick, David Rygalski, Nell Scovell, Paul Simms, Philip Vaughn, and Steve Young. Copyright © 1991 by National Broadcasting Company, Inc. and Cardboard Shoe Productions, Inc. Cover photo of David Letterman courtesy of The National Broadcasting Company, Inc., copyright © The National Broadcasting Company, Inc. Reprinted by permission of Pocket Books, a division of Simon & Schuster, Inc./ Photographs, AP/Wide World Photos.

ROBERT LUDLUM. Cover of *The Bourne Identity,* by Robert Ludlum. Bantam, 1981. Copyright © 1980 by Robert Ludlum. Cover artwork copyright © 1988 by Bantam Books. Reprinted by permission of Bantam Books, a division of Bantam Doubleday Dell Publishing Group, Inc./ Cover of *The Osterman Weekend,* by Robert Ludlum. Bantam, 1982. Copyright © 1972 by Robert Ludlum. Cover artwork copyright © 1985 by Bill Schmidt. Reprinted by permission of Bantam Books, a division of Bantam Doubleday Dell Publishing Group, Inc./ Cover of *The Bourne Supremacy,* by Robert Ludlum. Bantam, 1987. Copyright © 1986 by Robert Ludlum. Cover art copyright © 1986 by Bantam Books. Reprinted by permission of Bantam Books, a division of Bantam Doubleday Dell Publishing Group, Inc./ Jacket of *The Road to Omaha,* by Robert Ludlum. Copyright © 1992 by Robert Ludlum. Jacket art by Paul Bacon, copyright © 1992 by Random House, Inc. Reprinted by permission of Random House, Inc./ Photograph by Per Fronth./ Movie still courtesy of The Academy of Motion Pictures Arts And Sciences.

PENNY MARSHALL. Photograph, AP/Wide World Photos./ Movie still from ''Big,'' copyright © 1988 by 20th Century-Fox Film Corporation./ Movie still from ''Awakenings,'' photograph by Louis Goldman, copyright © 1990 by Columbia Pictures Industries, Inc./ Movie still from 'Jumpin' Jack Flash, photograph by Bruce McBroom, copyright © by 20th Century-Fox Film Corporation./ Movie still, Penny Marshall and Tom Hanks, photograph by Kerry Hayes, copyright © by 20th Century-Fox Film Corporation.

PABLO PICASSO. "The Family of Acrobats With Ape," 1905. SCALA/© 1992 ARS, NY/SPADEM, Paris; "The Dream," 1932. SCALA/Art Resource, NY./ "Woman Weeping". Copyright © 1992 ARS, NY/SPADEM, "Woman's Head With Self-Portrait." Copyright ARS, NY/SPADEM./ Picasso with sculptured portrait of Francoise, 1951, photograph by Douglas Glass, London./ Photograph of Picasso, copyright by Arnold Newman.

AYN RAND. Cover of *The Fountainhead*, by Ayn Rand. Copyright © 1943 by The Bobbs-Merrill Company. Copyright © renewed 1971 by Ayn Rand. Afterword copyright © 1993 by Leonard Peikoff. Used by permission of New American Library, a division of Penguin USA Inc./ Cover of *Atlas Shrugged*, by Ayn Rand. Copyright © 1957 by Ayn Rand. Reprinted by permission of Random House, Inc./ Cover of *We the Living*, by Ayn Rand. Copyright © 1936, 1959 by Ayn Rand O'Connor. Copyright renewed © 1983 by Eugene Winick, Paul Gitlin, Leonard Peikoff. Used by permission of New American Library, a division of Penguin USA Inc./ Photograph by Phyllis Cerf Wagner.

CYNTHIA RYLANT. Cover of *A Blue-Eyed Daisy*, by Cynthia Rylant. Dell, 1987. Copyright © 1985 by Cynthia Rylant. Reprinted by permission of Dell Publishing, a division of Bantam Doubleday Dell Publishing Group, Inc./ Cover of *A Fine White Dust*, by Cynthia Rylant. Dell, 1987. Copyright © 1986 by Cynthia Rylant. Reprinted by permission of Dell Publishing, a division of Bantam Doubleday Dell Publishing Group, Inc./ Jacket of *A Couple of Kooks and Other Stories about Love*, by Cynthia Rylant. Copyright © 1990 by Cynthia Rylant. Jacket photograph copyright © 1990 by Michele Jan Baylis. Reprinted by permission of Orchard Books, New York./ Jacket of *Soda Jerk*, by Cynthia Rylant. Copyright © 1990 by Cynthia Rylant. Jacket painting copyright © 1990 by Peter Catalanotto. Reprinted by permission of Orchard Books, New York./ Photograph courtesy of Cynthia Rylant.

JOHN SAUL. Cover of *The God Project*, by John Saul. Copyright © 1982 by John Saul. Cover art copyright © 1983 by Lisa Falkenstern. Reprinted by permission of Bantam Books, a division of Bantam Doubleday Dell Publishing Group, Inc./ Cover of *Second Child*, by John Saul. Bantam, 1991. Copyright © 1990 by John Saul. Cover art copyright © 1990 by Bob Hickson. Reprinted by permission of Bantam Books, a division of Bantam Doubleday Dell Publishing Group, Inc./ Cover of *Sleep Walk*, by John Saul. Bantam Books, 1991. Copyright © 1990 by John Saul. Cover art copyright © 1990 by Tom Hallman. Reprinted by permission of Bantam Books, a division of Bantam Doubleday Dell Publishing Group, Inc./ Cover of *Darkness*, by John Saul. Bantam, 1992. Copyright © 1991 by John Saul. Cover illustration copyright © 1991 by Tom Hallman. Cover design copyright © 1991 by One Plus One Studio. Reprinted by permission of Bantam Books, a division of Bantam Doubleday Dell Publishing Group, Inc./ Cover of *Shadows*, by John Saul. Bantam, 1992. Copyright © 1992 by John Saul. Book design by Stanley S. Drate/Folio. Graphics Co., Inc. Reprinted by permission of Bantam Books, a division of Bantam Doubleday Dell Publishing Group, Inc./ Photograph copyright © by Milkie Studio.

GARY SOTO. Cover of *Living Up the Street*, by Gary Soto. Dell, 1992. Copyright © 1985 by Gary Soto. Cover art by Carmen Lomas Garza. Reprinted by permission of Dell Publishing, a division of Bantam Doubleday Dell Publishing Group, Inc./ Cover of *Baseball in April and Other Stories*, by Gary Soto. Copyright © 1990 by Gary Soto. Cover illustration by Barry Root. Cover design by Carin Goldberg. Reprinted by permission of Harcourt Brace Jovanovich, Inc./ Jacket of *Neighborhood Odes*, by Gary Soto. Text copyright © 1992 by Gary Soto. Illustrations by David Diaz. Illustrations copyright © 1992 by Harcourt Brace Jovanovich, Inc. Jacket design by Michael Farmer. Reprinted by permission of Harcourt Brace Jovanovich, Inc./ Photograph reprinted from *The Elements of San Joaquin*, by Gary Soto, by permission of the University of Pittsburgh Press, copyright © 1977 by Gary Soto.

ART SPIEGELMAN. Cover of *Maus: A Survivor's Tale*, by Art Spiegelman. Reprinted by permission of Pantheon Books, a division of Random House, Inc./ Jacket by Art Spiegelman from his *Maus II*. Copyright © 1986, 1989, 1990, 1991 by Art Spiegelman. Reprinted by permission of Pantheon Books, a division of Random House, Inc./ Illustration by Art Spiegelman from his *Maus II*. Copyright © 1986, 1989, 1990, 1991 by Art Spiegelman. Reprinted by permission of Pantheon Books, a division of Random House, Inc./ Photograph © 1986 by Sylvia Plachy. Reprinted by permission./ Illustration from *The Comics Journal* copyright © by Art Spiegelman.

ROSEMARY SUTCLIFF. Cover of *The Eagle of the Ninth*, by Rosemary Sutcliff. Oxford University Press, 1954. Illustrations by Walter Hodges. Reprinted by permission of Oxford University Press./ Cover of *Flame-Colored Taffeta*, by Rosemary Sutcliff. Sunburst, 1989. Copyright © 1986 by Rosemary Sutcliff. Cover art copyright © 1986 by Rachel Birkett. Reprinted by permission of Farrar, Straus and Giroux, Inc./ Cover of *The Mark of the Horse Lord*, by Rosemary Sutcliff. Dell, 1989. Copyright © 1965 by Rosemary Sutcliff. Afterword copyright © 1989 by Scott O'Dell. Reprinted by permission of Dell Publishing, a division of Bantam Doubleday Dell Publishing Group, Inc./ Jacket of *The Shining Company*, by Rosemary Sutcliff. Text copyright © 1990 by Rosemary Sutcliff. Map copyright © 1990 by Claudia Carlson. Jacket art copyright © 1990 by Charles Mikolaycak. Reprinted by permission of Farrar, Straus and Giroux, Inc./ Jacket of *The Shield Ring*, by Rosemary Sutcliff. Reprinted by permission of Oxford University Press./ Photograph courtesy of Murry Pollinger Literary Agency.

MILDRED D. TAYLOR. Cover of *Song of the Tree*, by Mildred D. Taylor. Copyright © 1975 by Mildred D. Taylor. Illustrations copyright © 1975 by Jerry Pinkney. Cover art copyright © 1984 by Max Ginsburg. Reprinted by permission of Bantam Books, a division of Bantam Doubleday Dell Publishing Group, Inc./ Cover of *Roll of Thunder, Hear My Cry*, by Mildred D. Taylor. Copyright © 1976 by Mildred D. Taylor. Cover art copyright © 1984 by Sal Baracca. Reprinted by permission Bantam Books, a division of Bantam Doubleday Dell Publishing Group, Inc./ Cover of *Let the Circle Be Unbroken*, by Mildred D. Taylor. Copyright © 1981 by Mildred D. Taylor. Cover art by Wendell Minor, courtesy of The Dial Press. Reprinted by permission of Bantam Books, a division of Bantam Doubleday Dell Publishing Group, Inc./

Cumulative Index

Author/Artist Index

The following index gives the number of the volume
in which an author/artist's biographical sketch appears.